The Spiral Dance

The Spiral Dance

A Rebirth of the Ancient Religion of the Great Goddess

STARHAWK

20TH ANNIVERSARY EDITION

with New Introduction and
Chapter-by-Chapter Commentary

HarperSanFrancisco
A Division of HarperCollins*Publishers*

HarperCollins books may be purchased for educational, business, or sales promotional use. For information please write: Special Markets Department, HarperCollins Publishers Inc., 10 East 53rd Street, New York, NY 10022.

HarperCollins Web Site: http://www.harpercollins.com

HarperCollins®, ▦ ™, and HarperSanFrancisco™ are trademarks of HarperCollins Publishers Inc.

Library of Congress Cataloging in Publication Data

Starhawk.
    The spiral dance : a rebirth of the ancient religion of the great goddess / Starhawk.
    —20th anniversary ed., with new introd. and chapter-by-chapter commentary.
    Bibliography: p.
    Includes index.
    ISBN 0–06–250815–6 (cloth)
    ISBN 0–06–250814–8 (pbk.)
    1. Witchcraft. 2. Goddess religion.   I. Title
BF1566.S77   1989
299—dc20   89–45400

Designed by Kris Tobiassen

    02   03   RRDH   10

Contents

Thanks and Acknowledgments   *ix*

Introduction to the Twentieth Anniversary Edition   *1*

Introduction to the Tenth Anniversary Edition   *13*

1. Witchcraft as Goddess Religion   25

2. The World View of Witchcraft   41

3. The Coven   58

4. Creating Sacred Space   80

5. The Goddess   102

6. The God   119

7. Magical Symbols   135

8. Energy: The Cone of Power   154

9. Trance   166

10. Initiation   187

11. Moon Rituals   193

12. The Wheel of the Year   197

13. Creating Religion: Toward the Future   214

Ten Years Later: Commentary on Chapters One through Thirteen   *231*

Twenty Years Later: Commentary on Chapters One
through Thirteen   *263*

Tables of Correspondences   *283*

Select Bibliography   *295*

Suggested Reading   *301*

Resources   *309*

Index   *311*

EXERCISES

1. Shadow Play   44
2. Rhythm Play   44
3. Sensing Group Energy   67
4. Group Breath   67
5. Grounding: The Tree of Life   68
6. Power Chant   68
7. Earthing Power   69
8. Word Association Trance   71
9. Relaxation   73
10. Grounding and Centering   74
11. Simple Visualizations   74
12. The Apple   75
13. The Pentacle   75
14. The Knot   75
15. Candle Gazing   76
16. The Diamond   76
17. Mirror, Mirror   76
18. The Rock   77
19. The Hammer   77
20. Salt-Water Purification   84
21. Group Salt-Water Purification   84
22. Banishing   85
23. Air Meditation   87
24. *Athame* or Sword Meditation   88
25. Fire Meditation   88
26. Wand Meditation   88
27. Water Meditation   89
28. Cup Meditation   89
29. Earth Meditation   90
30. Pentacle Meditation— The Five Stages of Life   90
31. The Iron Pentagram   91
32. The Pentagram of Pearl   92
33. Transformation Meditation   93
34. Cauldron Meditation   93
35. The Circle Visualization Exercise   94
36. Consecrating a Tool   95
37. Protective Circle   100
38. Permanent Protective Circle   100
39. Waxing Moon Meditation   104
40. Full Moon Meditation   105
41. Waning Moon Meditation   105
42. The Double Spiral   107
43. Binding a Spell   141
44. Protective Filter   142
45. The Cone of Power   159
46. Womb Chant   160
47. Formal Grounding   160
48. Pendulum Exercise   162
49. Sensing the Aura: Pendulum Method   163
50. Sensing the Aura: Direct Method   163
51. Damping and Projecting Energy   163
52. Seeing the Aura   164
53. Cautions   176
54. The Rainbow: Trance Induction   177
55. Place of Power   178
56. The Rainbow: Emerging   178
57. Scrying   179
58. Suggestion   180
59. Memory   180
60. Trance into a Dream   181
61. Ritual Induction   182

INVOCATIONS, CHANTS, AND BLESSINGS

The Casting of the Circle   80, and
    240–241
A Circle for Healing During
    Struggle (Alan Acacia)   97
Valerie's Rhyming
    Invocations   98
Invocations from the Summer
    Solstice Ritual   99
The Charge of the Goddess   102
Repeating Chants
    (to the Goddess)   111
Repeating Cycle:
    "Green Bud Leaf"   112
Sumerian Chant   112
Invocation to the Dewy One   112
Honor to the Goddess
    (Karen Lynd Cushen)   113
Kore Chant   114
Invocation to the Goddess as
    Mother (Susan Stern)   115
Moonmother (Laurel)   116

Invocation to the Queen of
    Summer   118
Invocation to the God   119
Repeating Chants
    (to the God)   129
Repeating Cycle:
    "Sun Shine Day"   129
Equinox Invocation of the Male
    Aspect (Alan Acacia)   129
Invocation to the God of
    Summer   130
Invocation to the Goddess
    and God (Valerie)   130
Invocation to the Ground
    of Being   131
Song to Pan (Mark Simos)   131
Blessing over Cakes
    and Wine   184
Farewell to the Goddess
    and God   185
Opening the Circle   185

SPELLS

Anger Spell   143
The Indrinking Spell   143
Spell for Loneliness   144
Spell for Fallow Periods   145
Safe Space Spell   146

Spell to Know the
    Child Within   147
Spell to Be Friends with
    Your Womb   148

HERBAL CHARMS

To Attract Money   149
To Attract Love   149
To Heal a Broken Heart   149

For Protection   149
To Get a Job   150
For Inner Power   150

For Eloquence   150
To Win in Court   150
To Charge an Herbal Charm   151

Healing Image Spell   151
To Bind an Enemy   152

MYTHS

Creation   41
The Wheel of the Year   52, 236, and 257

The Goddess in the
   Kingdom of Death   187

PRINCIPLES

Reclaiming Principles of Unity   6

Thanks and Acknowledgments

This book could not have come into being without the love and support of my former husband, Ed Rahsman, and my mother, Dr. Bertha Simos.

For the opportunity to explore and strive to understand the Mysteries, I thank the members of my covens: in Compost, Guidot, Quest, Diane, Beth, Arden, Mother Moth, Amber, Valerie, and Paul; in Honeysuckle, Laurel, Brook, Susan, Zenobia, Diane, and especially Kevyn, for the added inspiration of her drawing.

I would also like to acknowledge those who have taught me the Craft: Victor and Cora Anderson, Ruth, Z. Budapest, and the others.

I am also grateful for the support and encouragement of the Bay Area Pagan community and Witches of the Covenant of the Goddess, and for friends and companions too numerous to be listed here. In particular, I want to thank my brother-in-spirit, Alan Acacia, and my brother-in-flesh, Mark Simos, for their contributions; Patty and Nada, for being there in the beginning; Ann, for her inspiration; and Carol Christ and Naomi Goldenberg, for their help in reaching a wider community.

Finally, I want to express my appreciation to my editor, Marie Cantlon, for her sensitivity and courage in taking on this subject, and to Sarah Rush, for all her help.

To all of you, to She Who Sings in the Heart, and He Who Dances, this work is dedicated.

Thanks for the Second Edition

Besides those listed above, I want to thank the members of Wind Hags, Matrix, and especially the Reclaiming Collective. The rituals we have made together, the work we have done teaching, writing, and organizing, and our arguments, conflicts, jokes, and discussions through the years form the matrix of community from which my own changes have been born.

I have been extremely fortunate in my associations in the publishing world. Marie Cantlon, who edited the first edition, has remained my good friend and editor throughout this decade and for all of my subsequent books. She has also edited many of the books listed in the bibliography, being a true mother of this movement. Jan Johnson and Yvonne Keller at Harper & Row have been supportive and understanding editors of this edition. My agent, Ken Sherman, has done his best over the last ten years to keep me solvent. Pleides Akasha assisted me in preparing this manuscript with great cheerfulness. Raven Moonshadow reviewed the Tables of Correspondences.

The Black Cats, members of my collective household, put up with my complaining and called me to dinner. And I want to thank my friend Kate Kaufman for suggesting the idea to do this edition.

While I was writing these revisions, two members of the old Honeysuckle coven have made the transition into Mother in a literal sense, giving birth to two beautiful daughters: Nora and Vivian Sarah. To all of you, thanks and love.

Thanks for the Third Edition

I want to thank my editor, Liz Perle, and all the folks at Harper San Francisco for their warm support for this new edition. I am also deeply grateful for the continuing friendship and inspiration and guidance of Marie Cantlon, who edited the first edition of this book. My agent, Ken Sherman, has also hung in with me for the long haul.

I am fortunate having the love and support of many people around me. My husband, David, keeps me smiling. My housemates and magical partners keep me going, and Madrone and Jodi Selene in different ways attempt to keep me organized. Mary Ellen Donald trained me in the magical skill of drumming. But most of all, I want to acknowledge the inspiration of working with the extended web of Reclaiming teachers, organizers, and community folks as we cocreate magic together.

And I acknowledge with sorrow the passing of my mother, Bertha Simos; of Raven Moonshadow; and of Mother Moth. All of them leave a legacy of contributions to this work.

STARHAWK
CAZADERO, MARCH 1999

Introduction to the Twentieth Anniversary Edition

Movements are like plants. Some, like annuals, spring up in a season, take over the garden, flourish, and die when winter comes. Others, and the Goddess movement is one of them, grow like perennials. In the first few years, most progress is underground. Only when they have developed strong roots do the plants spring into wild and exuberant growth. Perennials develop slowly, but they have staying power. They spring up anew when winter ends. Their deep roots let them withstand drought. They live long, and reproduce from roots and runners as well as seeds.

The Spiral Dance is a seed planted twenty years ago. Over the last two decades, the Goddess movement has grown from many seeds, like a garden of long-lived flowers and healing herbs. It's a big garden: I've tended only one corner of it. But twenty years is long enough for perennials to come into full blossom and for fruit trees to mature. We can look back now and see the results of our planting, weeding, and tending.

In 1979, I ended the book with a chapter called "Creating Religion: Toward the Future." One of the disconcerting things about life is that the future has a way of catching up with you. I wrote the book on an electric typewriter when White-Out was the leading-edge word-processing technology. I wrote the ten-year notes on an early model home computer with a minuscule screen and no hard drive, and I'm writing these notes on a Mac laptop that, at five years old, is already outdated. My source of power is the solar panels on my roof, and when I take a break from working I'll be checking into an online meeting of Witchcraft teachers and organizers from across the United States, Canada, and Europe, or possibly updating my Web page. The future is already here.

Besides technological changes, political changes have reshaped the world in the last two decades. This book was conceived during the Carter era. Since then, we've seen Reagan and Bush come and go, the waxing and waning of the revolutionary movements in Central America, the fall of the Soviet Union, the end of apartheid, and the impeachment of a popular president in a drama so sleazy and bizarre that no one in 1979 could possibly have imagined it.

In approaching this new edition, I wondered if the book would still make sense on the edge of a new millennium, and in the light of both world changes and the tremendous growth of the Goddess movement in the last two decades. Ten years ago, we were still putting down roots, growing steadily but not as visibly. Today we are in that fine flush of perennial growth when the roots reach deep for underground waters and runners begin to multiply and spread.

In 1979, I was in my twenties, and most of my coven sisters and brothers were also young. I was still inventing my own life and figuring out some basic things, like what I wanted to be when I grew up and how to get the dishes done before the supply of clean plates was exhausted. I'm amazed at how that person, that mere snip of girl I remember being, knew some of the things in this book and why, if she knew them, she didn't apply them more clearly and consistently in her own life.

Now I'm middle-aged. I'm wiser, neater, and less judgmental although far more irritable. I don't see or hear as well, although I'm probably stronger and in better shape (if thicker around the middle) than I was in my twenties. I already am what I'm going to be when I grow up. Now I think about who is going to carry on this work when I'm gone, and what I want to be in my next life. In this one, it's too late for me to become a surfer, a professional flamenco dancer, a biological mother. These are choices I must now accept. Middle age is a time for coming to peace with decisions and life choices. The garden beds are built, and the perennials have had time to settle in. Either you continue to tend them or you toss it all out and start all over again at a time in life when double digging throws your back out. Time runs differently. This year we planted a grove of olive trees: I'll be in my midfifties by the time they bear fruit, and an old woman when they reach full maturity. Recently a friend I thought of as a contemporary informed me that she was "raised on the Spiral Dance." Not long after, a young woman inquiring about a class asked a friend of mine if she was familiar with the work of a woman named Starhawk. "Oh yes, I know her well," my friend replied. "I work with her closely." "Oh—is she still alive?" the caller asked.

I am still alive, and hope to remain so for a good long while yet. So is this book. I'm gratified that I still want to work in this garden. The soil is still rich, and the structure, the theology, the ethics, the politics, and the magical training and exercises are sound.

The insights in this book form the basic framework of understanding that has supported me throughout my adult life. The perennials that took root twenty years ago still nourish me. I know more about magic, ritual, energy, and groups than I did then. But the more I know, the simpler magic becomes. I still use and teach the exercises given here, and when I've changed them it is not because they're ineffective but because I felt a personal need to do something new.

There are aspects of this book I wish were irrelevant. A major thrust of this work is its challenge to the spiritual supremacy of patriarchal males and male images. I would have hoped those issues would be outdated by now, but they are not. I'd like to think the introduction to the fiftieth anniversary edition might read:

"This classic work of the past millennium brings us back to a time when religious teachers, leaders, and deities were nearly all men. How hard it is to conceive of that era now, when women abound in the highest decision-making bodies of every major religion, when rape, incest, and domestic violence have become as rare and unthinkable as cannibalism, when religious language is so universally gender-inclusive, when children learn Solstice chants along with Christmas carols, Hanukkah songs, and Kwanza prayers, and new Goddess traditions spring up annually."

There are also plants that didn't grow and others that were probably a mistake to introduce into the garden. In the 1989 introduction, I wrote extensively about my shift away from a polarized view of the world as a dance of "female" and "male" qualities and energies, and toward a much more complex and inclusive view of gender and energy. That shift continues to deepen as I grow older, and it is still the major change I would make in this book. I have commented on others in the notes.

I also notice that throughout this book, I'm critical of Eastern traditions. In the seventies, they were the alternative people often turned to when mainstream religions left a void. There were new gurus every month, and I saw many women I knew fall into what seemed to me oppressive situations. Now, I have a lot more humility about judging something that's not my own. I've also grown to appreciate the deep wisdom and great diversity within those traditions.

Finally, were I writing today I would probably be more cautious about the history I present. In researching a film on the archaeologist Marija Gimbutas, I've become aware of the controversy that rages in academic circles around the history of the Goddess. When I wrote this book, I was not attempting to do historical scholarship or archaeology. Writing as a Witch, I felt free to involve my imagination in a reconstruction of the past. In reality, the most "objective" of historians do the same; they're just not so blatant about it. Today I might exhibit more middle-aged caution, but to do so might undercut the real power of this history, which lies in the awakening of imagination and a sense of possibilities. What I and many others are saying is simply, "Hey, it wasn't always like this. It doesn't always have to be like this! So—what culture do we want to live in? Let's create it!"

That statement could be read as the Short Form of the Origin Story of Contemporary Goddess Worship. Recent attacks on the Goddess tradition have tried to discredit our history, often with scholarship that is blatantly biased and inaccurate. The idea seems to be that if they can disprove our origin story, they can invalidate our spirituality. This is odd, because nobody applies the same standards to the origin myths of other religions. Is Buddhism invalid if we cannot find archaeological evidence of Buddha's existence? Are Christ's teachings unimportant if we cannot find his birth certificate or death warrant?

Witches, on the whole, are interested in discussions of our history. There are now conferences, magazines, articles, and panels at the American Academy of Religions on the subject. But that interest is separate from any sense that the validity of our spiritual choices depends on documenting their origins, their antiquity, or their provenance. This has sometimes been misquoted as "not caring about truth." In reality, it's simply saying that the truth of our experience is valid whether it has roots thousands of years old or thirty minutes old, that there is a mythic truth whose proof is shown not through references and footnotes but in the way it engages strong emotions, mobilizes deep life energies, and gives us a sense of history, purpose, and place in the world. What gives the Goddess tradition validity is how it works for us now, in the moment, not whether or not someone else worshipped this particular image in the past.

In the past twenty years, our rituals have taken on a life of their own separate from any question of origins. This year, on the Winter Solstice, the temperature suddenly dropped below freezing on Solstice Eve. Nevertheless, over two hundred people gathered on the beach, and most of us stripped off our clothes and went running into the ocean for our now-traditional ritual purification. The exhilaration of the cold, the wind, the beauty of the night, the sheer wild craziness of the plunge, and our naked ecstatic dance around the bonfire created an archetypal Pagan ritual that felt thousands of years old. I know this particular tradition was born out of a whim less than twenty years ago, not Divine Decree lost in ages past. On one of the first Solstices I celebrated with my early women's coven, we went to the beach to watch the sunset before our evening ritual. One woman said, "Let's take off our clothes and jump in. Come on, I dare you!" "You're out of your mind," I remember saying, but we did it anyway. After a few years, it occurred to us to light a fire, staving off hypothermia, and so a tradition was born. (Do something once, it's an experiment. Do it twice, and it's a tradition.) My knowledge of the less-than-celestial inspiration of this rite doesn't diminish the power of the ritual for me in the least. "What is the origin of this ancient custom?" is not something Pagans are likely to say, although we might well ask, "Whose idea was this, anyway?"

In the history of the reawakening of the Goddess, 1979 was a pivotal year. The ground had been fertilized by many people: Witches meeting secretly in small covens, a very few open Pagan groups, the hippies of the sixties, and the feminists of the early seventies. Z. Budapest had been teaching feminist Wicca in southern California for many years. Women were beginning to look at religion and spirituality as a feminist issue. Merlin Stone's book *When God Was a Woman* was published in 1976. In 1979, three important works were published. One was this book. Margot Adler's *Drawing Down the Moon* chronicled the growth of Witchcraft and Paganism through the seventies. And *Womanspirit Rising*, edited by Carol Christ and Judith Plaskow, introduced the world to the challenges women were posing to patriarchal religion both within and outside of the churches and synagogues.

The year 1979 was also when my friends and I organized a large public ritual. In part as a celebration of the publication of this book, we gathered artists, musicians, and dancers and wrote poetry and music for a Halloween ritual we called "The Spiral Dance Ritual." As in gardening, some things you plant persist and take on a life of their own. The Spiral Dance has now become an annual tradition in San Francisco, with its own body of music and liturgy. (See Resources.) Last year fifteen hundred people danced the double spiral.

The group that put on the first Spiral Dance evolved into a collective we called Reclaiming. Many of us participated in nonviolent direct action throughout the eighties, and the lessons we learned in empowerment, participatory organization, and consensus process strongly influenced our organization and the way we planned, taught, and created ritual. Over the years, Reclaiming also evolved. From teaching, training, and offering ritual in the San Francisco Bay Area, we began giving weeklong summer intensives, "Witch Camps," in other parts of North America and, later, Europe. Each camp, in turn, became the nucleus of teaching and organizing in other communities. Our local newsletter grew into a national magazine. Its latest issue reports classes and rituals in fifteen or sixteen communities throughout the United States, Canada, and Europe.

Reclaiming has become much more than a local collective. We are a tradition of the Craft. In the midnineties, we began a period of reorganizing and restructuring, struggling with the question of how to expand without becoming a hierarchy or a bureaucracy. In 1997, we reached consensus on the following statement of our core values:

> RECLAIMING PRINCIPLES OF UNITY
> "My law is love unto all beings . . ."
> The Charge of the Goddess

The values of the Reclaiming tradition stem from our understanding that the earth is alive and all of life is sacred and interconnected. We see the Goddess as immanent in the earth's cycles of birth, growth, death, decay, and regeneration. Our practice arises from a deep, spiritual commitment to the earth, to healing, and to the linking of magic with political action.

Each of us embodies the divine. Our ultimate spiritual authority is within, and we need no other person to interpret the sacred to us. We foster the questioning attitude, and we honor intellectual, spiritual, and creative freedom.

We are an evolving, dynamic tradition and proudly call ourselves Witches. Honoring both Goddess and God, we work with female and male images of divinity, always remembering that their essence is a mystery that goes beyond form. Our community rituals are participatory and ecstatic, celebrating the cycles of the seasons and our lives, and raising energy for personal, collective, and earth healing.

We know that everyone can do the life-changing, world-renewing work of magic, the art of changing consciousness at will. We strive to teach and practice in ways that foster personal and collective empowerment, to model shared power, and to open leadership roles to all. We make decisions by consensus, and balance individual autonomy with social responsibility.

Our tradition honors the wild and calls for service to the earth and the community. We value peace and practice nonviolence, in keeping with the Rede "Harm none, and do what you will." We work for all forms of justice: environmental, social, political, racial, gender, and economic. Our feminism includes a radical analysis of power, seeing all systems of oppression as interrelated, rooted in structures of domination and control.

We welcome all genders, all races, all ages and sexual orientations, and all those differences of life situation, background, and ability that increase our diversity. We strive to make our public rituals and events accessible and safe. We try to balance the need to be justly compensated for our labor with our commitment to make our work available to people of all economic levels.

All living beings are worthy of respect. All are supported by the sacred elements of air, fire, water, and earth. We work to create and sustain communities and cultures that embody our values, that can help to heal the wounds of the earth and her peoples, and that can sustain us and nurture future generations.

Reclaiming's coming of age reflects similar growth occurring among many Pagan groups. The nineties have seen Wiccan and Pagan groups continue to expand. More people began openly teaching and offering public rituals. The Internet supplied the safe meeting ground Pagans and Witches had not had for centuries. When people had a way to make connections without risk, the movement mushroomed. Now many groups are struggling with these same issues of growth and continuity as we move into the new century.

Amory Lovins says the primary design criteria he uses is the question "How do we love all the children?" Not just our children, not just the ones who look like us or who have resources, not just the human children but the young of birds and salmon and redwood trees. When we love all the children, when that love is truly sacred to us in the sense of being most important, then we have to take action in the world to enact that love. We are called to make the earth a place where all the children can thrive.

The Spiral Dance linked Goddess spirituality with political activism decades ago. In spite of fears by some political feminists that interest in the Goddess would divert energy from political work, Pagans and Witches have accrued a proud record of involvement in feminist issues, gay liberation, and antinuclear, antiwar, and environmental campaigns. Personally, I stopped counting my arrests in direct action when they numbered something like two dozen. I chronicled some of the work we did in nonviolent direct action in the introduction to the tenth anniversary edition of this book. Over the last ten years, our community's political work has broadened in scope. In the last few months, for example, I've gone up to the Headwaters forest base camp to offer support for the blockade protesting the clear-cutting of old-growth redwoods; spoken at rallies; circulated petitions, and picketed the GAP as part of a boycott protesting logging activities in Mendocino County; visited an action camp in Minneapolis, where a strong Pagan presence has been an integral part of the organizing, to offer support and ritual; helped to found an organization in our community to address land use issues; facilitated meetings; opened a dialogue with vineyard owners around their use of pesticides; traveled to El Salvador to visit the sister communities Reclaiming supports; passed out endless flyers; wrote to state, local, and federal representatives and the California Department of Forestry—not counting the petitions I've signed online, or the work of teaching and writing, which I consider highly political, or the hands-on organic gardening and permaculture I do on my own land. (And then there are the tree-climbing lessons—but we won't speak of those. Let us all pray that the survival of the redwoods never hinges on my ability to scale up a tree higher than about fifteen feet.) I'm more public than most Pagans, but not atypical. Our community has been deeply involved in direct action around nuclear power and weapons, Central American solidarity, and antimilitarism. We currently participate in an ongoing support program for a group in El Salvador that teaches sustainability. We are involved as well in feminist issues, gay liberation, and AIDS activism. The latest issue of the *Reclaiming Quarterly* reports on issues ranging from Headwaters to support for a local soup kitchen, from protesting the School of the Americas to an interview with the director of the Rainforest Action Network.

Not all Pagans or Goddesses are political activists, any more than all Christians, Jews, or secular humanists are. But in a cross section of the Pagan community you will find more activists per population than in just about any other spiritual tradition, except the Unitarians and Quakers, who have been breeding activists for centuries. And some are second-generation Pagans, among the first group of young people raised in the reemergent Goddess tradition.

The new areas I'm exploring arise from changes in my own life. A few years ago, while meditating in—where else?—my garden, I received this message: "You're teaching too much meditation and not enough observation." As a Witch, as a therapist, as a writer and novelist, I had spent years immersed in my own and others' internal imagery. I loved nature: I worshipped her and had often gone to jail defending her, but in many ways I really knew very little about her. My education had focused on art, psychology, and film, not biology, forestry, or horticulture. I grew herbs and made compost and took long walks in the hills, but often the garden, the forest, and the ocean were simply scenic backdrops to my own thoughts.

I shifted my personal practice to spend some time each day in nature, observing what is going on around me, whether I'm in the forest or in a backyard in the city. I began reading and studying, attending conferences; I took a permaculture design course that offered training in reading the land, working with nature, and in ecological design. The garden began talking louder and louder. "Grow food," the garden said. "Do you realize how much I travel?" "I don't care, just grow food. Because when you eat food grown on the land, you become the land."

Growing at least some food for myself and my friends and family became part of my personal spiritual practice. I began to look not just at food but at the herbs and plants we use in magic in a new way. They were no longer just names gleaned from old books but real characters that I had an ongoing relationship with. In David Abram's book *The Spell of the Sensuous*, he writes: "The traditional or tribal shaman, I came to discern, acts as an intermediary between the human community and the larger ecological field" (p. 7). I began to wonder what that role would look like in the high-tech world of the nineties.

These changes coincided with other personal changes. Somewhere in there

I fell in love with and married a sweet, supportive, and funny man who is also a Witch. David brought with him four wonderful stepdaughters. If you call the youngest of them on the phone, her answering machine invites you to "leave a message for any of these beautiful, empowered, and independent women . . . ," which describes them all. I have two—soon to be three—step-grandchildren and a tribe of Goddess daughters.

My mother died the summer I remarried. A couple of years later, the coven I'd been in for sixteen years dissolved. Covens, like any organism, have a life span, and ours had reached its end. At the same time, Reclaiming's activities were expanding. I found that after teaching five or six intensives a summer, what I needed as a counterbalance was nature and solitude. I began spending more and more time on our land in the coastal hills of northern California, living, as a proper Witch should, in a little hut in the woods, complete with skylights and solar panels.

Now nature was no longer an abstraction but a daily condition. The elements were no longer theoretical: fire meant the real danger of summer wildfire, and the fire I had to build in the woodstove out of wood, someone had to chop. Water meant the hundred or more inches we receive in a wet winter, the erosion it may cause, the spring that supplies our drinking and irrigation water, the pipeline that carries it, with its annoying tendency to break, the tanks that store it, and the drip system that distributes it. The imagery and symbolism I'd been working with for decades finally got real.

My current passion is to integrate more closely the worship of nature with knowledge that comes from the observation of nature, and to infuse science, ecological design, and environmental activism with the deep connectedness that comes from acknowledging the sacred.

Looking back at the past inevitably leads to looking forward to the future, especially on the edge of a new millennium. At one Brigid ritual, I was sitting with Allison, a child I've known and loved since her birth, who lived with us for her first two years. We were close to the cauldron, watching people come up to the fire to make a pledge. The Brigid doll, woven of wheat and grasses and dressed in white, was especially beautiful that year, and Allison was watching with a look of awe on her face. After a time, she gathered her courage and went to the fire to make her first pledge. I realized that this ritual was as central to her universe as the Jewish High Holidays were to me as a child. I remembered the origins of each piece of the ritual: I could say, oh yes, that year we began the pledges, that year we first made a doll. But to her, this was simply a core marker in every year of her life. (She is, after all, the child who at age two encountered the wild crowds that filled the streets of San Francisco after the 49ers won the Super Bowl and thought they were excited because the moon had come back.)

I realized that we who had begun these traditions now had a sacred responsibility. We could not abandon them if some year we simply weren't in the mood, or had other commitments. Or rather, we needed enough of a support system and structure so that if one person dropped back, others would be there to carry on.

In middle age, I no longer operate under the delusion of immortality that sustains the young. I know that I won't be here forever. My concern has shifted from "How do I learn to do this?" to "How do I pass this on?" How do I ensure that others will carry on the work, continue not just to tend the garden but to continue to create it, expand it, compost the plants that no longer thrive, and feed the deep-rooted ones that can live a thousand years?

I hope that in the next two decades our traditions will develop more resources for children and youth. We have not yet been able to love all the children because we have not been free to openly educate our own. Up until the present, the virulent prejudice against Pagans in the larger culture has made any kind of work with children or youth problematic and even dangerous.

That situation is slowly changing. More and more, Pagans are demanding to be seen as a religious tradition just as valid as any other. The ability to openly practice one's faith without fear is a basic religious freedom. At twenty-eight, I didn't mind being a rebel. The need for secrecy around Witchcraft just added to its charm. But at forty-eight, as I see the children grow up around us, I find the necessity for fear and secrecy around our tradition intolerable. We cannot pass on a tradition to the next generation unless we can be open, honest, and unafraid. We cannot continue to be forced to say to our children, "This is beautiful, sacred, and meaningful—but don't tell anyone about it!" Religious freedom is a political issue as much as any other. I'm deeply grateful to the many Pagan organizations that have stressed education, media outreach, and interfaith work in attempting to redress this problem.

I also hope that in the next years, we as a movement can become ever more inclusive, diverse, and accessible, that people of all backgrounds and ancestries will find a warm welcome in our communities and a deep understanding of the complex issues of race and class in our society. Twenty years ago, we often had agonized discussions about whether gays and lesbians and "straight people" could ever work together. Today, in the communities I work with, we take for granted that many different sexual orientations not only can work and celebrate together but also can enrich each other's understanding and broaden our perspectives. There are many other kinds of diversity, however, that are not yet well represented in our communities, and this is one of the greatest challenges we face in the coming years.

A few years ago, I participated in a public ritual for El Día de los Muertos organized by the Latino community in San Francisco and warmly supported by Reclaiming. That year, we mourned the youth who had died from violence on our streets that year, called their names, and grieved for the ways their deaths diminished our community. When the ritual was over, a woman approached me. She was obviously a street person, her face ravaged by years of hard living and pain. "Thank you for that ritual," she said. "I needed it. One of my babies died of an overdose, and one committed suicide, and I really needed that ritual."

Her comment stayed with me as the challenge we take with us into the next century—how to bring ritual and healing, how to bring the fruits we have grown to those who most desperately need them.

When young people ask me for advice today, I generally say, "Decide what is sacred to you, and put your best life energies at its service. Make that the focus of your studies, your work, the test for your pleasures and your relationships. Don't ever let fear or craving for security turn you aside." When you serve your passion, when you are willing to risk yourself for something, your greatest creative energies are released. Hard work is required, but nothing is more joyful than work infused by love.

My mother always hoped that Witchcraft was just a phase I was going through. After twenty years, it seems more in the nature of a lifework. What does it mean to have lived a life in service to the Goddess? In spite of all the anti-Craft prejudice, it has not generally meant great personal sacrifice or danger, although the possibility is always there. What the Goddess has asked of me is more a certain shamelessness, a willingness to stand up for ideas other people find weird, flaky, or silly, to look foolish, to refuse to be molded by others' judgments. New ideas always meet resistance, and one generation's woo-woo weirdness may be another generation's brilliant breakthrough (too often becoming the rigid orthodoxy of yet another era).

It was said of the Goddess Isis that "Her service is perfect freedom." Freedom is among the great rewards I've received in this life—along with love, friendship, good work with good companions, and the satisfaction of feeling my gifts are well used. I've always had what I needed. I'm not rich, but neither am I poor. I consider myself among the most fortunate human beings on this planet, and if I work hard it's out of the desire to give back a small part of what I have.

Twenty years ago, I ended this book with a vision of the future. We're not quite as far into that future as I imagined we would be, but we've made some steps. We have celebrated first blood rites for our daughters, and coming-of-age rituals for our sons. On the Winter Solstice and the full moon, many groups gather and celebrate, in San Francisco and around the world. There are many Witches working to love all the children, to heal the land, to defend the wilderness that remains, to succor the homeless, to comfort the dying, to feed the poor, to nurture the power and vision of women and men of goodwill.

But no, we cannot yet say that in our city no one goes hungry, that no one is left to die alone, that we can walk the dark streets without fearing violence, that the air is clean, that life has returned to the waters of the bay, that we are at peace.

The Goddess continues to awaken in infinite forms and a thousand disguises. We have tilled the garden bed, planted seeds, and tended the slow, early growth. But much work still remains.

STARHAWK
CAZADERO, FEBRUARY 1999

Introduction to the
Tenth Anniversary Edition

This new edition of *The Spiral Dance* has afforded me the opportunity of having a conversation with myself, one in which I hope you, the reader, will feel included. One of the things that fascinates me about writing is the way in which it collapses time. Rereading this, I hear my own voice of a decade past, remember insights I had forgotten and perceptions that had faded. Inevitably, I find ways in which I have changed.

At first, the idea of delving back into my own material of ten years ago seemed an alarming endeavor. On the one hand, I feared finding that many things that seemed absolute certainties at the time would be so changed that my earlier sentiments would seem juvenile or embarrassing. On the other hand, perhaps even more fearful was the thought that perhaps nothing had changed, that my beliefs, thoughts, and practices might have remained static all this time.

Rereading this book has proved reassuring. Yes, there are things that have changed, as the world has changed. But most of what I wrote still holds up. In fact, there is a lot that I had forgotten, having not really read the book in close to a decade, although I've used it as a reference. I find, after writing numerous drafts of a book, retyping three successive drafts (yes, this book was written before the days of home computers), and reading galley proofs and page proofs, that, frankly, I don't want to look at the thing again for a long time.

I was pleasantly surprised, however. My memory of *The Spiral Dance* was of a simple exercise book, an easy-to-read introduction to Witchcraft for beginners. Rereading it, I realize that it is actually a work of poetic thealogy, still a good introduction for beginners, but more complex than I realized. In fact, I'm quite surprised that I produced it when I was in my midtwenties and that it rings with such a tone of authority when I remember that time of my life as being quite insecure.

This book was really born the summer I was seventeen years old, the summer of 1968. I spent most of it hitchhiking up and down the California coast and camping on the beaches. For the first time, I lived in direct contact with nature, day and night. I began to feel connected to the world in a new way, to see everything as alive, erotic, engaged in a constant dance of mutual pleasuring, and myself as a special part of it all. But I didn't yet have a way to name my experience.

I returned home and started college at UCLA. A friend and I began teaching a class in Witchcraft as an independent project for our anthropology class. We didn't actually know anything about Witchcraft when we began teaching, but that didn't stop us from offering the course, which we ran as a sort of seminar, encouraging each of our fellow students to research some aspect of the subject and report. Thus we learned quite a lot, and even formed a coven, in spite of not knowing exactly what a coven was or what it was supposed to do. We improvised rituals, which as I recall involved a lot of banging on sticks and rhythm and group massage.

When we finally met real Wiccan Witches, they came to the converted fraternity house in which several of us were living in loose communal fashion and read us the Charge of the Goddess. As I heard the words, I had a strong sense, not of hearing something new, but of finding names and a framework for understanding the experiences I had already had.

The concept of a religion that worshipped a Goddess was amazing and empowering. Raised Jewish, I had been very religious as a child and had pursued my Jewish education to an advanced level. But as I reached young womanhood in the late sixties, something seemed lacking. The feminist movement had not yet entered its period of resurgence, and I had never heard the word *patriarchy*, but I sensed that the tradition as it stood then was somehow lacking in models for me as a woman and in avenues for the development of female spiritual power. (In subsequent years, certain branches of Judaism have opened up more directions for women's empowerment and broader ways of experiencing God, but at that time this process had not yet begun.)

The Goddess tradition opened up new possibilities. Now my body, in all its femaleness, its breasts, vulva, womb, and menstrual flow, was sacred. The wild power of nature, the intense pleasure of sexual intimacy, took center stage as paths to the sacred instead of being denied, denigrated, or seen as peripheral.

We began training with the Witches we met, but they wanted certain things from us that I was incapable of doing at the time: primarily, a regular discipline of meditation, study, and exercise. I drifted away but continued to treasure the introduction I had had to the religion of the Goddess.

In the early seventies, I lived in Venice, a section of Los Angeles that at that time was a strong community of many artists, writers, political activists, and generally eccentric characters. I had become deeply involved with the women's movement and identified myself as a feminist. To me, there seemed to be a natural connection between a movement to empower women and a spiritual tradition based on the Goddess.

While most feminists at that time were suspicious and critical of any turn toward spirituality, identifying it with either patriarchal control or apolitical escapism, some others were beginning to encounter the history and symbolism of the Goddess. In Venice, Z. Budapest, a hereditary Witch from Hungary, began teaching and training many women in a feminist tradition of Wicca. I met her one day close to the Spring Equinox, in her shop on a busy street, and she invited me to the first large all-women's ritual I attended. We walked to a beautiful hillside on the Santa Monica mountains, chanted, danced, and poured libations to the Goddess. I asked for healing for a friend who was going through an intense emotional crisis, and Z. looked me in the eye and said, "Ask for something for yourself." "No," I thought, "that's bad, selfish, and besides, I don't have any needs," but she was, wisely, adamant. "In our tradition it's good to have needs and desires," she said. "We are not a religion of self-abnegation."

I can't recall exactly what I asked for (which tells me how reluctant I was to own my own needs), but the ritual began a process of change and transformation, working in the way magic often does: by making everything fall apart. My relationship dissolved, my job ended, and I decided to leave town.

I had begun writing the week I turned twenty-one. My mother gave me an electric typewriter as a birthday and college graduation present. I was starting graduate school in filmmaking at UCLA, and I took a summer writing course. I sat down at the typewriter, and a feeling of doom overcame me. Something said, "You're going to spend a lot of your life here."

So that summer and fall I wrote a novel that won the Samuel Goldwyn Writing Award at UCLA, giving me what seemed at the time to be a staggering sum of money and illusory expectations of immediate success. I followed it with a second novel. Neither was ever published, which is just as well. They served their real purpose, which was to teach me the craft and discipline of writing.

But of course, nobody sits down and writes an entire novel with the idea that it is just an exercise. So, the summer I turned twenty-three, depressed by rejection slips, unsure what I wanted to do with my life, and eager for physical challenges and contact with nature, I took off with a bicycle to travel for a year.

That year was a formative one for *The Spiral Dance*, although I couldn't have imagined it at the time. It became an odd sort of vision quest. As I pedaled along in the wake of Winnebagos, camped in a leaking tent in the rain, and developed an expertise in getting taken in by strangers, as I spent every day out in the open air, tested the limits of my body, and encountered the intricate, untamed wild places of the West Coast, new dimensions of myself began to unfold. The year was an initiation during which I learned to trust my intuition and let it be my guide.

By winter, my intuition led me to New York City, where I tried unsuccessfully to find a publisher for my novels. I wanted to be a writer, which at the time seemed to be partly a function of living in New York and meeting the right people, but I didn't know how to go about meeting the right people or what to say to them if I met them. I cleaned house for an elderly woman for money and imposed on the hospitality of some very nice people who let me stay in their apartment far longer than they had any reason to. (I was, at that time in my life, the terrible sort of person who shows up to stay for a weekend and ends up living with you for three months. All I can say in my behalf is that since then I have more than repaid my karmic debts in this matter.)

I was cold, I was lonely, I was getting nowhere, and it seemed that everyone else was suddenly going to law school. Then I had a series of very powerful dreams. One told me to go back to the West Coast. In it I was standing by the ocean, looking out on a rock outcropping. Suddenly I realized that it was full of marvelous animals: sea lions, penguins, birds. "I didn't know all of these wonderful things were here," I thought.

In another dream I looked up to see a hawk flying across the sky. There was a feeling to the dream that I cannot capture in words, as if the universe shimmered and split to reveal some underlying shining pattern of things. The hawk swooped down and turned into an old woman. I felt that I was under her protection.

I made my way back to the West Coast (by car, not bicycle) and moved up to San Francisco with my friend Nada, where I began reading Tarot cards and palms at a series of psychic fairs and doing other odd forms of temporary jobs. One of the agents I'd met in New York had suggested I try nonfiction. She claimed it was easier to get published than fiction.

I decided that I wanted to write something about women, feminism, and spirituality, so I began researching the history and traditions of the Goddess. At first Nada collaborated, but after a short time she went on to other pursuits. At the same time I began teaching classes in ritual and related skills, and out of them the Compost coven was formed. For teaching I began using the name Starhawk, which I took from my dream about the hawk and from the Star card in the Tarot, which represents the Deep Self. And I began actually practicing some of the disciplines of magical training that had been suggested to me seven years earlier.

The Bay Area had a thriving Pagan community, and I soon met people from many other covens and traditions, including Victor and Cora Anderson, who trained me in the Faery tradition. Bay Area Witches formed the Covenant of the

Goddess, which incorporated as a legally recognized church. I was elected first officer in 1976 and became active as a spokesperson for the Craft.

All this time I was writing draft after draft of *The Spiral Dance*, sending out proposals and sample chapters and receiving rejections in return. One that I'll never forget said: "I don't think this author knows what she's trying to say and I doubt that she has the intelligence to say it if she did." In the fall of 1977 I finished an entire manuscript of the book and, in a flush of enthusiasm, got married three months later. This manuscript, like the earlier proposals, bounced from publisher to publisher for the next year or two, receiving no interest from anyone.

I was still teaching, still writing, still involved with my covens and with the small but growing community of people interested in ritual and Goddess religion. For money I did temporary secretarial work or wrote for technical films. But this was, to say the least, a discouraging time in my life. I had been writing seriously for five or six years with no success, as far as I could tell. In desperation, I applied to the creative writing program at San Francisco State University. They rejected me.

(Perhaps you, the reader, are in a similar phase in your life? Good luck!)

Finally, my luck turned. Carol Christ, coeditor of *Womanspirit Rising*, included an article I wrote about Witchcraft and Goddess religion. She invited me to present it as a paper at the annual meeting of the American Academy of Religion. There she introduced me to Marie Cantlon, her editor at Harper & Row, San Francisco. Marie was interested in seeing my book, and I sent it to her. Months passed.

Then, at last, I got the news I'd been hoping for: They wanted to publish the book. At that point, I sat down to revise the manuscript and wrote the version you read here.

The past ten years have seen enormous changes, in my own life, in the Craft and Pagan communities, and in the world as a whole. Interest in feminist spirituality, Paganism, earth religions, and Witchcraft has grown enormously. Nobody registers Witches or keeps official statistics of Pagans, but some indication of this growth can be seen in the number of books on the Goddess published since 1979. Many, many people have participated in circles and rituals. *The Spiral Dance* has sold over one hundred thousand copies and been translated into German and Danish. I have spoken and taught in communities all over the United States, in Canada, and in Europe. Pagan publications, newsletters, and even computer bulletin boards abound.

Feminist spirituality, Paganism, and Witchcraft overlap but are not identical communities. Many feminists explore their spirituality in the context of Christianity or Judaism, and within those traditions new avenues have opened up for women, although, of course, there are still many struggles to be waged. Others draw from Goddess traditions of many cultures or prefer to create their own rituals without identifying with any particular tradition.

Pagans, and even Witches, may or may not be feminists. Many people are drawn to earth-based spiritual traditions, to the celebration of seasonal cycles and the awakening of broader dimensions of consciousness, without an analysis of the interplay of power and gender. But the feminist Craft has also grown enormously, including many men as well as women and participating in many arenas of social and political struggle.

My own life has become much more politically focused in the past ten years. *The Spiral Dance* was written during the Carter era, a more sanguine time politically, before the right-wing backlash of the Reagan years. Many of us who had been politically active in the sixties felt that we could, perhaps, relax a bit. True, society was still full of inequalities, women's liberation was a process barely begun, and there had been no major shift in social organization, but perhaps the road to those changes needed to pass through the terrain of the interior and transform our cultural imagery as well as our economic system and national policy. Maybe, in fact, deep transformation of society could only come from an underlying transformation of culture.

I saw *The Spiral Dance* as a political book, in the sense that it brought into question the underlying assumptions on which systems of domination were based, and I still see it that way. But over the last decade, as the gap between rich and poor widened, as our nuclear arsenals were rebuilt, and the homeless began to die in our streets and the jobless to crowd the bread lines, as the United States moved into covert and overt wars in Latin America, and the AIDS virus spread while legislators sat on funds for education and treatment, as the environment deteriorated, the national debt quadrupled, and the hole in the ozone layer grew ominously, a more active political engagement seemed called for.

One of the core principles of the thealogy presented here is that the earth is sacred. Believing that, I felt that action to preserve and protect the earth was called for. So our commitment to the Goddess led me and others in our community to take part in nonviolent direct actions to protest nuclear power, to interfere with the production and testing of nuclear weapons, to counter military interference in Central America, and to preserve the environment. It led me down to Nicaragua and into ongoing work to build alliances with people of color and the native peoples whose own earth-based religions and traditional lands are being threatened or destroyed. It led me out of a faltering marriage to live collectively.

Many of these struggles are chronicled in my later books, *Dreaming the Dark* and *Truth or Dare*. If I were writing *The Spiral Dance* today, perhaps it would have a more overtly political focus. Yet in a way I'm pleased with the focus as it stands. Political awareness can become a tyranny of its own, not least because it locks us into the issues and perspectives of a particular time. But when we are looking at the questions of the sacred, we move beyond time. To create the changes in consciousness needed to transform society at a deep level, we need insights broader than those the issues of the moment can provide.

Spirituality and politics both involve changing consciousness. In fact, Dion Fortune's definition of magic as "the art of changing consciousness at will" could serve for both. Yet there are differences. Effective political action, of whatever sort, needs to offer directions and at least propose answers to current problems. But true spirituality must also take us beyond the will, down into the realms of mystery, of letting go, of echoing questions rather than resounding answers. So I'm glad to have written this book at a time when I had the luxury of pondering the mysteries.

Political activism does, however, increase our awareness in many respects, and for me this has happened especially around issues of inclusiveness and sensitivity to those who are different from myself. Over the last ten years, I've worked to build alliances between women of color and white women and have worked in groups with women and men of differing sexual preferences, class backgrounds, and life choices. I've learned that the viewpoints that arise from differing life situations are vital to complete our picture of reality, and the effort to include them, to take off our blinders and see through another's eyes, can be tremendously enriching.

So my major critique of this work now centers on questions of inclusiveness.

Inclusiveness is especially important when we consider the mysteries, the deep question of our lives. For these questions are meant not to generate dogma but to propel us on journeys. When we ask, "What is reality?" we are not so much looking for an ultimate definition as stating our willingness to be taken somewhere beyond the boundaries of our previous experiences. But that journey cannot be rich and varied unless we are willing to let go of seeing our own experience, our own answers and styles and insights, as defining reality for everyone. We need not deny our experience but must recognize that it is one facet of the gifts that are there for us in other perspectives. If I were writing *The Spiral Dance* today, I would include more material from many races, cultures, and traditions, especially in the historical sections.

When we ask the questions "What is femaleness? What is maleness?" we are stating our willingness to change in ways that may seem frightening, for our conditioning to experience our gender in culturally determined ways runs very deep and in a primary way determines how we experience ourselves. But Witches have a saying: "Where there's fear, there's power." In opening to these questions, we may encounter new aspects of ourselves that liberate our power-from-within.

The feminist movement has prompted the culture as a whole to reexamine questions of maleness and femaleness. For the definitions are no longer working. They are oppressive to women and confining to men.

In this process of transformation, the Goddess and the Old Gods can open doorways for us into new dimensions of our own possibilities, for they are not just symbols but channels of power. Yet we must also be willing to examine how our own interpretations have been shaped by the limitations of our vision. And that is, perhaps, the most central change I would make in this book and the one upon which many of my comments are focused.

When I originally wrote this book, I saw femaleness and maleness as reified qualities, like liquids that could fill us. I believed, along with Jung, that each women had within her a male self, and each man a female self. Now I find these concepts unhelpful and misleading.

Today I don't use the terms *female energy* and *male energy*. I don't identify femaleness or maleness with specific sets of qualities or predispositions. While I have found images of the Goddess empowering to me as a woman, I no longer look to the Goddesses and Gods to define for me what woman or man should be. For any quality that has been assigned to one divine gender can elsewhere be found in its opposite. If we say, for example, "Male energy is aggressive," I can easily find five aggressive goddesses without even thinking hard. If we say "Female energy is nurturing," we can also find male gods who nurture.

Our whole modern tendency to look at myths and deities as role models may be a misappropriation of the power of these images, born of our desperation at not knowing how to be in the world and culture in which we find ourselves. We are looking for permission to be more than our society tells us we are. But the Goddesses and Gods are not figures for us to copy—they are more like broomsticks: Grab hold, and they will take us away somewhere beyond the boundaries of our ordinary lives.

Why are there two sexes? For the same reason we cut the cards before we shuffle the deck. Sexual reproduction is an elegant method of ensuring maximum biological diversity. Yet I would no longer describe the essential quality of the erotic energy flow that sustains the universe as one of female/male polarity. To do so enshrines heterosexual human relationships as the basic pattern of all being, relegating other sorts of attraction and desire to the position of deviant. That description not only makes invisible the realities of lesbians, gay men, and bisexual people; it also cuts all of us off, whatever our sexual preference, from the intricate dance of energy and attraction we might share with trees, flowers, stone, the ocean, a good book or a painting, a sonnet or a sonata, a close friend or a faraway star. For erotic energy inherently generates and celebrates diversity. And Goddess religion, at its heart, is precisely about the erotic dance of life playing through all of nature and culture.

In a world in which power and status are awarded according to gender, we necessarily identify with our gender in a primary way. In a world in which sexual preference is a grounds for either privilege or oppression, we necessarily identify with our sexual orientation. But to take one particular form of sexual union as the model for the whole is to limit ourselves unfairly. If we could, instead, take the whole as the model for the part, then whomever or whatever we choose to love, even if it is ourselves in our solitude, all our acts of love and pleasure could reflect the union of leaf and sun, the wheeling dance of galaxies, or the slow swelling of bud to fruit.

The Spiral Dance was written before the AIDS epidemic surfaced. It is harder today, but perhaps even more necessary, to affirm the sacredness of the erotic. For to say that something is sacred is to say that it is what we deeply value. And AIDS, which is an immune system disease passed on in many ways, only some of which are sexual, has become an excuse for an attack on the erotic, especially on those forms that do not meet society's approval. Out of fear of both the disease and the stigma attached to it, we close off options for ourselves and others.

If society valued the erotic as sacred, AIDS research would be a top priority, as would research on safe forms of birth control. Support would be given to those living with AIDS without extracting from them payment in the form of humiliation or guilt.

AIDS can be a teacher. By confronting us with death, one of the great mysteries, it challenges us to respond with courage, caring, and compassion. Because of AIDS we must speak openly, honestly, and publicly about sexuality. And as one of many immune system diseases we see arising at this time, it serves as a warning that the immune system of the earth herself is under attack from toxins and pollution. So AIDS challenges us on many levels to become healers, of ourselves, our communities, and the earth.

Another healing challenge that the Pagan community has begun to face over the last decade is that of confronting our addictions. Many Pagans are involved with Twelve-Step Programs such as Alcoholics Anonymous and have found their spiritual approach to recovery one that can deepen Craft practice. The Goddess can be a Higher Power, or perhaps we might say a Deeper Power. The language of the Twelve Steps and the traditional forms of meetings may not always work for Pagans, but their insights are extremely valuable to anyone struggling with addictions or codependence and can be adapted to fit our needs.

Awareness of these issues is reflected in one of the overall changes I have made to this edition of the book—the substitution of other drinks for wine in rituals and the change of what we used to call Cakes and Wine to Feasting. I do this not because I think no one should ever drink but so that ritual becomes a safe space for those who are struggling toward recovery from addictions. Those who choose to may still drink wine, but, out of our recognition that to some people in the circle it may be destructive, we no longer pass it in the ritual chalice.

Another overall change has been the elimination of the terms *High Priestess* and *High Priest*. Today, we work nonhierarchically. Any participant might take on the roles once designated for "leaders." Now that we have a core group of highly experienced ritual makers, power, inspiration, and recognition can be more equitably shared. (Which is not to say that we always reach this goal, but we aspire to it.)

The three core principles of Goddess religion are immanence, interconnection, and community. Immanence means that the Goddess, the Gods, are embodied, that we are each a manifestation of the living being of the earth, that nature, culture, and life in all their diversity are sacred. Immanence calls us to live our spirituality here in the world, to take action to preserve the life of the earth, to live with integrity and responsibility.

Interconnection is the understanding that all being is interrelated, that we are linked with all of the cosmos as parts of one living organism. What affects one of us affects us all. The felling of tropical forests disturbs our weather patterns and destroys the songbirds of the North. No less does the torture of a prisoner in El Salvador or the crying of a homeless child in downtown San Francisco disturb our well-being. So interconnection demands from us compassion, the ability to feel with others so strongly that our passion for justice is itself aroused.

And Goddess religion is lived in community. Its primary focus is not individual salvation or enlightenment or enrichment but the growth and transformation that comes through intimate interactions and common struggles. Community includes not only people but also the animals, plants, soil, air and water and energy systems that support our lives. Community is personal—one's closest friends, relatives, and lovers, those to whom we are accountable. But in a time of global communications, catastrophes, and potential violence, community must also be seen as reaching out to include all the earth.

The health of the earth has declined alarmingly over the last ten years, and the next decade may see us take an irrevocable turn, either toward destruction or toward regeneration. We are beginning to reap the results of exploitation and environmental callousness. The ozone layer is being depleted. We see tropical rain forests, the earth's lungs, destroyed at a rapid rate. Everywhere we find deforestation and poisoning of the rivers, lakes and aquifers, and oceans. Every day species become extinct. The sacred lands of native peoples are strip mined or taken as sites for military bases and nuclear tests. If we saw the earth as our extended body, perhaps we would treat her better. Or, given how many of us abuse and harm our own bodies, perhaps we would need a global Twelve-Step Program to counter our collective addiction to ecological destruction.

The problems are overwhelmingly clear, but to solve them we need both tools and vision. I see this book as a tool chest for visionaries, containing many processes for engaging our collective imagination, developing rituals, communities of support, spaces in which to create and enact something new.

Ultimately, the reemergence of the Goddess religion is a conscious attempt to reshape culture. In the past, culture has been reshaped by force. The Witch perse-cutions of the sixteenth and seventeenth centuries are themselves one example. They can be viewed as a mass brainwashing, a conversion through terror to the idea that women's power, and any power not approved of by the authorities, is dangerous, dirty, and sinful.

But *we* cannot reshape consciousness by force or through fear, for to do so would only reinforce what we are trying to change. We must bring about change through nonviolence, physical and spiritual. We are called to take a radical leap of faith, to believe that people, given the opening to dream of new possibilities, with tools and visions will create a living future.

Since divination is a traditional part of the Craft, I decided to consult the Tarot cards for an indication of what to expect for the next ten years. The card that turned up was the Priestess, the Moon Goddess who sits between the pillars of duality, guarding the veil of the mysteries. I take that as an indication that in the next decade we will go deeper into magic and mystery, into explorations of the spirit and forms of knowledge that go beyond the rational. But because the mysteries of earth religion are not separate from this world and this life, that deepened knowledge must lead us into the active work of change.

The renewal of the Goddess religion and other earth-based spiritual traditions will continue to grow over the next decade. As the community grows, our spiritu-ality becomes more embedded in every aspect of our lives. As more children are born and grow up in the Goddess tradition, we will develop more materials for them and more rituals rooted in life cycles and transitions. And of course, the Goddess of inspiration continually moves us to create music, art, theater, and dance as well as creative actions to resist the destruction of the earth and her peoples and to make manifest our visions of what could be.

The possibility also exists that we will experience more repression as we become more visible. But we should never let fear silence us—or we do the oppressors' work for them. Personally, as I've become more public and more visible, I have at times experienced negative reactions, but they have been far outweighed by positive support.

The times we face are both exciting and alarming. The next decade will see crucial decisions made about the future of the environment, the social structure, and the health of the world we leave to the generations that follow. With courage, vision, humor, and creativity, we can use our magic, our ability to change our consciousness, our world view, and our values to reinstate the living web of all interconnected life as the measure by which all choices are judged.

Except in a few cases, I have not changed the original text of this book. Instead, I have added a running commentary, which you will find at the end, keyed to page numbers and phrases in the text. Throughout the text, asterisks mark sections for which new commentary appears, beginning on page 231. Single asterisks mark notes from the tenth anniversary edition; double asterisks mark notes from the twentieth anniversary edition. I suggest that you read each chapter through first and then glance back at the notes to find out what has changed in my thinking. Of course, some of you may want to read the notes first and then read the chapters. And if you're already familiar with the material in the original edition, reading through the notes as a whole will give you a picture of my current thoughts.

In some places I have given new versions of old myths or new interpretations of the material. You are, of course, free to prefer either the new or the old version and to use it as the basis for your own rituals and meditations. In general, all of the material in this book is presented so that you can take it and make it your own, adapt it and change it if need be to fit your inclinations and circumstances, add to what works and discard what doesn't. I consider this a book of tools, not dogma.

I have used these tools myself now for many years and have found that they work in my own life and community. Of course, as you will see, some have undergone change. Other tools continue to be developed. For a living tradition is not static or fixed. It changes and responds to changing needs and changing times.

Many years ago I had a vision of the Goddess, although I didn't know what it was at the time, and I have followed it ever since. I have no regrets. The Goddess continually offers us challenges, but knowing that she is within us as well as around us, we find the strength to meet them, to transform fear into power-from-within, to create communities in which we can grow, struggle, and change, to mourn our losses and celebrate our advances, to generate the acts of love and pleasure that are her rituals. For she is no longer sleeping but awake and rising, reaching out her hands to touch us again. When we reach for her, she reveals herself to us, in the stones and the soil beneath our feet, in the whitewater rapids and limpid pools of the imagination, in tears and laughter, ecstasy and sorrow, common courage and common struggle, wind and fire. Once we have allowed ourselves to look into her open eyes, we can never lose sight of her again. For she faces us in the mirror, and her steps echo each time we place foot to ground. Try to leap away, and she will pull you back. You cannot fall away from her—there is nowhere she is not.

And so it is no accident that this is the moment in history when she arises again, and stretches. For great as the powers of destruction may be, greater still are the powers of healing. Call her the Resilient One, for she is the circle of birth, growth, death, and regeneration. We, as cells of her body, if we listen to our deepest hearts, cannot help but serve the cycles of renewal. May our dreams and visions guide us, and may we find the strength to make them real.

CHAPTER 1

Witchcraft as Goddess Religion

Between the Worlds

The moon is full. We meet on a hilltop that looks out over the bay. Below us, lights spread out like a field of jewels, and faraway skyscrapers pierce the swirling fog like the spires of fairytale towers. The night is enchanted.

Our candles have been blown out, and our makeshift altar cannot stand up under the force of the wind, as it sings through the branches of tall eucalyptus. We hold up our arms and let it hurl against our faces. We are exhilarated, hair and eyes streaming. The tools are unimportant; we have all we need to make magic: our bodies, our breath, our voices, each other.

The circle has been cast. The invocations begin:

> *All-dewy, sky-sailing pregnant moon,*
> *Who shines for all.*
> *Who flows through all . . .*
> *Aradia, Diana, Cybele, Mah . . .*
>
> *Sailor of the last sea,*
> *Guardian of the gate,*
> *Ever-dying, ever-living radiance . . .*
> *Dionysus, Osiris, Pan, Arthur, Hu . . .*

The moon clears the treetops and shines on the circle. We huddle closer for warmth. A woman moves into the center of the circle. We begin to chant her name:
"Diana . . ."
"Dee-ah-nah . . ."
"Aaaah . . ."
The chant builds, spiraling upward. Voices merge into one endlessly modulated harmony. The circle is enveloped in a cone of light.
Then, in a breath—silence.
"You are Goddess," we say to Diane, and kiss her as she steps back into the outer ring. She is smiling.
She remembers who she is.

One by one, we will step into the center of the circle. We will hear our names chanted, feel the cone rise around us. We will receive the gift, and remember:
"I am Goddess. You are God, Goddess. All that lives, breathes, loves, sings in the unending harmony of being is divine."

In the circle, we will take hands and dance under the moon.
> "To disbelieve in witchcraft is the greatest of all heresies."
> *Malleus Maleficarum* (1486)

On every full moon, rituals such as the one described above take place on hilltops, on beaches, in open fields, and in ordinary houses. Writers, teachers, nurses, computer programmers, artists, lawyers, poets, plumbers, and auto mechanics—women and men from many backgrounds come together to celebrate the mysteries of the Triple Goddess of birth, love, and death, and of her Consort, the Hunter, who is Lord of the Dance of life. The religion they practice is called *Witchcraft*.*†

Witchcraft is a word that frightens many people and confuses many others. In the popular imagination, Witches are ugly, old hags riding broomsticks, or evil Satanists performing obscene rites. Modern Witches are thought to be members of a kooky cult, primarily concerned with cursing enemies by jabbing wax images with pins, and lacking the depth, the dignity, and seriousness of purpose of a true religion.

But Witchcraft is a religion, perhaps the oldest religion extant in the West. Its origins go back before Christianity, Judaism, Islam—before Buddhism and Hinduism, as well, and it is very different from all the so-called great religions.

†Throughout the text, one asterisk marks sections for which ten-year commentary appears, beginning on page 231. Two asterisks mark the twenty-year commentary, beginning on page 263.

The Old Religion, as we call it, is closer in spirit to Native American traditions or to the shamanism of the Arctic. It is not based on dogma or a set of beliefs, nor on scriptures or a sacred book revealed by a great man. Witchcraft takes its teachings from nature, and reads inspiration in the movements of the sun, moon, and stars, the flight of birds, the slow growth of trees, and the cycles of the seasons.* **

According to our legends, Witchcraft began more than thirty-five thousand years ago, when the temperature of Europe began to drop and the great sheets of ice crept slowly south in their last advance. Across the rich tundra, teeming with animal life, small groups of hunters followed the free-running reindeer and the thundering bison. They were armed with only the most primitive of weapons, but some among the clans were gifted, could "call" the herds to a cliffside or a pit, where a few beasts, in willing sacrifice, would let themselves be trapped. These gifted shamans could attune themselves to the spirits of the herds, and in so doing they became aware of the pulsating rhythm that infuses all life, the dance of the double spiral, of whirling into being, and whirling out again. They did not phrase this insight intellectually, but in images: the Mother Goddess, the birthgiver, who brings into existence all life; and the Horned God, hunter and hunted, who eternally passes through the gates of death that new life may go on.

Male shamans dressed in skins and horns in identification with the God and the herds; but female priestesses presided naked, embodying the fertility of the Goddess.[1] Life and death were a continuous stream; the dead were buried as if sleeping in a womb, surrounded by their tools and ornaments, so that they might awaken to a new life.[2] In the caves of the Alps, skulls of the great bears were mounted in niches, where they pronounced oracles that guided the clans to game.[3] In lowland pools, reindeer does, their bellies filled with stones that embodied the souls of deer, were submerged in the waters of the Mother's womb, so that victims of the hunt would be reborn.[4]

In the East—Siberia and the Ukraine—the Goddess was Lady of the Mammoths; She was carved from stone in great swelling curves that embodied her gifts of abundance.[5] In the West, in the great cave temples of southern France and Spain, her rites were performed deep in the secret wombs of the earth, where the great polar forces were painted as bison and horses, superimposed, emerging from the cave walls like spirits out of a dream.[6]

The spiral dance was seen also in the sky: in the moon, who monthly dies and is reborn; in the sun, whose waxing light brings summer's warmth and whose waning brings the chill of winter. Records of the moon's passing were scratched on bone,[7] and the Goddess was shown holding the bison horn, which is also the crescent moon.[8]

The ice retreated. Some clans followed the bison and the reindeer into the far north. Some passed over the Alaskan land bridge to the Americas. Those who remained in Europe turned to fishing and gathering wild plants and shell-fish. Dogs guarded their campsites, and new tools were refined. Those who had the inner power learned that it increased when they worked together. As iso-lated settlements grew into villages, shamans and priestesses linked forces and shared knowledge. The first covens were formed. Deeply attuned to plant and animal life, they tamed where once they had hunted, and they bred sheep, goats, cows, and pigs from their wild cousins. Seeds were no longer only gath-ered; they were planted, to grow where they were set. The Hunter became Lord of the Grain, sacrificed when it is cut in autumn, buried in the womb of the Goddess and reborn in the spring. The Lady of the Wild Things became the Barley Mother, and the cycles of moon and sun marked the times for sow-ing and reaping and letting out to pasture.

Villages grew into the first towns and cities. The Goddess was painted on the plastered walls of shrines, giving birth to the Divine Child—her consort, son, and seed.[9] Far-flung trade brought contact with the mysteries of Africa and West Asia.

In the lands once covered with ice, a new power was discovered, a force that runs like springs of water through the earth Herself. Barefoot priestesses trace out "ley" lines on the new grass.* It was found that certain stones increase the flow of power. They were set at the proper points in great marching rows and circles that mark the cycles of time. The year became a great wheel divided into eight parts: the solstices and equinoxes and the cross-quarter days between, when great feasts were held and fires lit. With each ritual, with each ray of the sun and beam of the moon that struck the stones at the times of power, the force increased. They became great reservoirs of subtle energy, gateways between the worlds of the seen and the unseen. Within the circles, beside the menhirs and dolmens and passage graves, priestesses could probe the secrets of time, and the hidden structure of the cosmos. Mathematics, astronomy, poetry, music, medicine, and the understanding of the workings of the human mind developed side by side with the lore of the deeper mysteries.[10]

But later, cultures developed that devoted themselves to the arts of war. Wave after wave of Indo-European invasions swept over Europe from the Bronze Age on. Warrior Gods drove the Goddess peoples out from the fertile lowlands and fine temples, into the hills and high mountains where they became known as the Sidhe, the Picts or Pixies, the Fair Folk or Faeries.[11] The mythological cycle of Goddess and Consort, Mother and Divine Child, which had held sway for thirty thousand years, was changed to conform to the values of the conquering patriarchies. In Greece, the Goddess, in her many guises, "married" the new gods—the result was the Olympian Pantheon. In the

British Isles, the victorious Celts adopted many features of the Old Religion, incorporating them into the Druidic mysteries.

The Faeries, breeding cattle in the stony hills and living in turf-covered, round huts, preserved the Old Religion. Clan mothers, called "Queen of Elphame," which means Elfland, led the covens, together with the priest, the Sacred King, who embodied the dying God, and underwent a ritualized mock death at the end of his term of office. They celebrated the eight feasts of the Wheel with wild processions on horseback, singing, chanting, and the lighting of ritual fires. The invading people often joined in; there were mingling and intermarriage, and many rural families were said to have "Faery blood." The Colleges of the Druids, and the Poetic Colleges of Ireland and Wales, preserved many of the old mysteries.

Christianity, at first, brought little change. Peasants saw in the story of Christ only a new version of their own ancient tales of the Mother Goddess and her Divine Child who is sacrificed and reborn. Country priests often led the dance at the Sabbats, or great festivals.[12] The covens, which preserved the knowledge of the subtle forces, were called *Wicca* or *Wicce*, from the Anglo-Saxon root word meaning "to bend or shape." They were those who could shape the unseen to their will. Healers, teachers, poets, and midwives, they were central figures in every community.

Persecution began slowly. The twelfth and thirteenth centuries saw a revival of aspects of the Old Religion by the troubadours, who wrote love poems to the Goddess under the guise of living noble ladies of their times. The magnificent cathedrals were built in honor of Mary, who had taken over many of the aspects of the ancient Goddess. Witchcraft was declared a heretical act, and in 1324 an Irish coven led by Dame Alice Kyteler was tried by the Bishop of Ossory for worshipping a non-Christian god. Dame Kyteler was saved by her rank, but her followers were burned.

Wars, Crusades, plagues, and peasant revolts raged over Europe in the next centuries. Joan of Arc, the "Maid of Orleans," led the armies of France to victory, but was burned as a Witch by the English. "Maiden" is a term of high respect in Witchcraft, and it has been suggested that the French peasantry loved Joan so greatly because she was, in truth, a leader of the Old Religion.[13] The stability of the medieval Church was shaken, and the feudal system began to break down. The Christian world was swept by messianic movements and religious revolts, and the Church could no longer calmly tolerate rivals.

In 1484, the Papal Bull of Innocent VIII unleashed the power of the Inquisition against the Old Religion. With the publication of the *Malleus Maleficarum*, "The Hammer of the Witches," by the Dominicans Kramer and Sprenger in 1486, the groundwork was laid for a reign of terror that was to hold all of Europe in its grip until well into the seventeenth century. The persecution was most strongly directed against women: Of an estimated nine million Witches executed,* eighty percent were women, including children and young girls, who were believed to inherit the "evil" from their mothers. The asceticism of early Christianity, which turned its back on the world of the flesh, had degenerated, in some quarters of the Church, into hatred of those who brought that flesh into being. Misogyny, the hatred of women, had become a strong element in medieval Christianity. Women, who menstruate and give birth, were identified with sexuality and therefore with evil. "All witchcraft stems from carnal lust, which is in women insatiable," stated the *Malleus Maleficarum*.

The terror was indescribable. Once denounced, by anyone from a spiteful neighbor to a fretful child, a suspected Witch was arrested suddenly, without warning, and not allowed to return home again. She† was considered guilty until proven innocent. Common practice was to strip the suspect naked, shave her completely in hopes of finding the Devil's "marks," which might be moles or freckles. Often the accused were pricked all over their bodies with long, sharp needles; spots the Devil had touched were said to feel no pain. In England, "legal torture" was not allowed, but suspects were deprived of sleep and subjected to slow starvation, before hanging. On the Continent, every imaginable atrocity was practiced—the rack, the thumbscrew, "boots" that broke the bones in the legs, vicious beatings—the full roster of the Inquisition's horrors. The accused were tortured until they signed confessions prepared by the Inquisitors, until they admitted to consorting with Satan, to dark and obscene practices that were never part of true Witchcraft. Most cruelly, they were tortured until they named others, until a full coven quota of thirteen were taken. Confession earned a merciful death: strangulation before the stake. Recalcitrant suspects, who maintained their innocence, were burned alive.

Witch hunters and informers were paid for convictions, and many found it a profitable career. The rising male medical establishment welcomed the chance to stamp out midwives and village herbalists, their major economic competitors. For others, the Witch trials offered opportunities to rid themselves of "uppity women" and disliked neighbors. Witches themselves say that few of those tried during the Burning Times actually belonged to covens or were members of the Craft. The victims were the elderly, the senile, the mentally ill, women whose looks weren't pleasing or who suffered from some handicap, village beauties who bruised the wrong egos by rejecting advances, or who had roused lust in a celibate priest or married man. Homosexuals and

†Generically, Witches are female—this usage is meant to include males, not to exclude them.

freethinkers were caught in the same net. At times, hundreds of victims were put to death in a day. In the Bishopric of Trier, in Germany, two villages were left with only a single female inhabitant apiece after the trials of 1585.

The Witches and Faeries who could do so escaped to lands where the Inquisition did not reach. Some may have come to America. It is possible that a genuine coven was meeting in the woods of Salem before the trials, which actually marked the end of active persecution in this country. Some scholars believe that the family of Samuel and John Quincy Adams were members of the megalithic "Dragon" cult, which kept alive the knowledge of the power of the stone circles.[14] Certainly, the independent spirit of Witchcraft is very much akin to many of the ideals of the "Founding Fathers": for example, freedom of speech and worship, decentralized government, and the rights of the individual rather than the divine right of kings.

This period was also the time when the African slave trade reached its height and the conquest of the Americas took place. The same charges leveled against the Witches—charges of savagery and devil worship—were used to justify the enslavement of the Africans (who were brought to the New World, supposedly, to Christianize them) and the destruction of cultures and wholesale genocide of Native Americans. African religions took on a protective cloak of Catholic nomenclature, calling their *orishas* saints, and survived as the traditions of Macumba, Santeria, Lucumi, and Voudoun, religions that have been as unfairly maligned as the Craft.

Oral tradition tells us that some European Pagans, brought over as indentured servants or convict labor, fled to join the Indians whose traditions were similar in spirit to their own. In some areas, such as the American South, black, white Pagan, and Native American elements combined.

In America, as in Europe, the Craft went underground, and became the most secret of religions. Traditions were passed down only to those who could be trusted absolutely, usually to members of the same family. Communications between covens were severed; no longer could they meet on the Great Festivals to share knowledge and exchange the results of spells or rituals. Parts of the tradition became lost or forgotten. Yet somehow, in secret, in silence, over glowing coals, behind closed shutters, encoded as fairy tales and folk songs, or hidden in subconscious memories, the seed was passed on.

After the persecutions ended, in the eighteenth century, came the age of disbelief. Memory of the true Craft had faded; the hideous stereotypes that remained seemed ludicrous, laughable, or tragic. Only in this century have Witches been able to "come out of the broom closet," so to speak, and counter the imagery of evil with truth. The word *Witch* carries so many negative connotations that many people wonder why we use it at all. Yet to reclaim the word *Witch* is to reclaim our right, as women, to be powerful; as men, to know the feminine within as divine. To be a Witch is to identify with nine million victims of bigotry and hatred and to take responsibility for shaping a world in which prejudice claims no more victims. A Witch is a "shaper," a creator who bends the unseen into form, and so becomes one of the Wise, one whose life is infused with magic.**

Witchcraft has always been a religion of poetry, not theology. The myths, legends, and teachings are recognized as metaphors for "That-Which-Cannot-Be-Told," the absolute reality our limited minds can never completely know. The mysteries of the absolute can never be explained—only felt or intuited. Symbols and ritual acts are used to trigger altered states of awareness, in which insights that go beyond words are revealed. When we speak of "the secrets that cannot be told," we do not mean merely that rules prevent us from speaking freely. We mean that the inner knowledge literally *cannot* be expressed in words. It can only be conveyed by experience, and no one can legislate what insight another person may draw from any given experience. For example, after the ritual described at the opening of this chapter, one woman said, "As we were chanting, I felt that we blended together and became one voice; I sensed the oneness of everybody." Another woman said, "I became aware of how different the chant sounded for each of us, of how unique each person is." A man said simply, "I felt loved." To a Witch, all of these statements are equally true and valid. They are no more contradictory than the statements "Your eyes are as bright as stars" and "Your eyes are as blue as the sea."

The primary symbol for "That-Which-Cannot-Be-Told" is the Goddess. The Goddess has infinite aspects and thousands of names—She is the reality behind many metaphors. She *is* reality, the manifest deity, omnipresent in all of life, in each of us. The Goddess is not separate from the world—She *is* the world, and all things in it: moon, sun, earth, star, stone, seed, flowing river, wind, wave, leaf and branch, bud and blossom, fang and claw, woman and man. In Witchcraft, flesh and spirit are one.

As we have seen, Goddess religion is unimaginably old, but contemporary Witchcraft could just as accurately be called the New Religion. The Craft, today, is undergoing more than a revival; it is experiencing a renaissance, a re-creation. Women are spurring this renewal, and actively reawakening the Goddess, the image of "the legitimacy and beneficence of female power."[15]

Since the decline of the Goddess religions, women have lacked religious models and spiritual systems that speak to female needs and experience. Male images of divinity characterize both Western and Eastern religions.** Regardless of how abstract the underlying concept of God may be, the symbols, avatars, preachers, prophets, gurus, and Buddhas are overwhelmingly male. Women are not encouraged to explore their own strengths and realizations; they are taught to submit to male authority, to identify masculine perceptions as their spiritual ideals, to deny their bodies and sexuality, to fit their insights into a male mold.

Mary Daly, author of *Beyond God the Father,* points out that the model of the universe in which a male God rules the cosmos from outside serves to legitimize male control of social institutions. "The symbol of the Father God, spawned in the human imagination and sustained as plausible by patriarchy, has in turn rendered service to this type of society by making its mechanisms for the oppression of women appear right and fitting."[16] The unconscious model continues to shape the perceptions even of those who have consciously rejected religious teachings. The details of one dogma are rejected, but the underlying structure of belief is imbibed at so deep a level it is rarely questioned. Instead, a new dogma, a parallel structure, replaces the old. For example, many people have rejected the "revealed truth" of Christianity without ever questioning the underlying concept that truth is a set of beliefs revealed through the agency of a "Great Man," possessed of powers or intelligence beyond the ordinary human scope. Christ, as the "Great Man," may be replaced by Buddha, Freud, Marx, Jung, Werner Erhard, or the Maharaj Ji in their theology, but truth is always seen as coming from someone else, as only knowable secondhand. As feminist scholar Carol Christ points out, "Symbol systems cannot simply be rejected, they must be replaced. Where there is no replacement, the mind will revert to familiar structures at times of crisis, bafflement, or defeat."[17]

The symbolism of the Goddess is not a parallel structure to the symbolism of God the Father. The Goddess does not rule the world; She *is* the world. Manifest in each of us, She can be known internally by every individual, in all her magnificent diversity. She does not legitimize the rule of either sex by the other and lends no authority to rulers of temporal hierarchies. In Witchcraft, each of us must reveal our own truth. Deity is seen in our own forms, whether female or male, because the Goddess has her male aspect. Sexuality is a sacrament. Religion is a matter of relinking, with the divine within and with her outer manifestations in all of the human and natural world.

The symbol of the Goddess is *poemagogic,* a term coined by Anton Ehrenzweig to "describe its special function of inducing and symbolizing the ego's creativity."[18] It has a dreamlike, "slippery" quality. One aspect slips into another: She is constantly changing form and changing face. Her images do not define or pin down a set of attributes; they spark inspiration, creation, fertility of mind and spirit: "One thing becomes another,/In the Mother . . . In the Mother . . ." (ritual chant for the Winter Solstice).

The importance of the Goddess symbol for women cannot be overstressed. The image of the Goddess inspires women to see ourselves as divine, our bodies as sacred, the changing phases of our lives as holy, our aggression as healthy, our anger as purifying, and our power to nurture and create, but also to limit and destroy when necessary, as the very force that sustains all life. Through the Goddess, we can discover our strength, enlighten our minds, own our bodies, and celebrate our emotions. We can move beyond narrow, constricting roles and become whole.

The Goddess is also important for men. The oppression of men in Father God–ruled patriarchy is perhaps less obvious but no less tragic than that of women. Men are encouraged to identify with a model no human being can successfully emulate: to be minirulers of narrow universes. They are internally split, into a "spiritual" self that is supposed to conquer their baser animal and emotional natures. They are at war with themselves: in the West, to "conquer" sin; in the East, to "conquer" desire or ego. Few escape from these wars undamaged. Men lose touch with their feelings and their bodies, becoming the "successful male zombies" described by Herb Goldberg in *The Hazards of Being Male:* "Oppressed by the cultural pressures that have denied him his feelings, by the mythology of the woman and the distorted and self-destructive way he sees and relates to her, by the urgency for him to 'act like a man,' which blocks his ability to respond to his inner promptings both emotionally and physiologically, and by a generalized self-hate that causes him to feel comfortable only when he is functioning well in harness, not when he lives for joy and personal growth."[19]

Because women give birth to males,* and ** nurture them at the breast, and in our culture are primarily responsible for their care as children, "every male brought up in a traditional home develops an intense early identification with his mother and therefore carries within him a strong feminine imprint."[20] The symbol of the Goddess allows men to experience and integrate the feminine side of their nature, which is often felt to be the deepest and most sensitive aspect of self. The Goddess does not exclude the male; She contains him, as a pregnant woman contains a male child. Her own male aspect embodies both the solar light of the intellect and wild, untamed animal energy.

Our relationship to the earth and the other species that share it has also been conditioned by our religious models. The image of God as outside of nature has given us a rationale for our own destruction of the natural order, and justified our plunder of the earth's resources. We have attempted to "conquer" nature as we have tried to conquer sin. Only as the results of pollution and ecological destruction become severe enough to threaten even urban humanity's adaptability have we come to recognize the importance of ecological balance and the interdependence of all life. The model of the Goddess, who is immanent in nature, fosters respect for the sacredness of all living things. Witchcraft can be seen as a religion of ecology.** Its goal is harmony with nature, so that life may not just survive, but thrive.

The rise of Goddess religion makes some politically oriented feminists uneasy.** They fear it will sidetrack energy away from action to bring about social change. But in areas as deeply rooted as the relations between the sexes, true social change can only come about when the myths and symbols of our culture are themselves changed. The symbol of the Goddess conveys the spiritual power both to challenge systems of oppression and to create new, life-oriented cultures.

Modern Witchcraft* is a rich kaleidoscope of traditions and orientations. Covens, the small, closely knit groups that form the congregations of Witchcraft, are autonomous; there is no central authority that determines liturgy or rites. Some covens follow practices that have been handed down in an unbroken line since before the Burning Times. Others derive their rituals from leaders of modern revivals of the Craft—the two whose followers are most widespread are Gerald Gardner and Alex Sanders, both British. Feminist covens are probably the fastest-growing arm of the Craft. Many are Dianic: a sect of Witchcraft that gives far more prominence to the female principle than the male. Other covens are openly eclectic, creating their own traditions from many sources. My own covens are based on the Faery tradition,** which goes back to the Little People of Stone Age Britain, but we believe in creating our own rituals, which reflect our needs and insights of today.

The myths underlying philosophy and *thealogy* (a word coined by religious scholar Naomi Goldenburg from *thea*, the Greek word for Goddess) in this book are based on the Faery tradition. Other Witches may disagree with details, but the overall values and attitudes expressed are common to all of the Craft. Much of the Faery material is still held secret, so many of the rituals, chants, and invocations come from our creative tradition. In Witchcraft, a chant is not necessarily better because it is older. The Goddess is continually revealing Herself, and each of us is potentially capable of writing our own liturgy.

In spite of diversity, there are ethics and values that are common to all traditions of Witchcraft. They are based on the concept of the Goddess as immanent in the world and in all forms of life, including human beings.

Theologians familiar with Judeo-Christian concepts sometimes have trouble understanding how a religion such as Witchcraft can develop a system of ethics and a concept of justice.** If there is no split between spirit and nature, no concept of sin, no covenant or commandments against which one can sin, how can people be ethical? By what standards can they judge their actions, when the external judge is removed from his place as ruler of the cosmos? And if the Goddess is immanent in the world, why work for change or strive toward an ideal? Why not bask in the perfection of divinity?

Love for life in all its forms is the basic ethic of Witchcraft. Witches are bound to honor and respect all living things, and to serve the life force. While the Craft recognizes that life feeds on life and that we must kill in order to survive, life is never taken needlessly, never squandered or wasted. Serving the life force means working to preserve the diversity of natural life, to prevent the poisoning of the environment and the destruction of species.

The world is the manifestation of the Goddess, but nothing in that concept need foster passivity. Many Eastern religions encourage quietism not because they believe the divine is truly immanent, but because they believe she/he is not. For them, the world is Maya, Illusion, masking the perfection of the Divine Reality. What happens in such a world is not really important; it is only a shadow play obscuring the Infinite Light. In Witchcraft, however, what happens in the world is vitally important. The Goddess is immanent, but she needs human help to realize her fullest beauty. The harmonious balance of plant/animal/human/divine awareness is not automatic; it must constantly be renewed, and this is the true function of Craft rituals. Inner work, spiritual work, is most effective when it proceeds hand in hand with outer work. Meditation on the balance of nature might be considered a spiritual act in Witchcraft, but not as much as would cleaning up garbage left at a campsite or marching to protest an unsafe nuclear plant.

Witches do not see justice as administered by some external authority, based on a written code or set of rules imposed from without. Instead, justice is an inner sense that each act brings about consequences that must be faced responsibly. The Craft does not foster guilt, the stern, admonishing, self-hating inner voice that cripples action. Instead, it demands responsibility. "What you send, returns three times over" is the saying—an amplified version of "Do unto others as you would have them do unto you." For example, a Witch does not steal, not because of an admonition in a sacred book, but because the threefold harm far outweighs any small material gain. Stealing diminishes the thief's self-respect and sense of honor; it is an admission that one is incapable of providing honestly for one's own needs and desires. Stealing creates a climate of suspicion and fear, in which even thieves have to live. And, because we are all linked in the same social fabric, those who steal also pay higher prices for groceries, insurance, taxes. Witchcraft strongly imbues the view that all things are interdependent and interrelated and therefore mutually responsible. An act that harms anyone harms us all.

Honor is a guiding principle in the Craft. This is not a need to take offense at imagined slights against one's virility—it is an inner sense of pride and self-respect. The Goddess is honored in oneself, and in others. Women, who embody the Goddess, are respected, not placed on pedestals or etherealized but valued for all their human qualities. The self, one's individuality and unique way of being in the world, is highly valued. The Goddess, like nature, loves diversity. Oneness is attained not through losing the self, but through realizing it fully. "Honor the Goddess in yourself, celebrate your self, and you will see that Self is everywhere," says Faery priest Victor Anderson.

In Witchcraft, "All acts of love and pleasure are My rituals." Sexuality, as a direct expression of the life force, is seen as numinous and sacred. It can be expressed freely, so long as the guiding principle is love. Marriage is a deep commitment, a magical, spiritual, and psychic bond. But it is only one possibility out of many for loving, sexual expression.

Misuse of sexuality, however, is heinous. Rape, for example, is an intolerable crime because it dishonors the life force by turning sexuality to the expression of violence and hostility instead of love. A woman has the sacred right to control her own body, as does a man. No one has the right to force or coerce another.

Life is valued in Witchcraft, and it is approached with an attitude of joy and wonder, as well as a sense of humor. Life is seen as the gift of the Goddess. If suffering exists, it is not our task to reconcile ourselves to it, but to work for change.

Magic, the art of sensing and shaping the subtle, unseen forces that flow through the world, of awakening deeper levels of consciousness beyond the rational, is an element common to all traditions of Witchcraft. Craft rituals are magical rites: they stimulate an awareness of the hidden side of reality, and awaken long-forgotten powers of the human mind.

The magical element in Witchcraft is disconcerting to many people. Much of this book is devoted to a deep exploration of the real meaning of magic, but here I would like to speak to the fear I have heard expressed that Witchcraft and occultism harbor fascist tendencies or are linked to Nazism.** There does seem to be evidence that Hitler and other Nazis were occultists—that is, they may have practiced some of the same techniques as others who seek to expand the horizons of the minds. Magic, like chemistry, is a set of techniques that can be put to the service of any philosophy. The rise of the Third Reich played on the civilized Germans' disillusionment with rationalism and tapped a deep longing to recover modes of experience Western culture had too long ignored. It is as if we had been trained, since infancy, never to use our left arms: The muscles have partly atrophied, but they cry out to be used. But Hitler perverted this longing and twisted it into cruelty and horror. The Nazis were not Goddess worshippers; they denigrated women, relegating them to the position of breeding animals whose role was to produce more Aryan warriors. They were the perfect patriarchy, the ultimate warrior cult—not servants of the life force. Witchcraft has no ideal of a "superman" to be created at the expense of inferior races. In the Craft, all people are already seen as manifest gods, and differences in color, race, and customs are welcomed as signs of the myriad beauty of the Goddess. To equate Witches with Nazis because neither are Judeo-Christians and both share magical elements is like saying that swans are really scorpions because neither are horses and both have tails.

Witchcraft is not a religion of masses—of any sort.* Its structure is cellular, based on covens, small groups of up to thirteen members that allow for both communal sharing and individual independence. "Solitaries," Witches who prefer to worship alone, are the exception.** Covens are autonomous, free to use whatever rituals, chants and invocations they prefer. There is no set prayer book or liturgy.

Elements may change, but Craft rituals inevitably follow the same underlying patterns. The techniques of magic, which has been termed by occultist Dion Fortune "the art of changing consciousness at will," are used to create states of ecstasy, of union with the divine. They may also be used to achieve material results, such as healings, since in the Craft there is no split between spirit and matter.

Each ritual begins with the creation of a sacred space, the "casting of a circle," which establishes a temple in the heart of the forest or the center of a covener's living room. Goddess and God are then invoked or awakened within each participant and are considered to be physically present within the circle and the bodies of the worshippers. Power, the subtle force that shapes reality, is raised through chanting or dancing and may be directed through a symbol or visualization. With the raising of the cone of power comes ecstasy, which may then lead to a trance state in which visions are seen and insights gained. Food and drink are shared, and coveners "earth the power" and relax, enjoying a time of socializing. At the end, the powers invoked are dismissed, the circle is opened, and a formal return to ordinary consciousness is made.**

Entrance to a coven is through an initiation, a ritual experience in which teachings are transmitted and personal growth takes place. Every initiate is considered a priestess or priest; Witchcraft is a religion of clergy.

This book is structured around those elements that I feel are constants among all the varied traditions of the Craft. Interest in Witchcraft is growing rapidly. Colleges and universities are beginning to feature courses in the Craft in their religious studies departments. Women in ever greater numbers are turning to the Goddess. There is a desperate need for material that will intelligently explain Witchcraft to non-Witches in enough depth so that both the practices and the philosophy can be understood. Because entrance to a coven is a slow and delicate process, there are many more people who want to practice the Craft than there are covens to accommodate them. So this book also contains exercises and practical suggestions that can lead to a personal Craft practice. A person blessed with imagination and a moderate amount of daring could also use it as a manual to start her or his own coven.** It is not, however, meant to be followed slavishly; it is more like a basic musical score, on which you can improvise.

Mother Goddess is reawakening, and we can begin to recover our primal birthright, the sheer, intoxicating joy of being alive. We can open new eyes and see that there is nothing to be saved *from*, no struggle of life *against* the universe, no God outside the world to be feared and obeyed; only the Goddess, the Mother, the turning spiral that whirls us in and out of existence, whose winking eye is the pulse of being—birth, death, rebirth—whose laughter bubbles and courses through all things and who is found only through love: love of trees, of stones, of sky and clouds, of scented blossoms and thundering waves; of all that runs and flies and swims and crawls on her face; through love of ourselves; life-dissolving world-creating orgasmic love of each other; each of us unique and natural as a snowflake, each of us our own star, her Child, her lover, her beloved, her Self.

Notes

1. The female figure is almost always shown naked in Paleolithic art. Examples include: the bas-reliefs of Laussel, Dordogne, France—see Johannes Maringer and Hans-George Bandi, *Art in the Ice Age* (New York: Frederick A. Praeger, 1953), pp. 84–85, for photograph; nude figures in La Magdaleine and Angles-Sur-Anglin, Dordogne, France, described by Philip Van Doren Stern in *Prehistoric Europe: From Stone Age Man to the Early Greeks* (New York: W. W. Norton, 1969), p. 162; engraved figures in the underground sanctuary of Pech-Merle, France, described by Stern, pp. 174–75; and the Aurignacian sculptured "fat Venuses" such as that of Willendorf, shown by Maringer and Bandi on p. 28 and Lespugue, see Maringer and Bandi, p. 29.

   Examples of male "sorcerors" are found painted in the cave of Le Trois Freres, Dordogne, France (Stern, p. 115), and the chamois-headed figures of Abu Mege, Teyjat, France (Stern, p. 166), among many other examples.

   References are given for the purpose of indicating descriptions and illustrations of archaeological and anthropological finds that corroborate Craft oral tradition. The interpretations given here of the meanings of finds and customs illustrate Craft traditions of our history, and are by no means meant to be taken as academically accepted or proven. If scholars agree on anything, it is that they don't know what many of these figures meant, or how they were used.

2. See descriptions of La Ferassie, Dordogne, France, in Stern, pp. 85, 95; also La Barma Grande, France, in Grahame Clark and Stuart Piggott, *Prehistoric Societies* (London: Hutchinson & Co., 1967), pp. 77–79; and Grimaldi, Calabria, Italy, in Clark and Piggott, pp. 77–79.

3. As at Drachenloch, Switzerland, described by Stern, p. 89.

4. At Meindorf and Stellmoor, Germany; see Alberto C. Blanc, "Some Evidence for the Ideologies of Early Man," in Sherwood L. Washburn, ed., *The Social Life of Early Man* (Chicago: Aldine Publications, 1961), p. 124.

5. Finds of the Mammoth Goddess near the Desna River in the Ukraine are described by Joseph Campbell, *The Masks of God: Primitive Mythology* (New York: Penguin Books, 1976), p. 327.

6. Annette Laming, *Lascaux*, trans. by Eleanor Frances Armstrong (Harmondsworth, Middlesex: Penguin Books, 1959); André Leroi-Gourhan, "The Evolution of Paleolithic Art," in *Scientific American* 218, no. 17 (1968): 58–68.

7. Gerald S. Hawkins, *Beyond Stonehenge* (New York: Harper & Row, 1973), see descriptions of engraved mammoth tusks (15,000 B.C.) from Gontzi in the Ukraine, Russia, pp. 263–67; red ochre markings at Abri de las Vinas, Spain (8000–6000 B.C.), pp. 232–33; and wall paintings at Canchal de Mahoma, Spain (7000 B.C.), pp. 230–31.

8. Laussel, Dordogne, France: see Maringer and Bandi, pp. 84–85.

9. James Mellaart, *Catal Hüyük, a Neolithic Town in Anatolia* (New York: McGraw-Hill, 1967).

10. Alexander Thom, "Megaliths and Mathematics," *Antiquity* 40 (1966): 121–28.

11. Margaret A. Murray, *The Witch-Cult in Western Europe* (New York: Oxford University Press, 1971), pp. 238–46.

12. Murray, p. 49.

13. Murray, pp. 270–76.

14. Andrew E. Rothovius, "The Adams Family and the Grail Tradition: The Untold Story of the Dragon Persecution," *East-West* 7, no. 5 (1977): 24–30; Andrew E. Rothovius, "The Dragon Tradition in the New World," *East-West* 7, no. 8 (1977): 42–54.

15. Carol P. Christ, "Why Women Need the Goddess," in Carol P. Christ and Judith Plaskow, eds. *Womanspirit Rising: A Feminist Reader in Religion* (San Francisco: Harper & Row, 1979), p. 278.

16. Mary Daly, *Beyond God the Father* (Boston: Beacon Press, 1973), p. 13.

17. Christ, p. 275.

18. Anton Ehrenzweig, *The Hidden Order of Art* (London: Paladin, 1967), p. 190.

19. Herb Goldberg, *The Hazards of Being Male* (New York: Signet, 1977), p. 4.

20. Goldberg, p. 39.

CHAPTER 2

The World View of Witchcraft

Between the Worlds

CREATION[1]

Alone, awesome, complete within Herself, the Goddess, She whose name cannot be spoken, floated in the abyss of the outer darkness, before the beginning of all things. And as She looked into the curved mirror of black space, She saw by her own light her radiant reflection, and fell in love with it. She drew it forth by the power that was in Her and made love to Herself, and called Her "Miria, the Wonderful."

Their ecstasy burst forth in the single song of all that is, was, or ever shall be, and with the song came motion, waves that poured outward and became all the spheres and circles of the worlds. The Goddess became filled with love, swollen with love, and She gave birth to a rain of bright spirits that filled the worlds and became all beings.

But in that great movement, Miria was swept away, and as She moved out from the Goddess She became more masculine. First She became the Blue God, the gentle, laughing God of love. Then She became the Green One, vine-covered, rooted in the earth, the spirit of all growing things. At last She became the Horned God, the Hunter whose face is the ruddy sun and yet dark as Death. But always desire draws Him back toward the Goddess, so that He circles Her eternally, seeking to return in love.

All began in love; all seeks to return to love. Love is the law, the teacher of wisdom, and the great revealer of mysteries.

"The Sioux idea of living creatures is that trees, buffalo and men are temporary energy swirls, turbulence patterns . . . that's an early intuitive recognition of energy as a quality of matter. But that's an old insight, you know, extremely old—probably a Paleolithic shaman's insight. You find that perception registered so many ways in archaic and primitive lore. I would say that it is probably the most basic insight into the nature of things, and that our more common, recent Occidental view of the universe as consisting of fixed things is out of the main stream, a deviation from basic human perception."

Gary Snyder[2]

The mythology and cosmology of Witchcraft are rooted in that "Paleolithic shaman's insight": that all things are swirls of energy, vortexes of moving forces, currents in an ever-changing sea. Underlying the appearance of separateness, of fixed objects within a linear stream of time, reality is a field of energies that congeal, temporarily, into forms. In time, all "fixed" things dissolve, only to coalesce again into new forms, new vehicles.

This view of the universe as an interplay of moving forces—which, incidentally, corresponds to an amazing degree with the views of modern physics—is a product of a very special mode of perception. Ordinary waking consciousness sees the world as fixed; it focuses on one thing at a time, isolating it from its surroundings, much like viewing a dark forest with a narrow flashlight beam that illuminates a lone leaf or a solitary stone. Extraordinary consciousness, the other mode of perception that is broad, holistic, and undifferentiated, sees patterns and relationships rather than fixed objects. It is the mode of starlight: dim and silvery, revealing the play of woven branches and the dance of shadows, sensing pathways as spaces in the whole.

The magical and psychic aspects of the Craft are concerned with awakening the starlight vision, as I like to call it, and training it to be a useful tool. Magic is not a supernatural affair; it is, in Dion Fortune's definition, "the art of changing consciousness at will"—of switching the flashlight off and on, of picking out details, of seeing by the stars.

Ordinary consciousness is highly valued in the Craft, but Witches are aware of its limitations. It is, in a sense, a grid through which we view the world, a culturally transmitted system of classification. There are infinite ways to look at the world; the "other vision" frees us from the limits of our culture.

"Our fellow men are the black magicians," Don Juan, the Yaqui shaman, tells his student Castaneda in *Tales of Power.** "Think for a moment. Can you deviate from the path that they've lined up for you? No. Your thoughts and your actions are fixed forever in their terms. I, on the other hand, brought you freedom. Freedom is expensive, but the price is not impossible.

So fear your captors, your masters. Don't waste your time and your power fearing me."[3]

In Witchcraft, the "price of freedom" is, first of all, discipline and responsibility. Starlight vision is a natural potential inherent in each of us, but much work is required to develop and train it. Powers and abilities gained through heightened awareness must also be used responsibly; otherwise, like the Ring of Sauron (in Tolkien's *Lord of the Rings*), they will destroy their possessors. Those who would be free must also be willing to stand slightly aside from the mainstream of society, if need be. In modern Western culture, artists, poets, and visionaries, let alone Witches, mystics, and shamans, are often somewhat alienated from their culture, which tends to devalue intangibles in favor of the solid, monetary fruits of success.

But the final price of freedom is the willingness to face that most frightening of all beings, one's own self. Starlight vision, the "other way of knowing," is the mode of perception of the unconscious, rather than the conscious mind. The depths of our own beings are not all sunlit; to see clearly, we must be willing to dive into the dark, inner abyss and acknowledge the creatures we may find there. For, as Jungian analyst M. Esther Harding explains in *Woman's Mysteries*, "These subjective factors . . . are potent psychical entities, they belong to the totality of our being, they cannot be destroyed. So long as they are unrecognized outcasts from our conscious life, they will come between us and all the objects we view, and our whole world will be either distorted or illuminated."[4]

Perhaps the most convincing way to present the Craft conception of the self is to examine some of the recent experimental findings of biologists and psychologists.* *and* ** Robert Ornstein, in *The Psychology of Consciousness*, describes experiments with brain-damaged and epileptic subjects, demonstrating that the two hemispheres of the brain appear to specialize in precisely the two modes of consciousness we have discussed. "The left hemisphere (connected to the right side of the body) is predominantly involved with analytic, logical thinking, especially in verbal and mathematical functions. Its mode of operation is primarily linear. This hemisphere seems to process information sequentially."[5] Like our flashlight beam, it focuses on one subject at a time, excluding others. It perceives the world as made of separate things, which we may fear or desire, which can be manipulated to suit our purposes. "It seems to have been evolved for the primary purpose of ensuring biological survival."[6]

"The right hemisphere (again, remember, connected to the left side of the body) seems specialized for holistic mentation. Its language ability is quite limited. This hemisphere is primarily responsible for our orientation in space, artistic endeavors, crafts, body image, recognition of faces. It processes information more diffusely than does the left hemisphere, and its responsibilities demand a ready integration of many inputs at once."[7] This is the starlight vision, which sees the universe as a dance of swirling energies, which "does not postulate duration, a future or a past, a cause or an effect, but a patterned, 'timeless' whole."[8]

This mode of awareness is vital to creativity. As Anton Ehrenzweig states in *The Hidden Order of Art*, "The complexity of any work of art, however simple, far outstrips the powers of conscious attention, which with its pin-point focus, can attend to only one thing at a time. Only the extreme undifferentiation of unconscious vision can scan these complexities. It can hold them in a single, unfocused glance and treat figure and ground with equal impartiality."[9]

The following exercise, used to train artists, is helpful in learning to experience the mode of awareness just described.

EXERCISE 1: SHADOW PLAY**

Take a blank sheet of paper and a soft pencil or stick of charcoal. Sit down and observe a scene that interests you. Forgetting about objects, names, and things, observe only the play of light and shadow over various forms. Block in the shadows, not with lines but with patches of broad strokes. Do not be distracted by local color; do not worry about reproducing "things." Let the patches of shade create forms. Spend at least ten minutes on this exercise. Remember, the point is not to create a "good" drawing or to prove your artistic talent (or lack of it); the point is to experience another way of seeing, in which separate objects disappear and only pattern remains.

People who are less visually oriented may find themselves more comfortable with the following exercise.

EXERCISE 2: RHYTHM PLAY

Close your eyes. Listen to the sounds around you, forgetting what they represent. Be conscious only of the vast rhythm they create. Even in the city, forget that the whooshes, thumps, clacks, chirrupings, rumbles, and bangs are passing cars, workmen's hammers, footsteps, sparrows, trucks, and slamming doors—hear only the intricate, organic pattern in which each is a separate beat.

As we have said, both modes of perception are valued in the Craft, but the holistic vision of the right hemisphere is considered to be more in touch with underlying reality than the linear vision of the left hemisphere. This view is borne out by experiments with biofeedback, which gives people visual information about their involuntary body processes, allowing them to monitor and eventually control such functions as heartbeat or brain waves. Barbara Brown, in *New Mind, New Body,* describes experiments showing that "long before conscious recognition, the body and its subconscious substructure both recognize and make judgments about what goes on in the environment."[10] Subjects were monitored as "naughty" words were flashed on a screen, too briefly to be recognized consciously. Their skin, heart rates, brain waves, and muscles all showed reactions to the "unseen" words. The subconscious can respond correctly to reality even when it is given incorrect information by the conscious mind. In one experiment, subjects were told that they would be given a series of shocks that varied in intensity. Consciously, they perceived that the shocks grew weaker; in reality, the shocks were of the same intensity each time. Skin reactions proved that the subconscious was not fooled—monitors recorded exactly the same skin response to each shock, even when the conscious reaction was different."[11]

In the Faery tradition of Witchcraft, the unconscious mind is called Younger Self; the conscious mind is called Talking Self.** Because they function through different modes of awareness, communication between the two is difficult. It is as if they speak different languages.*

It is Younger Self that directly experiences the world, through the holistic awareness of the right hemisphere. Sensations, emotions, basic drives, image memory, intuition, and diffuse perception are functions of Younger Self. Younger Self's verbal understanding is limited; it communicates through images, emotions, sensations, dreams, visions, and physical symptoms. Classical psychoanalysis developed from attempts to interpret the speech of Younger Self. Witchcraft not only interprets, but teaches us how to speak back to Younger Self.

Talking Self organizes the impressions of Younger Self, gives them names, classifies them into systems. As its name implies, it functions through the verbal, analytic awareness of the left hemisphere. It also includes the set of verbally understood precepts that encourage us to make judgments about right and wrong. Talking Self speaks through words, abstract concepts, and numbers.

In the Faery tradition, a third "self" is recognized: the Deep Self or God Self, which does not easily correspond to any psychological concept. The Deep Self is the Divine within, the ultimate and original essence, the spirit that exists beyond time, space, and matter. It is our deepest level of wisdom and compassion and is conceived of as both male and female, two motes of consciousness united as one. It is often symbolized as two linked spirals, or as the infinity sign, the 8 on its side. In the Faery tradition, it is called Dian Y Glas, the Blue God. Blue symbolizes spirit; the Deep Self was said to appear blue when psychically "seen." The Picts stained themselves blue with woad, according to our traditions, in order to identify with the Deep Self. "Dian" is related to both Diana and Tana, the Faery name of the Goddess; also to Janicot, the Basque name of the Horned God, and to the given names Jean, Joan, and Jonet, which Margaret Murray documents as being popular in Witch families.[12]

In the esoteric Judaism of the Cabalah, the Deep Self is named the Neshamah, from the root *Shmh*, "to hear or listen": The Neshamah is She Who Listens, the soul who inspires and guides us. In modern occultism, the Deep Self often appears as the "Spirit Guide," sometimes in dual form, as in John C. Lilly's account of his LSD experiences in an isolation tank, where he reports meeting two helpful beings: "They say that they are my guardians, that they have been with me before at critical times and that in fact they are with me always, but that I am not usually in a state to perceive them. I am in a state to perceive them when I am close to the death of the body. In this state there is no time. There is an immediate perception of the past, present, and future as if in the present moment."[13]

Lilly is describing the holistic, right-hemisphere awareness linked to Younger Self. The Faery tradition teaches that the Deep Self is connected to Younger Self, and not directly linked to Talking Self. We do not, fortunately, have to be nearly dead before we can perceive the Deep Self, once we learn the trick of communication. It is not the conscious mind, with its abstract concepts, that ever actually communicates with the Divine; it is the unconscious mind, the Younger Self that responds only to images, pictures, sensations, tangibles.** To communicate with the Deep Self, the Goddess/God Within, we resort to symbols, to art, poetry, music, myth, and the actions of ritual that translate abstract concepts into the language of the unconscious.

Younger Self—who can be as balky and stubborn as the most cantankerous three-year-old—is not impressed by words. Like a native of Missouri, it wants to be *shown*. To arouse its interest, we must seduce it with pretty pictures and pleasurable sensations—take it out dining and dancing, as it were. Only in this way can the Deep Self be reached. For this reason, religious truths have not been expressed throughout time as mathematical formulas, but in art, music, dance, drama, poetry, stories, and active rituals. As Robert Graves says, "Religious morals, in a healthy society, are best enforced by drums, moonlight, fasting, dancing, masks, flowers, divine possession."[14]

Witchcraft has no sacred book. Its allegiance is not to "The Word" of the Gospel of John, but to the power of symbolic action that unlocks the starlit awareness of Younger Self, and opens a free flow of communication between all three selves at once. The myths and stories that have come down to us are not dogma to be taken literally, any more than we are meant to take literally the statement that "my love is like a red, red rose." They are poetry, not theology—meant to speak to Younger Self, in Joseph Campbell's words "to touch and exhilarate centers of life beyond the reach of vocabularies of reason and coercion."[15]

Aspects of Witchcraft rituals may sometimes seem silly to very serious-minded people, who fail to realize that ritual is aimed at Younger Self. The sense of humor, of play, is often the key to opening the deepest states of consciousness. Part of the "price of freedom," then, is the willingness to play, to let go of our adult dignity, to look foolish, to laugh at nothing. A child makes believe that she is a queen; her chair becomes a throne. A Witch makes believe that her wand has magic power, and it becomes a channel for energy.

Of course, balance is necessary. There is a difference between magic and psychosis—and that difference lies in maintaining the ability to step back, at will, into ordinary consciousness, to return to the awareness that, as my high school health education teacher used to affirm in the height of the psychedelic era, "Reality is that when you jump off a roof, you break your leg." Drugs can open the holistic awareness of Younger Self, but often at the expense of Talking Self's survival judgment: If we "play" at flying in the body, we may smash a femur. But a trained awareness has no quarrel with ordinary reality; it flies further, in the spirit, and gains insights and perceptions that can later be verified by Talking Self.

Humor and play awaken the sense of wonder, the basic attitude that Witchcraft takes to the world. For example, last night my coven held a May Eve ritual, the central action of which involved winding a "Maypole," and weaving into it those things we wish to weave into our lives.** Instead of a pole, we used a central cord, and instead of ribbons we had strings of colored yarn, anchored to a central hook on the ceiling of our meeting room. We also had eleven people in the circle. Of course, we knew perfectly well that it is impossible to wind a Maypole with an odd number of people, but we did not want to leave anybody out. So, with a cavalier disregard for ordinary reality, we went right ahead.

The result, to begin with, was chaos and confusion. Everyone was laughing as we dodged in and out, creating a tangled knot of yarn. It was scarcely a scene of mystical power; a ritual magician would have blanched pale and turned in his wand on the spot. But an odd thing began to happen as we continued. The laughter began to build a strange atmosphere, as if ordinary reality was fading away. Nothing existed but the interplay of colored cords and moving bodies. The smiles on faces that flashed in and out of sight began to resemble the secret smiles of archaic Greek statues, hinting at the highest and most humorous of Mysteries. We began to sing; we moved in rhythm and a pattern evolved in the dance—nothing that could ever be mapped or plotted rationally; it was a pattern with an extra element that always and inevitably would defy explanation. The snarl of yarn resolved itself into an intricately woven cord. The song became a chant; the room glowed, and the cord pulsed with power like a live thing, an umbilicus linking us to all that is within and beyond. At last the chant peaked and died; we dropped into trance. When we awoke, all together, at the same moment, we faced each other with wonder.

The Creation myth that heads this chapter clearly expresses the attitude of wonder, to the world, which is divine, and to the divine, which is the world.* *and* **

In the beginning, the Goddess is the All, virgin, meaning complete within Herself. Although She is called *Goddess,* She could just as easily be called *God*—sex has not yet come into being. As yet, there is no separation, no division, nothing but the primal unity. Yet the female nature of the ground of being is stressed—because the process of creation that is about to occur is a *birth* process. The world is born, not made, and not commanded into being.

The Goddess sees her reflection in the curved mirror of space, which may be a magical insight into the form of the universe, the curved space of modern physics. The mirror is an ancient attribute of the Goddess, according to Robert Graves, in her aspect as "the ancient pagan Sea Goddess Marian . . . Miriam, Mariamne (Sea Lamb), Myrrhine, Myrtea, Myrrha, Maria, or Marina, patroness of poets and lovers and proud mother of the Archer of Love. . . . A familiar disguise of this same Marian is the merry-maid, as 'mermaid' was once written. The conventional figure of the mermaid—a beautiful woman with a round mirror, a golden comb and a fish-tail—expresses 'The Love-Goddess rises from the Sea.' Every initiate of the Eleusinian mysteries, which were of Pelasgian [the indigenous, matrifocal people of Greece] origin, went through a love rite with her representative after taking a cauldron bath. . . . the mirror did also form part of the sacred furniture of the Mysteries, and probably stood for 'Know thyself.'"[16] The same mermaid/ocean mother is named Yemaya in West Africa and Iamanja in Brazil.

Water is the original mirror; the image conveyed is also that of the moon floating over the dark sea, watching her reflection in the waves. A faint echo can be heard in the opening of Genesis: "The earth was unformed and void, and the spirit of God floated on the face of the water."

There is yet another aspect to the mirror: A mirror image is a reversed image, the same, but opposite, the reverse polarity. The image expresses the paradox: All things are one, yet each thing is separate, individual, unique. Eastern religions tend to focus on the first part of the paradox, holding the view that in reality all things are one and that separation and individuality are illusions. Western religions stress individuality and tend to see the world as composed of fixed and separate things. The Western view tends to encourage individual effort and involvement with the world; the Eastern view encourages withdrawal, contemplation, and compassion. Witchcraft holds to the truth of paradox and sees each view as equally valid. They reflect and complement each other; they do not contradict each other. The world of separate things is the reflection of the One; the One is the reflection of the myriad separate things of the world. We are all "swirls" of the same energy, yet each swirl is unique in its own form and pattern.

The Goddess falls in love with Herself, drawing forth her own emanation, which takes on a life of its own. Love of self for self is the creative force of the universe. Desire is the primal energy, and that energy is erotic: the attraction of lover to beloved, of planet to star, the lust of electron for proton. Love is the glue that holds the world together.

Blind *eros*, however, becomes *amor*,[17] the love that, in Joseph Campbell's terminology, is personal, directed to an individual, rather than the universal, sexless charity of *agape*, or indiscriminate, sexual desire. The Goddess's reflection takes on its own being and is given a name. Love is not only an energizing force, but an individualizing force. It dissolves separation and yet creates individuality. It is, again, the primal paradox.

Miria, "The Wonderful," is of course, Marian-Miriam-Mariamne, who is also Mari, the full moon aspect of the Goddess in the Faery tradition. The sense of wonder, of joy and delight in the natural world, is the essence of Witchcraft. The world is not a flawed creation, not something from which we must escape, not in need of salvation or redemption. However it might appear from day to day, by the nature of its deepest being it fills us with wonder.

Divine ecstasy becomes the fountain of creation, and creation is an orgasmic process. Ecstasy is at the heart of Witchcraft—in ritual, we turn paradox inside out and become the Goddess, sharing in the primal, throbbing joy of union. "The fundamental characteristic of shamanism is ecstasy," according to Mircea Eliade, and although he interprets the state somewhat narrowly as "the soul forsaking the body," he admits that "in all probability the ecstatic experience in its many aspects, is coexistent with the human condition, in the sense that it is an integral part of what is called man's gaining consciousness of his specific mode of being in the world. Shamanism is not only a technique of ecstasy; its theology and its philosophy finally depend on the spiritual value that is accorded to ecstasy."[18] Witchcraft is a shamanistic religion, and the spiritual value placed on ecstasy is a high one. It is the source of union, healing, creative inspiration, and communion with the divine—whether it is found in the center of a coven circle, in bed with one's beloved, or in the midst of the forest, in awe and wonder at the beauty of the natural world.

Ecstasy brings about harmony, the "music of the spheres." Music is a symbolic expression of the vibration that is a quality of all beings. Physicists inform us that the atoms and molecules of all things, from an unstable gas to the Rock of Gibraltar, are in constant motion. Underlying that motion is an order, a harmony that is inherent in being. Matter sings, by its very nature.

The song is carried forth on waves that become spheres. The waves are the waves of orgasm, light waves, ocean waves, pulsating electrons, waves of sound. The waves form spheres as swirling gases form stars. It is a basic insight of Witchcraft that energy, whether physical, psychic, or emotional, moves in waves, in cycles that are themselves spirals. (An easy way to visualize this is to borrow a child's "Slinky" toy—a coiling spiral of very thin metal. When stretched and viewed from the side, the spirals appear very clearly as wave forms.)

The Goddess swells with love and gives birth to a rain of bright spirits, a rain that awakens consciousness in the world as moisture awakens green growth on earth. The rain is the fructifying menstrual blood, the moon's blood that nourishes life, as well as the bursting waters that herald birth, the ecstatic giving forth of life.

The motion, the vibration, becomes so great that Miria is swept away. As She moves farther from the point of union, She becomes more polarized, more differentiated, more male. The Goddess has projected Herself; her projected Self becomes the Other, her opposite, who eternally yearns for reunion. Differentness awakens desire, which pulls against the centrifugal force of projection. The energy field of the cosmos becomes polarized; it becomes a conductor of forces exerted in opposite directions.

The view of the All as an energy field polarized by two great forces, Female and Male, Goddess and God, which in their ultimate being are aspects of each other, is common to almost all traditions of the Craft.** The Dianic tradition, however, while recognizing the Male Principle, accords it much less importance than the Female. Some modern, self-created traditions, especially those stemming from a feminist-separatist political orientation, do not recognize the Male at all. If they work with polarity, they visualize both forces as contained within the female. This is a line of experimentation that has great value for many women, particularly as an antidote to thousands of years of Western culture's exclusive concentration on the Male. However, it has never been the mainstream view of the Craft. I personally feel that, in the long run, a female-only model of the universe would prove to be as constricting and oppressive, to women as well as men, as the patriarchal model has been. One of the tasks of religion is to guide us in relationship to both that which is like ourselves, and that which is unlike ourselves. Sex is the most basic of differences; we cannot become whole by pretending difference does not exist, or by denying either male or female.

It is important, however, to separate the concept of polarity from our culturally conditioned images of male and female. The Male and Female forces represent difference, yet they are not different, in essence: They are the same force flowing in opposite, but not opposed, directions.** The Chinese concept of Yin and Yang is somewhat similar, but in Witchcraft the description of the forces is very different. Neither is "active" or "passive," dark or light, dry or moist—instead, each partakes of all those qualities. The Female is seen as the life-giving force, the power of manifestation, of energy flowing into the world to become form. The Male is seen as the death force, in a positive, not a negative sense: the force of limitation that is the necessary balance to unbridled creation, the force of dissolution, of return to formlessness. Each principle contains the other: Life breeds death, feeds on death; death sustains life, makes possible evolution and new creation. They are part of a cycle, each dependent on the other.

Existence is sustained by the on-off pulse, the alternating current of the two forces in perfect balance. Unchecked, the life force is cancer; unbridled, the death force is war and genocide. Together, they hold each other in the harmony that sustains life, in the perfect orbit that can be seen in the changing cycle of the seasons, in the ecological balance of the natural world, and in the progression of human life from birth through fulfillment to decline and death—and then to rebirth.

Death is not an end; it is a stage in the cycle that leads on to rebirth. After death, the human soul is said to rest in "Summerland," the Land of Eternal Youth, where it is refreshed, grows young, and is made ready to be born again. Rebirth is not considered to be condemnation to an endless, dreary round of suffering, as in some Eastern religions. Instead, it is seen as the great gift of the Goddess, who is manifest in the physical world. Life and the world are not separate from Godhead; they are immanent divinity.

Witchcraft does not maintain, like the First Truth of Buddhism, that "All life is suffering." On the contrary, life is a thing of wonder. The Buddha is said to have gained this insight after his encounter with old age, disease, and death. In the Craft, old age is a natural and highly valued part of the cycle of life, the time of greatest wisdom and understanding. Disease, of course, causes misery, but it is not something to be inevitably suffered: The practice of the Craft was always connected with the healing arts, with herbalism and midwifery. Nor is death fearful: It is simply the dissolution of the physical form that allows the spirit to prepare for a new life. Suffering certainly exists in life—it is a part of learning. But escape from the Wheel of Birth and Death is not the optimal cure, any more than hara-kiri is the best cure for menstrual cramps. When suffering is the result of the social order or human injustice, the Craft encourages active work to relieve it. Where suffering is a natural part of the cycle of birth and decay, it is relieved by understanding and acceptance, by a willing giving-over to both the dark and the light in turn.

The polarity of the Female and Male Principles should not be taken as a general pattern for individual female and human beings. We each contain both principles; we are female and male both.** To be whole is to be in touch with both forces—creation and dissolution, growth and limitation. The energy created by the push-pull of forces flows within each of us. It can be tapped individually in rituals or meditations, and it can be attuned to resonate with others. Sex, for instance, is far more than a physical act; it is a polarized flow of power between two people.

The Male Principle is first seen as a nearly androgynous figure: the Child, the flute-playing Blue God of love.** His image is connected with that of the personal Blue God, the Deep Self, which is also androgynous. Gentle youth, beloved son, He is never sacrificed.

The Green aspect is the vegetation God—the corn spirit, the grain that is cut and then replanted; the seed that dies with every harvest and is eternally reborn each spring.

The Horned God, the most "male" in the conventional sense, of the Goddess's projections, is the eternal Hunter, and also the animal who is hunted. He is the beast who is sacrificed that human life may go on, as well as the sacrificer, the one who sheds blood. He is also seen as the sun, eternally hunting the moon across the sky. The waxing and waning of the sun throughout the seasons manifest the cycle of birth and death, creation and dissolution, separation and return.

Goddess and God, Female and Male, Moon and Sun, Birth and Death swing in their orbits—eternal, yet ever changing. Polarity, the force that holds the cosmos together, is love, erotic, transcendent, and individual. Creation did not happen once in a fixed point in time; it goes on eternally, occurring in each moment, revealed in the cycle of the year:

The Wheel of the Year [19]* and **

In love, the Horned God, changing form and changing face, ever seeks the Goddess. In this world, the search and the seeking appear in the Wheel of the Year.

She is the Great Mother who gives birth to Him as the Divine Child Sun at the Winter Solstice. In spring, He is sower and seed who grows with the growing light, green as the new shoots. She is the Initiatrix who teaches Him the mysteries. He is the young bull; She the nymph, seductress. In summer, when light is longest, they meet in union, and the strength of their passion sustains the world. But the God's face darkens as the sun grows weaker, until at last, when the grain is cut for harvest, He too sacrifices Himself to Self that all may be nourished. She is the reaper, the grave of earth to which all must return. Throughout the long nights and darkening days, He sleeps in her womb; in dreams, He is Lord of Death who rules the Land of Youth beyond the gates of night and day. His dark tomb becomes the womb of rebirth, for at Midwinter She again gives birth to Him. The cycle ends and begins again, and the Wheel of the Year turns, on and on.

The rituals of the eight solar holidays, the Sabbats, are derived from the myth of the Wheel of the Year. The Goddess reveals her threefold aspects: As Maiden, She is the virgin patroness of birth and initiation; as Nymph, She is the sexual temptress, lover, siren, seductress; as Crone, She is the dark face of life, which demands death and sacrifice. The God is son, brother, lover, who becomes his own father: the eternal sacrifice eternally reborn into new life.

Sir James Frazer, in *The Golden Bough*, traces many variations of this myth. Most, like the version expounded by Robert Graves in *The White Goddess*, present the God as split into rival Twins embodying his two aspects. The Star Son, Lord of the Waxing Year, vies with his brother the Serpent for the love of the Goddess. On the Summer Solstice, they battle, and the Dark Serpent defeats the Light and supplants Him in the Goddess's favor, only to be Himself defeated at Midwinter, when the Waxing year is reborn.

This variation is not, in essence, different from the variation we have presented, as long as the Dark and Light Twins are clearly understood to be aspects of the same divinity. But when we see the God as split, we run the risk of suffering a split within ourselves: of identifying totally with the Light and ascribing the Dark to an agent of evil. Star Son and Serpent too easily become Christ-Satan figures. In Witchcraft, the dark, waning aspect of the God is not evil—it is a vital part of the natural cycle.

The essential teaching of the myth is connected with the concept of sacrifice. To Witches, as to other peoples who live close to nature, all things—plants, animals, stones, and stars—are alive, are on some level conscious beings. All things are divine, are manifestations of the Goddess. The death of the grain in the harvest, or the death of a deer in the hunt, was considered a divine sacrifice, freely made out of love. Ritualistic and mythical identification with the sacrificing God honors the life spark, even in death, and prepares us to give way gracefully to new life, when the time comes for each of us to die. Waxing and waning, birth and death, take place within the human psyche and life cycle. Each is to be welcomed in its proper time and season, because life is a process of constant change.

The God chooses to sacrifice in order to remain within the orbit of the Goddess, within the cycle of the natural world, and within the ecstatic, primal union that creates the world. Were He to cling to any point on the wheel and refuse to give way to change, the cycle would stop; He would fall out of orbit and lose all. Harmony would be destroyed; union would be broken. He would not be preserving Himself; He would be denying his true self, his deepest passion, his very nature.

It is vitally important not to confuse this conception of sacrifice with the masochistic self-sacrifice that is so often preached as the ideal by patriarchal religions. In the Craft, the sacrifice of one's nature or individuality is never demanded. Instead, one sacrifices *to* nature. There is no conflict, in Witchcraft, between the spiritual and the material; we do not have to give up one to gain the other. The spirit manifests in matter: The Goddess is seen as giving us abundance. But the most abundant summer is followed by winter, as the longest day ends in night. Only when one gives way to the other can life go on.

In Witchcraft, sacrifice is most definitely not the submission to external power held by another person or institution. Nor does it mean giving up one's will or self-respect. Its emotional tone is not self-pity, but pride: it is the sacrifice of Mettus Curtius, who, when told by the augurs that the bottomless crack that had suddenly opened in the Forum was a sign that the Gods demanded the sacrifice of Rome's finest, unhesitatingly leapt into the chasm on horseback, fully armed. He had not a moment's doubt as to his own self-worth; he knew what "Rome's finest" must be, and acted accordingly, out of an inner sense of what was right.

Witchcraft does not demand poverty, chastity, or obedience, but it is not a "looking out for Number One" philosophy, either. It developed in a close-knit clan society, where resources were shared and land held in common. "Charity" was an unknown concept, because sharing was an integral part of society, a basic expectation. "Number One" existed only within the fabric of society and within the web of all life. Witchcraft recognizes that we are all interdependent, and even the most avid member of the "me generation" must ultimately serve the life force, if only as compost.**

The sacrifice of the God was represented in human society by the "Sacred King" or priest, who served as consort to the High Priestess, religious leader, and at times, war leader for the clan. Since Frazer compiled *The Golden Bough*, his classic work of folklore and anthropology first published in 1900, writers on the subject of "primitive" religions, especially those oriented toward a Goddess, have generally accepted his thesis that human sacrifice was a vital and regular institution in matrifocal culture. Even well-meaning, sensitive, and thinking men—including Robert Graves,* who has probably been the greatest force for revival of interest in the Goddess in this century—perpetuate the myths. Joseph Campbell, author of the fine series *The Masks of God*, goes so far as to say that "human sacrifice . . . is everywhere characteristic of the worship of the Goddess."[20]

Craft tradition and archaeological evidence do not support this picture of Goddess worship as bloody and barbaric. The many Paleolithic sites associated with Goddess figures—Laussel, Angles-Sur-Anglin, Cogul, La Magdaleine, Malta, to name just a few—show no evidence of human sacrifice. In the Neolithic, Catal Hüyük is one of the earliest (circa 6500–5700 BC) and most clearly matriarchal sites excavated. The many shrines decorated with figures of the Mother Goddess and her son-paramour have no provisions for either human or animal sacrifice; no altars, no pits for blood, and no caches of bones. Nor do the Goddess temples of Malta and Sardinia, the passage graves and stone circles of the megalith builders, or the excavated sites of Crete show any evidence that human beings were ever ritually murdered. Where human sacrifice is clearly evident—for example, in the Royal Tombs of the Sumerian city Ur, where entire courts followed the king into death—it is associated with cultures that have already made the shift to patriarchy.

Reconstructing culture from buried bones and artifacts is, of course, difficult; reconstruction from surviving folk customs, which Frazer often attempts, is just as liable to error. If peasants burn corn dollies in the harvest fire, it does not necessarily follow that they once burned living men. To Younger Self, a corn dollie is a perfectly effective symbol of the God's sacrifice; a live victim is not required.

Historical reports of matrifocal cultures most often come from their enemies and conquerors, who are likely to paint a negative picture of the religious customs of their foes. If our knowledge of medieval Judaism was limited to historical reports by Catholic Churchmen, we would be bound to conclude that the blood of Christians was needed to bake the ritual matzohs. Today we recognize this fiction for the libel that it was, but slurs against matrifocal religions have become deeply embedded in religion and mythology and are often hard to identify. For example, the Greek myth of Theseus and the Minotaur was believed to represent Cretan sacrifice of captives to their bull God. But frescoes excavated in the Palace of Minos reveal, instead, the practice of bull-leaping: no doubt a dangerous sport, but one that could hardly be called human sacrifice any more than its modern descendent, bullfighting.

In the Faery tradition, oral teachings say that in early times the Sacred King or Priest held office for nine years, after which he underwent a ritual mock death, abdicated, and joined the Council of Elders.** Ritual mock death may be the origin of many folk customs involving symbolic sacrifices. In times of great need or disaster, a king might, if his inner being prompted, sacrifice himself. The willingness to give over one's personal existence to serve the people was the true test of kingship, and this requirement lessened the attraction of power for corrupt and selfish individuals. Kingship was not originally an opportunity to make a killing in the bronze market or collect personal slaves; it was a ritual, mystical identification with the underlying forces of death and life.

Women were never sacrificed in Witchcraft. Women shed their own blood monthly and risk death in service to the life force with every pregnancy and birth. For this reason, their bodies were considered sacred, and held inviolate.

Unfortunately, newspapers, motion pictures, and television today continue to perpetuate the association of Witchcraft and Goddess religion with horror and human sacrifice. Every Manson-like murderer is called a "witch." Outright psychopaths claim to be practicing Witchcraft with degraded rites, and may at times mislead gullible people into believing them. Witchcraft as a religion may not have a universal creed or set liturgy, but on some points there is unanimity. No true Witches today practice human sacrifice, torture, or any form of ritual murder. Anyone who does is not a Witch, but a psychopath.**

The world view of Witchcraft is, above all, one that values life. The cosmos is a polarized field of forces that are constantly in the process of swirling into form and dissolving back into pure energy. Polarity, which we call Goddess and God, creates the cycle that underlies the movements of the stars and the changing of the seasons, the harmony of the natural world and the evolution within our human lives. We perceive the interplay of forces in two basic modes, the holistic, intuitive "starlight" mode of the right hemisphere and the unconscious; and the linear, analytic, conscious mode of the left hemisphere. Communication between conscious and unconscious, between Talking Self and Younger Self, and through the latter to the Deep Self, the spirit, depends on an openness to both modes of awareness. Verbal concepts must be translated into symbols and images; unconscious images must be brought to the light of consciousness. Through open communication, we can become attuned to the cycles of nature, to the primal, ecstatic union that is the force of creation. Attunement requires sacrifice, the willingness to change, to let go of any point on the Wheel and move on. But sacrifice is not suffering, and life in all its aspects, light and dark, growing and decaying, is a great gift. In a world where the endlessly transforming, erotic dance of God and Goddess weaves radiant through all things, we who step to their rhythm are enraptured with the wonder and mystery of being.

Notes

1. Oral teaching of the Faery tradition of Witchcraft.
2. Lee Bartlett, "Interview—Gary Snyder," *California Quarterly* 9 (1975): 43–50.
3. Carlos Castaneda, *Tales of Power* (New York: Simon & Schuster, 1974), pp. 28–29.
4. M. Esther Harding, *Woman's Mysteries, Ancient & Modern* (New York: Pantheon, 1955), p. 6.

5. Robert E. Ornstein, *The Psychology of Consciousness* (San Francisco: W. H. Freeman, 1972), pp. 51–52.
6. Ornstein, p. 17.
7. Ornstein, pp. 51–52.
8. Ornstein, p. 79.
9. Anton Ehrenzweig, *The Hidden Order of Art* (London: Paladin, 1967), p. 35.
10. Barbara Brown, *New Mind, New Body* (New York: Harper & Row, 1974), p. 75.
11. Brown, p. 75.
12. Margaret A. Murray, *The Witch-Cult in Western Europe* (New York: Oxford University Press, 1971), p. 255.
13. John C. Lilly, *The Center of the Cyclone* (New York: Julian Press, 1972), p. 27.
14. Robert Graves, *Food for Centaurs* (New York: Doubleday, 1960), p. 6.
15. Joseph Campbell, *The Masks of God: Creative Mythology* (New York: Viking Press, 1970), p. 4.
16. Robert Graves, *The White Goddess* (New York: Farrar, Straus & Giroux, 1966), p. 395.
17. Campbell, pp. 176–77.
18. Mircea Eliade, *Rites & Symbols of Initiation*, translated by William R. Trask (New York: Harper & Row, 1958), p. 101.
19. Oral teaching of the Faery tradition.
20. Joseph Campbell, *The Masks of God: Oriental Mythology* (New York: Penguin Books, 1970), p. 160.

CHAPTER 3

The Coven

Between the Worlds

NEW MOON

"We met tonight in the rented storefront. For a long time, we just talked—about our fears and doubts about magic and ourselves: that it isn't real, that it is real, that it will stop, that it's an ego-trip, that we're crazy, that what we really want is power, that we'll lose our sense of humor and become pompous about it, that we won't be able to take it seriously, that it won't work, that it will work. . . .

At one point, we all took hands, and started breathing together. Suddenly we realized that a circle had been cast. We passed around the oil, for anointing, and kissed. Someone began a low humming, and Pat started tapping out a rhythm on the drum. And we were all chanting, interweaving voices and melodies, as if different words were coming through each of us:

Isis . . . Astarte . . . Ishtar
Dawn and darkness . . . dawn and darkness . . .
Moo-oo-oon, Crescent Moo-oo-oon . . .
Pour out your light and your radiance upon us. . . .
Shine! Shine! Shine! Shine! Shine!

and through it and behind it all, Beth was wailing on her kazoo, and it sounded like some strange, Arabian oud, or a sobbing jazz saxophone, but we were smiling at the humor of it.

At the same moment, we all fell silent. Then we shared fruit, laughed, and talked about humor. We were thinking about a coven name, and someone suggested Compost. It was perfect! Earthy, organic, nurturing—and discouraging to self-inflation.

We are now the Compost coven!

The ritual worked. Whatever magic brings, it will not take away our ability to laugh at ourselves. And those fears grow less and less all the time."

From my Book of Shadows

The coven is a Witch's support group, consciousness-raising group, psychic study center, clergy-training program, College of Mysteries, surrogate clan, and religious congregation all rolled into one. In a strong coven, the bond is, by tradition, "closer than family": a sharing of spirits, emotions, imaginations. "Perfect love and perfect trust" are the goal.

The coven structure makes the organization of Witchcraft very different from that of most other religions.* The Craft is not based on large, amorphous masses who are only superficially acquainted; nor is it based on individual gurus with their devotees and disciples. There is no hierarchical authority, no Dalai Lama, no Pope. The structure of Witchcraft is cellular, based on small circles whose members share a deep commitment to each other and the Craft.

Witchcraft tends to attract people who, by nature, do not like to join groups. The coven structure makes it possible for rabid individualists to experience a deep sense of community without losing their independence of spirit. The secret is its small size. A coven (usually pronounced so as to rhyme with oven), by tradition, never contains more than thirteen members. In such a small group, each person's presence or absence affects the rest. The group is colored by every individual's likes, dislikes, beliefs, and tastes.

At the same time, the coven becomes an entity in itself, with a personality of its own. It generates a *raith* form,† an energy swirl that exists over and beyond its membership. There is a quality of synergy about a strong coven. It is more than the sum of its parts; it is an energy pool on which its members can draw.

To become a member of a coven, a Witch must be initiated, must undergo a ritual of commitment, in which the inner teachings and secrets of the group are revealed.** Initiation follows a long training period, during which trust and group security are slowly built. When properly timed, the ritual also becomes a rite of passage that marks a new stage in personal growth. Witchcraft grows slowly; it can never be a mass-market religion, peddled on streetcorners or between flights at the airport. Witches do not proselytize. Prospective members are expected to seek out covens and demonstrate a deep

---

† See page 161 for a full discussion and explanation of the *raith*.

level of interest. The strength of the Craft is felt to be in quality, not quantity.

Originally, coveners were the teachers and priestesses/priests of a large Pagan population of noninitiates.** They were the councils of elders within each clan, the wise women and wise men who delved beneath the surface of their rites and sought the deeper meanings. At the large solar festivals, the Sabbats, they led the rituals, organized the gatherings, and expounded the meanings of the ceremonies. Each coven had its own territory, which by tradition extended for a league. Neighboring covens might join for the great Sabbats, in order to share knowledge, herbs, spells, and, of course, gossip. Federations of covens were sometimes linked together under a Witch "Queen," or Grandmaster. On full moons, covens met alone for Esbats, when they studied the inner teachings and practiced magic.

During the Burning Times, the great festivals were stamped out or Christianized. Persecution was most strongly directed against coven members, because they were seen as the true perpetuators of the religion. The strictest secrecy became necessary. Any member of a coven could betray the rest to torture and death, so "perfect love and perfect trust" were more than empty words. Covens were isolated from one another, and traditions became fragmented, teachings forgotten.

Today, there is a growing effort throughout the Craft to reestablish communication between covens and share knowledge. But many individual Witches still cannot afford to "come out of the broom closet." Public recognition may mean the loss of their jobs and livelihoods. Known Witches are easy targets for violent crackpots: A Southern California couple were firebombed out of their home after appearing on a television talk show. Other Witches face harassment by the authorities for traditional practices such as divination, or become scapegoats for local crimes. Unfortunately, prejudice is still widespread.** Sensitive people never identify anyone as a Witch without first asking permission privately. In this book, my own friends and coveners have generally been referred to by coven names in order to protect their privacy.

Every coven is autonomous. Each functions as its own authority in matters of ritual, thealogy, and training. Groups of covens that follow the same rites may consider themselves part of the same tradition. To ensure legal protection for their members, many covens band together and incorporate as a church, but the rights of separate covens are always jealously guarded.

Covens usually develop a specific orientation and focus. There are covens that concentrate on healing or teaching; others may lean toward psychic work, trance states, social action, or creativity and inspiration. Some simply seem to throw good parties; after all, "all acts of love and pleasure" are rituals of the Goddess. Covens may include both men and women or be limited to women only. (There are very few all-male covens, for reasons to be discussed in Chapter Six.)*

A coven is a group of peers, but it is not a "leaderless group." Authority and power, however, are based on a very different principle from that which holds sway in the world at large. Power, in a coven, is never power *over* another. It is the power that comes from within.

In Witchcraft, power is another word for energy, the subtle current of forces that shape reality. A powerful person is one who draws energy into the group. The ability to channel power depends on personal integrity, courage, and wholeness. It cannot be assumed, inherited, appointed, or taken for granted, and it does not confer the right to control another. Power-from-within develops from the ability to control ourselves, to face our own fears and limitations, to keep commitments, and to be honest. The sources of inner power are unlimited. One person's power does not diminish another's; instead, as each covener comes into her own power, the power of the group grows stronger.**

Ideally, a coven serves as the training ground in which each member develops her or his personal power. The support and security of the group reinforce each member's belief in herself. Psychic training opens new awarenesses and abilities, and feedback from the group becomes the ever-present mirror in which we "see ourselves as others see us." The goal of a coven is not to do away with leaders, but to train every Witch to be a leader, a Priestess, or a Priest.

The issue of leadership has plagued the feminist movement and the New Left. Exemplars of power-from-within are sadly lacking on the American political scene. Power-over-others is correctly seen to be oppressive, but too often the "collective ideal" is misused, to tear down the strong instead of to build strength in the weak. Powerful women are attacked instead of supported: "Am I a traitor? They ought to shoot me. Made me into a leader. We're not supposed to have leaders. I will be executed in some underground paper, my character assassinated subterraneously."[1]

The concept of power-from-within encourages healthy pride, not self-effacing anonymity; joy in one's strength, not shame and guilt. In Witchcraft, authority means responsibility. The coven leader must have the inner power and sensitivity to channel the group's energy, to start and stop each phase of the ritual, adjusting the timing to the mood of the circle. A ritual, like a theater production, needs a director.

In practice, leadership is passed from one covener to another in a fully developed group. The wand representing the authority of the leader may be passed to each covener in turn. Different sections of the ritual may be led by different people.

For example, our last Fall Equinox ritual was inspired by Alan, who is an apprentice but not yet an initiate of Compost coven. Alan is very much involved with the men's liberation movement and wanted a ritual centered around changing the sex-role conditioning we have each received. Eight of us, from Compost, from Honeysuckle, my women's coven, and from Alan's men's group, planned the ritual together. Here is my account:

Fall Equinox, 1978

A hot night. Seventeen of us met at Guidot's, nine women and eight men. After some socializing, we went upstairs to the ritual room.

Alan, aided by Guidot and Paul, cast the circle, using beautiful invocations, which I think he improvised on the spot. Three or four of us had explained the ritual to the rest, so they were ready. I led the invocation to the Goddess, using the Kore Chant. I began speaking it, and as I switched into the sung chant, it was as if something came in from behind and lifted me out of myself. My voice physically changed, became a low, deep throbbing, with power pouring through into the circle, and then, as everyone picked up the chant, pouring through all of us—the dark moaning wail of summer's passing, sad but beautiful. . . .

Change is . . . touch is . . .
Touch us . . . change us . . .

Alan, Paul, and Guidot invoked the God, Alan calling Him as the Gentle Brother, the Rape Fighter. He wrote a powerful invocation (included in Chapter Six).

We began a banishing dance, widdershins around the circle. As we moved, one person would throw out a phrase—the group took it up and repeated it, chanted it rhythmically, building it, shrieking it, then letting it die away until its power to control us faded with it. Alan began it:

"You must be successful!"

"You must be successful!" "You must be successful!" "Must be! Must be! Must be!" "Must!"

"Nice girls don't do that!" "Nice girls don't do that!" "Big boys don't cry!" "You're not a real woman!" "Sissy! Sissy! Sissy!"

Sixteen howling echoes took up every cry, frenzied, mocking voices that became, in the dim light, the pursuing Furies of our own minds, taunting, laughing, screaming—then vanishing, like wisps of smoke. By the end we were stamping, shouting—seventeen stark-naked adults, jumping up and down, yelling "No! No! No! No! No!"

Younger Self was awake in its full, primal glory, all right.

Val has come into her own, her power as the Crone. She performed the Mystery (which is secret), aided, I think, by Alan and Paul. I never saw. Laurel, Brook, and I led the trance, a soft, whispered, three-voiced induction:

Your fingers are dissolving into . . .
Dream deep, and sleep the magic sleep . . .
Dissolving into water, and your toes are . . .

Valerie awakened us. We formed into two groups, for the male and female Mysteries. The men took a long time—I think they got involved in a historical discussion of the rites of Dionysus. When they finished, we one by one moved back into the circle, sitting man and woman alternately. We went around the circle, each saying how we become strong.

"I become strong through facing my fears."
"I become strong through my friends."
"I become strong through making mistakes."
"I become strong through taking a stand."
"I become strong through dreaming."

Then we chanted, raising power to actualize the visions we had seen in trance, of our true, free selves. The chant went on and on, it was so physically pleasurable, feeling the flow of power, the low resonance of the deep male voices, the high, bell-like notes of the women—it swirled around us like a great, warm wave.

After, Alan and I blessed the wine and cakes. As the cup went around the circle, we each said what we were thankful for. The cup went around many times. Then we relaxed, ate, laughed, talked as usual. Alan ended the ritual and opened the circle.

Afterward, I was amazed at how smoothly it all went, with everyone taking different parts. It feels good to be able to step back and let other people take the center, to see them developing their power.

At the present time, both Compost and the women's coven, called Honeysuckle, are covens of elders.* and ** Each initiate is capable of leading rituals, directing the energy, and training newcomers. The process of development in each group, however, was very different.

Compost was typical of many of the new, self-initiatory covens that are springing up today without benefit of formal Craft training. I had been taught by Witches many years previously, when I was a college student, but never actually initiated. Most of my knowledge came from dream figures and trance experiences. I had been unable to find a coven I felt was right for me, and for many years I had worked alone. Finally, I decided to see if I could start my own coven, whether or not I was "authorized" to do so. I began teaching a class in Witchcraft through the Bay Area Center for Alternative Education.

Within a few weeks, a group of interested individuals began meeting weekly. Our rituals were collective and spontaneous, like the one described at the opening of this chapter. We resisted set forms and set words.

After a few months had passed, a strong core group developed, and we performed a formal initiation. Our rituals had also taken on a regular pattern, and we decided to set the structure of the rites so that we would have a collective framework, within which we could all be spontaneous and open. Before, the leader—usually me—had decided what was going to happen at any given moment, and everyone else had followed along.

We met many Witches from other covens, and I began studying with a teacher from the Faery tradition. I began to come into a sense of my own power. As a group, we also realized that the energies we were raising were *real*, not merely symbolic. The group felt a need for an acknowledged leader; at the same time, I felt the need to have my newfound inner power recognized. The coven confirmed me as Priestess.

Like most people whose sense of inner strength is developing quickly, I occasionally went to extremes. From being a collectivist nonleader, I became a rather heavy-handed Priestess at times. There are days when my records of rituals read quite differently from either of the two presented in this chapter: "I cast the circle . . . I invoked the Goddess . . . I led the chant . . . I directed the Cone of Power . . ." Fortunately, my coveners were both tolerant enough to let me make mistakes and honest enough to tell me when they didn't like what I was doing. We began sharing responsibilities: One covener would bring the salt and water and purify the circle, another would bring the incense and charge the space. The men invoked the Horned God, and we took turns invoking the Goddess and directing the cone of power. I became more relaxed in the role of leader.

As other coveners developed their own strengths, we decided to "pass the wand." Diane, a tremendously warm individual, who radiates a sense of caring, was our unanimous choice. She had always liked our simple, spontaneous rituals best, and under her leadership we let go of a lot of structure and experimented. "I don't feel like formally casting the circle tonight," she might say, "let's just tap the four walls, and chant. Why don't we chant each other's names?" And so we would chant—sometimes for hours, in the process developing one of the simplest and most beautiful rituals we use today.

Diane left for the summer, and we passed the wand to Amber, the youngest member of our coven. Diane warmed the circle with a steady glow; Amber lit it up with skyrockets, fireworks, and colored flames. Talented, charming, lovable, and unsteady, she is a fine musician with an operatic singing voice and a flair for drama. She inspired us to the creation of more theatrical rituals, like many of those presented in Chapter Twelve. But Amber had difficulty functioning at the high level of responsibility that coven leadership demands. She was going through a tense period in her personal life, and, while she usually carried through her commitments, doing so caused her a lot of anxiety and stress. In retrospect, we did her a disservice by not allowing her a longer period of training.

Honeysuckle underwent a different process of formation. It began as a class in the Great Goddess, at a time when I had been Priestess of Compost for many months, and was already an initiate of the Faery tradition. I was coming from a much stronger position as a leader, and it took a much longer time before anyone questioned my authority. I was determined not to rush the training of this group, and it was almost a year before I so much as mentioned the word *initiation*. When each woman in turn felt ready to take on more responsibility, was able to question my authority, and was willing to move out from the role of student, she was initiated. A new ritual was created for each member, and each rite crystallized a period of growth.

Finding a coven to join can be difficult.* Witches are not listed in the Yellow Pages, although today groups can easily be found on the World Wide Web (see Resources). Often, however, they do give classes through Open Universities or metaphysical bookstores. Some universities sponsor Pagan student groups. Occult shops sometimes also furnish leads and Unitarian churches may have CUUPs chapters (see Resources). The best route, of course, is through personal contacts. Witches feel that when a person is internally ready to join the Craft she will be drawn to the right people.

Unfortunately, a lot of people claim to be Witches who are merely unsavory characters. When you meet someone who calls herself a Witch, listen carefully to your underlying feelings and intuitions. The rituals of many covens are secret, but you should be told or shown enough about them to form a fairly clear picture of what goes on. A true coven will never ask you to do something you feel is wrong for you. Any form of force, coercion, or high-pressure sales tactics is contrary to the spirit of Witchcraft. Real Witches will let you take the initiative in seeking them out.

Witchcraft is not for sale. There are no fees for initiation, and it is considered a breach of ethics to charge money for coven training. Of course, Witches who teach public classes or work as psychic counselors are allowed to charge a fair fee for their time and labor. They will not, however, sell you "blessed" candles for large sums of money or ask you to hand over your life savings in order to remove a curse: Those are favorite dodges of the con artists who prey on the gullible public. A coven may charge dues to cover candles, incense, and other expenses, but the Priestess will *not* be driving a Mercedes bought by the contributions of her faithful followers.**

In a strong coven, members will feel close to each other and turn naturally to each other in times of stress. They generally spend time together socially outside of group meetings and enjoy each other's company. But they also have varied and interesting outside friends and lives and do not spend all of their time together. A coven should not be a retreat from the world, but a supportive structure that helps each member function in the world more fully.

At the present time, there are far more people who want to join covens than there are groups capable of taking in newcomers. If you cannot find a congenial coven, you can either practice the Craft alone or start your own coven.

Working alone is not ideal. Opening up the starlight vision is much more difficult without the support of a group. Those who travel the uncharted pathways of the mind alone run more risk of being caught in subjectivity. Also, working with other people is much more fun.

But, as one Witch who has practiced the Craft by herself for many years says, "Working alone has its good points as well as bad. Your training is rather erratic—but then it is in a lot of covens, anyway. The advantage is that you learn to depend on yourself and learn your limitations. When you do join a coven, you know what you want and what works best for you."

Solitary meditation and visualization practice are part of every Witch's training. Most of the exercises in this book can be done alone, and even the rituals can be adapted. Solitary worship is far preferable to joining the wrong group.

You do not have to be a hereditary or even an initiated Witch in order to start your own coven. Naturally, training helps. But the school of trial and error is also a very fine one.

When a group of interested but inexperienced people come together, the first task is to establish a feeling of security. Openness and trust develop slowly, through both verbal and nonverbal sharing. People need time to socialize, as well as work magic. I often start groups with a potluck dinner, so that everyone can share a very tangible form of energy: food. Consciousness-raising techniques can also be very effective. We may go around the circle, letting each person tell why she or he came to the group and what she or he hopes to get out of it. Everyone is allowed to speak for a limited period of time without interruptions, so that quieter people are encouraged to express themselves and more voluble individuals do not dominate the conversation. Questions and comments come after everyone has had a turn to speak.

Nonverbal sharing is also important in creating group trust. The following exercises teach the sensing and sharing of energy, which is the basis of Craft rituals. They can be done singly or flow into a smooth sequence. I have written down what I say when leading a group through the exercise. In guiding a group, the actual words spoken are less important than the rhythm of your voice and the timing of pauses. The only way to learn this is by practice. Read through the exercises, become familiar with them, and then improvise in your own natural speech patterns.

EXERCISE 3: SENSING GROUP ENERGY

"The energy we talk about in Witchcraft is real, a subtle force that we can all learn to perceive. Right now, as we are sitting in the circle, be aware of the energy level in the group. Do you feel alert? Aware? Excited? Calm or anxious? Tense, or relaxed? (Pause.)

"Energy travels up and down your spine. Now sit up, as erect as you can without straining. Good. Notice how the energy level has changed. Do you feel more alert? More aware? (Pause.)

"Your breath moves energy in and out of your body. It wakens your body's centers of power. So take a deep breath. Breathe deep . . . breathe all the way down. Breathe from your diaphragm . . . from your belly . . . from your womb. Your stomach should push in and out as you breathe . . . loosen your pants if you need to. Fill your belly with breath. Feel yourself relaxing, recharging. Now notice how the energy of the group has changed. (Pause.)

"Now let's reach out and take hands, linking ourselves together around the circle. Continue to breathe deeply. Feel the energy move around the circle. It may seem like a subtle tingling, or a low heat, or even a sensation of cold. We may all perceive it differently. Some of us may see it—dancing like sparks in the center of the circle. (Long pause.)

(To end here:) "Now take a deep breath, and suck in the power, as if you were sucking through a straw. Feel it travel down your spine, and flow into the earth. Relax."

(Or go on to the next exercise.)

EXERCISE 4: GROUP BREATH

(To begin here, say:) "Let's take hands around the circle and sit (or stand) up straight.

"And now, closing your eyes, let's breathe together—breathing the deep breath of the belly, of the womb. Inhale . . . (slowly), exhale . . . inhale . . . exhale . . . inhale . . . exhale . . . feel yourself relax, as you breathe. Feel yourself become strong with each breath . . . become refreshed . . . with each breath . . . feel your worries floating away . . . with each breath . . . become revitalized . . . as we breathe together . . . inhale . . . exhale . . . inhale . . . exhale . . .

"And feel our breath as it meets in the center of the circle . . . as we breathe as one breathing one breath . . . inhale . . . exhale breathing one circle . . . breathing one, living organism . . . with each breath . . . becoming one circle . . . with each breath . . . becoming one . . ." (long pause).

(End as in Exercise 3, or go on.)

EXERCISE 5: GROUNDING: THE TREE OF LIFE*

(This is one of the most important meditations, which is practiced individually, as well as in the group. In solitary practice, begin by sitting or standing erect, and breathing deeply and rhythmically.)

"And as we breathe, remember to sit erect, and as your spine straightens, feel the energy rising . . . (pause).

"Now imagine that your spine is the trunk of a tree . . . and from its base roots extend deep into the earth . . . into the center of the earth Herself . . . (pause).

"And you can draw up power from the earth, with each breath . . . feel the energy rising like sap rising through a tree trunk . . .

"And feel the power rise up your spine . . . feel yourself becoming more alive . . . with each breath . . .

"And from the crown of your head, you have branches that sweep up and back down to touch the earth . . . and feel the power burst from the crown of your head . . . and feel it sweep through the branches until it touches the earth again making a circle . . . making a circuit . . . returning to its source . . .

(In a group:) "And breathing deeply, feel how all our branches intertwine . . . and the power weaves through them . . . and dances among them, like the wind . . . feel it moving . . ." (long pause).

(End as in Exercise 3, or go on.)

EXERCISE 6: POWER CHANT

(This should always begin with a Group Breath—Exercise 4.)

"Now let your breath become sound . . . any sound that you like . . . a moan . . . a sigh . . . a giggle . . . a low hum . . . a howl . . . a melody . . . chant the word-less sounds of the vowels . . ."

(Wait. In a new group, there may be silence for a moment. Slowly, someone will begin to sigh, or hum very quietly. Others will gradually join in. The chant may develop into a strong hum, or a swelling wave of open-throated notes. People may begin to chortle, bark, or howl like animals, if they feel so inclined. The chant may peak suddenly, and drop to silence, or it may rise and fall in several tides of power. Let it direct itself.

When everyone is silent, allow a quiet time of relaxation. Before the group has time to get restless, earth the power as in Exercise 7.)

EXERCISE 7: EARTHING POWER

(Also called *grounding*, earthing power is one of the basic techniques of magic. Power must be earthed every time it is raised. Otherwise, the force we feel as vitalizing energy degenerates into nervous tension and irritability. In the earlier exercises, we grounded the energy by sucking it in and letting it flow through us into the earth. That technique is often useful when working alone.)

"Now sink to the ground and relax. Place your palms flat on the ground, or lie flat. Let the power sink through you into the earth." (Even if you are meeting in a penthouse fifteen floors above the earth, visualize the energy flowing down to the actual ground.) "Relax, and let the force flow through you . . . let it flow deep into the earth . . . where it will be cleansed and renewed. Relax and let yourself drift peacefully."

These five exercises contain the essence of a Craft ritual. The circle is cast by taking hands; power is raised, shared, and earthed. Sharing of drink and food generally follows—magic is hungry work! As the cup is passed around, toasts are made and people express thanks to the Goddess for good things that have come to them. This part of the meeting is relaxed and informal, a good time for sharing impressions and discussing what has gone on. People may move out of the circle at this time, but the meeting *must* be formally ended before anyone goes home. Meetings that dribble off at the end leave people without a sense of closure and completion. If magic has been worked, the energy absorbed then tends to turn into anxiety and irritation, instead of peace and vitality. A meeting can be ended quite simply by having everyone take hands and say together:

> The circle is open, but unbroken,
> May the peace of the Goddess go in our hearts;
> Merry meet, and merry part.
> And merry meet again. Blessed be.

A kiss is then passed around the circle (clockwise).

Sharing poems, songs, stories, pictures, and creative work in the circle also helps build a feeling of closeness. In Honeysuckle, when we are taking in a group of new members we devote an evening to sharing our life stories in the circle. We also jog together regularly and have gone backpacking as a group. Compost occasionally makes "excursions"—for example, to the Chinese Moon Festival parade. We devoted one meeting to watching *The Wizard of Oz* on television and to skipping down the street singing "Follow the Yellow Brick Road."

As the group grows more unified, certain interpersonal conflicts will inevitably arise.* *and* ** The very cohesiveness of the group itself will make some members feel left out. Each person is part of the whole, but also an individual, partly separated from the rest. Some people tend to see the group as a solid entity that completely enfolds everyone else, while they alone are partly left out. Sexual attraction often arises between coveners, and, while the first bright flush of love will draw power into the group, a quarreling couple will cause disruption. If the two break up, and no longer feel they can work in the group together, a real problem arises. A coven leader who is strong and charismatic often becomes the focus of other members' projections. She may be seen as the all-giving earth mother, the eternally-desirable-yet-unattainable woman, or the all-wise prophetess. It is always tempting for her to believe these flattering images and psychically feed on the energy charge they contain, but if she does she stunts her own growth as a real human being. Sooner or later, she will fumble and the image will be shattered; the results can be explosive.

A certain amount of group time and energy spent on resolving interpersonal conflicts is necessary and desirable, part of the growth process that goes on in a healthy coven. But it is all too easy for a group to degenerate into a sort of amateur encounter session or shouting match. A coven cannot function as a therapy group. Problems between members can sometimes be solved more effectively by using magic than by endless discussion. For example, instead of verbally reassuring an insecure covener, place her in the center of the circle and chant her name. If two members cannot work together, but neither wants to leave, the group may need to cast lots; leaving the decision up to the Goddess.* And if a Priestess seems in danger of being seduced by her own public relations campaign, the less star-struck members of the group should gently tell her so. Objective, constructive criticism is one of the great benefits of the coven structure.**

A coven becomes a safe space in which members feel free to release their inhibitions: laugh, dance, act silly, burst into song, chant spontaneous poetry, make bad puns, and let Younger Self come out and play. Only then can the higher states of awareness be reached. Many techniques have been developed to drop the "censor" of Talking Self and to let the inner voice speak freely.

Nudity is one such technique. When we take off our clothes, we drop our social masks, our carefully groomed self-images. We become open. The mystical meaning of the naked human body is "truth." Different people need different levels of private space; while some romp happily on nude beaches, others cannot feel comfortable naked until trust has been built over a long period of time. In our covens, public rituals are always clothed. If guests invited to private "sky-clad" ceremonies feel uncomfortable disrobing, they are welcome to wear whatever they like. Vulnerability cannot be forced on anyone, except destructively.

Here is one of the exercises we use to begin opening the inner voice and releasing the blocks to expression:

EXERCISE 8: WORD ASSOCIATION TRANCE

(Everyone should lie down and position themselves comfortably. Turn off the lights. Begin with a Group Breath—Exercise 4. When everyone is relaxed, proceed:)

"Now we're going to go around the circle, clockwise. I'll start by saying a word, and the next person will say the first word that pops into her mind. Then the person after that will respond to her word, and so on, around the circle. Don't think about the word, just relax, breathe deep, and let it come."

(Start. The sequence might go like this:)

"Green/Pea/Soup/Hot/Cold/Ice/Snow/White/Black/Bird/Fly/Sky/Starry/Night/Dark."

(After a few rounds:)

"Now we're each going to repeat the last person's word before we add our own."

(The sequence might go like this:)

"Dark Cave/Cave Bury/Bury Deep/Deep Sea/Sea Wave/Wave Flag/Flag Star/Star Light/Light Ray/Ray Sun."

(After a few rounds:)

"Now we're each going to repeat the last two words before adding our own."

(Now the sequence might run like this:)

"Ray Sun Shine/Sun Shine Day/Shine Day Forever/Day Forever Night/Forever Night Sky/Night Sky Star/Sky Star Light."

(This is an actual invocation we use, which was created by a group during this exercise. As the trance continues, words become entities in themselves. The combinations form constantly shifting scenes, which flash vividly before the inner eye. Gradually, the cycle may die away, and people simply describe what they see:)

"I see a dark sky, dotted with a million stars—one of them shoots across the sky . . ."

"I see a blazing comet, with a golden tail trailing behind . . ."

"I see a trailing peacock's tail with iridescent eyes . . ."

"I see an eye looking at me . . ."

"I see a face, the dark face of a beautiful woman . . ."

(Descriptions may be elaborate or simple. Some may obtain striking visions, others hear sounds or voices, or feel new sensations. A few people may drift off to sleep. After a time, the group will fall silent, each member floating in her own vision. Allow time for everyone to fully experience her inner world, then say:)

"Now breathe deeply and say farewell to your visions. In a moment, we're going to open our eyes and awaken, fully and completely, feeling refreshed and renewed. When I count to three, we will open our eyes and wake up. Now take a deep breath . . . inhale . . . exhale . . . one . . . two . . . three. . . . Open your eyes, and awaken, refreshed and renewed."

It is extremely important to bring everyone fully back into ordinary consciousness. Turn on the lights and change the atmosphere completely. Share food and drink (but not alcohol); move around and talk. Otherwise, participants may remain slightly entranced, a condition that becomes draining and depressing.

This is especially good for opening up the creative imagination and could be used in art or writing classes as well as in covens.

Ritual is partly a matter of performance, of theater. Some people delight in this aspect of Witchcraft; others become shy and frozen in front of a group. The quieter coveners, however, may channel power in other ways. Brook, for example, rarely wants to cast the circle or invoke the Goddess, but when she chants, her voice, ordinarily pleasant but unremarkable, becomes an eerie, more-than-human channel for power.

Magical training varies greatly from coven to coven, but its purpose is always the same: to open up the starlight consciousness, the other-way-of-knowing that belongs to the right hemisphere and allows us to make contact with the Divine within. The beginner must develop four basic abilities: relaxation, concentration, visualization, and projection.

Relaxation is important because any form of tension blocks energy. Muscular tension is felt as mental and emotional stress, and emotional stresses cause physical and muscular tension and dis-ease. Power trying to move through a tense body is like an electric current trying to force its way through a line of resistors. Most of the juice is lost along the way. Physical relaxation also seems to change brain wave patterns and activate centers that aren't ordinarily used.

EXERCISE 9: RELAXATION

(This can be done in a group, alone, or with a partner. Begin by lying down on your back. Do not cross your limbs. Loosen any tight clothing.)

"In order to know how relaxation feels, we must first experience tension. We are going to tense all the muscles of the body, one by one, and keep them tense until we relax our entire bodies with one breath. Don't clench the muscles so they cramp, just tense them lightly.

"Start with your toes. Tense the toes in your right foot . . . and now your left foot. Tense your right foot . . . and your left foot. Your right ankle . . . and your left ankle . . ."

(Continue throughout the whole body, part by part. From time to time, remind the group to tense any muscles that they have let slack.)

"Now tense your scalp. Your whole body is tense . . . feel the tension in every part. Tense any muscles that have gone slack. Now take a deep breath . . . inhale . . . (pause) . . . exhale . . . and relax!

"Relax completely. You are completely and totally relaxed." (In a sing-song tone:) "Your fingers are relaxed, and your toes are relaxed. Your hands are relaxed, and your feet are relaxed. Your wrists are relaxed, and your ankles are relaxed."

(And so on, throughout the entire body. Periodically pause and say:)

"You are completely and totally relaxed. Completely and totally relaxed. Your body is light; it feels like water, like it is melting into the earth.

"Allow yourself to drift and float peacefully in your state of relaxation. If any worries or anxieties disturb your peace, imagine they drain from your body like water and melt into the earth. Feel yourself being healed and renewed."

(Remain in deep relaxation for ten to fifteen minutes. It is good to practice this exercise daily, until you can relax completely simply by lying down and letting go, without needing to go through the entire process. People who have difficulty sleeping will find this extremely helpful. However, do not allow yourself to drift off into sleep. You are training your mind to remain in a relaxed but alert state. Later, you will use this state for trance work, which will be much more difficult if you are not in the habit of staying awake. If you practice this at night before sleeping, sit up, open your eyes, and consciously end the exercise before dozing.

Many of the other exercises can be most effectively practiced in a state of deep relaxation. Experiment to find what works best for you.)

Visualization is the ability to see, hear, feel, touch, and taste with the inner senses. Our physical eyes do not *see*; they merely transmit nerve impulses touched off by light stimuli to the brain. It is the brain that *sees*, and it can see inner images as clearly as those in the outer world. In dreams, all five senses are vivid. With practice, most people can develop the ability to use the inner senses vividly while awake.

Some people naturally see images; others may hear or feel impressions. A few people find it difficult or impossible to visualize, but most find the facility will improve with exercise.

Visualization is important because it is through internal images and sensations that we communicate with Younger Self and the Deep Self. When the inner senses are fully awake, we may see visions of extraordinary beauty, smell the blossoms of the Isle of Apples, taste ambrosia, and hear the songs of the Gods.

EXERCISE 10: GROUNDING AND CENTERING

Before beginning visualization practice, we should ground and center ourselves. This is again one of the basic techniques of magical work. *Grounding* means to establish an energy connection with the earth. The Tree of Life exercise is one method of grounding. Another is to visualize a cord or pole extending from the base of your spine into the center of the earth. Center yourself by aligning your body along its center of gravity. Breathe from your center—from your diaphragm and abdomen. Feel energy flow up from the earth and fill you.

Grounding is important because it allows you to draw on the earth's vitality, rather than depleting your own. When channeling energy, it serves as a psychic lightning rod—forces run through you into the earth, rather than "burning out" your mind and body.

EXERCISE 11: SIMPLE VISUALIZATIONS

This exercise is for those of you who have difficulty visualizing. Ground and center. Close your eyes, and imagine that you are looking at a white wall or a blank screen. Practice visualizing simple geometric forms: a line, a dot, a circle, a triangle, an ellipse, and so on.

When you are able to see the forms clearly, visualize the screen in color: red, yellow, blue, orange, green, violet, and black in turn. It may help to look at a colored object with your eyes open, first—then close your eyes and mentally see the color.

Finally, practice visualizing the geometric forms in various colors. Change the colors and forms until you can mentally picture them at will.

EXERCISE 12: THE APPLE

Visualize an apple. Hold it in your hands; turn it around; feel it. Feel the shape, the size, the weight, the texture. Notice the color, the reflection of light on its skin. Bring it up to your nose and smell it. Bite into it, taste it; hear the crunch as your teeth sink in. Eat the apple; feel it slide down your throat. See it grow smaller. When you have eaten it down to the core, let it disappear.

Repeat with other foods. Ice cream cones are also excellent subjects.

EXERCISE 13: THE PENTACLE

Visualize a line of flickering blue flame, like a gas flame from a Bunsen burner. Now mentally draw a pentacle, a five-pointed star with one point up, in the invoking direction, starting at the top and moving down to the left. Watch it form out of the blue flame. Hold the image in your mind for a few moments.

Now retrace it in the banishing direction, starting at the lower left-hand corner and moving up. As you do so, watch it disappear.

Practice until it comes to you easily. This visualization is part of casting a circle.

INVOKING PENTACLE   BANISHING PENTACLE

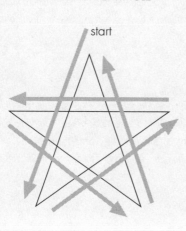

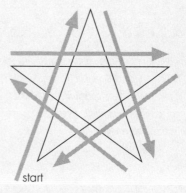

EXERCISE 14: THE KNOT

Visualize yourself tying a knot—any knot you can tie easily in reality. Try not to see a mental picture of yourself from outside; instead, put yourself in the picture. See your hands moving, and feel the string. Feel every movement you would make, then draw the knot closed, and feel the string pull taut.

This visualization is used to bind spells.

More complex visualizations are given in later chapters.

Concentration is the ability to focus on an image, thought, or task, to narrow one's field of awareness and shut out distractions. Like a muscle, it grows stronger with exercise.

Many people today practice forms of Eastern meditation—yoga, Zen, Transcendental Meditation—which are excellent for developing concentration. The more you practice the visualizations, the easier it is to concentrate on the images. The following three exercises will help improve your inner focus:

EXERCISE 15: CANDLE GAZING

In a quiet, darkened room, light a candle. Ground and center, and gaze quietly at the candle. Breathe deeply, and let yourself feel warmed by the light of the candle. Let its peaceful radiance fill you completely. As thoughts surface in your mind, experience them as if they came from outside. Do not let the flame split into a double image: keep your eyes focused. Remain for at least five to ten minutes, then relax.

EXERCISE 16: THE DIAMOND

Again, light a candle in a dim, quiet room. Ground and center. Gaze at the candle, and visualize a diamond in the center of your forehead, between and just above your eyebrows. The diamond reflects the light of the candle, and the candle reflects the light of the diamond. Feel the reverberation of energy. Hold for at least five to ten minutes, then relax.

EXERCISE 17: MIRROR, MIRROR

Ground and center. In a mirror, gaze into your own eyes. Focus your attention on the space between them. Repeat your own name to yourself, over and over. Again, as thoughts surface, experience them as if they were outside you. After five to ten minutes, relax.

Projection is the ability to send out energy. It comes quite naturally to most people, once they are aware of its "feel." Projection is also used in another sense to mean the ability to travel "out-of-body": That form of projection will be discussed in Chapter Nine. In the Tree of Life exercise and during the Group Breath and Power Chant, we have already experienced what it feels like to send out energy. Here are two other exercises:

EXERCISE 18: THE ROCK

Ground and center. Imagine that you are standing on the seashore, looking out over the waves. In your strongest hand, you hold a heavy rock. Pick it up, inhale, and as you exhale, let it fly! Watch it splash into the sea just below the horizon.

Now look up again. Realize that you can see a horizon twice as far away. Mentally stretch to see it. In your hand, you hold a rock twice as large as the first. Again, take a deep breath, and, as you exhale, throw with all your might. Watch it splash into the far waves.

Once again, look up and realize that you can see a horizon twice as far away again. In your hand, you hold a rock twice as heavy. Take one more deep breath, and as you exhale, throw hard! Watch it splash.

Practice this exercise until you can feel the release of power that goes with the rock.

EXERCISE 19: THE HAMMER

Ground and center. Visualize a heavy hammer in your hand. A stubborn nail is sticking out of a board in front of you. With all your strength, drive the nail into the board. Repeat, doing it three times in all.

Covens have many different ways of taking on new members.* Some hold open classes or study groups. We prefer to have initiates take on individual apprentices. Each newcomer gets individualized instruction, tailored to her particular needs. And each coven member has a chance to be an authority, and is forced to conceptualize her own knowledge of the Craft in order to teach it. Apprentices and their teachers develop a strong bond, so each newcomer feels she has a special relationship to one group member. Apprentices also develop a bond with each other as a group. They attend rituals together, so that nobody has to be the "only new kid on the block."

When I train an apprentice, I think of myself as being somewhat like a dance teacher. I suggest a regular discipline, including many of the exercises in this chapter, the "basic barre-work" of magic. Also, I try to identify areas of weakness and imbalance, and prescribe corrective exercises. For example, for one student whose mind continually wanders I might suggest concentration practice. For Paul, on the other hand, who studied for years with a sect of Buddhists and can, in his own words, "bore holes through walls," I suggested daily jogging. During rituals, apprentices have a chance to combine skills learned in solitary practice into an intricate dance of power with the coven and each other.

As a basic, daily discipline,* and ** I recommend three things. The first is regular physical exercise. The importance of this cannot be overstressed. Unfortunately, it is one of the hardest things to get people to do. The Craft tends to attract mental and spiritual types rather than brawny athletes. But magic and psychic work require tremendous vitality—literally, the energy of the *raith*, of Younger Self. That vitality is replenished and renewed by physical activity—much as the motion of an automobile's wheels turns the generator, which recharges the batteries. Too much mental and spiritual work that is not balanced by physical exercise drains our etheric batteries. Yoga is sometimes good, but it is usually taught as a spiritual discipline that opens the psychic centers, rather than increasing physical vitality. For our purposes, jogging, swimming, bicycling, tennis, or roller-skating are better—something active and enjoyable that gets us out into the elements. Witches who are physically disabled can find a regime appropriate to their needs and abilities. If you can spend some time each day outdoors, on the grass or under a tree where you can soak up elemental energies, you will reap many of the same benefits as the marathon runners.

The second thing I recommend for students is daily relaxation practice and a daily meditation, visualization, or concentration exercise. These often change as the student develops. Some people practice several at once, but one is enough. Too many are cumbersome. At one point in my own training, I woke up in the morning and did a trance exercise at my typewriter for up to an hour, then twenty minutes of yoga, including meditations on the four elements and the Circle Visualization in Chapter Four. Later in the day I practiced deep relaxation and a lying-down trance. At night, I did a candle-gazing, a water purification, and a variety of personal spells. Unfortunately, I had very little time left for actually *living*. After a few weeks, I decided that moderation was the essence of wisdom, in magic, as in other things.

The third practice I suggest is the keeping of a magical diary, called a Book of Shadows. Traditionally, this was the "recipe book" of rituals, spells, chants, and incantations, hand-copied by each Witch from her teacher. Today, although I blush to admit it, such information is generally xeroxed for coven distribution.** The Book of Shadows is more of a personal journal. It may include descriptions of rituals, records of dreams, reactions to exercises, poems, stories, and trance journeys. Solitary Witches can use their Book of Shadows to develop some of the objectivity that generally comes from working in a coven. Trances and meditations can be written out in the journal. Tristine Rainer, in *The New Diary*, even describes techniques for using journal writing to remember past lives.[2]

Womb, support group, magical training college, and community of friends—the coven is the heart of the Craft. Within the circle, each Witch is trained to develop her inner power; her integrity of mind, body, and spirit. Like families, covens sometimes have their squabbles. But whenever the circle is cast, whenever they raise the cone and call on the Gods together, they recognize in each other the Goddess, the God, the life spirit of all. And so, when every initiate is challenged at the gate to the circle, she speaks the only password: "Perfect love and perfect trust."

Notes

1. Kate Millett, *Flying* (New York: Ballantine Books, 1974), p. 14.
2. Tristine Rainer, *The New Diary* (Los Angeles: Tarcher, 1978), pp. 259–61.

CHAPTER 4

Creating Sacred Space

Between the Worlds
THE CASTING OF THE CIRCLE*

The room is lit only by flickering candles at each of the cardinal points. The coveners stand in a circle, their hands linked. With her athame, her consecrated knife, unsheathed, the Priestess† steps to the altar and salutes sky and earth. She turns and walks to the Eastern corner, followed by two coveners, one bearing the chalice of salt water, the other the smoldering incense. They face the East. The Priestess raises her knife and calls out:

> Hail, Guardians of the Watchtowers of the East,
> Powers of Air!
> We invoke you and call you,
> Golden Eagle of the Dawn,
> Star-seeker,
> Whirlwind,
> Rising Sun,
> Come!
> By the air that is Her breath,
> Send forth your light,
> Be here now![1]

† For literary convenience, I have designated the Priestess as casting the circle. But any qualified covener, female or male, may take her role.

As she speaks, she traces the invoking pentagram in the air with her knife. She sees it, glowing with a pale blue flame, and through it feels a great onrush of wind, sweeping across a high plain lit by the first rays of dawn. She breathes deeply, drawing in the power, then earths it through her knife, which she points to the ground.

As she sprinkles water three times, the first covener cries out, "With salt and water, I purify the East!" The second covener draws the invoking pentagram with incense, saying,

"With fire and air, I charge the East!"

The Priestess, knife held outward, traces the boundaries of the circle. She sees it take shape in her mind's eye as they continue to each of the four directions, repeating the invocation, the purification, and the charging:

> Hail, Guardians of the Watchtowers of the South,
> Powers of Fire!
> We invoke you and call you,
> Red Lion of the noon heat,
> Flaming One!
> Summer's warmth,
> Spark of life,
> Come!
> By the fire that is Her spirit,
> Send forth your flame,
> Be here now!
>
> Hail, Guardians of the Watchtowers of the West,
> Powers of Water!
> We invoke you and call you,
> Serpent of the watery abyss,
> Rainmaker,
> Gray-robed Twilight,
> Evening Star!
> By the waters of Her living womb,
> Send forth your flow,
> Be here now!
>
> Hail, Guardians of the Watchtowers of the North,
> Powers of Earth,
> Cornerstone of all Power.
> We invoke you and call you,
> Lady of the Outer Darkness,
> Black Bull of Midnight,

North Star,
Center of the whirling sky.
Stone,
Mountain,
Fertile Field,
Come!
By the earth that is her body,
Send forth your strength,
Be here now!

The Priestess traces the last link of the circle, ending in the East. Again she salutes sky and earth, turns and touches the tip of her athame to the central cauldron, and says,

The circle is cast.
We are between the worlds,
Beyond the bounds of time,
Where night and day,
Birth and death,
Joy and sorrow,
Meet as one.

The second covener takes a taper to the South point candle and with it lights candles in the central cauldron and on the altar, saying,

The fire is lit,
The ritual is begun.

They return to the circle. The first covener smiles at the person on her left, and kisses her or him, saying,

"In perfect love and perfect trust."
The kiss is passed around the circle.

"The unfolding of God . . . involves the creation of new space, in which women are free to become who we are. . . . Its center is on the boundary of patriarchal institutions . . . its center is the lives of women who begin to liberate themselves toward wholeness."²
    "Entry into the new space . . . also involves entry into new time. . . . The center of the new time is on the boundary of patriarchal time. . . . It is our life-time. It is whenever we are living out of our own sense of reality, refusing to be

possessed, conquered, and alienated by the linear, measured-out, quantitative time of the patriarchal system."[3]

Mary Daly

In Witchcraft, we define a new space and a new time whenever we cast a circle to begin a ritual. The circle exists on the boundaries of ordinary space and time; it is "between the worlds" of the seen and unseen, of flashlight and starlight consciousness, a space in which alternate realities meet, in which the past and future are open to us. Time is no longer measured out; it becomes elastic, fluid, a swirling pool in which we dive and swim. The restrictions and distinctions of our socially defined roles no longer apply; only the rule of nature holds sway, the rule of Isis who says, "What I have made law can be dissolved by no man."[4] Within the circle, the powers within us, the Goddess and the Old Gods, are revealed.

Casting the circle is an enacted meditation. Each gesture we make, each tool we use, each power we invoke, resonates through layers of meaning to awaken an aspect of ourselves. The outer forms are a cloak for inner visualizations, so that the circle becomes a living mandala, in which we are centered.

When we cast a circle, we create an energy form, a boundary that limits and contains the movements of subtle forces. In Witchcraft, the function of the circle is not so much to keep *out* negative energies as to keep *in* power so that it can rise to a peak. You cannot boil water without putting it in a pot, and you cannot raise power effectively unless it is also contained. Leaving the circle during the ritual is discouraged because it tends to dissipate the energy, although cats and very small children seem to pass across without disturbing the force field. Adults usually cut a "gate" in pantomime with an *athame*, should they need to leave the circle before the ritual is ended.

The casting of the circle is the formal beginning of the ritual, the complex "cue" that tells us to switch our awareness into a deeper mode. In ritual, we "suspend disbelief" just as we do when watching a play: We allow the critical and analytical functions of Talking Self to relax so that Younger Self may respond fully and emotionally to what happens. Younger Self, as we have seen, responds best to actions, symbols, tangibles—so this change in consciousness is acted out, using a rich array of tools and symbols.

In the permanent stone circles of the Megalithic era, where rituals were enacted for hundreds of years, great reservoirs of power were built up. Because the stones defined the sacred space, there was no need to draw out the circle as we do. The form of circle casting most Witches use today probably originated during the Burning Times, when meetings were held secretly, indoors, and it became necessary to create a temple in a simple hut. Witches may have taken over some forms from Cabalists. It is said that Witches often harbored Jews from Christian persecution and that they exchanged knowledge. (I must admit that, while Witches in general like to believe this is true, Jews don't seem to have heard of it—or, if they have, aren't advertising the fact.)

Before any ritual there is always a period of purification, during which participants can clear away worries, concerns, and anxieties that may hamper their concentration.** Some covens simply aspurge (sprinkle) each member with salt water while casting the circle. At very large rituals, this is the only practical method. But for small groups and important workings, we use a more intense meditative exercise called the Salt-Water Purification.

Salt and water are both cleansing elements. Water, of course, washes clean. Salt preserves from decay and is a natural disinfectant. The ocean, the womb of life, is salt water, and so are tears, which help us purify the heart of sorrow.

EXERCISE 20: SALT-WATER PURIFICATION

(This is one of the basic individual meditations that should be practiced regularly. During periods of high anxiety or depression or when undertaking heavy responsibilities, it is helpful to practice this daily.)

Fill a cup with water. (Use your ritual chalice, if you have one.) With your *athame* (or other implement), add three mounds of salt, and stir counterclockwise.

Sit with the cup in your lap. Let your fears, worries, doubts, hatreds, and disappointments surface in your mind. See them as a muddy stream, which flows out of you as you breathe and is dissolved by the salt water in the cup. Allow yourself time to feel deeply cleansed.

Now hold up the cup. Breathe deeply, and feel yourself drawing up power from the earth (as in the Tree of Life exercise). Let the power flow into the salt water, until you can visualize it glowing with light.

Sip the water. As you feel it on your tongue, know that you have taken in the power of cleansing, of healing. Fear and unhappiness have become transformed into the power of change.

Empty the leftover water into a running stream. (Alas, in these decadent times the nearest stream is usually running out of the kitchen faucet and down the drain.)

EXERCISE 21: GROUP SALT-WATER PURIFICATION*

Coveners assemble in a circle, with incense and point candles lit. The Priestess goes to the altar, grounds and centers herself. She takes the cup of water in her right hand, saying, "Blessed be, thou creature of water." She takes the dish of salt in her left hand, and says, "Blessed be, thou creature of earth." She holds them both up to the sky with arms outstretched, and lets power flow into them, saying,

> Salt and water,
> Inner and outer,
> Soul and body,
> Be cleansed!
> Cast out all that is harmful!
> Take in all that is good and healing!
> By the powers of life, death, and rebirth*
> So mote it be!†

She sets them down on the altar, and takes her *athame* in her strongest hand, saying, "Blessed be, thou creature of art." She spills three mounds of salt into the water and stirs it counterclockwise, saying,

> May this *athame* be purified,
> And may these tools and this altar be purified,

as she shakes a few drops over the altar, then salutes sky and earth:

> In the names of Life and Death, so mote it be!

She then holds the cup to her heart and charges the water with power. When she can feel it glowing, she returns to the circle. The cup is sent around, and each person performs her or his private purification. Others may sing softly as the cup goes around. In a large group, three or four cups of water are charged at the same time; otherwise the cup may take hours to go around the circle.

When the cup returns to the Priestess, she sends a kiss around the circle. Then she begins the casting of the circle. If the meeting space is felt to need special cleansing, the following Banishing can be performed.

EXERCISE 22: BANISHING**

After the purification, the Priestess takes the sword or *athame* and goes to the center of the circle. She points the blade to earth and sky, and says, forcefully,

> Spirits of evil,
> Unfriendly beings,
> Unwanted guests,

---

†"So mote it be" means "So must it be" and is traditional for ending a spell or magical working in the Craft.

> Begone!
> Leave us, leave this place, leave this circle,
> That the Gods may enter.
> Go, or be cast into the outer darkness!
> Go, or be drowned in the watery abyss!
> Go, or be burned in the flames!
> Go, or be torn by the whirlwind!
> By the powers of life, death, and rebirth,

All the coven together shouts:

> We banish you! We banish you! We banish you!
> Begone!

All scream, shout, clap hands, ring bells, and make noise to frighten away negative forces.

Bath water can be "charged,"[†] and a few salt crystals added, and coveners can take a ritual bath before entering the circle. This is more fully described in Chapter Ten, on Initiation. Due to the limitations of time and hot water, it is best done at home.

The concept of the quartered circle is basic to Witchcraft, as it is to many cultures and religions.* The four directions and the fifth, the center, each correspond and resonate to a quality of the self, to an element, a time of day and year, to tools of the Craft, symbolic animals, and forms of personal power. Constant visualization of these connections creates deep internal links, so that physical actions trigger inner states. The action of casting the circle then awakens all parts of the self, and puts us in touch with mind, energy, emotions, body, and spirit, so that we are constantly made whole.

The "Guardians of the Watchtowers" are energy forms, the *raiths* or spirits of the four elements. They bring the elemental energy of earth, air, fire, and water into the circle, to augment our human power. The vortex of power created when we invoke the four directions guards the circle from intrusions, and draws in the higher powers of the Goddess and God.

Each movement in a ritual has meaning. When we move "sunwise" or clockwise, "deosil," we follow the direction the sun appears to move in the Northern Hemisphere, and draw in power. Deosil is the direction of increase, of fortune, favor, and blessing. When we move "widdershins" or counterclockwise, we are

---

[†] To magically "charge" an object means to imbue it with energy.

going against the sun, and this direction is used for decrease and banishings.

The tools, the physical objects we use in Witchcraft, are the tangible representatives of unseen forces. The mind works magic, and no elaborately forged knife or elegant wand can do any more than augment the power of a trained mind. The tools are simply aids in communicating with Younger Self, who responds much better to tangibles than to abstracts.

There are two basic schools of thought about tools in the Craft: the ceremonial Magic school and what I call the kitchen magic school. Ceremonialists are purists, who feel that magical tools should never be handled by others or used for any but ritual purposes. Objects can become reservoirs of psychic power, which may be dissipated by, for example, slicing fruit with your *athame*. Kitchen magic Witches, on the other hand, feel that the Goddess is manifest in ordinary tasks as well as magic circles. When you slice fruit with your *athame*, you consecrate the fruit, and a kitchen chore becomes a sacred task. Whichever school of thought you follow, it is a breach of manners to handle another Witch's tools without asking permission.

Tools may be bought, hand-made yourself, given as gifts, or found, sometimes in unusual circumstances. Mother Moth of Compost found her *athame* lying on the white line in the middle of the freeway when she was driving home late one night. A set of tools are sometimes given to a new initiate by the coven. When buying magical tools, never haggle over the price.

Correspondences may differ in varying traditions, and interpretations of symbolism may not always agree. The following are the correspondences used in the Faery tradition (complete tables are given beginning on page 283).

The East*

The East corresponds to the element Air, to the mind, dawn, spring, to pale, airy colors, white and violet, to the eagle and high-flying birds, and the power to *know*. Its tools are the *athame* and the sword, which are used interchangeably. The *athame* is traditionally a double-bladed, black-handled knife, but people use anything from kitchen knives to Swiss Army knives complete with corkscrew, so indispensable for opening ritual wine.** Many Witches do not own a sword; they are dramatic at large, open rituals but awkward in close quarters.

EXERCISE 23: AIR MEDITATION

Face East. Ground and center. Breathe deep, and be conscious of the air as it flows in and out of your lungs. Feel it as the breath of the Goddess, and take in the life force, the inspiration, of the universe. Let your own breath merge with the winds, the clouds, the great currents that sweep over land and ocean with the turning of the earth. Say, "Hail, Arida, Bright Lady of the Air!"

EXERCISE 24: *ATHAME* OR SWORD MEDITATION*

Ground and center. Hold your *athame* or sword in your strongest hand. Breathe deeply and take in the power of Air, the power of the mind. The power of this tool is that of discrimination, of drawing lines, setting limits, making choices, and carrying them out. Remember choices you have made and carried through in spite of difficulties. Feel the power of your mind to influence others and the strength of your responsibility not to misuse that power. You have the force to act ethically, in accord with what you believe is right. Let the power of your intelligence, your knowledge, your moral courage, flow into your tool.

The South

The South corresponds to the element Fire, to energy or spirit, to noon, summer, fiery reds and oranges, to the solar lion and the quality of *will*. Its tool is the wand, which may be a slender branch of hazel, a stout oak staff, or a magically shaped piece of driftwood. The wand is used to channel energy, to direct a cone of power, and to invoke God or Goddess.

EXERCISE 25: FIRE MEDITATION

Face South. Ground and center. Be conscious of the electric spark within each nerve as pulses jump from synapse to synapse. Be aware of the combustion within each cell, as food burns to release energy. Let your own fire become one with candle flame, bonfire, hearth fire, lightning, starlight, and sunlight, one with the bright spirit of the Goddess. Say, "Hail, Tana, Goddess of Fire!"

EXERCISE 26: WAND MEDITATION

Ground and center. Hold your wand in your strongest hand. Breathe deeply, and feel the power of Fire, of energy. Be aware of yourself as a channel of energy. You can change spirit into matter, idea to reality, concept into form. Feel your own power to create, to do, to be an agent of change. Be in touch with your *will*—your power to do what you must, to set a goal and work toward it. Let your will flow into your wand.

The West

The West corresponds to the element Water, to emotions, to twilight, autumn, to blues, grays, deep purples, and sea greens, to sea serpents, dolphins, fish, to the power to *dare*. From the West comes the courage to face our deepest feelings. Its tool is the cup or chalice, which holds the salt water or ritual drink.

EXERCISE 27: WATER MEDITATION

Face West. Ground and center. Feel the blood flowing through the rivers of your veins, the liquid tides within each cell of your body. You are fluid, one drop congealed out of the primal ocean that is the womb of the Great Mother. Find the calm pools of tranquility within you, the rivers of feeling, the tides of power. Sink deep into the well of the inner mind, below consciousness. Say, "Hail, Tiamat, Serpent of the Watery Abyss!"

EXERCISE 28: CUP MEDITATION

Ground and center. Hold your cup cradled in both hands. Breathe deep, and feel the power of Water, of feeling and emotion. Be in touch with the flow of your own emotions: love, anger, sorrow, joy. The cup is the symbol of nurturing, the overflowing breast of the Goddess that nourishes all life. Be aware of how you are nurtured, of how you nurture others. The power to feel is the power to be human, to be real, to be whole. Let the strength of your emotions flood the cup.

The North

The North is considered the most powerful direction. Because the sun never reaches the Northern Hemisphere, it is the direction of Mystery, of the unseen. The North Star is the center, around which the skies revolve. Altars face North in the Craft. North corresponds to Earth, to the body, to midnight, winter, brown, black, and the green of vegetation. From the North comes the power to keep silent, to listen as well as speak, to keep secrets, to know what not to say. The Goddess as Dark Maiden, the new moon that is not yet visible, and the God as Sacred Bull are the totems of the North, and its tool is the pentacle, the prime symbol of the Craft. A five-pointed star with one point up, set within the circle of the full moon, the pentacle can be engraved on a plate, glazed on a ceramic platter, or molded out of "baker's clay"—bread dough and salt. It is used for grounding energy or as a platter for serving the sacred cakes.

EXERCISE 29: EARTH MEDITATION

Face North. Ground and center. Feel your bones, your skeleton, the solidity of your body. Be aware of your flesh, of all that can be touched and felt. Feel the pull of gravity, your own weight, your attraction to the earth that is the body of the Goddess. You are a natural feature, a moving mountain. Merge with all that comes from the earth: grass, trees, grains, fruits, flowers, beasts, metals, and precious stones. Return to dust, to compost, to mud. Say, "Hail, Belili, Mother of Mountains!"

EXERCISE 30: PENTACLE MEDITATION— THE FIVE STAGES OF LIFE

Ground and center. Hold your pentacle in both hands. Breathe deep, and feel the power of earth, of the body. The pentacle is your own body, four limbs and head. It is the five senses, both inner and outer. Be in touch with your own power to see, to hear, to smell, to taste, to touch. The pentacle is the four elements plus the fifth— essence. And it is the five stages of life, each an aspect of the Goddess:

1. *Birth:* the beginning, the time of coming into being
2. *Initiation:* adolescence, the time of individuation
3. *Love Ripening:* the time of union with another, of full adulthood, sexuality, responsibility, and love
4. *Reflection:* the time of advancing age, of repose, integration, wisdom
5. *Death:* the time of ending, of letting go, of moving on toward rebirth

Look at your pentacle, or draw one on a sheet of paper. Label the five stations, going clockwise around the points, and experience each stage in turn, as it occurs in a life span and within the span of each new activity or relationship. Trace the interlocking lines and reflect on their meanings. Love is linked to Birth and Death. Death is linked to Love and Initiation.

In the Goidelic† tree alphabet,* each of the five stages was symbolized by a tree, whose name began with one of the five vowels:⁵

A: Birth—*ailm*, silver fir
O: Initiation—*onn*, gorse or furze
U: Love—*ura*, heather
E: Repose—*eadha*, the aspen
I: Death—*idho*, the yew

Chant the sounds of the vowels and feel the power of each stage in turn. Touch your pentacle to your body, and let the life force of your own flesh flow into it.

EXERCISE 31: THE IRON PENTAGRAM

(A pentagram is a drawn or written pentacle. This is a meditative tool of the Faery tradition and an important training exercise.)

Ground and center. In your Book of Shadows, draw a pentacle with interlocking lines and label the points, in order, clockwise: "Sex," "Self," "Passion," "Pride," and "Power."

Sex is the manifestation of the driving life force energy of the universe. It is polarity, the attraction of God and Goddess, the on-off pulse that sustains the universe, the orgasmic, ecstatic harmony that sings within each being.*

Self is identity, individuality. Each of us is a unique manifestation of the Goddess, and that individuality is highly valued in the Craft. Self-love is the foundation of all love. "Celebrate yourself, and you will see that Self is everywhere."

Passion is the force of emotion that gives color and depth and vitality to life. Joy, sorrow, ecstasy, anger, fear, pain, love—the Goddess manifests in all human emotions. We cannot feel any of them in their full intensity unless we are willing to face them all.

Pride encourages us to create, to do, to share, to grow, and to enjoy the rightful fruits of our achievements. True pride is not based on comparisons or competition; it is an absolute sense of one's inner worth. Pride carries with it the responsibility of acting in accordance with one's self-respect and respect for Self in others.

Power is energy, inner power, not power over others. When the five points are in balance, the life force flows freely, filling us with vitality. Power is integrity, creativity, courage: the mark of a person who is whole.

Meditate on each of the points in turn, and then explore the links and connections: "Sex—Passion," "Self—Pride," "Passion—Power," and so on. Lie down with your arms

---

† Goidelic refers to the Gaelic Celts (Irish, Scots, Manx) as opposed to the Brythonic Celts (Welsh, Cornish, and Bretons).

and legs outstretched so that you form a star. Let your head and each of your limbs be a point on the pentacle. When you are "on the points," they will all be in balance. If some points feel weak, work on developing those qualities. Absorb the strength of the Iron Pentagram.

EXERCISE 32: THE PENTAGRAM OF PEARL

The Pentagram of Pearl is a meditative tool, like the Iron Pentagram. Its points are Love, Wisdom, Knowledge, Law, and Power.

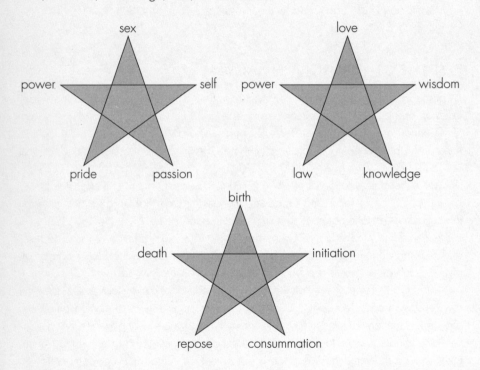

Begin as for the Iron Pentagram.

Love is the moving energy of life. It is both blindly erotic and deeply personal, a passionate, prideful, powerful caring for oneself and others. It is the law of the Goddess and the essence of magic.

Wisdom and *Knowledge* can best be understood together. Knowledge is learning, the power of the mind to understand and describe the universe. Wisdom is knowing how to apply knowledge—and how not to apply it. Knowledge is knowing what to say; wisdom is knowing whether or not to say it. Knowledge gives answers; wisdom asks questions. Knowledge can be taught; wisdom grows out of experience, out of making mistakes.

Law is natural law, not human law. When we break natural laws, we suffer the consequences as a natural result of our actions, not as a punishment. If you break the law of gravity, you will fall. Magic functions within natural law, not outside of it. But natural law may be broader and more complex than we realize.

Power, again, is the power that comes from within, when love, knowledge, wisdom, and law are united. Power, rooted in love and tempered by knowledge, law, and wisdom, brings growth and healing.

Again, meditate on the points and the links between them. Lie in the pentacle position, feel the points as part of yourself, and become aware of your own imbalances. Absorb the beauty of the Pentagram of Pearl.

Center

The center of the circle is the point of transformation. It corresponds to pure essence, to timelessness, to transparent light, to the power to *go*, to move, change, transform. Its magical tool is the cauldron, which may be the traditional three-legged cast iron pot, or a clay or metal bowl. The cauldron holds fire: a candle, incense, smoldering herbs, or a bonfire. It may also be a cooking pot, in which fire transforms the food we will eat.

EXERCISE 33: TRANSFORMATION MEDITATION

Ground and center. Whisper softly, over and over, "She changes everything She touches, and everything She touches, changes." Feel the constant processes of change within yourself, in your body, your ideas and emotions, your work and relationships. Within every unmoving stone, atoms are in constant flux. Feel the changes all around you, changes you have made, are about to make. Even ending the meditation is part of the process of change that is life. Say, "Hail, Kore, whose name cannot be spoken, the Ever-Changing One!"

EXERCISE 34: CAULDRON MEDITATION

Ground and center. Hold the cauldron in both hands. Breathe deep, and feel the power of transformation. You hold the Cauldron of Ceridwen, where the dead come to life. You hold the cauldron in which was brewed the broth that imparts all knowledge and understanding. The cauldron is the womb of the Goddess, the gestation ground of all birth. Think of the transformations you undergo every day. In a moment, you die and are reborn a thousand times. Feel your power to end and begin anew, your ability to gestate, to create, to give birth to new things, and let that power flow into your cauldron.

Meditations on the elements are part of the training of every Witch. After experiencing the energy of each magical element separately, the apprentice is taught to combine them, in preparation for learning to cast a circle.

EXERCISE 35: THE CIRCLE VISUALIZATION EXERCISE

(You may lie down, sit comfortably, or get up and enact this exercise. Face each direction either physically or mentally.)

Ground and center. Face East. Visualize your *athame* in your strongest hand, and draw an Invoking Pentacle (as in Exercise 13). See it burning with a pale, blue flame. Say, "Hail, Guardians of the Watchtowers of the East, Powers of Air."

Walk through the pentacle, and see a great wind sweeping across a vast plain of waving grass. Breathe deeply, and feel the air on your face, in your lungs, through your hair. The sun is rising, and in its rays a golden eagle shines as it flies toward you. When you are filled with the power of air, say, "Hail and farewell, Shining Ones." Walk back through the pentacle.

Turn and face the South. Again, draw the Invoking Pentacle. Say, "Hail, Guardians of the Watchtowers of the South, Powers of Fire."

Walk through the pentacle. You are on a blazing veldt under the hot sun. It is high noon. Feel the sun's fire on your skin and absorb its power. In the distance, red-gold lions sun themselves. When you feel attuned to fire, say, "Hail and farewell, Radiant Ones." Walk back through the pentacle.

Turn and face the West, and again draw the pentacle. Say, "Hail, Guardians of the Watchtowers of the West, Powers of Water."

Walk through the pentacle. You are on a cliff above a pounding sea. Feel the spray and the force of the waves. It is twilight, and the blue-green waves are edged with violet as the sun disappears. Dolphins and sea serpents dive and play in the foam. When you feel attuned to the power of water, say, "Hail and farewell, Flowing Ones" and walk through the pentacle.

Turn and face North. Draw the pentacle, and say, "Hail, Guardians of the Watchtowers of the North, Powers of Earth."

Walk through the pentacle. You are in the midst of a lush, fertile landscape, on the slopes of a mountain. Around you are green, growing herbs nourished by fresh springs, and tall, silent trees fed by the minerals and nutrients in the earth. In the distance, grain is waving in the fertile fields. Wild goats cling to the craggy heights above you, while below, herds of wild cattle thunder across the plain. It is midnight;

the moon is hidden but the stars are bright. The Great Bear and Little Bear circle the North Star, the still center point of the whirling wheel of the sky. Say, "Hail and farewell, Silent Ones."

Visualize all four pentacles around you in a circle of blue flame. Above your head is an eight-rayed star. Breathe deep, and draw in power from the star. Let it fill you; feel it flood every cell of your body with light, a cone of light that extends deep into the earth around you. Thank the star, and let the light return to its source. Open the circle by visualizing the pentacles flying off into space.

Additional tools* *and* ** used in most covens include a cord, a necklace, a censer, and a Book of Shadows, which has been discussed in Chapter Three. The cord is the symbol of binding, of belonging to a particular coven. In some traditions, the color of the cord reflects the degree of advancement in the Craft of its bearer. The censer is used to hold the incense, and is identified with either the East or the South, Air or Fire. The necklace is the circle of rebirth, the sign of the Goddess. It can be of any design that is personally pleasing.

Of course, candles, herbs, oils, and incenses are also used in Witchcraft. Unfortunately, I don't have space to go into a detailed discussion of their uses and correspondences, especially as that information is given in the Tables of Correspondences and is available from other sources.[6] In general, a Witch depends less on traditional associations of herbs, odors, and colors than on her own intuition. If the "proper" materials aren't available, we improvise.

The tools are usually kept on an altar, which may be anything from a hand-carved antique chest to a box covered with a cloth. When used for regular meditation and magical practice, the altar becomes charged with energy, a vortex of power. Generally, a Witch's altar faces north, and the tools are placed in their corresponding directions. Images of the Goddess and God—statues, shells, seeds, flowers, or a minor—take a central position.

EXERCISE 36: CONSECRATING A TOOL

(Tools can be charged—imbued with psychic energy—and consecrated within a group ritual, during an initiation, or individually. I will describe the rite for an *athame:* for other tools, simply make the necessary adjustments.)

Set up the altar as you want it, and light the candles and incense. Perform the Salt-Water Purification, and cast a circle by doing the Circle Visualization. Ask the Goddess to be with you.

Hold your *athame* in your strongest hand, saying, "Blessed be, thou creature of art." Do the *Athame* or Sword Meditation.

Touch it to the symbols of each of the four elements in turn: incense for Air, the wand for Fire, the cup for Water, and the pentacle for Earth. Meditate on the power of each element, and visualize that power flowing into the *athame*. Say, "May you be charged with the power of (Air, Fire, etc.) and serve me well in the (East, South, etc.), between the worlds, in all the worlds. So mote it be."

Pass your *athame* through the candle flame, and touch it to the central cauldron. Visualize white light filling and charging it. Say, "May you be charged from the center of all, above and below, throughout and about, within and without, to serve me well between the worlds, in all the worlds. So mote it be."

Draw or inscribe your own personal symbols on the blade or hilt. Trace over them with your own saliva, sweat, menstrual blood, or other secretions, to create the link with your tool. Breathe on it, and imagine your own personal power flowing into it.

Touch it to your heart, and your lips. Raise it to sky, and point it to earth. Wrap your cord around it (or imagine it, if you don't have a cord) and visualize a shield of light binding the power. Say, "Cord go round, power be bound, light revealed, now be sealed."

Earth the power, thank the Goddess, and open the circle by thanking each of the directions and visualizing the pentacles dissolving.

In casting a circle, the outer forms used are less important than the strength of the inner visualization. When the Priestess calls the Guardians of the East, for example, she feels the wind and sees the sun rising with her inner sight. She is also visualizing the flaming pentacles and the circle of light surrounding the coven. In a strong coven, one person may perform the outward actions, but all will be internally visualizing the circle and attuning themselves to the elements.

The outer forms can be very simple. Alone, it may be enough to simply visualize a ring of white light around the room, or turn to each direction in turn and tap the wall. A group may join hands and picture the circle, or one member may walk around the others. The circle may be marked out ahead of time with chalk, stones, string, flowers, leaves, or shells, or drawn invisibly with the *athame* as it is cast.

This chapter opens with a description of a formal circle casting. At first, trying to remember the words and actions, visualize the elements, and feel the power will be far more difficult than trying to pat your head and rub your stomach at the same time. But with practice your concentration will improve until the entire sequence flows easily and naturally. You may wish to create your own invocations, instead of using the ones given. Here are other examples:

A CIRCLE FOR HEALING DURING STRUGGLE
by Alan Acacia

hail guardians of the watchtower of the east, powers of air:

blow the staleness away, fill our lungs.
help us bring freshness
into our lives.
let there be clear skies, clear minds
for us to see our way.
let our words create a safe space.
blessed be.

hail guardians of the watchtower of the south, powers of fire:

come into our hearts, warm us.
help us emerge from hibernation, isolation,
to greet each other.
let passion glow on our birthright
as we fight injustice.
let our emotions out
from all their hiding places.
blessed be.

hail guardians of the watchtower of the west, powers of water:

rain on us, quench our thirst.
help us remember
the ocean womb from which we come.
now let all of us be connected.
let our moods be flowing back & forth
until all is one.
let the drought of separation be over.
blessed be.

hail guardians of the watchtower of the north, powers of earth:

strengthen our resolve, keep us centered.
help us be here, now.
let our bodies be strong
for loving each other.
let the dizziness of the workday pass,

& all of us find ourselves together
on one planet.
because of our struggles & magic
may a greater circle be cast
of love & social harmony.
blessed be.

Valerie's Rhyming Invocations to the Four Quarters

East:
Quicksilver messenger
Master of the crossroads
Springtime step lightly
Into my mind
Golden One whisper
Airy ferryman
Sail from the East on the wings of the wind.

South:
Desert flower, flaming will
Crackle with energy under my skin
Red lion roaring
Pulses racing
Roaming the South
I am open: come in.

West:
Pearl-gray warrior
Ghostly quest
Prince of Twilight
Sailing West
Intuition, sundown lady
Ancient serpent of the Sea
Pearly Queen of twilight waters
Silverfoot come silently.

North:
Mother of mountains, mother of trees,
Mother of midnight, mother of earth.

Root and leaf and flower and thorn,
Come to us, come to us, out of the North.

INVOCATIONS FROM THE SUMMER SOLSTICE RITUAL (STARHAWK)

[With these, begin in the North]
Earth my bone, my body,
Mountain my breast
Green grass and leafy tree
My trailing hair,
Rich dark dust, oozing mud
Seed sending white root deep,
Carpet of molding leaves,
Be our bed!
By the earth that is Her body,
Powers of the North send forth your strength.

Air, my breath, breeze of morning,
Stallion of the dawn star,
Whirlwind, bearing all that soars in flight,
Bee and bird,
Sweet fragrance,
Wailing storm's voice,
Carry us!
By the air that is Her breath,
Powers of the East send forth your light.

Fire my heart, burn bright!
My spirit is a flame,
My eye misses nothing.
A blaze leaps from nerve to nerve
Spark of the solar fire!
An answering heat rises, unbearable delight!
The flames sing, consume us!
By the fire that is Her spirit,
Powers of the South, send forth your flame.

Water my womb, my blood,
Wash over us, cool us.

Waves sweep ashore on white wings,
The rush, hiss, the rumble of stones
As the tide recedes,
That rhythm, my pulse,
Flood, gushing fountain,
We pour ourselves out,
Sweep us away!
By the waters of Her living womb,
Powers of the West, send forth your flow.

The energy field created by a circle can also be used for protection. This can be done very simply:

EXERCISE 37: PROTECTIVE CIRCLE

Visualize a circle or bubble of white light around yourself, with the energy running clockwise. Tell yourself it is an impenetrable barrier no harmful forces can cross. If you have time, perform the Circle Visualization or quickly call each of the four elements in turn.

EXERCISE 38: PERMANENT PROTECTIVE CIRCLE

(A permanent circle of protection can be established around your home or place of work. The following ritual can be done alone, or in a group with each person carrying one of the objects.)

Ground and center. Go around the house widdershins with a bell, a broom, and charged salt water. Ring the bell to scare away negative energies. Sweep away unwanted forces with the broom—or use a wand to wave them out. Sprinkle each entrance—each window, door, mirror, and major water outlets—with salt water. Also sprinkle the corners of every room. If necessary, perform a Banishing as in Exercise 22. Do the Salt-Water Purification.

Now go around the house clockwise, with salt water, *athame*, and incense. Draw an invoking pentacle at each entrance with the *athame*, and then with salt water. Concentrate on forming a seal of protection that cannot be broken. Finally, with the incense, charge each entrance and corner, inviting good forces to enter. Say,

Salt and sea,
Of ill stay free,

Fire and air,
Draw all that is fair.
Around and around,
The circle is bound.

Formally cast a circle in the room you will use for rituals. Chant and raise power to fill the house with protection. Then thank the Goddess, earth the power, and open the circle.

You can reinforce a protective circle by visualizing it. Do so before magical work or sleep.

The circle is cast; the ritual is begun. We have created the sacred space, a space fit for the Gods to enter. We have cleansed ourselves and centered ourselves; our mental bonds have dropped away. Free from fear, we can open to the starlight. In perfect love, and perfect trust, we are prepared to invoke the Goddess.

Notes

1. This set of invocations is written and paraphrased by me from traditional Faery invocations.
2. Mary Daly, *Beyond God the Father* (Boston: Beacon Press, 1973), p. 40.
3. Daly, p. 41.
4. Helen Diner, *Mothers and Amazons* (New York: Anchor Press, 1973), p. 169.
5. Robert Graves, *The White Goddess* (New York: Farrar, Straus & Giroux, 1966), Chaps. 10–11.
6. As a good general reference on traditional materials, and an excellent source book for Dianic Witchcraft, see Z. Budapest, *The Feminist Book of Lights and Shadows* (Venice, Calif.: Luna Publications, 1976)—reissued by Wingbow Press, Berkeley, Calif.

CHAPTER 5

The Goddess* *and* **

Between the Worlds
THE CHARGE OF THE GODDESS¹*

Listen to the words of the Great Mother, who of old was called Artemis, Astarte, Dione, Melusine, Aphrodite, Ceridwen, Diana, Arionrhod, Brigid, and by many other names:

"Whenever you have need of anything, once in the month, and better it be when the moon is full, you shall assemble in some secret place and adore the spirit of Me who is Queen of all the Wise. You shall be free from slavery, and as a sign that you be free you shall be naked in your rites. Sing, feast, dance, make music and love, all in My presence, for Mine is the ecstasy of the spirit and Mine also is joy on earth. For My law is love unto all beings. Mine is the secret that opens upon the door of youth, and Mine is the cup of wine of life that is the Cauldron of Ceridwen that is the holy grail of immortality. I give the knowledge of the spirit eternal and beyond death I give peace and freedom and reunion with those that have gone before. Nor do I demand aught of sacrifice, for behold, I am the mother of all things and My love is poured upon the earth."

Hear the words of the Star Goddess, the dust of whose feet are the hosts of heaven, whose body encircles the universe:

"I who am the beauty of the green earth and the white moon among the stars and the mysteries of the waters, I call upon your soul to arise and come unto me. For I am the soul of nature that gives life to the universe. From Me all things proceed and unto Me they must return. Let My worship be in the heart that rejoices, for behold—

*all acts of love and pleasure are My rituals. Let there be beauty and strength, power
and compassion, honor and humility, mirth and reverence within you. And you who
seek to know Me, know that your seeking and yearning will avail you not, unless you
know the Mystery: for if that which you seek, you find not within yourself, you will
never find it without. For behold, I have been with you from the beginning, and I am
that which is attained at the end of desire."*

(Adapted by Starhawk from Doreen Valiente)

The symbolism of the Goddess has taken on an electrifying power for modern
women. The rediscovery of the ancient matrifocal civilizations has given us a
deep sense of pride in woman's ability to create and sustain culture. It has
exposed the falsehoods of patriarchal history, and given us models of female
strength and authority. Once again in today's world, we recognize the
Goddess—ancient and primeval; the first of deities; patroness of the Stone Age
hunt and of the first sowers of seeds; under whose guidance the herds were
tamed, the healing herbs first discovered; in whose image the first works of art
were created; for whom the standing stones were raised; who was the inspiration of song and poetry. She is the bridge, on which we can cross the chasms
within ourselves, which were created by our social conditioning, and reconnect
with our lost potentials. She is the ship, on which we sail the waters of the
Deep Self, exploring the uncharted seas within. She is the door, through
which we pass into the future. She is the cauldron, in which we who have
been wrenched apart simmer until we again become whole. She is the vaginal
passage, through which we are reborn.

A historical and/or cross-cultural overview of the Goddess and her symbols
would itself require several volumes, and I will not attempt it in the limited
space of this book, especially as much good material is already available.[2]
Instead, I will limit myself to discussing the Goddess as seen through
Witchcraft, and focus on her function and meaning for women and men today.

People often ask me if I *believe* in the Goddess. I reply, "Do you believe in
rocks?" It is extremely difficult for most Westerners to grasp the concept of a
manifest deity. The phrase "believe *in*" itself implies that we cannot *know* the
Goddess, that She is somehow intangible, incomprehensible. But we do not
believe in rocks—we may see them, touch them, dig them out of our gardens,
or stop small children from throwing them at each other. We know them; we
connect with them. In the Craft, we do not *believe* in the Goddess—we connect with Her; through the moon, the stars, the ocean, the earth, through
trees, animals, through other human beings, through ourselves. She is here.
She is within us all. She is the full circle: earth, air, fire, water, and essence—
body, mind, spirit, emotions, change.

The Goddess is first of all earth, the dark, nurturing mother who brings forth all life. She is the power of fertility and generation; the womb, and also the receptive tomb, the power of death. All proceeds from Her; all returns to Her. As earth, She is also plant life; trees, the herbs and grains that sustain life. She is the body, and the body is sacred. Womb, breast, belly, mouth, vagina, penis, bone, and blood—no part of the body is unclean, no aspect of the life processes is stained by any concept of sin. Birth, death, and decay are equally sacred parts of the cycle. Whether we are eating, sleeping, making love, or eliminating body wastes, we are manifesting the Goddess.

The Earth Goddess is also air and sky, the celestial Queen of Heaven, the Star Goddess, ruler of things felt but not seen: of knowledge, mind, and intuition. She is the Muse, who awakens all creations of the human spirit. She is the cosmic lover, the morning and evening star, Venus, who appears at the times of lovemaking. Beautiful and glittering, She can never be grasped or penetrated; the mind is drawn ever further in the drive to know the unknowable, to speak the inexpressible. She is the inspiration that comes with an indrawn breath.

The celestial Goddess is seen as the moon, who is linked to women's monthly cycles of bleeding and fertility. Woman is the earthly moon; the moon is the celestial egg, drifting in the sky womb, whose menstrual blood is the fertilizing rain and the cool dew; who rules the tides of the oceans, the first womb of life on earth. So the moon is also Mistress of Waters: the waves of the sea, streams, springs, the rivers that are the arteries of Mother Earth; of lakes, deep wells, and hidden pools, and of feelings and emotions, which wash over us like waves.

The Moon Goddess has three aspects: As She waxes, She is the Maiden; full, She is the Mother; as She wanes, She is the Crone. Part of the training of every initiate involves periods of meditation on the Goddess in her many aspects. I don't have space to include all of these, but I will share with you the meditations on the three aspects of the moon:

EXERCISE 39: WAXING MOON MEDITATION

Ground and center. Visualize a silver crescent moon, curving to the right. She is the power of beginning, of growth and generation. She is wild and untamed, like ideas and plans before they are tempered by reality. She is the blank page, the unplowed field. Feel your own hidden possibilities and latent potentials; your power to begin and grow. See her as a silver-haired girl running freely through the forest under the slim moon. She is Virgin, eternally unpenetrated, belonging to no one but herself. Call her name "Nimuë!" and feel her power within you.

EXERCISE 40: FULL MOON MEDITATION

Ground and center, and visualize a round full moon. She is the Mother, the power of fruition and of all aspects of creativity. She nourishes what the New Moon has begun. See her open arms, her full breasts, her womb burgeoning with life. Feel your own power to nurture, to give, to make manifest what is possible. She is the sexual woman; her pleasure in union is the moving force that sustains all life. Feel the power in your own pleasure, in orgasm. Her color is the red of blood, which is life. Call her name "Mari!" and feel your own ability to love.

EXERCISE 41: WANING MOON MEDITATION

Ground and center. Visualize a waning crescent, curving to the left, surrounded by a black sky. She is the Old Woman, the Crone who has passed menopause, the power of ending, of death. All things must end to fulfill their beginnings. The grain that was planted must be cut down. The blank page must be destroyed, for the work to be written. Life feeds on death—death leads on to life, and in that knowledge lies wisdom. The Crone is the Wise Woman, infinitely old. Feel your own age, the wisdom of evolution stored in every cell of your body. Know your own power to end, to lose as well as gain, to destroy what is stagnant and decayed. See the Crone cloaked in black under the waning moon; call her name "Anu!" and feel her power in your own death.

The triad of the moon becomes the pentad, the fivefold star of birth, initiation, ripening, reflection, and death.** The Goddess is manifest in the entire life cycle. Women are valued and respected in old age, as well as youth.

Birth and childhood, of course, are common to all cultures. But our society has not, until recently, conceptualized the stage of initiation, of personal exploration and self-discovery, as necessary for women.** Girls were expected to pass directly from childhood to marriage and motherhood—from control by their fathers to control by their husbands. An initiation demands courage and self-reliance, traits that girls were not encouraged to develop. Today, the stage of initiation may involve establishing a career, exploring relationships, or developing one's creativity. Women who have missed this stage in their youth often find it necessary to go back to it later in life. The later stages of life can only fully be experienced after the initiation is completed and an individualized self has been formed.

The stage of ripening is also called *consummation*, and it is the stage of full creativity. Relationships deepen and take on a sense of commitment. A woman may choose to mother children or to nurture a career, a project, or a cause. An artist or writer reaches her mature style.

Creations, whether they are children, poems, or organizations, take on a life of their own. As they become independent, and their demands diminish, the stage of reflection is reached. With age comes a new initiation, this one less physically active but deepened by the insights of experience. Old age, in Witchcraft, is seen very positively, as the time when activity has evolved into wisdom. It brings about the final initiation, which is death.**

These five stages are embodied in our lives, but they can also be seen within every new enterprise or creative project. Each book, each painting, each new job is born first as an idea. It undergoes an initiatory period of exploration, which is frightening at times, because we are forced to learn new things. As we grow comfortable with a new skill or concept, the project can be consummated. It exists independently; as we let go, other people read the book, view the painting, eat the food, or apply the knowledge we have taught. Finally, it is over; it dies, and we go on to something new.

The pentacle, all five-lobed leaves, and five-petaled flowers are sacred to the Goddess as pentad. The apple is especially her emblem, because, when it is sliced crosswise, the embedded seeds form a pentacle.

The nature of the Goddess is never single. Wherever She appears, she embodies both poles of duality—life in death, death in life. She has a thousand names, a thousand aspects. She is the milk cow, the weaving spider, the honeybee with its piercing sting. She is the bird of the spirit and the sow that eats its own young. The snake that sheds its skin and is renewed; the cat that sees in the dark; the dog that sings to the moon—all are Her. She is the light and the darkness, the patroness of love and death, who makes manifest *all* possibilities. She brings both comfort and pain.

It is easy to respond to the concept of Goddess as Muse or Mother, to inspiration, nurturing, and healing power. It is more difficult to understand the Goddess as Destroyer. Judeo-Christian dualism has conditioned us to think of destruction as synonymous with evil. (Although, Goddess knows, the Jehovah of the Old Testament was far from all sweetness and light.) Most of us live removed from nature, cut off from the experiences that constantly remind more "primitive" people that every act of creation is an act of aggression. To plant a garden, you must dig out the weeds, crush the snails, thin the seedlings as they reach toward the light. To write a book, you must destroy draft after draft of your own work, cutting apart paragraphs and striking out words and sentences. Creation postulates change; and any change destroys what went before.

The Creatrix-Destroyer is manifest in fire, which destroys all it feeds on in order to create warmth and light. Fire is the nurturing hearth, the creative fire of the forge, the joyous bonfire of celebration. But the Goddess is also the raging fire of anger.

The power of anger is difficult to face. We identify anger with violence, and women have been conditioned to feel that our anger is wrong and unacceptable. Yet anger is a manifestation of the life force. It is a survival emotion, a warning signal that something in our environment is threatening. Danger triggers a physical, psychic, and emotional response that mobilizes our energy to change the situation. Being human, we respond to verbal and emotional attacks as threats, which arouse anger. But when we cannot admit our own anger, instead of recognizing the threat in the environment, we experience ourselves as wrong. Instead of flowing outward to change the environment, our energy becomes locked into internal efforts at repression and control.

The Goddess liberates the energy of our anger. It is seen as sacred, and its power is purified. Like a forest fire in undisturbed wilderness, it sweeps away the underbrush so that the seedlings of our creativity can receive the nourishing sunlight. We control our *actions*; we do not attempt to control our *feelings*. Anger becomes a connecting force that spurs honest confrontations and communications with others.

I have spoken of the Goddess as psychological symbol and also as manifest reality. She is both. She exists, *and* we create Her. The symbols and attributes associated with the Goddess speak to Younger Self and, through it, to the Deep Self. They engage us emotionally. We know the Goddess is not the moon—but we still thrill to its light glinting through branches. We know the Goddess is not a woman, but we respond with love as if She were, and so connect emotionally with all the abstract qualities behind the symbol.

Many shapes and symbols represent the Goddess. Eyes, which schematically are also breasts, symbolize her nurturing powers and the gift of inner sight. The crescent represents the moon: a waxing and waning crescent, back to back, becomes the labrys or double ax, the weapon of Goddess cultures. Triangles, ovals, and lozenges, the shapes of the female genitals, are her symbols, as well. As part of an initiate's training, she is taught to visualize symbols, to meditate on them and play with them in her imagination until they reveal their meaning directly. Any symbol or aspect of the Goddess can be a basis for meditation, but as I have space for only one example, I will choose the double spiral:

EXERCISE 42: THE DOUBLE SPIRAL

Ground and center. Visualize a double spiral. When you see it clearly, let it grow until you stand within it, and follow it inward, moving counterclockwise. It becomes a maze of high, clipped hedges, then a labyrinth of stone walls; its winding turns are the passageway to a hidden secret. As you move through the spiral, the world dissolves, form dissolves, until you are in the hidden heart where birth and death are one. The center of the spiral shines; it is the North Star, and the arms of the spiral are the Milky Way, a myriad of stars slowly revolving around the still center point. You are in Spiral Castle, at the back of the North Wind. Explore it in your imagination. See who you meet, what you learn. You are in the womb of the Goddess, floating free. Now feel yourself pushed and squeezed, moving out through the spiral, which is now the vaginal passage of rebirth. Move clockwise through the double spiral of your DNA. Now it becomes a whirlwind—fly with it. Let it become the twining tendril of a plant—a crystal—a shell—an orbiting electron. Time is a spiral—the cycles endlessly repeating, yet always moving. Know the spiral as the underlying form of all energy. As you emerge, let it return to its small, abstract, symbolic form. Thank it, and let it disappear.

The Charge of the Goddess, at the opening of this chapter, reflects the Craft understanding of the Goddess. It begins with a long list of Goddess names, drawn from many cultures. These are not seen as separate beings but, rather, as different aspects of the same Being that is all beings. The names used may change with the seasons or preferences of the speaker: for example, the Goddess might be named Kore in the spring, after the Maiden aspect of the Greek Goddess. A Witch of Jewish heritage might call on the ancient Hebrew Goddess as Ashimah or Asherah; an Afro-American Witch might prefer Yemaya, the West African Goddess of the sea and love.[3] In most traditions of the Craft, the inner name of the Goddess is recognized to embody great power, and so is kept secret, revealed only to initiates. The outer names often used are Diana, for the Goddess of the moon, and Aradia, her daughter, whom legends say was sent to earth to liberate people by teaching them the arts of magic.[4]

"Need of anything" refers to both spiritual and material needs. In Witchcraft, there is no separation. The Goddess is manifest in the food we eat, the people we love, the work we do, the homes in which we live. It is not considered ignoble to ask for needed goods and comforts. "Work for yourself, and you will see that Self is everywhere," is a saying of the Faery tradition. It is through the material world that we open ourselves to the Goddess. But Witchcraft also recognizes that when material needs are satisfied deeper needs and longings may remain. These can only be satisfied by connection with the nurturing, life-giving forces within, which we call *Goddess*.

The coven meets at the full moon, in honor of the Goddess at the height of her glory. The tides of subtle power are considered to be strongest when the moon is full. The Goddess is identified with the fructifying lunar energy that illumines the secret dark; the feminine, tidal, pulsating power that waxes and wanes in harmony with woman's menstrual flow. The sun is identified with her male, polar self, the God, whose festivals are celebrated at eight points of power in the solar cycle.

The Goddess is the liberator, and it has been said that "Her service is perfect freedom."[5] She is the liberator because She is manifest in our deepest drives and emotions, which always and inevitably threaten the systems designed to contain them. She is love and anger, which refuse to fit comfortably into the social order. To be "free from slavery" once meant that, within the ritual circle, all were equal, whether they were peasant, serf, or noble in the outside world. Slavery, today, can be mental and emotional as well as physical: the slavery of fixed perceptions, of conditioned ideas, of blind beliefs, of fear. Witchcraft demands intellectual freedom and the courage to confront our own assumptions. It is not a belief system; it is a constantly self-renewed attitude of joy and wonder to the world.

The naked body represents truth, the truth that goes deeper than social custom. Witches worship naked for several reasons: as a way of establishing closeness and dropping social masks, because power is most easily raised that way, and because the human body is itself sacred.** Nakedness is a sign that a Witch's loyalty is to the truth before any ideology or any comforting illusions.

Rituals are joyful and pleasurable. Witches sing, feast, dance, laugh, joke, and have fun in the course of rituals. Witchcraft is serious—but not pompous or solemn. As in Hasidic Judaism or Bhakti Yoga, joy and ecstasy are seen as the pathways to the Divine. The "ecstasy of the spirit" is not separate from "joy on earth." One leads to the other—and neither can truly be realized without the other. Earthly joys, unconnected with the deep, feeling power of the Goddess, become mechanical, meaningless—mere sensations that soon lose their appeal. But spiritual ecstasies that attempt to escape the senses and the body become equally arid and rootless, draining vitality instead of nourishing it.

The law of the Goddess is love: passionate sexual love, the warm affection of friends, the fierce protective love of mother for child, the deep comradeship of the coven. There is nothing amorphous or superficial about love in Goddess religion; it is always specific, directed toward real individuals, not vague concepts of humanity. Love includes animals, plants, the earth itself—"all beings," not just human beings. It includes ourselves and all our fallible human qualities.

Ceridwen is one of the forms of the Celtic Goddess, and her cauldron is the womb-cauldron of rebirth and inspiration. In early Celtic myth, the cauldron of the Goddess restored slain warriors to life. It was stolen away to the Underworld, and the heroes who warred for its return were the originals of King Arthur and his Knights, who quested for its later incarnation, the Holy Grail. The Celtic afterworld is called the Land of Youth, and the secret that opens its door is found in the cauldron: The secret of immortality lies in seeing death as an integral part of the cycle of life. Nothing is ever lost from the universe: Rebirth can be seen in life itself, where every ending brings a new beginning. Most Witches do believe in some form of reincarnation. This is not so much a doctrine as a gut feeling growing out of a world view that sees all events as continuing processes. Death is seen as a point on an ever-turning wheel, not as a final end. We are continually renewed and reborn whenever we drink fully and fearlessly from "the cup of wine of life."

The love of the Goddess is unconditional. She does not ask for sacrifice—whether human or animal—nor does She want us to sacrifice our normal human needs and desires. Witchcraft is a religion of self-celebration, not self-abnegation. Sacrifice is *inherent* in life, in constant change that brings constant losses. Offerings: A poem, a painting, a pinch of grain may express our thankfulness for her gifts, but only when they are made freely, not from a sense of obligation.

In the Star Goddess passage, we see the imagery of the celestial encircler, the moon, the waters, the green earth from which all proceeds and to which all must return. She is the "soul of nature," which vivifies all things.

Any act based on love and pleasure is a ritual of the Goddess. Her worship can take any form and occur anywhere; it requires no liturgy, no cathedrals, no confessions. Its essence is the recognition, in the midst of pleasure, of its deepest source. Pleasure, then, is not superficial but becomes a profound expression of the life force; a connecting power linking us to others, not the mere sensation of satisfying our own isolated needs.

Witchcraft recognizes that any virtue becomes a vice unless it is balanced by its own opposite. Beauty, when unsustained by strength, is vapid, lifeless. Power is insufferable when untempered by compassion. Honor, unless balanced by humility, becomes arrogance; and mirth, when not deepened by reverence, becomes mere superficiality.

Finally we learn the Mystery—that unless we find the Goddess within ourselves we will never find Her without. She is both internal and external; as solid as a rock, as changeable as our own internal image of Her. She is manifest within each of us—so where else should we look?

The Goddess is "the end of desire," its goal and its completion. In Witchcraft, desire is itself seen as a manifestation of the Goddess. We do not seek to conquer or escape from our desires—we seek to fulfill them. Desire is the glue of the universe; it binds the electron to the nucleus, the planet to the sun—and so creates form, creates the world. To follow desire to its end is to unite with that which is desired, to become one with it, with the Goddess. We are already one with the Goddess—She has been with us from the beginning. So fulfillment becomes, not a matter of self-indulgence, but of self-*awareness*.

For women, the Goddess is the symbol of the inmost self, and the beneficent, nurturing, liberating power within woman. The cosmos is modeled on the female body, which is sacred. All phases of life are sacred: Age is a blessing, not a curse. The Goddess does not limit women to the body; She awakens the mind and spirit and emotions. Through Her, we can know the power of our anger and aggression, as well as the power of our love.

For a man, the Goddess, as well as being the universal life force, is his own, hidden, female self.* She embodies all the qualities society teaches him *not* to recognize in himself. His first experience of Her may therefore seem somewhat stereotyped; She will be the cosmic lover, the gentle nurturer, the eternally desired Other, the Muse, all that he is not. As he becomes more whole and becomes aware of his own "female" qualities, She seems to change, to show him a new face, always holding up the mirror that shows what to him is still ungraspable. He may chase Her forever, and She will elude him, but through the attempt he will grow, until he too learns to find Her within.

To invoke the Goddess is to awaken the Goddess within, to become, for a time, that aspect we invoke.** An invocation channels power through a visualized image of Divinity. In some covens, one Priestess is chosen to represent the manifest Goddess to the rest. In our covens, She is invoked into each member of the circle.

An invocation can be a set piece of poetry or music, sung or spoken by an individual or the group. In our covens, we usually chant as a group, sometimes wordlessly and spontaneously, sometimes using a set phrase that is repeated over and over again. A multivoiced chant will sometimes involve one Priestess repeating a simple "bass" line—"All That Is Wild and Free," for example— while another chants a repeating cycle—"Green Bud Leaf/Bud Leaf Bright," and so on (see below)—and a third chanting a long poetic piece, while the entire coven softly chants the vowel sounds. It is impossible to reproduce the effect on the printed page, unfortunately, but the bare words follow. When you use the invocations given here, please play with them, experiment with melodies and plain-song incantings, rearrange them, combine them, interweave them, change them, and take inspiration from them to make your own:

REPEATING CHANTS (TO THE GODDESS)**

MOON Mother Bright Light Of All Earth Sky We CALL You.
LUNA Momma Shiny Shine COME.
HAIL Old Moon Secret WISE One HAIL Old Moon Secret
    WISE One.
She SHINES For All She FLOWS Through All.
All That Is WILD And Free All That Is WILD And Free.

REPEATING CYCLE: "GREEN BUD LEAF"

(This developed out of a Word Association Trance, as in Exercise 8. Words should be stressed evenly, with no breaks between groups, which are separated for ease of memorization. The entire cycle repeats over and over.)

Green Bud Leaf/Bud Leaf Bright/Leaf Bright Flower/
Bright Flower Grow/Flower Grow Fruit/Grow Fruit Ripe/
Fruit Ripe Seed/Ripe Seed Die/Seed Die Earth/
Die Earth Dark/Earth Dark Waken/Dark Waken Green/
Waken Green Bud . . .

SUMERIAN CHANT

(Half-sung on two or three notes—repeat entire chant.)
NAMmu NAMmu O NamMU AE EE AE EE O NamMU
NINmah NINmah O NinMAH AE EE AE EE O NinMAH
MAmi MAmi O MaMI AE EE AE EE O MaMI
MAma MAma O MaMA AE EE AE EE O MaMA
MAH MAH O MAH MAH AE EE AE EE O MAH MAH . . .

INVOCATION TO THE DEWY ONE

All-dewy Sky-sailing Pregnant Moon
Who shines for all,
Who flows through all.
Light of the world which is yourself.
Maiden, Mother, Crone,
The Weaver   The Green One
Isis Astarte Ishtar
Aradia Diana Cybele
Kore Ceridwen Levanah
Luna Mari Anna
Rhiannon Selena Demeter Mah
See with our eyes, Hear with our ears,
Touch with our hands, Breathe with our nostrils,
Kiss with our lips, Open our hearts,
Come into us!
Touch us, Change us, Make us whole.

HONOR TO THE GODDESS, LADY OF MANY NAMES TO
DEMETER, THE IMMEASURABLE ONE, & TO THE MAIDEN
by Karen Lynd Cushen

'Take, Eat, This is My Body   'Take, Drink, This is My Blood
Which shall Rise in You   The emptied Cup shall be
& Be Made Whole'   Refilled'

Goddess of the Harvest,
the fruit of Whose joy in the return of Your Daughter,
sustains us even as You make bleak the earth
at Her leaving

The earth is rent
& Persephone
the Maiden Whose name may not be spoken
is swallowed by the land of the dead

She will come again,
in Whose footfalls spring the flowers & the grain
carrying up with Her
dark memories of whence She came

Demeter
Near in our grief
because yearly we see Your own sorrow
ravage the face of earth
& Your Daughter
Close at the hour of our death
because yearly death claims Her
We know hope because we remember
again & again
Persephone healing Herself
& You with Her, rising

Demeter, Mother
We who have lain on Your knees
& slept in Your arms, give You honor,
Anoint us & place us at night
in the red heart of Your fire;
we shall not flinch

& let none in terror
snatch us from that hearth.
Anneal us at unspeakable heat
& give us a slow cooling
that pliant we may return
evergreen with the spring

We Your holy grain
honor You not in slaughter
but as we plow, plant our feet, scatter Your seed
in Your Daughter's returning footsteps
& reap

We the threshing floor
Ground of Your Being
where you stand smiling with sheaves & poppies in Your hand
watching the winnowing

In the heat of the morning we wake
our parched throats thirsty for the cup of Eleusis
cooling draught of the reaper
Our limbs longing to sway again in the wind
in Your ancient dances

Out of our dreams, our myths, our nursery tales
those ghettoes in which survive Your memory
we behold the Ear of Corn
we know the song You sung,
Song of the Sacred Body
Yours & Our Own
& honor You, Lady of Many Names,
Maiden & Immeasurable One.

KORE CHANT: SPRING AND FALL EQUINOX

Her name cannot be spoken,
Her face was not forgotten,
Her power is to open,
Her promise can never be broken.

(Spring)
All sleeping seeds She wakens,
The rainbow is Her token,
Now winter's power is taken,
In love, all chains are broken.

(Fall)
All seeds She deeply buries,
She weaves the thread of seasons.
Her secret, darkness carries,
She loves beyond all reason.

She changes everything She touches, and
Everything She touches, changes. [Repeat—chant.]
Change is, touch is; Touch is, change is.
Change us! Touch us! Touch us! Change us!

Everything lost is found again,
In a new form, In a new way.
Everything hurt is healed again,
In a new life, In a new day.
[Repeat any and all verses.]

INVOCATION TO THE GODDESS AS MOTHER
by Susan Stern

Mama!
From my heart,
From my blood, Mama
I call you . . .

My heart of your heat
Limb of your Northwind
Water of your Water
Cunt of your Hillside
Cock of your Springtime
Eyes of Your Stars,
Mama
Eyes of your sun,

Mama
Of your Sol, Mama
My soul of your Sol
Mama
Come Mama!
Come into our circle
Our womb
Be with us now, Mama
Be with us now!

MOONMOTHER
by Laurel

moonmother
i am your child of innocence
your natural born
no laws but yours can tame me
no love but your own

everlasting
everchanging
thousand formed
your eyes are ducks on the wing
your foot is dancing foam
i am your dancer
you are the dance
song without limit
drummer and tune
a whole orchestra
of your love
i could walk
your golden path
straight to the sun
two-step my way
to your heart

o send me away
let me swing on your star
inconstant ripple

stream lake pond
ocean
whirlpool
crashing great one
earthsucker
the one and only true love
you leave treasure everywhere
sand dollars
smooth stone
your edible green hair

this is our life mama
yours and mine
all the flickering powers
all the shimmering lights
currents alternate
and direct
i might hold the cork
but you are the flow
the circuit
the breaker
the spare dry cell
insanity at midnight
prayers at dawn
ecstasy in the noon heat
mirage that points
to the real splendor
gold and saffron
ruby and red
sunrise
moonset
the single song of all
that is
was
and ever shall be

Blessed be.

INVOCATION TO THE QUEEN OF SUMMER

Queen of Summer
Queen Bee
Sweet-smelling
Flowering One
Honey Nectar
Overflowing fountain
Full-blown rose
Intoxicating dancer
Whispering wind
Singer
Spell-binder
Blossom and thorn
Rhiannon
Arianrhod
Aphrodite
Ishtar
Cybele
Come into us
Carry us off!

Notes

1. The Charge of the Goddess was written by Doreen Valiente. It appears in many vary-ing forms; in this version, I have slightly changed the language. It is loved by Witches because it so perfectly expresses our concept of the Goddess.
2. One of the best recent historical sources on the Goddess is Merlin Stone, *When God Was a Woman* (New York: Dial Press, 1976). Also see the Suggested Readings for resources published in the twenty years after the first publication of this book.
3. Many books are available that explore Goddess religion historically and cross-culturally. The classic work is still Robert Graves, *The White Goddess* (New York: Farrar, Straus & Giroux, 1966).
4. Charles Leland, *Aradia, Gospel of the Witches* (New York: Weiser, 1974).
5. "It was said of the lotus-crowned Goddess in the Corinthian Mysteries, long before the phrase was applied to the ideally benign Father-God, 'Her service is perfect freedom'" (Graves, p. 485).

CHAPTER 6

The God*

Between the Worlds

INVOCATION TO THE GOD

The Priest steps into the center of the circle and picks up the drum. Beating a strong, pounding rhythm, he begins the chant:

> Seed sower, grain reborn,
> Horned One Come!

Other voices join his. Hands clap out the rhythm on bare thighs; feet stamp the floor. There is one great shout:

> "Io! Evohe!"

Silence. A soft tenor begins to sing:

> Bright sun, Dark death,
> Lord of winds, Lord of the dance,
> Sun child, Winter-born king,
> Hanged One,
> Untamed! Untamed!
> Stag and stallion, Goat and bull,
> Sailor of the last sea, Guardian of the gate,
> Lord of the two lands,

Ever-dying, Ever-living, Radiance!
Dionysus, Osiris, Pan, Dumuzi, Arthur,
Robin, Janicot, Hou!
Move us! Touch us! Shake us!
Bring us through!

All is quiet. The Priest sets down the drum, and says simply, "He is here." The coven echoes, "He is here!" "Blessed be."

I grow old, I grow old,
I shall wear the bottoms of my trousers rolled.

Shall I part my hair behind? Do I dare to eat a peach?
I shall wear white flannel trousers, and walk upon the beach.
I have heard the mermaids singing, each to each.

I do not think that they will sing to me.

T. S. Eliot[1]

"It is very much in style today to urge men to feel. However, this urging is partially reminiscent of taunting a crippled man to run."

Herb Goldberg[2]

The image of the Horned God in Witchcraft is radically different from any other image of masculinity in our culture. He is difficult to understand, because He does not fit into any of the expected stereotypes, neither those of the "macho" male nor the reverse-images of those who deliberately seek effeminacy.[3] He is gentle, tender, and comforting, but He is also the Hunter. He is the Dying God—but his death is always in the service of the life force. He is untamed sexuality—but sexuality as a deep, holy, connecting power. He is the power of feeling, and the image of what men could be if they were liberated from the constraints of patriarchal culture.

The image of the Horned God was deliberately perverted by the medieval Church into the image of the Christian Devil. Witches do not believe in or worship the Devil—they consider it a concept peculiar to Christianity. The God of the Witches is sexual—but sexuality is seen as sacred, not as obscene or blasphemous. Our God wears horns—but they are the waxing and waning crescents of the Goddess Moon, and the symbol of animal vitality. In some aspects, He is black, not because He is dreadful or fearful, but because darkness and the night are times of power, and part of the cycles of time.[4]

There have always been traditions of the Craft in which the God is given little recognition.[5] In the Craft, separate Women's Mysteries and separate Men's Mysteries may be performed.[6] But in most Witch traditions the God is seen as the other-half of the Goddess, and many of the rites and holidays are devoted to Him as well as to Her.

In the medieval Witch cult, the God may have obtained prominence over the Goddess for a time. Most Witch confessions speak of "the devil," as the Christian priests transcribed the Witches' words for their non-Christian God. Fewer mention the Goddess, who is usually called "The Queen of Elphame." However, the interrogators of Witches were looking for evidence of Devil worship, not Goddess worship. They recorded evidence that supported their accusations of Satanism and ignored or twisted other evidence. Tortured suspects who reached the end of their endurance were often given already prepared statements to sign, which expressed what the Christian Priests wished to believe, rather than the truth.

A common practice in the medieval Craft was for the Priest and Priestess to enact the parts of God and Goddess, who were believed to be physically incarnate in the rites.* and ** One old account cited by Margaret Murray expresses the importance of this custom to illiterate peasants, for whom seeing was believing: The Priest mocked those "who offered to trust in God who left them miserable in the world, and neither he nor his son Jesus Christ ever appeared to them when they called on him, as he had, who would not cheat them."[7] For most Witches, "that earthly Sabbath was to her the true Paradise, where there was more pleasure than she could express, and she believed also that the joy which she took in it was but the prelude to a much greater glory, for her god so held her heart that no other desire could enter in."[8]

In the women's movement, Dianic/separatist Witchcraft[9] has become the fashion, and some women may have difficulty understanding why a feminist would bother with the Horned God at all.* Yet there are few if any women whose lives are not bound up with men, if not sexually and emotionally, then economically. The Horned God represents powerful, positive male qualities that derive from deeper sources than the stereotypes and the violence and emotional crippling of men in our society. If man had been created in the Horned God's image, he would be free to be wild without being cruel, angry without being violent, sexual without being coercive, spiritual without being unsexed, and able to truly love. The mermaids, who are the Goddess, would sing to him.

The Goddess is the Encircler, the Ground of Being; the God is That-Which-Is-Brought-Forth, her mirror image, her other pole. She is the earth; He is the grain. She is the all-encompassing sky; He is the sun, her fireball. She is the Wheel; He is the Traveler. His is the sacrifice of life to death that life may go on. She is Mother and Destroyer; He is all that is born and is destroyed.*

For men, the God is the image of inner power and of a potency that is more than merely sexual. He is the undivided Self, in which mind is not split from body, nor spirit from flesh. United, both can function at the peak of creative and emotional power.

In our culture, men are taught that masculinity demands a lack of feeling. They are conditioned to function in a military mode; to cut off their emotions and ignore the messages of their bodies; to deny physical discomfort, pain, and fear, in order to fight and conquer most efficiently. This holds true whether the field of conquest is the battlefield, the bedroom, or the business office.*

It has become something of a cliché to say that men have been trained to be aggressive and dominant and women have been taught to be passive and submissive, that men are allowed to be angry and women are not. In patriarchal culture, both women and men learn to function within a hierarchy, in which those at the top dominate those below. One aspect of that dominance is the privilege of expressing anger. The general chews out the sergeant; the private cannot. The boss is free to blow his stack, but not his assistant. The boss's wife yells at her maid, not vice versa. Because women have usually been at the bottom of hierarchies, from the business world to the traditional family, they have borne the brunt of a great deal of male anger, and been the ultimate victims of violence. Anger can be seen as a response to an attack; very few men are in positions where they can afford to directly confront their attackers.

Men's anger, then, becomes twisted and perverted. It is threatening to recognize the true source of his rage, because he would then be forced to recognize the helplessness, powerlessness, and humiliation of his position. Instead, he may turn his anger on safer targets—women, children, or still less powerful men. Or his anger may turn to self-destruction: disease, depression, alcoholism, or any of a smorgasbord of readily available addictions.

Patriarchy literally means "rule of the fathers," but in a patriarchy, very few men are allowed to enact the role of "father" outside the limited family sphere. The structure of hierarchical institutions is pyramidal: One man at the top controls many below. Men compete for money and power over others; the majority, who do not reach the top of the chain of command, are forced to remain immature, enacting the roles of either dutiful or rebel sons. The good sons eternally seek to please the father by obedience; the bad sons seek to overthrow him and take his place. Either way, they are cut off from their own true desires and feelings.

And so our religions reflect a cosmos in which Father God exhorts his "children" to obey the rules and do what they are told, lest they align themselves with the Great Rebel. Our psychology is one of war between sons and fathers who eternally vie for exclusive possession of the mother, who, like all women under patriarchy, is the ultimate prize for success. And progressive politics are reduced to alignments of rebel sons, who overthrow the father only to institute their own hierarchies.

The Horned God, however, is born of a Virgin mother. He is a model of male power that is free from father-son rivalry or oedipal conflicts. He has no father; He is his own father.* and ** As He grows and passes through his changes on the Wheel, He remains in relationship to the prime nurturing force. His power is drawn directly from the Goddess: He participates in Her.

The God embodies the power of feeling. His animal horns represent the truth of undisguised emotion, which seeks to please no masters. He is untamed. But untamed feelings are very different from enacted violence. The God is the life force, the life cycle. He remains within the orbit of the Goddess; his power is always directed toward the service of life.

The God of the Witches is the God of love. This love includes sexuality, which is also wild and untamed as well as gentle and tender.* His sexuality is fully *felt*, in a context in which sexual desire is sacred, not only because it is the means by which life is procreated but also because it is the means by which our own lives are most deeply and ecstatically realized. In Witchcraft, sex is a sacrament, an outward sign of an inward grace. That grace is the deep connection and recognition of the wholeness of another person. In its essence, it is not limited to the physical act—it is an exchange of energy, of subtle nourishment, between people. Through connection with another, we connect with all.

In the Craft, the male body, like the female body, is held sacred, not to be violated. It is a violation of the male body to use it as a weapon, just as it is a violation of the female body to use it as an object or a proving ground for male virility. To feign desire when it is absent violates the body's truth, as does repression of desire, which can be fully felt even when it cannot be satisfied. But to *feel* desire and longing is to admit need, which is threatening to many men in our culture.

Under patriarchy, men, while encouraged to expect a great deal of nurturing care from women, are taught not to admit their need for nurturing, their need to be passive at times, to be weak, to lean on another. The God, in Witchcraft, embodies longing and desire for union with the prime, nurturing force. Instead of seeking unlimited mothering from actual, living women, men in Witchcraft are encouraged to identify with the God and, through Him, to attain union with the Goddess, whose mother-love knows no bounds. The Goddess is both an external and an internal force: When her image is taken into a man's mind and heart, She becomes part of him. He can connect with his own nurturing qualities, with the inner Muse who is a source of unfading inspiration.

The God is Eros, but He is also Logos, the power of the mind. In Witchcraft, there is no opposition between the two. The bodily desire for union and the emotional desire for connection are transmuted into the intellectual desire for knowledge, which is also a form of union. Knowledge can be both analytic and synthetic; can take things apart and look at differences, or form a pattern from unintegrated parts and see the whole.

For women raised in our culture, the God begins as a symbol of all those qualities that have been identified as male and that we have not been encouraged to own.* The symbol of the God, like that of the Goddess, is both internal and external. Through meditation and ritual, a woman who invokes the God creates his image within herself and connects with those qualities she lacks. As her understanding moves beyond culturally imposed limitations, her image of the God changes, deepens. He is the Creation, which is not simply a replica of oneself, but something different, of a different order. True creation implies separation, as the very act of birth is a relinquishment, a letting go. Through the God, the woman knows this power in herself. His love and desire stretch across the abyss of separation, taut as a harpstring, humming one note which becomes the single song, the uni-verse, of all. That vibration is energy, the true source of power-from-within. And so the God, like the Goddess, empowers woman.

For both women and men, the God is also the Dying God. As such, He represents the giving over that sustains life: Death in the service of the life force. Life is characterized by many losses, and, unless the pain of each one is fully felt and worked through, it remains buried in the psyche, where, like a festering sore that never fully heals, it exudes emotional poison.[10] The Dying God embodies the concept of loss. In rituals, as we enact his death over and over again, we release the emotions surrounding our own losses, lance the wounds, and win through to the healing promised by his rebirth. This psychological purging was the true purpose of dramatic tragedy, which originated, in Greece, out of the rites of the dying God Dionysus.

In Witchcraft, death is always followed by rebirth, loss by restitution. After the dark of the moon, the new crescent appears. Spring follows winter; day follows night. Not all Witches believe in literal reincarnation; many, like Robin Morgan, view it as "a *metaphor* for that mystically cellular transition in which the dancers DNA and RNA immortally twine themselves."[11] But in a world view that sees everything as cyclical, death itself cannot be a final ending, but rather some unknown transformation to some new form of being. In enacting and reenacting the death of the God, we prepare ourselves to face that transformation, to live out the last stage of life. The God becomes the Comforter and Consoler of Hearts, who teaches us to understand death through his example. He embodies the warmth, tenderness, and compassion that are the true complement of male aggression.

The Dying God puts on horns and becomes the Hunter, who metes out death as well as suffering it. Few of us today directly participate in life processes; we no longer raise or hunt our own meat, but get it plastic-wrapped at the supermarket. It is difficult for us to understand the concept of the Divine Hunter. But in a culture of hunters the hunt meant *life*, and the hunter was the life giver of the tribe.* The tribe identified with its food animals; hunting involved tremendous skill and knowledge of the habits and psychology of the prey. Animals were never killed needlessly, and no parts of the kill were wasted. Life was never taken without recognition and reverence for the spirit of the prey.

Today, the only thing most of us hunt for regularly is parking places. But the Hunter has another aspect: that of searching, of seeking. He embodies all quests, whether physical, spiritual, artistic, scientific, or social. His image is *poemagogic*: It both symbolizes and sparks the creative process, which is itself a Quest. The God seeks for the Goddess, as King Arthur seeks for the Grail, as each of us seeks for that which we have lost and for all that has never yet been found.

Like the Goddess, the God unifies all opposites. As in the invocation that opens this chapter, He is both the bright sun, the light-giving, energizing force, and the darkness of night and death. The two aspects, as I have said before, are complementary, not contradictory. They cannot be identified as "good" and "evil": both are part of the cycle, the necessary balance of life.

As Lord of Winds, the God is identified with the elements and the natural world. As Lord of the Dance, He symbolizes the spiral dance of life, the whirling energies that bind existence in eternal motion. He embodies movement and change.

The Sun Child is born at the Winter Solstice, when, after the triumph of darkness throughout the year's longest night, the sun rises again.* In Witchcraft, the celebrations of the Goddess are lunar; those of the God follow the mythological pattern of the Wheel of the Year.

At the Winter Solstice, he is born as the embodiment of innocence and joy, of a childlike delight in all things. His is the triumph of the returning light. At Brigid or Candlemas (February 2)[12] his growth is celebrated, as the days grow visibly longer. At the Spring Equinox, He is the green, flourishing youth who dances with the Goddess in her Maiden aspect. On Beltane (May 1), their marriage is celebrated with Maypoles and bonfires, and on the Summer Solstice it is consummated, in a union so complete it becomes a death. He is named Summer-Crowned King instead of Winter-Born, and the crown is of roses: the bloom of culmination coupled with the stab of the thorn.

He is mourned at Lughnasad (August 1), and at the Fall Equinox He sleeps in the womb of the Goddess, sailing over the sunless sea that is her womb. At Samhain (Halloween, October 31), He arrives at the Land of Youth, the Shining Land in which the souls of the dead grow young again, as they wait to be reborn. He opens the gates that they may return and visit their loved ones, and rules in the Dreamworld as He too grows young, until at the Winter Solstice He is again reborn.[13]

This is the myth: the poetic statement of a process that is seasonal, celestial, and psychological. Enacting the myth in ritual, we enact our own transformations, the constant birth, growth, culmination, and passing of our ideas, plans, work, relationships. Each loss, each change, even a happy one, turns life upside down. We each become the Hanged One: the herb hung up to dry, the carcass hung to cure, the Hanged Man of the Tarot, whose meaning is the sacrifice that allows one to move on to a new level of being.

The association of love and death is a strong one in the mythology of many cultures. In Witchcraft, love is never associated with actual physical violence, and nothing could be more antithetical to the spirit of the Craft than the current rash of violent pornography. The God does not perpetrate acts of sadomasochism on the Goddess or preach to Her the "power of sexual surrender." It is He that surrenders, to the power of his own feeling. Nowhere but in love do we live so completely in the all-consuming present; and at no time but when we are in love are we so searingly conscious of our own mortality. For even if love lasts—and both popular songs and personal experience assure us it does not—or metamorphoses into a sweeter and deeper, if less fiery form, sooner or later one lover will die and the other will be left alone. The Craft does not try to resolve that dilemma, but to intensify it, because only through that bittersweet realization, through the embrace of Pan whose hairy thighs rub us raw even as they bring us ecstasy, can we learn to be fully alive.

And so the God is the proud stag who haunts the heart of the deepest forest, that of the Self. He is the stallion, swift as thought, whose crescent hooves leave lunar marks even as they strike sparks of solar fire. He is the goat-Pan, lust and fear, the animal emotions that are also the fostering powers of human life; and He is the moon-bull, with its crescent horns, its strength, and its hooves that thunder over the earth. These are only a few of his animal aspects.

Yet He is untamed. He is all that within us that will never be domesticated, that refuses to be compromised, diluted, made safe, molded, or tampered with. He is free.

As God of the waning year, He sails the Last Sea for the Dreamland, the Otherworld, the internal space in which creativity is generated. The mythic Shining Isle is our own internal source of inspiration. He is the Self voyaging the dark waters of the unconscious mind. The gates He guards are the threshold that divides the unconscious from the conscious, the gates of night and day through which we pass to go beyond the illusion of duality, the gates of form through which we pass in and out of life.

While He is ever-dying, He is also ever-reborn, ever-living. In the moment of his transformation, He becomes immortal, as love is immortal although its objects may fade. He glows with the radiance that sparks life.

The God, like the Goddess, has many names. He appears, linked with Her, throughout time, from the Paleolithic caves to the bulls of ancient Crete to the medieval tales of Robin Hood and his merry men.[14] Any of his names or aspects can be used as a focus for meditation.

Although there are many men in modern Witchcraft, in general they are less immediately attracted to the Craft than women. No matter how simplistically or superstitiously the Craft is understood, it offers women a model of female strength and creative power; in that, it has remarkably little competition from other religions. But for men, it demands a giving up of traditional forms of power and traditional concepts of religion. What it offers men is more subtle and not always easy to comprehend.

Men are not subservient or relegated to second-class spiritual citizenship in Witchcraft.[15] But neither are they automatically elevated to a higher status than women, as they are in other religions. Men in the Craft must interact with strong, empowered women who do not pretend to be anything less than what they are. Many men find the prospect disconcerting.

The Craft also demands a new relationship to the female body. No longer can it be seen as an object or vilified as something dirty. A woman's body, its odors, secretions, and menstrual blood, are sacred, are worthy of reverence and celebration. Women's bodies belong to themselves alone; no spiritual authority will back a man's attempt to possess or control her.

The body is not to be celebrated in isolation. Men in the Craft must come to terms with woman's power: the power of a whole woman, a completed woman, whose mind and spirit and emotions are fully awakened. A man must also know and accept the power of his own, inner, female self; to generate a source of nurturing and inspiration within, rather than demanding it exclusively from without.*

Witchcraft also means losing the "Great Man" model of spirituality. Jesus, Buddha, Krishna, Moses, and the whole horde of preachers, prophets, gurus, and group leaders who claim to teach in their names, or the names of secular descendents, lose their halos. In Witchcraft, there are no comforting, all-knowing father figures who promise answers for everything at the price of one's personal autonomy. The Craft calls on each of us to be our own authority, and that can be an uncomfortable position.

In fact, there is no more God the Father. In the Craft, the cosmos is no longer modeled on external male control. The hierarchy is dissolved; the heavenly chain of command is broken; the divinely revealed texts are seen as poetry, not truth. Instead, a man must connect with the Goddess, who is immanent in the world, in nature, in woman, in his own feelings—in all that childhood religions taught him needed to be overcome, transcended, conquered, in order to be loved by God.

But the very aspects of Witchcraft that seem threatening also hold out to men a new and vibrant spiritual possibility: that of wholeness, connection, and freedom. Men of courage find relationships with strong, powerful women exhilarating. They welcome the chance to know the Female within, to grow beyond their culturally imposed limitations and become whole.

Attempts to live out the model of God-father isolate men in emotionally frozen life situations. Many men welcome release from the eternal son-father conflict of patriarchy. They delight in a model of male power that is nonhierarchical, that is neither slave nor master. While individuals may not escape external authority in their own lives, they see it for what it is: an arbitrary set of rules to a complex game. They may play or withdraw, but their identities and self-esteem no longer depend on their place in the power pyramid.

In the Craft, the split between mind and body, flesh and spirit, is healed. Men are free to be spiritual without being unsexed, because God and Goddess embody the deeply moving force of passionately felt sexuality. They can connect with their own true feelings, their needs, their weaknesses as well as strengths. Rituals are active, physical, energetic, and cathartic. Ecstasy and wild, untamed energy are given a spiritual value, not relegated to the football field or the corner bar.

It is uncomfortable to be one's own authority, but it is the only condition under which true personal power can develop. Men and women are no longer content to be tame dogs or whipping boys: to place life-and-death decisions in the hands of a "fearless leader," a Pope, or a Jim Jones. Personal authority demands integrity and responsibility, but without it we cannot be free.

Within covens, men can experience group support and the affection of other men, as well as women. They can interact in situations that are not competitive or antagonistic. Men in covens can become friends with other men.

Finally, Witchcraft is fun. It offers men a chance to play, to act silly, to let the inner child come out. There are no fronts to uphold, no masculine dignity that must remain unbreached. Out of foolishness and play, creativity is born.

The God is within and without. Like the Goddess, He is invoked in many ways: singing, chanting, drumming, dancing, a whispered poem, a wild shout. However we call Him, He awakens within us:

REPEATING CHANTS (TO THE GOD)**

SEED Sower GRAIN Reborn HORNED ONE COME!

BRIGHT Sun DARK Death Lord Of the Winds COME

HAR HAR HOU HOU
DANCE Ici DANCE La!
JOUE Ici JOUE La!
HAR HAR HOU HOU!
DANCE Here DANCE There!
PLAY Here PLAY There![16]

The SUN Child The Winter-Born KING
[or] The SUN Child The Summer-Crowned KING

IO! EVOHE IO! EVOHE!
[Pronounced Yoh! Ay-VOH-hay!]

Evohe is one of the names of the God, derived from an ancient name of Dionysus, and cited as a Witches' cry in accounts of the Burning Times.[17]

REPEATING CYCLE

Sun Shine Day/Shine Day Forever/Day Forever Night/
Forever Night Sky/Night Sky Star/Sky Star Light/
Star Light Sun/Light Sun Shine/

EQUINOX INVOCATION OF THE MALE ASPECT
by Alan Acacia

horned god, tamed by love, fierce with passion
join us now

gentle one, sharer, one without possessions
be here now

lover to men as well as women, little child, old man
join us now

strong in struggle, proud of earth from which you
    spring, and to which you fall
be here now

loyal son, caring father, loving brother, rape fighter
join us now

rebel, seed sower, sissy, one who gives support to us,
we need your energy, we call for your presence
be here now

INVOCATION TO THE GOD OF SUMMER

Lord of the colors of day
Untamed Awakener of Hearts
Comforter of sorrows
The namer
Clear-sighted dancer
Morning's son
Vine-ripened Seed
Many-jeweled one
Hunter Wild beast
Guide
Come to us!
You are dry Drink of us!
We are the dew-filled flowers
That open To your golden shaft

INVOCATION TO THE GODDESS AND GOD
by Valerie

Kouros seedsower, Kore underground
Leaflight, bloodroot, grain reborn
Turning the Wheel we keep you in mind,
Lovelight, spermshine, flower & thorn.

Spinning the web we call you forth,
Turning the Wheel with ageless love.

Earth Her body, Air Her breath,
Fire Her spirit, Water Her flow,
Transformed in the halls of Death,
Life on life we come and go.

Spinning the Web we call you forth,
Turning the Wheel with ageless love.

Kouros Horned One, Kore above,
Starlight, heart's joy, ancient mirth,
Spinning the Web we call you forth,
Turning the Wheel with ageless love.

INVOCATION TO THE GROUND OF BEING*

Nameless One	of many names
Eternal	and ever-changing One
Who is found nowhere	but appears everywhere
Beyond	and within all.
Timeless	circle of the seasons,
Unknowable mystery	known by all.
Lord of the dance,	Mother of all life,
Be radiant within us,	Engulf us with your love,

See with our eyes, Hear with our ears, Breathe with
our nostrils, Touch with our hands, Kiss with our lips,
Open our hearts!
That we may live free at last
Joyful in the single song
Of all that is, was, or ever shall be!

SONG TO PAN**
by Mark Simos

Should the raven catch your hair
And seat a king of scarlet
Upon the heart's steep stair
Then, oh, the sights will you see there—
A breaking of the crystal
Under a dark green glare.

A dark green glare, from eyes on fire,
From pools of deepest amber—
Circle your castle round with briar,
Still Pan will find your chamber.

Fill it to the brim, don't say when,
Drink your fill and drink again,
Hear the ocean roaring.
Fill it to the brim, don't say when,
It's Pan that keeps on pouring.

Walnut hands, the eyes of a bear—
He who seeks his sorrows out
May find the lion's share.
With self-same breath He tempts and warns—
The fire that keeps the chill at bay
Is the very flame that burns.

The flame that burns, the song that slays,
When you hear what it is saying—
Let Panic chase us through the maze,
But Pan is only playing.

Fill it to the brim, don't say when,
Drink your fill and drink again,
Hear the ocean roaring.
Fill it to the brim, don't say when,
It's Pan that keeps on pouring.

Dark watcher with tangled brows
Puts his finger to his lips,
Let's hear no more of vows,
Of promises we'll never keep,
Nor of the secret dream
That slips away as we rise from sleep.

As we rise from sleep,
As we rub our eyes,
To set the salt tears falling,
You can cover your ears to drown his cries—
Yet Pan just keeps on calling.

Notes

1. T. S. Eliot, *The Waste Land, and Other Poems* (New York: Harcourt Brace Jovanovich, 1958), p. 8.
2. Herb Goldberg, *The Hazards of Being Male* (New York: New American Library, 1977), p. 58.
3. In San Francisco, certain groups of male transvestites and transsexuals see deliberately adopted effeminacy as a conscious, political identification with the Female life principle. The Horned God, however, while partaking of the Female, is in essence the image of the Male, not a denial of masculinity in favor of the feminine.
4. As many black leaders and thinkers have pointed out, the constant identification of "black" with "evil" is rooted in racism and perpetuated by Judeo-Christian religious imagery. The Craft has always valued the dark as well as the light: Both Goddess and God have aspects in which they are imaged as black, and these are aspects of power and wonder, not horror.
5. All traditions of the Craft recognize the Goddess, and all, except for some lesbian-feminist traditions that originated in the past few years, recognize the God to some extent. But there are broad variations in how much attention and ritual time is given to the God. In some covens, He is never invoked; in others, He may be called in only on the Summer and Winter Solstices, or only on the other solar holidays. Other traditions, however, give Him "equal time"; He may rule the winter months while the Goddess rules the summer, or He may simply be invoked at every ritual. In our tradition, He is usually invoked at rituals where men are present, and often, but not always, in women-only rituals.
6. At the present time, there are many all-women covens devoted to the practice of Women's Mysteries. There are very few all-male covens; the ones I know of are gay, and are more devoted to the Goddess than the Horned God. Male "mysteries" abound in American society—but the concept of such groups in a spiritual context that honors the Female Principle is open for exploration.
7. Margaret Murray, *The Witch-Cult in Western Europe* (New York: Oxford University Press, 1971), p. 30.
8. Murray, p. 15.
9. Not all Dianic traditions are separatist: In Morgan McFarland's tradition, for example, covens include men, but the Horned God is considered subordinate to the Goddess and is invoked only on the Summer and Winter Solstices.
10. My understanding of the concept of loss derives from personal discussions with my mother, over the course of the research and writing of her book. See Dr. Bertha Simos, *A Time to Grieve: Loss as a Universal Human Experience* (New York: Family Service Association Press, 1979).
11. Robin Morgan, *Going Too Far* (New York: Random House, 1977), p. 306.
12. Holidays begin on the eve of the date given (except for Halloween, for which I have given the commonly known date).
13. There are many variations of this myth known throughout the Craft—in some, the God becomes warring twins; in other traditions, aspects of his transformation may be celebrated on other dates. Whatever the superficial differences, the underlying poetic truth remains the same.
14. A more complete explanation of the identification of Robin Hood with the Horned God of the Witches is given by Margaret Murray in *The God of the Witches* (New York: Oxford University Press, 1970), pp. 41–42.

15. Some covens, of course, do not admit men; I am speaking of the Craft as a whole—apart from the separatist traditions.
16. Murray, *The God of the Witches*, p. 40.
17. In Burning Time accounts, it often appears as "A' boy"—an obvious mishearing of *Evohe* (see Murray, *The God of the Witches*, p. 141). The true meaning of the name is connected with the esoteric meanings of the vowels. Chant it—and see what happens.

CHAPTER 7

Magical Symbols*

Between the Worlds
WORDPLAY

i/mage mag/ic magician imagination mage mag/net imagic imagnetic imagenetic imagenesis

Imagic—the image is the heart of magic which is made by imagination—what we see in
the mind's eye makes magic—makes us magic—the mage—who casts the net—the
magenet—magic magnet—net of subtle power dipping into the life-stream—glowing
in the dark—a web that surrounds the earth Her body—magnetic field—imagnetic—
how we are attracted to magic—it draws us in—we are fish caught in a magic net—
imagenetic—because our genes remember, our cells remember, the source, the origin,
the beginning—imagenesis—creation out of image—creation of the image—from the
image all is born—all is magic—imagnosis—this, through what we imagine, we know.

Smooth stone with a hole in the center/candles of blue, green, gold/musk/silver/a
round mirror/myrrh/seven-pointed star/silk cord/eight-spoked wheel/the number of
increase/the red cord/silk/gold/lead/the planetary symbols/drums/the shapes of let-
ters/the shapes of eyes/the shape of a heart/the shape of a sound/shape of magic.

> "Do you know the old language?
> I do not know the old language.
> Do you know the language of the old belief?"
>
> Robert Duncan[1]

"Do you believe in an invisible reality behind appearances?"

Dion Fortune[2]

"No ideas, but in things."

William Carlos Williams

"White magic is poetry, black magic is anything that actually works."

Victor Anderson (Priest of the Faery tradition)

"Black is beautiful."

Aphorism of the Black Power Movement

"It's our limitations that keep us sane."

Dr. Bertha Simos (Starhawk's mother)

Magic is the craft of Witchcraft, and few things are at once so appealing, so frightening, and so misunderstood. To work magic is to weave the unseen forces into form; to soar beyond sight; to explore the uncharted dream realm of the hidden reality; to infuse life with color, motion, and strange scents that intoxicate; to leap beyond imagination into that space between the worlds where fantasy becomes real; to be at once animal and god. Magic is the craft of shaping, the craft of the wise, exhilarating, dangerous—the ultimate adventure.

The power of magic should not be underestimated. It works, often in ways that are unexpected and difficult to control. But neither should the power of magic be overestimated. It does not work simply, or effortlessly; it does not confer omnipotence. "The art of changing consciousness at will" is a demanding one, requiring a long and disciplined apprenticeship. Merely waving a wand, lighting a candle, and crooning a rhymed incantation do nothing in and of themselves. But when the force of a trained awareness is behind them, they are far more than empty gestures.

Learning to work magic is a process of neurological repatterning, of changing the way we use our brains. So, for that matter, is learning to play the piano—both processes involve the development of new pathways for neurons to follow, both require practice and take time, and both, when mastered, can be emotional and spiritual channels for great beauty. Magic requires first the development and then the integration of right-hemisphere, spatial, intuitive, holistic, patterning awareness. It opens the gates between the unconscious and the conscious minds, between the starlight and flashlight vision. In so doing, it deeply influences an individual's growth, creativity, and personality.

The language of the old belief, the language of magic, is expressed in symbols and images. Images bridge the gap between the verbal and nonverbal modes of awareness; they allow the two sides of the brain to communicate, arousing the emotions as well as the intellect.** Poetry, itself a form of magic, is imagic speech. Spells and charms worked by Witches are truly concrete poetry.

A spell is a symbolic act done in an altered state of consciousness, in order to cause a desired change. To cast a spell is to project energy through a symbol. But the symbols are too often mistaken for the spell. "Burn a green candle to attract money," we are told. The candle itself, however, does nothing—it is merely a lens, an object of focus, a mnemonic device, the "thing" that embodies our idea. Props may be useful, but it is the mind that works magic.

Particular objects, shapes, colors, scents, and images do work better than others to embody particular ideas. Correspondences between colors, planets, metals, numbers, plants, and minerals make up a great body of magical lore. I have included some sets of correspondences beginning on page 283. But the most powerful spells are often improvised, out of materials that feel right or that simply happen to come to hand.**

Spells are an important aspect of magical training. They require the combined faculties of relaxation, visualization, concentration, and projection (see the exercises in Chapter Three), and so they provide practice in coordinating these skills and developing them further.

Spell casting also forces us to come to terms with the material world. Many people who are attracted to the spiritual path of Witchcraft find themselves uneasy with the idea of using magic for practical ends or toward material goals. Somehow it seems wrong to work for oneself, to want things and to get things. But this attitude is a holdover of the world view that sees spirit and matter as separate and that identifies matter with evil and corruption. In Witchcraft, the flesh and the material world are not sundered from the Goddess; they are the manifestation of the divine. Union with the Goddess comes through embracing the material world. In Witchcraft, we do not fight self-interest; we follow it, but with an awareness that transmutes it into something sacred.

"Work for yourself, and soon you will see that Self is everywhere," is a saying of the Faery tradition. The paradox is that in spell casting we may start with the personal self, but in order to work the magic we are forced to expand and recognize the Self that moves through all beings. Magic involves a deliberate self-identification with other objects and people. To do a healing, we must *become* the healer, the one who is healed, and the energy of healing. To attract love, we must become love.

Spell casting is the lesser, not the greater, magic; but the greater magic builds on the less. Spells are extremely sophisticated psychological tools that have subtle but important effects on a person's inner growth.

A spell may highlight otherwise hidden complexes. A person who has con-flicts about success, for example, will find great difficulty in concentrating on a money spell. Practical results may be far less important than psychological insights that arise during the magical working. Discovering our inner blocks and fears is the first step in overcoming them.

Spells also go one step further than most forms of psychotherapy. They allow us not only to listen to and interpret the unconscious but also to speak to it, in the language it understands. Symbols, images, and objects used in spells communicate directly with Younger Self, who is the seat of our emotions and who is barely touched by the intellect. We often under-stand our feelings and behavior but find ourselves unable to change them. Through spells, we can attain the most important power—the power to change ourselves.

The practice of magic also demands the development of what is called the magical *will*. Will is very much akin to what Victorian schoolmasters called "character": honesty, self-discipline, commitment, and conviction.

Those who would practice magic must be scrupulously honest in their per-sonal lives. In one sense, magic works on the principle that "it is so because I say it is so." A bag of herbs acquires the power to heal because I say it does. For my word to take on such force, I must be deeply and completely convinced that it is identified with truth as I know it. If I habitually lie to my lovers, steal from my boss, pilfer from supermarkets, or simply renege on my promises, I cannot have that conviction.

Unless I have enough personal power to keep commitments in my daily life, I will be unable to wield magical power. To work magic, I need a basic belief in my ability to do things and cause things to happen. That belief is generated and sustained by my daily actions. If I say I will finish a report by Thursday and I do so, I have strengthened my knowledge that I am a person who can do what I say I will do. If I let the report go until a week from next Monday, I have undermined that belief. Of course, life is full of mistakes and miscalculations. But to a person who practices honesty and keeps commit-ments, "As I will, so mote it be" is not just a pretty phrase; it is a statement of fact.

Spells work in two basic ways. The first, which even the most confirmed skeptics will have no trouble accepting, is through suggestion. Symbols and images implant certain ideas in Younger Self, in the unconscious mind. We are then influenced to actualize those ideas. Obviously, psychological spells and many healing spells work on this principle. It functions in other spells, too. For example, a woman casts a spell to get a job. Afterward, she is filled with new self-confidence, approaches her interviewer with assurance, and creates such a good impression that she is hired.

However, spells can also influence the external world. Perhaps the job hunter "just happens" to walk into the right office at the right time. The cancer patient, without knowing that a healing spell was cast, has a spontaneous remission. This aspect of magic is more difficult to accept. The theoretical model that Witches use to explain the workings of magic is a clear one and coincides in many ways with the "new" physics. But I do not offer it as "proof" that magic works—nor do I wish to convince anyone to drop their doubts. (Skeptics make better magicians.) It is simply an elaborate—but extremely useful—metaphor.

That metaphor is based on the world view that sees things not as fixed objects, but as swirls of energy. The physical world is formed by that energy as stalactites are formed by dropping water. If we cause a change in the energy patterns, they in turn will cause a change in the physical world—just as, if we change the course of an underground river, new series of stalagtites will be formed in new veins of rock.

When our own energy is concentrated and channeled, it can move the broader energy currents. The images and objects used in spells are the channels, the vessels through which our power is poured and by which it is shaped. When energy is directed into the images we visualize, it gradually manifests physical form and takes shape in the material world.

Directing energy is not a matter of simply emoting. ** It is fashionable in some occult circles to proclaim piously that "thoughts are things, and therefore we should think only positive thoughts, because the negative things we think will come to pass." It is hard to imagine a philosophy that could more swiftly produce extreme paranoia. Were it true, the death rate would rise phenomenally. Overpopulation would be the least of our worries—and no elected politicians would survive long enough to be inaugurated. If thoughts and emotions alone could cause things to happen, thousands of my contemporaries would have married the Beatles in 1964. And I would not be writing at this desk—I would be sunning myself in Tahiti, where the crowds would undoubtedly be fierce.

Emotion is a strobe light; directed energy is a laser beam.* No matter how much hate, envy, and rage we direct at tailgaters, business competitors, ex-lovers, and close relations, we will not esoterically affect either their physical or their mental health—although we may affect our own.

Even concentrated power is a small stream compared with the vast surges of energy that surround us. The most adept Witch cannot be successful in all her spells; the opposing currents are often too strong. As John C. Lilly says, "It is all too easy to preach 'go with the flow.' The main problem is identifying what the flow is, here and now."[3] Witchcraft teaches us first to identify the flow and then to decide whether or not it is going where we want to go. If not, we can try to deflect it, or we may have to change our course.

To twist our metaphor slightly, casting a spell is like sailing a boat. We must take into account the currents—which are our own unconscious motivations, our desires and emotions, our patterns of actions, and the cumulative results of all our past actions. The currents are also the broader social, economic, and political forces that surround us. The winds that fill our sails are the forces of time and climate and season; the tides of the planets, the moon, and the sun. Sometimes all the forces are with us; we simply open our sail and run before the wind. At other times, the wind may run against the current, or both run counter to our direction, and we may be forced to tack back and forth, or furl the sail and wait.

Sensing the energy climate is a matter of intuition and experience. Some Witches make a detailed study of astrology in an effort to plan their magical workings at the optimum times. Personally, I prefer simply to work when I feel the time is right. Of all the planets, the moon's influence on subtle energies is the strongest.** Subtle power increases as the moon waxes, so the time of the waxing moon is best for spells involving growth or increase, such as money spells. The power peaks when the moon is full, and that is the best time for workings of culmination and love. During the waning moon, power subsides and turns inward: the waning period is used for banishing, binding, and discovering hidden secrets.

Spells can be adjusted to fit the time. For example, if you are obsessed with the need to do a money spell on the waning moon, focus on banishing poverty. A friend of mine whose business had been limping along for two years did precisely that and realized soon afterward that most of his problems stemmed from his partner's miscalculations and lack of management. At the same time, his partner decided to quit. The waning moon had done its work. By the next full moon, the business had begun to turn around.

Energy pursues the path of least resistance. Material results are more easily achieved through physical actions than through magical workings. It is simpler to lock your door than to protect your house with psychic seals. No magic spell is going to bring results unless channels are open in the material world. A job spell is useless unless you also go out and look for a job. A healing spell is no substitute for medical care.

The visualization we create in a spell should be that of the desired end— not necessarily the means by which it will come about. We picture the accident victim running on the beach—not the bones knitting. We keep our focus on our destination, without attempting to chart every movement we will make on the way. Spells usually work in unexpected ways. In order to assure that the power does not inadvertently cause harm, we bind the spell. We "set" the form we have created, so that the energy becomes fixed in the pattern we desire.

EXERCISE 43: BINDING A SPELL

When you have finished casting a spell, visualize yourself tying a knot in a cord wrapped around the symbol or image on which you have focused. Tell yourself you are setting the form of the spell, as a clay pot is set when it is fired. Say,

> By all the power
> Of three times three,
> This spell bound around
> Shall be.
> To cause no harm,
> Nor return on me.
> As I do will,
> So mote it be!

Spells that influence another person depend on a psychic link. Power pours through you toward another—but in order for the connection to be made you must be at least partly identified with that other person. You *become* the other, as well as becoming the energy you send. For this reason, "What you send returns on you, three times over." The energy you project to another affects *you* even more strongly than the other person—because you have generated it, you have become it, and you have become its object. If you send out healing energy, you are healed in turn. If you hex or curse, you yourself are cursed.

Witches, therefore, are extremely reluctant to hex anybody.[4] Some traditions expressly forbid hexing, cursing, or even healing another without their consent. Other Witches feel strongly that "a Witch who cannot hex, cannot heal." By that they mean that to use magic for destruction is not synonymous with using it for evil. Cancer must be destroyed for healing to take place. A person who threatens the safety of others must be stopped. This is most safely done with a binding spell, focused on the image of preventing him or her from doing harm. The returning energy, then, will be basically protective. If you bind a rapist, you may find yourself prevented from committing rape, but if that interferes with your daily activities you have no business practicing Witchcraft anyway. The spell may work itself out in many different ways: The rapist may be caught and convicted, or he could become impotent or even undergo a religious conversion. *How* it works is not your concern, as long as it accomplishes your goal.

Even binding spells should never be undertaken lightly. It is best to discuss them thoroughly in the coven, and proceed only when everyone is in agreement. *Never* hex someone just because they annoy you, because you dislike them or they cause you inconvenience, or in order to profit at their expense.

Such misuses of magic are demeaning, dangerous, and self-defeating. They will do far more harm to you than to anybody else.

Magic should not be used to gain power over others—it should be seen as part of the discipline of developing "power-from-within." Spells that attempt to control another person should be avoided. This particularly applies to love spells focused on a specific person. More than any other form of spells, these work far more strongly on the person who casts them than they do on the intended object. They inevitably backfire, complicating one's life beyond belief. Of course, if you feel you have grown too emotionally complacent, and need to be thoroughly shaken up . . . go ahead. Look on it as a "learning experience."

General spells to attract love create fewer problems, although they tend to be more effective for attracting sex than love per se. Love itself is a discipline, requiring an internal readiness. Unless you yourself are open to love, no spell will bring it into your life. It may, however, bring you a lot of amusement.

People often worry about being attacked magically. Actually, psychic attacks occur extremely rarely and are even more rarely effective. Paranoia is a far more pressing danger than psychic warfare. However, people can be attacked in many subtle ways. Envy and hostility need not be focused in a spell to create an uncomfortable emotional climate. Protective meditations and spells can be helpful in many mundane situations (see Chapter Four). The following meditation is effective whenever negative energy is being directed at you:

EXERCISE 44: PROTECTIVE FILTER

Ground and center. Visualize yourself surrounded by a net of glowing white light. See it as a semiporous energy field. Any force that hits this barrier is transmuted into pure creative energy. Whatever anger or hostility is sent to you, it only feeds your own power. Take in that power; absorb it; glow with it. Maintain the filter around yourself as you go through the day.

In the following spells, raise power by breathing or chanting, as in the exercises given previously. You can cast a circle formally or simply by visualizing it. Don't forget to earth the power and open the circle at the end. Names of materials used are given in capital letters, for ease of reference.

Spell casting is the lesser magic, but imagery and symbols are also used in the greater magic of rituals, where they become the keys to self-transformation and the links that connect us to the divine, within and without.

ANGER SPELL

Visualize a circle of light around yourself.

Cup a BLACK STONE in your hands and raise it to your forehead.

Concentrate and project all your anger into the stone.

With all your might, hurl it out of the circle into a lake, stream, river, or the ocean. Say:

> With this stone
> Anger be gone.
> Water bind it,
> No one find it.

Earth the power.

Release the circle.
    (To be done alongside flowing water.)

THE INDRINKING SPELL

(For self-acceptance when you've made a mistake or are filled with guilt or regrets.)

Cast a circle.

Sit facing North, and light a BLACK or WHITE CANDLE.

Hold in both hands your CUP, filled with CLEAR WATER. You should have before you an IMAGE OF THE GODDESS and a GREEN PLANT, in earth.

Visualize all the negative things you are feeling about yourself, the mistakes you have made, the things you have done wrong. Talk to yourself and admit you feel bad. Tell yourself, out loud, exactly what you have done wrong, and why. Let your emotion build energy, and project it all into the cup. Breathe on the water.

Raise power.

Visualize the Goddess as forgiving Mother. Imagine her hands cover yours. Hear Her say,

> I am the Mother of all things,
> My love is poured out upon the earth.
> I drink you in with perfect love,
> Be cleansed. Be healed. Be changed.

Pour out the water onto the plant, and feel your self-hate draining out of you. (It is possible this ritual will kill the plant.)

Fill the CUP with MILK or JUICE.

Raise more power, and visualize yourself as you would like to be, free of guilt and sorrow, changed so that you will not repeat the same errors. Charge the cup with strength and the power to be the person you want to be.

Again, visualize the Goddess. Her hands cover yours, and She says,

> Mine the cup, and Mine the waters of life.
> Drink deep!

Drink the juice or milk. Feel yourself filled with strength. Know that you have changed, that you are, from that very moment, a new person, not bound by the patterns and errors of the past.

Bind the spell.

Earth the power.

Open the circle.

SPELL FOR LONELINESS

Cast a circle.

Raise energy.

Sit facing North and light a GRAY CANDLE.

In a MORTAR AND PESTLE, grind a SHARK'S TOOTH (or other sharp bone) to powder. Say,

> You
> have no bones
> and never sleep.
> You
> swim always
> within me.

Allow loneliness to fill you and project it into the powder. Chant,

> Fire take you!
> Fire have you!
> Fire free you!

Shout, "Now be gone!" and release the feeling into the powder.

Spit three times into the powder and burn it in a BRASS BOWL, with ALOES, NETTLES, and THORNS.

Douse the fire with SALT WATER.

Earth the power.

Bind the spell.

Release the circle.

You will feel light of heart and free of loneliness.

SPELL FOR FALLOW PERIODS

On the first day of the dark of the moon, begin to sprout some seeds of wheat, barley, rye, or alfalfa.

Keep them in the dark three days, and then three days in the light.

On the morning of the seventh day, rise at dawn and bathe in water infused with CLOVER, BASIL, and ROSE PETALS.

Wear white, or go naked.

Cast a circle.

Raise energy.

Sit facing East, and light a WHITE CANDLE. Say,

> As the grain grows,
> As the sun grows,
> As the moon grows.

Chant,

> I grow,
> I reap,
> I receive.

Visualize each stage concentrating and projecting the image into the SPROUTS.

Eat the sprouts. Say,

> Bud in me,
> Blossom in me,
> Fruit in me.

Say each line three times, visualizing and concentrating.

Save SEVEN SPROUTS and wrap in BLACK SILK.

Bind the spell.

Earth the power.

Release the circle.

That night, bury the sprouts with a SILVER COIN (a dime is OK).

SAFE SPACE SPELL

(Can be done on a Sunday, Monday, or Friday.)

Cast a circle.

Raise energy.

Sit facing South, and light a GREEN, BLUE, or YELLOW CANDLE.

Hold in both hands a CUP of MILK mixed with SUGAR and SAFFRON.

Visualize, one after another, all the people and places who have made you feel safe and secure. Concentrate and project the feeling into the milk.

Raise the cup to your mouth and breathe the feeling of security into it.

Look at the candle flame and visualize three women, one dressed in black, one in white, one in red. They more toward you and merge into one figure. Imagine She places her hands over yours and lifts the cup to your lips.

Say, "I have been with you from the beginning."

Drink the milk.

Earth the power and feel the safe space within yourself.

Bind the spell.

Release the circle.

SPELL TO KNOW THE CHILD WITHIN

Cast a circle.

Sit facing south, and light a GREEN or BLUE CANDLE.

You should have a child's DOLL or STUFFED ANIMAL. Take it in your hands and sprinkle it with SALT WATER.

Say, "I name you _____." (Use your own childhood name or nickname.)

Hold it in your arms, croon to it, rock it, and talk to it. Tell it everything you would have liked to hear as a child. Let it talk to you, and tell you how it feels and what it wants. Let your voice change. Play.

Raise energy, and visualize that you are pouring it into the doll, who is your own child self. Create an image of your child self as you would have liked to be, and project it into your doll. Continue until the doll is glowing with white light and love.

Kiss the doll. Wrap it in WHITE CLOTH and lay it to rest on your altar.

Bind the spell.

Earth the power.

Open the circle.

(Repeat as often as you need or want to.)

SPELL TO BE FRIENDS WITH YOUR WOMB

(To be done on the first night of your menstruation. Especially helpful for those women who suffer from cramps, or irregular or excessive bleeding.)

Cast a circle.

Light a RED CANDLE. Face South.

With the third finger of your left hand, rub a few drops of your menstrual blood on the candle.

Raise power. Feel the blood's essence drawn into the flame. Let the light warm you and fill you. Feel your own blood as the essence of the life force.

Draw light from the candle into your womb. Let it fill you and spread slowly through your entire body from your womb center, charging you with energy and warmth.

Bind the spell.

Earth the power.

Open the circle.

Herbal Charms**

Herbal charms, as I make them, are small bags filled with herbs and other symbolic objects. They are made of a simple square or circle of cloth of the proper color, tied with thread of the proper color, and then charged with energy. They can be worn on the person or kept in the house to attract what you desire. If you wish, they can be made of silk or velvet and elaborately embroidered with symbols—or they can be simple cotton tied with string. You can create your own herbal charms tailored to your own needs. Here are some suggested combinations:

TO ATTRACT MONEY

Use a square of green cloth, filled with borage, lavender, High John the Conqueror Root, and saffron (or any four appropriate herbs), a few crystals of rock salt, and three silver coins. (Dimes, although no longer solid silver, seem to work fine.) Tie with gold and silver thread in eight knots.

TO ATTRACT LOVE

Use a circle of rose-colored or red (for more sexually passionate love) cloth. Fill it with acacia flowers, myrtle, rose petals or buds, jasmine flowers, and lavender. Add a red felt heart and a copper coin or ring. Tie it with blue thread or ribbon, in seven knots.

TO HEAL A BROKEN HEART

Use a circle of blue cloth, filled with All-Heal, Balm of Gilead buds, feverfew, myrtle, and rose petals (white). Take a white felt heart cut into two pieces, sew it together with blue thread while charging the charm, and add it to the herbs. Add a copper coin to draw new love. Tie it with white thread.

FOR PROTECTION

Use a circle of blue cloth, filled with nine protective herbs. Add a silver coin, or better, a silver crescent moon (perhaps an earring). Tie it with white or silver thread.

TO GET A JOB

Use a square of green cloth. Fill it with bay laurel, lavender, and High John the Conqueror Root. Add four other herbs governed by—

- *Mercury*—for a job involving communications
- *The Moon*—for a job involving healing, women's work or health, or psychology
- *Jupiter*—for a job involving leadership and responsibility, or the law
- *Mars*—for a job requiring aggressive, assertive action
- *The Sun*—for a job outdoors, in agriculture or nature, or for an easygoing, enjoyable job
- *Saturn*—for architecture, history, or any job where you will be limiting others' actions or freedom (police work, for example)

Add a silver coin, for wealth, and pictures of any important tools you may use in your work. Tie it with purple thread.

FOR INNER POWER

Use a square of royal purple cloth, filled with bay leaf, Dragon's Blood, elder flowers, High John the Conqueror Root, rosemary, vervain, oak leaf, holly leaf or berries, and mistletoe. Tie with blue thread, and embroider or draw on your own personal symbol.

FOR ELOQUENCE

Use a circle of yellow or iridescent cloth. Fill it with fennel, hazel, mandrake, and valerian. Add a silver coin, and tie with orange and violet thread.

TO WIN IN COURT

Use a square of blue cloth, filled with bay laurel, High John the Conqueror Root, St. John's Wort, and vervain. If you are being persecuted by an enemy, add a pine nut or part of a cone, some tobacco, and some mustard seed. Put in a small picture of an open eye, so that justice will look favorably on you. Tie with purple thread.

Feel free to improvise on these charms to add symbols of your own or to try other combinations of herbs. What feels best to you will work best.

TO CHARGE AN HERBAL CHARM

Assemble all your materials on your altar.

Cast a circle.

Light a CANDLE of an appropriate color. If you wish, burn INCENSE.

Raise energy.

In MORTAR and PESTLE, grind together all the herbs for your charm. Visualize the image or emotion you desire, and project it into the herbs as you grind them together. Draw or create any other symbols you may wish.

Gather together the herbs and other objects into the cloth. Twist the top around them and tie it once with thread.

Breathe on the charm and charge it with air.

Pass it through the candle flame, and charge it with fire.

Spinkle a few drops of WATER on it, and charge it with water.

Dip it into SALT, or touch it to your PENTACLE, and charge it with earth.

Hold it in your hands, breathe on it, and charge it fully with all the energy you can raise, concentrating on your visualization.

Drop to the ground, relax, and earth the power.

Bind the spell, tying it as you do so.

Open the circle.

HEALING IMAGE SPELL

Create your poppet (a wax or cloth doll) to represent the person you wish to help already completely healed and whole. Do not represent the problem; rather, create the image of the solution. Concentrate as you make the poppet.

Cast a circle.

Light a BLUE CANDLE.

Sprinkle your POPPET with SALT WATER. Say, "Blessed be, thou creature made by art. By art made, by art changed. Thou art not wax (cloth, wood, etc.) but flesh and blood, I name thee _____ (name the person you wish to heal). Thou art s(he), between the worlds, in all the worlds. Blessed be."

Hold the poppet in your hands. Breathe on it, and charge it with energy. Visualize your friend completely healed, completely well. Charge particular parts of the doll especially strongly to correspond with the parts of your friend that are hurt or diseased.

Visualize your friend completely charged with white light, well, happy, and filled with energy.

Bind the spell.

Earth the power.

Open the circle.

Keep the poppet on your altar until your friend is healed. Then, cast another circle, again take the poppet, sprinkle it with water, and say, "Blessed be, child of light. By art changed, by art unmade. I take from thee thy name _____ (your friend's name) and name thee poppet, creature of wax (or cloth, or whatever). Between the worlds, in all the worlds, so mote it be. The link is broken. Blessed be."

Open the circle. If the poppet contains physical links, burn it in an open fire. If not, dispose of it any way you wish, or give it to your friend as a keepsake.

TO BIND AN ENEMY

Cast a circle.

Light a BLACK CANDLE. Burn INCENSE of Saturn.

Sprinkle your POPPET with SALT WATER. Say, "Blessed be, thou creature made by art. By art made, by art changed. Thou art not wax (cloth, etc.) but flesh and blood. I name thee _____ (the person you are binding). Thou art s(he), between the worlds, in all the worlds, So mote it be."

Hold the poppet in your hands. Visualize a silver net falling over it, and binding the person it represents.

Take RED RIBBON and wrap it around the poppet, tying it firmly, and binding all parts of the body that could conceivably harm others. Charge the binding with power.

Say,

> By air and earth,
> By water and fire,
> So be you bound,
> As I desire.
> By three and nine,
> Your power I bind.
> By moon and sun,
> My will be done.
> Sky and sea
> Keep harm from me.
> Cord go round,
> Power be bound,
> Light revealed,
> Now be sealed.

Earth the power.

Open the circle.

Bury the poppet during a waning moon, far from your house, under a heavy rock.

Notes

1. Robert Duncan, "The Fire: Passages 13," in Hayden Carruth, ed., *The Voice That Is Great Within Us* (New York: Bantam Books, 1971).
2. Dion Fortune, *Moon Magic* (New York: Weiser, 1972), p. 117.
3. John C. Lilly, *The Center of the Cyclone* (New York: Julian Press, 1972), p. 218.
4. The word *hex* actually derives from the Latin word for "six," and became identified with spell casting because of the six-sided symbolic forms used in German and Pennsylvania Dutch magic. In those traditions, it does not have a negative connotation, but in general usage it is identified with cursing or sending negative energy and bad luck. The word *hex* is also related, in German, to the roots of the words *hag* and *hedge* and *hexxe*— Witch. The hag was the wise woman who sat on the hedge—the boundary between the village and the wild, the human world and the spirit world.

CHAPTER 8

Energy:
The Cone of Power

Between the Worlds

The chant begins as a low crooning, a deep vibration barely heard. One by one, voices take it up:

    "Aaaaaaaah. . . ."

    "Ooooooooh. . . ."

    "Eeeeeeeeee. . . ."

    It rises, an eerie nonharmony. The air seems to thicken, to dance with electric sparks that begin to fly, circle, spin, careen madly in the center of the circle.

    "Eeeeeeeooooooooh. . . ."

    The air glows, a luminous cloud that pulsates, burning with a black heat. The chant opens, full-throated, a ringing chord . . .

    The light begins to spin, a shining wheel of breath, turning and turning. Voices rise higher. The light spirals upward, faster, faster, as it narrows toward the top. The sound is indescribable; the voices are the shrieking wind, the howling of wolves, the high cries of tropical birds, the swarming of bees, the sigh of receding waves. The cone builds and builds a pulsing spiral, a unicorn's horn, rare and marvelous. Its tip cannot be seen. It is flooded with color: red, blue, green, sunlight, moonlight. It rises—

    "Now!" A voice cries out. A final shriek. The cone flies off, an arrow loosed to do its work, sucking the air clean. The coven collapses, limp dolls, sprawled on the floor. They smile, deliciously relaxed.

They have sent the cone of power.

"Four laws of ecology: (1) everything is connected to everything else, (2) everything must go somewhere, (3) nature knows best, and (4) there is no such thing as a free lunch."

Barry Commoner[1]

The primary principle of magic is connection. The universe is a fluid, ever-changing energy pattern, not a collection of fixed and separate things. What affects one thing affects, in some way, all things: All is interwoven into the continuous fabric of being. Its warp and weft are energy, which is the essence of magic.

Energy is ecstasy. When we drop the barriers and let power pour through, it floods the body, pulsing through every nerve, arousing every artery, coursing like a river that cleanses as it moves. In the eye of the storm, we rise on the winds that roar through mind and body, throbbing a liquid note as the voice pours out shimmering honey in waves of golden light, that as they pass, leave peace. No drug can take us so high, no thrill pierce us so deep because we have felt the essence of all delight, the heart of joy, the end of desire. Energy is love, and love is magic.

Of all the disciplines of magic, the art of moving energy is the simplest and most natural. It comes as easily as breathing, as making sound. Picture the power in motion, and it moves. Feel it flowing, and it flows, cleansing, healing, renewing, and revitalizing as it passes.

Witches conceive of the subtle energies as being, to a trained awareness, tangible, visible, and malleable. They are, as Dion Fortune says, "more tangible than emotion—less tangible than protoplasm." We can learn to sense them and mold them into form.

The laws of ecology are the laws of energy. Everything is interconnected; every action, every movement of forces, changes the universe. "You must not change one thing, one pebble, one grain of sand, until you know what good and evil will follow on that act. The world is in balance, in Equilibrium. A Wizard's power of changing and summoning can shake the balance of the world. It is dangerous, that power. It is most perilous. It must follow knowledge and serve need. To light a candle is to cast a shadow."[2]

Yet the equilibrium of the universe is not static, but dynamic. Energy is constantly in motion. It cannot be stopped. Again, using water as our metaphor, when we block its flow it becomes stagnant and foul. When it flows freely, it cleanses and purifies. The rituals, spells, and meditations of the Craft center on aiding energy to flow.

Energy flows in spirals. Its motion is always circular, cyclical, wavelike. The spiral motion is revealed in the shape of galaxies, shells, whirlpools, DNA. Sound, light, and radiation travel in waves—which themselves are spirals viewed in a flat plane.[3] The moon waxes and wanes, as do the tides, the economy, and our own vitality.

The implications of the spiral model are many. Essentially, it means that no form of energy can be exerted indefinitely in one direction only. Always, it will reach a peak, a point of climax, and then turn. In personal terms, activity is balanced by passivity. Exertion must be followed by rest; creativity by quiescence. Men cannot live entirely in the active mode, nor women in the passive—as patriarchal culture expects—and be whole. No one can be constantly creative, constantly sexual, constantly angry—or constantly *anything* that requires energy. Recognizing this alternation can help us sustain a dynamic, healthy balance.

Socially and politically, movement toward greater freedom is usually followed by movement toward greater security. Expansion is followed by contraction. The wise can learn to take advantage of this alternation, instead of being buffeted by it and forfeiting gains during every period of reaction. Freedom and security are not mutually exclusive goals.

Political actions could be more effective if they were consciously understood to be energy workings. Power can move through a group as it does through an individual, renewing and revitalizing group energy. An important aspect of this movement is grounding the energy after it is raised, consciously recognizing its fall as well as its peak, and returning it to the earth, its elemental source. When energy is not grounded, the group remains "charged"—like a room full of static electricity, with what soon becomes felt as tension and anxiety. Instead of generating a useful current, such groups short-circuit themselves, and their members "burn out."

Rallies, meetings, conferences, and demonstrations raise power—but rarely do organizers think about grounding it afterward. Grounding does not have to be elaborate—simply remembering to formally end each working session will help earth the power. Group members might simply take hands in a circle and sit quietly for a moment. Recently, there has been a growing tendency in the feminist movement to incorporate ritual into conferences and demonstrations, for the express purpose of grounding and channeling the power raised. The following is an account of a ritual several women[4] and I created in November 1978, as part of a conference on violence and pornography, with the theme "Take Back the Night!" The climax of the weekend was a march through the North Beach section of San Francisco, the heart of the topless-bottomless and massage parlor scene. The ritual took place in Washington Square Park, at the end of the march.*

The women pour in from the street. It takes so much longer than we expected. I had no conception of three thousand women in a mass. . . .

Witches, at the front of the march, asperge North Beach with salt water. They chant Laurel's couplet:

> Wipe the slate clean,
> Dream a new dream!

At Broadway and Columbus, the artists create a mini-ritual around their float. In the front, it is a giant, candle-lit Madonna; behind, slabs of dead meat and pornographic magazines. A strong symbol of images that squeeze women into narrow, hurtful roles. They bring out the float, chant, tear the pornography into confetti. Holly Near sings.

We wait at the park, too nervous to leave and risk not getting back in time. The Witches arrive at the entrance to the park, form a double line, a birth canal. They hold lighted candles and incense and sprinkle the women with salt water as they enter:

> From a woman you were born into this world,
> By women you are born into this circle.

We are onstage (the back of Anne's truck). Our backdrop is the lit facade of the church: an irony. Lennie Schwendinger of Lighten Up has created beautiful lighting for us—it is the first time I have done a ritual so theatrical, where the bright lights cut us off from the crowd, who become "audience." Our pool of light seems the only world—and I'm not sure I like it. Behind us, in the trees, a woman's acrobatic troupe, Fly By Night, perform a slow, aerial dance.

Nina leads the chant:

> We're taking back the night,
> The night is ours!

The women are not dancing, as we had hoped. The audience-performer image is too strong—they are watching us. I feel awkward, unsure of what to do. The chant dies away—still, crowds are flowing into the park. . . .

Toni Marcus begins to play her violin. The sound carries over the park, electric, magical. . . .

We can put off starting no longer. I take the microphone, and say that we should turn for a moment and look at each other, at how beautiful we are, how real we are. . . .

I say, "We have been taught that women's bodies are unclean, that our sexuality degrades us, that we must be either Virgins or whores. But we accept neither image! Instead we raise the banner of the naked Goddess, whose body is truth, who is within us, in the human spirit.

"We say that our bodies are sacred, because they bring forth life, because they are life, because they give us pleasure, because with them we make, build, think, laugh, create, and do."

Lee and I lead the responsive chant:

> Our bodies are sacred,
> Our breasts are sacred,
> Our wombs are sacred,
> Our hands are sacred. . . .

It builds and builds.

> Our voices are sacred,
> Our voices carry power!
> The power to create!
> The power to change the world!
> Let go—let them become sound—
> Chant without words—let them be heard!

The voices roar into the night! Not a cone—it is too strong, too amorphous—a tidal wave sweeping out of the park.

It stops. Quietly, I lead a soft, low chant. A humming—the buzz of two thousand bees, a deep throb. . . .

Over it, Hallie leads the meditation:

"Softly, softly now begin to feel the earth's energy beneath your feet as She dances with us. . . .

"Close your eyes . . . feel your strength sparkling through your body and women around you. This is the power generated by our marching, our chanting, our dancing, our destruction of the symbols of violence. . . . Know that each of us, and all of us together, have the power to change the world. Feel the effects of your action rippling out into the world . . . reflect on how your life will be different. . . .

"Open your eyes and look around you . . . see our strength in one another's face . . . know that we are strong. Know what the women of old knew . . . that the night must belong to us. Know that we are women who take back the night. Know that the night is ours!"

Cheers, laughter, screams, kisses. Some of us touch the earth. The women follow. The ritual is done.

Nature knows best. Magic is part of nature; it does not controvert natural laws. It is through study and observation of nature, of the visible, physical reality, that we can learn to understand the workings of the underlying reality.

Magic teaches us to tap sources of energy that are unlimited, infinite. Nevertheless, there is no "free lunch." To raise energy, we must expend energy. We cannot get without giving. In working magic, we expend our own physical and emotional energy and must take care to replenish it. Magic is an art and a discipline, that demands work, practice, and effort before it can be perfected. Every change brings consequences; some seen and some unforeseen.

In coven rituals, energy raised is most often molded into the form of a cone, the Cone of Power. The base of the cone is the circle of coveners; its apex can focus on an individual, an object, or a collectively visualized image. At times, the cone is allowed to rise and fall naturally, as in the power chant described in Chapter Three. It may also be sent off in a burst of force, directed by one person, who may be part of the circle, or may stand at its center. When a group is familiar with the exercises given in Chapter Three, the following will prepare members for more advanced energy workings:

EXERCISE 45: THE CONE OF POWER*

All ground and center. Standing or sitting in a circle, take hands. Begin with a Group Breath, and gradually build a wordless Power Chant.

As the energy builds, visualize it swirling clockwise around the circle. *See* it as a blue-white light. It spirals up into a cone form—an upright shell, a cornucopia. Hold the visualization until it glows.

The energy forms we build have a reality of their own. As the power rises, people will intuitively sense the form that takes shape. As the peak is reached, the chant becomes a focused tone. If you have an image that represents your intent for the working, focus on it. Sometimes words or phrases come through. Let the power move until it falls, suddenly or gradually.

Let the energy go, fall to the ground, and relax completely, allowing the cone to fly off to its objective. Breathe deeply, and let the residue of power return to the earth, for her healing.

Rhythm, drums, hand claps, and dance movements may also be used in building the cone. Covens should experiment, and feel free to try many methods. Other words, names, Goddess or God names, or simple incantations can be used to raise power. The energy can also be molded into other forms: for example, a fountain, that rises and flows back on the coveners, a wave form, or a glowing sphere. Possibilities are infinite.

EXERCISE 46: WOMB CHANT

(Coveners lie in a wheel, with heads at center, on their backs.)

Stretch out your arms and touch the womb of the person next to you. If he is a man, place your hand on the spot where his womb would be, which is the womb center of his energy body. Clasp hands on each other's bellies.

Ground and center. Begin with a Group Breath and Power Chant. As you breathe, imagine that you breathe through the womb. See it glow white, like the moon, as you inhale power. See it glow red with blood, with creative fire. Feel the power of the womb to create—not the physical womb only, but the inner womb where ideas and visions are generated. Let your breath become a sound that resonates in the womb.

With each breath—feel its power—feel the woman or man next to you—feel her power—feel how we are linked—how strong we are when we are linked—breathe the power of vision—breathe the womb power of creation—and let your voice carry that power. . . .

The chant will build and die naturally. Earth the power and end.

EXERCISE 47: FORMAL GROUNDING

(This is for use in rituals and group workings.)

All clasp hands. If you wish, all take hold of the coven wand. Raise them high, and visualize the power flowing downward through your hands. Ground and center, and Leader gives the line, and coveners repeat:

> Source to source
> Flow through me
> Above and below,
> Turn to return,
> Clearly
> Fade to grow.
> As I will,
> So it shall be.
> Spell make it so!

Lower hands as you speak, until they (the wand) touch the ground. Exhale, and feel the power flow down.

Witches conceive of subtle energy as being of three basic types. Again, this is meant as a conceptual model, not a doctrine. Each person is also seen as an energy field, with subtle bodies that surround and interpenetrate the physical body.

The first type of energy is "elemental" or *raith* energy, also called *etheric substance* and *ectoplasm* by some occultists. It is the subtle force of the elements; earth, air, water, and fire, of plants and animals. Elemental vitality sustains the physical body. We feed off of it, and its movement through our bodies "primes the pump," so to speak, drawing the higher forms of power.

The *raith*, the elemental energy body, is also called the etheric body and the vital body, because through it we receive our vitality, our physical and emotional energy. It is the body of Younger Self, and it perceives through the starlight consciousness of the right hemisphere. Its perceptions are often more accurate than our conscious perceptions—but its ability to express them in words is limited. The *raith* extends out from the physical body for only about a centimeter, and appears to most psychics as a blue-gray glow.

Animals, plants, clean air and water, physical exercise, and sex increase vital energy. When *raith* energy is low, people become physically ill, tired, and emotionally depressed. Magic uses a great deal of vital energy, and anyone who practices magic regularly must take care not to become depleted. Regular physical exercise is one of the best methods of increasing vital energy. Being outdoors, consciously making contact with nature and the elements, also restores vitality.** Witches also traditionally keep special pets, "familiars,"[5] in part as a source of elemental energy.

Grounding before every magical working or psychic exercise prevents us from becoming depleted. Instead of draining our own vitality, we tap directly into the unlimited sources of elemental energy in the earth. Power flows through us, not out of us.

The second type of energy can be thought of as the energy of consciousness, of thoughts, dreams, fantasies, mind—auric or astral energy. The astral body, as it is called by occultists, can be thought of as the body of Talking Self. It is the force that makes up the "astral plane," the hidden reality behind appearances, the dream realm, sometimes called the Overworld,** or the Other Side. The *raith* and astral body together make up a person's aura,[6] or energy field. The astral body is less dense than the *raith* and extends out about nine inches from the physical body. If the truth were known, I believe that every psychic would see it somewhat differently. To me, it appears like a glowing, misty cloud, sometimes obscuring a person's features. Colors, unlike any seen with the physical eyes, shift and play within the aura. It is strongest about the head and easiest to see in dim light, against a plain background, especially when either I or the subject is in a light trance.

The astral body can be projected away from the physical body. Consciousness is not bound by the limitations of the physical senses. Out-of-body experiences may be vividly sensual, or they may simply involve awareness without sight or sound. The region of travel may be astral or material; purely subjective, purely objective, or a mixture of both.

The third type of energy is that of the Deep Self, of the Gods. It is the finest of vibrations, yet the most powerful. When we invoke the Goddess and god in rituals, we connect with this energy. That connection is the heart of the greater magic, of mystical ecstasy.

Generally, Younger Self is far more aware of subtle energy than Talking Self. We are all psychic, unconsciously. The difficulty is in finding ways to translate that awareness into terms the conscious mind can understand. Yogis and Eastern occultists talk about opening "the third eye," the psychic center located in the pineal gland, in the center of the forehead. For me, this is secondary to opening the energy centers in the womb and solar plexus, which connect directly with Younger Self. To put it less esoterically, when the conscious and unconscious minds can communicate freely, in a healthy, highly vital physical body, the higher consciousness will awaken naturally, in its own time. A useful tool in establishing this communication is a pendulum.

EXERCISE 48: PENDULUM EXERCISE

(A pendulum can be a necklace, a ring, key, watch, or crystal on a string or chain—anything that will swing freely and that is emotionally appealing.)

Ground and center, and breathe deeply, from the diaphragm and belly. Hold the pendulum lightly by the top of its chain, so that it hangs about two inches above the open palm of your other hand.

Relax, and tell yourself that the pendulum will begin to swing sunwise, reflecting the energy in your hand. Wait quietly. For most people, it will soon begin to circle. (While it seems to move of its own volition, actually involuntary movements of your own hand cause its motion. Don't attempt to control it consciously—the purpose is to let your unconscious speak to you through your own muscle movements, reflected in the pendulum.

If it does not move, deliberately make it circle a few times, showing Younger Self what you want. Wait. Some people will need several sessions before the pendulum will work.)

EXERCISE 49: SENSING THE AURA: PENDULUM METHOD

(Two people are needed for this exercise, a sender and a receiver. Both should be successful at Exercise 48.)

Sender sits in a relaxed position, breathing deeply from the belly. The receiver holds the pendulum so that it swings about two feet over the sender's head. Both ground and center.

Slowly, the receiver lowers the pendulum, telling herself that it will begin to swing when it hits the sender's aura. Practice until you can feel the edge or corona of the aura. When the pendulum reacts consistently, explore the outlines of the astral body. Search out areas of tension, and note vortexes of energy.

Exchange positions and repeat.

EXERCISE 50: SENSING THE AURA: DIRECT METHOD

Again, the sender sits in a relaxed position, breathing deeply. Both ground and center. The receiver lowers her hand, palm toward the sender, into the field of the aura. Stop when you can feel the outer, radiating edge of the astral body. The "feel" will at first be extremely subtle—a slight tingling, heat, an almost imperceptible difference, perhaps only a sudden urge to stop. Scan the astral body with your hands— again feeling for areas of tension, which may register as cold, as absence of energy, or simply as uneasiness. Sense the body's power centers, as well. Share your impressions with the sender, and compare results with the pendulum method.

Exchange positions and repeat.

EXERCISE 51: DAMPING AND PROJECTING ENERGY

The sender sits in a relaxed position. The receiver can use either the pendulum or the direct method of sensing the aura.)

Ground and center. The receiver locates the sender's aura, above the crown of her head. Ask the sender to do the Tree of Life Meditation, and, as the energy rises, to visualize and feel it as a strong stream of flowing water, bursting up from her head like a fountain. The receiver observes the pendulum's swing become stronger and faster as the energy increases—or feels the difference through her hand.

Ask the sender to damp the energy—visualize herself swathed in cotton wool or smothered in mashed potatoes. Feel the change—see the motion of the pendulum decrease.

Practice until the sender becomes adept at projecting and damping energy, and the receiver becomes adept at sensing the change. Test yourself by having the sender either damp or project power without first telling the receiver, who should be able to feel which is happening. Exchange positions, and also practice projecting and damping energy through other power centers you have discovered.

EXERCISE 52: SEEING THE AURA

(This exercise is best practiced in a group. Each of the members can take turns being the subject. All should first be proficient at sensing the aura.)

Set up a plain background—a black cloth or a white sheet. The subject should stand against it or lie down on it, and if possible, be nude. Everyone should ground and center, and relax with one of the exercises in Chapter Three, which will produce a light state of trance. The lighting should be dim.

Breathe deeply, from your diaphragm, and let your eyes relax. Lightly scan the space around the subject. You may see a thin, glowing line around her body—the *raith*. Around it, look for the cloudlike astral body, which may appear to glow, or may seem like a shadow, oddly lighter than the background. To some, the astral body will simply appear as a subtle difference between foreground and background—a wavering, like heat waves over a radiator. It may appear and blank out, shift, move, and change, but will gradually become more stable as you accustom yourself to astral vision.

The colors in the aura have many interpretations. Rather than following a set rule, "feel-see" them for yourself. The quality of the color is most illuminating—is it clear and bright, or muddy and dull? What does it make you think of? Feel? Are you attracted or repelled by it? What associations does it have? Share perceptions and feedback, and with time and experience you will be able to interpret what you see.

The subject can practice projecting and damping energy, and the viewers can learn to see the energy move. In later sessions, subjects can also practice projecting colors and energy forms. The more group members practice, the more acute their perceptions will become.

When you have learned to sense or see energy on individuals, you will be more sensitive to the forms and levels of power in rituals. Inanimate objects also can store a charge of subtle power. (See Chapter Four.) Examine your magical tools, and sense the aura of power.

Awareness of energy is awareness of the great dance of the universe. Seemingly intangible, it underlies all that we can touch. It is the only constant, although it is constant change, eternal flux. Awareness of your own energy is the awareness that flesh and spirit are one, that thou art Goddess, eternally linked, connected, at one with the moving spirit of All.

Notes

1. Barry Commoner, *The Closing Circle* (New York: Knopf, 1971), p. 18.
2. Ursula K. LeGuin, *A Wizard of Earthsea* (New York: Bantam Books, 1975), p. 44.
3. An easy way to visualize this is to examine a child's Slinky toy: a spiral formed of thin metal coils. Stretch it out and look at it from the side: You will see wave forms.
4. Besides myself, Hallie Iglehart, Nina Wise, Ann Hershey, Lee Schwing, Helen Dannenberg, Diane Broadstreet, Lennie Schwendinger, and Toni Marcus, as well as others, participated in planning and executing the ritual.
5. "Familiars" have many uses. They can divine; a cat can point out herbs for spells or Tarot cards with her paw, for example. They may "ground" negative energy; cats are especially good at this, and it does not harm them. Dogs exude vitality, and you can no more drain them than you can outrun them. During rituals and magical workings, however, animals often will try to enter the circle and soak up the power. Animals often become nervous when people trance and leave their bodies, and will attempt to "bring them back" by leaping on their stomachs, nipping their feet, and licking their faces. Animals should be either extremely well trained or excluded from the room during trance work.
6. Some occult systems postulate a further hierarchy of "mental" and "spiritual" bodies. I have attempted to present a conceptual system that is simple enough to be easily grasped and workable and consistent with both Craft tradition and my own experience. Again, this is an elaborate metaphor, not a Sacred Truth. If some other metaphor works better for you, use it!

CHAPTER 9

Trance

Between the Worlds

I say, "Relax, breathe deep, and look into the well—the well beyond the world's end. . . . Call up the shadow you saw in the dream."

Valerie sinks deeper into trance. Her aura glows—the face disappears beneath it. She sighs; a shadow clouds the glow.

"She's here . . . now I see it—the same shadow I saw months ago—it's the woman who appeared in my dream last night, and stole my work from me."

"What does she look like?"

"Tall, icy—her face is made of knives, clashing and revolving."

"How do you feel?"

"Afraid."

"What must you do?"

"Fight her—defeat her."

"Ask her name."

We wait. The shadow grows darker.

"She won't tell me."

"Demand it."

"I can't—can't get it."

"What do you need to get it?"

"Power."

"Where is power?"

"In—my wand."

Quietly I cross the room, take her wand from the altar, and place it in the limp hand. Her fingers close around it. Sparks from an inner battle dance around her head.

"Her name is anger," Valerie says softly.

"Who is she?"

"Me."

"What must you do?"

"Become her, take her in."

"How do you feel?"

"Afraid. The knives will cut me."

"Yes."

"I won't be strong enough."

"You are."

"How can I be sure?"

"Because you were able to learn her name."

She sucks in her breath. Her aura explodes in fireworks of red and violet. Her body shakes; she sobs, screams, gasps.

"She's choking me."

"Keep breathing—deep—relax."

She pants. Her face is sweating. Gently I wipe it off. There is a white flash over her head—she sighs, relaxing. Her face is clear again.

"I've done it. I've taken her in. She is me."

"How do you feel?"

"Strong. At peace."

> "The seekers of new mind states—the mind control devotees, encounter group enthusiasts, the drug takers, the psychics, the meditators—all are on a journey into the interior universe trying to burst the limits of the socially conditioned mind. Whether acceptable or unacceptable, moral or immoral, wise or foolish, the mind of man is stirring toward a new evolution."
>
> Dr. Barbara Brown[1]

The universe is a dance of energy, a uni-verse, a single song of ever-changing rhythms and harmonies. Sustaining the melody of the physical world is a rich interplay of counterpoint and descant. We see only a fraction of the band of radiation that makes up the spectrum; we hear only a small range of possible frequencies of sound. Ordinarily, we are conscious of only one, isolated melody; we listen to only the piccolo out of an infinite orchestra. To trance is to shift and expand our awareness: to pick out the beat of the drum, the throbbing violins, the cry of saxophones, to know the interwoven harmonies played in new keys, to thrill to the soaring symphony itself.

Trance states, states of nonordinary consciousness, have been called by many names: expanded awareness, meditation, hypnosis, "getting high." Trance techniques are found in every culture and religion—from the rhythmic chant of a Siberian shaman to free association on a Freudian analyst's couch. The pull to burst beyond the limits of the socially conditioned mind seems to be a deep-seated human need. There are an infinite variety of possible states of trance. We all experience light trance whenever we are daydreaming; concentrating deeply; watching a play, film, or television show; turning attention inward; and forgetting the sensory world. In deep states, we may have experiences such as John C. Lilly describes:

"I moved into a region of strange life forms, neither above nor below the human level, but strange beings, of strange shapes, metabolisms, thought forms, and so forth. These beings reminded me of some of the drawings I had seen of Tibetan gods and goddesses, of ancient Greek portrayals of their gods and of some of the bug-eyed monsters of science fiction."[2]

Deeper levels of trance may open up paranormal senses, psychic awareness, precognition. We may empathize and connect with other beings and life forms; in Balinese, the word for *trance* means "to become."

Occultists and metaphysicians delight in attempting to order, define, and rank the various states of consciousness, a process somewhat like attempting to measure a cloud with a ruler. I will not indulge in it here, because I feel it creates an erroneous impression that we know more than we do about these states. When we impose a left-brain, linear order on a right-brain, complex pattern, we tend to feel that we have gained control of the phenomenon—when we have done nothing more than point out a few stars with the beam of our flashlight. Classifying consciousness also encourages "higher than Thou" games of one-upmanship. People waste energy defining which state they are in, as if consciousness were a cosmic grammar school, in which third-graders were entitled to look down on kindergartners. The point is not what level we are on, but what we are learning.

Sharing and comparing trance experiences, and reading descriptions of altered states of awareness, can, however, yield useful insights. One of the most important realizations is that trance states are both subjective and objective. There is a continuum of experience, part of which is relevant only to the individual's interior world, and part of which can be shared and agreed on by others. What begins in the imagination becomes real—even though that reality is of a different order than the reality of the physical senses. It is the reality of the underlying energy currents that shape the universe.

Ordinary perception is a process of the physical senses. What we see, hear, feel, smell, or taste is further conditioned by language, the set of cultural symbols that allows us to name what we have perceived. The name shapes an amorphous sensory stimulus into something recognizable and familiar—and guides our response. But perception in the trance state is not bound by the physical senses. "Astral colors" are not seen with the physical eyes; sounds are "heard" only in our minds. The currents of subtle energy fit no sensory modes. Our language does not name them or contain words that adequately describe them.

Trance perception must be translated into the modes we know. In essence, we construct an elaborate metaphor world, to represent the reality of what is called the *astral*. If we are adept enough, we create metaphor senses that "see," "hear," "feel," "smell," and "taste." Those pseudosensory perceptions are then further interpreted in a symbolic system that fits our expectations. For example, Lilly describes meeting two helpful "guides," who "may be two aspects of my own functioning at the supraself level. They may be entities in other spaces, other universes than our consensus reality. They may be helpful constructs, helpful concepts that I use for my own future evolution. They may be representatives of an esoteric hidden school. They may be concepts functioning in my own human biocomputer at the supraspecies level. They may be members of a civilization a hundred thousand years or so ahead of ours."[3] A devout Christian, however, might call the same entities "angels" or perhaps "Blessed saints," and "see" them with wings, harps, haloes, and all the appropriate trappings. A Witch might call them the two linked motes of consciousness within the Deep Self, and "see" them in female and male human forms that glow blue.

Astral vision is always a mixture of the subjective and the objective.** Sensory forms and symbolic interpretations are subjective, the cloak of objective energies and entities. Whether those entities are internal forces or external beings depends on how one defines the self. It is more romantic and exciting (and probably truer) to see them as at least partly external; it is psychologically healthier and probably wiser to see them as internal. A thing can be internal and still be objective, still be real. A neurosis or conflict, for example, may be verified as real by others even before it is perceived by the self. And nothing external can be admitted into the psyche unless a corresponding internal force admits it. No "entity" can possess a soul that denies it entrance.

Astral energies can be molded into forms that will last and be perceived by more than one person. Collective beliefs and images also shape astral energies and create "places" and beings. Heaven, hell, and the Land of Youth all exist in the astral. The energy forms we collectively create, in turn, shape us and the world we live in.

Astral forms can be "anchored" into physical objects. When ancient people held that idols *were* their gods, they meant that the astral form of the god was keyed into the statue. In *Moon Magic*, Dion Fortune describes the anchoring of an energy form into a place of magical working, which "has to have the astral temple built over it, and that is the really important part; and this is how we do it—we sit down and imagine it—nothing more—*but*—it is the imagination of a trained mind!

> So we sat down, my friend and I . . . and we pictured the temple of Isis as we had known it near the Valley of the Kings in the great days of the cult. We pictured it in its broad outline, and then we pictured it in all its detail, describing what we saw till we made each other see it more and more clearly. We pictured the approach through the avenue of ram-headed sphinxes; the great pylon gate in the temenos wall; the court with its lotus pool; shadowed colonnades, and the great hall with its pillars. And as we did this, alternately watching and describing—the phantasied scenes began to take on the semblance of objective reality and we found ourselves in them—no longer looking at them with the mind's eye, but walking about in them. After that there was no more effort of concentration, for the astral vision took charge.[4]

Consciousness can travel in the astral in many different ways. "Astral projection," described by many occultists, involves the separation of the astral body from its physical housing, retaining only a cord of etheric energy as a connection. In other words, it is the creation of a complete, vivid, sensory metaphor state, through which all perceptions can be understood. The astral body may move through the physical universe, although with difficulty. Most often, it remains within the realm of energy and thought forms that is the astral.

It is also possible to project consciousness alone, without the construction of a "body." Physical "sensation" is lessened, and a great deal of practice may be required in order to achieve clarity and learn to interpret perceptions, but this method is less draining of vitality and less dangerous.

The astral body, when projected, "feeds" off of the *raith*, and the practice can be devitalizing if it is engaged in too often. It is common to return feeling extremely cold and ravenously hungry. When learning to enter trance states, it is important to protect the health of the physical body by eating well, sleeping sufficiently, and exercising regularly.

Trance work of any kind should be conducted only in a safe, private place, where you can remain undisturbed. As trance temporarily lessens your perceptions of the outer world and its dangers, city parks, public beaches, streets, and busses where you may be mugged, robbed, or molested are not suitable locations. Cast a protective circle around your body before leaving it, with either an elaborate ritual or a simple visualization. This will create an energy barrier, assuring safety on the astral as you have assured it in the physical realm.

Trance states offer many possibilities besides astral projection.** Trance unlocks the tremendous potential inherent in our unused awareness. We can augment our sensitivity, growth, and creativity.

In trance, we are more suggestible—a fact that underlies the most common uses of hypnosis. Suggestibility can seem frightening if we see it as opening people to control and exploitation by others. Actually, the self overrides any suggestions that contradict deeply ingrained moral or ethical principles or personal desires. Suggestion alone will not make an honest person a thief, nor an unwilling person a murderer. The Craft teaches the use of suggestion to help us consciously direct our own minds, not the minds of others. As we increase our awareness of the functioning of suggestion and learn to use it deliberately on ourselves, our suggestibility to others seems to decrease. The unconscious is no longer split off, but is in constant communication with the conscious mind and can no longer be easily programmed without our conscious consent.

We can use our own suggestibility for both physical and emotional healing. Mind and body are linked, and our emotional state contributes to disease, whether it is purely physical or psychosomatic. Suggestion can aid learning, increase concentration, and further creativity. It can also open up new forms of awareness and awaken the psychic senses.

Trance stimulates vision and imagination and opens up new sources of creativity. When the barriers between the unconscious and the conscious are crossed, ideas, images, plans, and solutions to problems arise freely. As the right-hemisphere, holistic vision is awakened, it becomes a rich source of insight, of new and original approaches to situations.

The psychic abilities also increase under trance. We are all psychic, unconsciously. Younger Self is aware of energy flows, communicates without words, senses the currents of the future, and knows how to channel power. In trance, we can become aware of that awareness and can perceive and shape the currents that move our lives.

Finally, in trance we find revelation. We invoke and become Goddess and God, linked to all that is. We experience union, ecstasy, openness. The limits of our perception, the fixation on a single note of the song, dissolve: We not only hear the music, but we dance the whirling, exhilarating, spiral dance of existence.

Trance can be dangerous, however, for the same reason it can be valuable—because it opens the gates to the unconscious mind. To pass through the gates, we must confront what has been called by occultists the Guardian, or the Shadow on the Threshold: the embodiment of all the impulses and qualities we have thrust into the unconscious because the conscious mind finds them unacceptable. All that we are and feel we should not be—sexual, angry, hostile, vulnerable, masochistic, self-hating, guilty, and even, perhaps, powerful or creative—squats in the doorway between Younger Self and Talking Self, refusing to let us pass until we have looked it in the face and acknowledged our own essential humanness. No fear is stronger than our fear of our own Shadow, and nothing is more destructive than the defenses we adopt in order to avoid the confrontation.*

The real dangers of magic stem not from the Guardian or Shadow itself, nor from external entities or forces. They stem from our own defense strategies, which can be intensified and rigidified by trance and magic as they can by drugs or fanaticism. Magic can also help us dissolve those strategies, confront the Guardian—a process that is never as frightening in actuality as it is in anticipation—and win clear. But unless people are willing to face fear, and confront their own negative qualities, they will be defeated by what Yaqui sorceror Don Juan calls "the first of his natural enemies: Fear! A terrible enemy— treacherous, and difficult to overcome. It remains concealed at every turn of the way, prowling, waiting."[5]

There are many ways of running from the Shadow. Some people simply deny it and never approach a confrontation. Others attempt to destroy the Shadow by destroying themselves with drugs or alcohol.

A defense strategy favored by many "spiritual" people is an elaborate form of denial, an assertion that the individual has "gone beyond" the shadow qualities of sexuality, anger, passion, desire, and self-interest. Many religions cater exclusively to this strategy. Priests, ministers, gurus, and "enlightened masters" who adopt a posture of transcendent superiority have great appeal to people with similar defense systems, who are able to escape their personal confrontations by identifying as members of an elite, "enlightened" group. Thus are cults born and perpetuated.

But this strategy of avoidance is accompanied by tremendous anxiety. However much we assert our transcendence and detachment, the Shadow remains. We may attempt to be more than human—even achieve great success, near miracles—but we remain fallible, vulnerable. That vulnerability becomes terrifying and fascinating. It may lead us to spurious acts of self-sacrifice and masochism, or self-embraced martyrdom, as a desperate attempt to ourselves control that shadow fear.

Victor Anderson, Faery Priest, tells the story that when he was a young man beginning to study the Craft, he met two shining, beautiful guides on the astral, who told him that he must make a choice. If he wanted great magical power, he must give up the hope of a lasting love in his life. His reply was, "Powers of evil, begone! Get you to the Outer Darkness! I will have both power and love."

"How did you know that they were evil?" I asked him.

"No truly helpful being will demand that you give up something that is natural and beautiful," he said.

"Evil spirits" are not necessarily outside entities: They may be elements of the unconscious mind. Groups that reinforce feelings of superiority, separation from the mainstream of human life, and removal from ordinary frailties and fallibilities reinforce their members' defenses and stunt their personal growth.

The flip side of the strategy of superiority is that of sickness and weakness. Instead of denying or pretending to transcend the shadow qualities, this type of person admits them, but interprets them as physical or mental illness. The seduction of sickness is that it absolves the individual from responsibility and allows her or him to luxuriate in passivity. Too often, self-definition of illness is fostered by therapists and "helping professionals," who after all have a vested interest in seeing others as sick.

Sickness as a defense is characterized by guilt. Such people often feel responsible for things that are, in reality, not under their control. Their shadow is their own, feared power, which they perceive in inflated, omnipotent terms. This defense often masks, and can undermine, great creativity and intelligence. If the practice of magic is misused to reinforce feelings of omnipotence, it can be devastating to these people.

Projection is another favorite strategy. When the negative qualities of the Guardian are sensed, it is easy to simply propel them outward and assign them to some other person or group. The special appeal of this strategy is that projection creates conflict, which is dramatic, exciting, and distracting. At its most extreme, however, it degenerates into paranoia. Such people never feel completely safe or accepted. Because their own anger and hostility are projected outward, they sense hostility everywhere around them.

Of course, all of us use many strategies, but most of us favor a particular mode. No one can be forced into a confrontation with the Shadow, nor can the process by hurried. It must happen in its own good time. As an example, the trance confrontation that opens this chapter is the record of an actual session between myself and one of my coveners. It was, however, the culmination of several months of work and training. In earlier sessions, Valerie managed to call up the Shadow, but could not get its name. She was not yet ready to confront and absorb it. Had we tried to force the confrontation, it might have been extremely destructive or simply useless. But when the timing was right, she found herself capable of taking in the qualities that before had seemed so threatening. The process marked a deep integration in her personality, and a flowering of her personal and creative power, to such an extent that I was moved to "pass the wand" of the coven to her, and she is now Priestess of Compost.*

One of the functions of a coven is to support and guide each other through the confrontation(s) with the Guardian. This is not always done so directly as in the preceding example; in fact, untrained coveners should not work with each other in this fashion, because it can be as harmful as amateur psycho-analysis. Coveners help each other best simply by not being seduced into each other's defense strategies. "Transcenders" should never be idolized or placed on a pedestal (even if they happen to be Priestesses). What they most need is to be loved for their weaknesses, their mistakes, and their humanness as well as their strengths.

Projectors sometimes have to literally fight out their confrontation with another person. The process can shatter a coven unless it is perceived cor-rectly. Other members of the group should avoid taking sides or focusing on the outward cause of the quarrel. It is equally important to resist the tempta-tion to toss one or both of them out of the group, except as a last resort. In a true Shadow fight, emotions will run far deeper than events seem to warrant. It is characterized by statements such as "I can't stand the way she makes me feel" or "She brings out the worst in me." The group should not accept the projections of the embroiled parties. If they are committed to the group and to their own growth, they will eventually come to confront the shadow of their own anger. They need to be loved throughout the battle.

It is a great temptation to love, smother, and coddle those people who define themselves as sick. It is also a temptation to lose patience with them, to urge them to "buck up," quit whining, and start off each day with a smile. Neither approach is helpful. Such people need to have their power recognized for what it is, and need to have its limits also recognized. They need support to struggle and function, not to retreat into illness or crippling guilt. They need to be loved for their power.

In learning to trance, we are indeed learning to "change consciousness at will," which implies control. Mind-altering drugs are *not* used in magic (at least, not by the wise), because they destroy that control.* and ** No drug can force a confrontation with the Guardian; it can at best strip away a defense that may be all that stands between the self and stark terror. More often, it simply reinforces existing defenses at a deeper and more destructive level. Superiority becomes a savior-complex; sickness may become psychosis; projec-tion may become true paranoia. In traditional societies, where drugs are used to bring on mystical visions and religious ecstasy, the experience is controlled and firmly structured along mythological lines. Shamans and priestesses have a deep understanding of the many states the mind may reach, and they know how to guide people through those states. But we do not live in a traditional society. We live in a society based on commodities, in which even enlighten-ment can purportedly be encapsulated and bought and sold. But what is bought and ingested is not really enlightenment, not really magic. The work, training, and discipline of magic can lead to a sensual trance similar to that produced by marijuana, and the goal of ritual is the ecstatic vision and high sense of wonder like that found on the highest LSD trips. But magic also opens up infinitely more subtle, sublime states, and teaches us not only how to go forth through the gate but also how to return. Consciousness is not, as Timothy Leary proclaims, a chemical phenomenon. Chemistry is a phenomenon of consciousness.

The best protection, when learning to trance—or learning anything else— is a sense of humor. Nothing you can laugh at, whether it is a demon, spirit, UFO, angel, guide, guru, teacher, vision, discorporate entity, or aspect of yourself, can possess you. No one can be whole who is incapable of laughing at him- or herself.

Expanded awareness begins with dreams. "This we call the Door Without a Key, which is also the Door of Dreams; Freud found it, and he used it for the coming forth by day; but we who are initiates use it for going forth by night."[6] Volumes have been written about the "coming forth by day": the bringing into waking consciousness of dream material from the unconscious. Here, I will restrict myself to pointing out aspects of interpretation that pertain especially to magic.

Dreams, while our most direct line into the subjective processes of Younger Self, may also contain objective elements. Some dreams reflect in symbolic language a direct cognition of astral currents. They may give insights into other people's motives, plans, or emotions, or given information about external events. Dream figures are not always an aspect of the individual: sometimes they are the person or thing they seem to be, although generally there is something in the individual that resonates with the external force.

Once we begin consciously working with magical symbols and mythology, our dreams reflect those images and should be interpreted in that light. To a Witch, for example, a snake is far more than a Freudian phallic symbol: It is a symbol of the Goddess, of renewal and regeneration.

Keeping a dream log, remembering dreams, sharing them in the coven, and reentering them in trance or guided fantasy all are ways of opening the door without a key. Learning to take active charge of our dreams, to suggest subjects, to change dreams as they happen, to confront attackers and defeat enemies, are ways of "going forth by night."[7]

There are many methods of trance induction, but all seem to function on one or more of four related principles: relaxation, sensory restriction, rhythm, and boredom. Physical tension blocks the trance state. Most inductions begin with deliberate relaxation, as in Exercise 9. When trance follows exertion, as after raising the Cone of Power, relaxation may occur naturally.

Sensory restriction has been explored in research described by Robert Ornstein in *The Psychology of Consciousness*. When subjects stared at a fixed image, after a time it seemed to disappear. At the same time, alpha waves showed on their electroencephalograms. The alpha rhythm has been shown to be characteristic of meditation and deep relaxation. Ornstein concludes that "one consequence of the way our central nervous system is structured seems to be that, if awareness is restricted to one unchanging source of stimulation, a 'turning off' of consciousness of the external world follows. The common instructions for concentrative meditation all underscore this."[8]

Not enough is known about the neurophysiology of awareness. But the ancient techniques of trance and scrying (crystal gazing) always involved restricting sensory awareness, often to one unchanging source of stimulation: a candle flame, a crystal ball, a black mirror, a dark bowl of water, or a bright sword.

Rhythm, whether experienced in motion, song, drumming, chanting, or poetic meter, also induces a state of heightened awareness.* Afro-American religions depend heavily on rhythmic drumming and dancing to induce a trance state in which worshippers become "mounted" or possessed by the orishas, the Gods and Goddesses. The metrical rhythm of poetry, according to Robert Graves, induces a trance of heightened sensitivity. In Craft tradition, it was believed that certain rhythms could induce particular emotional states. Drummers originally accompanied armies because their rhythms could make men fighting mad. (This secret, as far as I can tell, has been lost to the military and Witch covens alike, only to be rediscovered by the producers of disco music.)** Spoken trance inductions are always soft, singsong, and rhythmic.

Boredom can also bring on trance—as generations of daydreaming schoolchildren have discovered. When we are not stimulated, sensorily, emotionally, or mentally, awareness turns elsewhere. Repetition is important in inducing trance—it creates a state of security and familiarity. The mind "tunes out" the repeated stimulus and "tunes in" on another channel.

The trance state is most easily learned in a group, with help from others. Later, it is easy to lead yourself through the same exercises alone. I will present the following exercises as if a leader were speaking to a group. A circle should be cast before beginning, and cautions should be repeated after everyone is relaxed:

EXERCISE 53: CAUTIONS*

"You are about to enter into a very deep, very comfortable state of mind, where you will be perfectly safe and perfectly protected.

"You will be aware of any danger in the outer world and will awaken immediately, perfectly alert, and able to react and function.

"You will remain lucid and conscious at all times, able to concentrate fully.

"You will remember everything you experience.[9]

"At any time you should need to or want to, you can awaken fully and completely.

"When you awake, you will feel refreshed, renewed, and filled with energy."

Inductions vary widely. Use any set of imagery that works for you: diving into water, descending in an elevator, going down Alice's rabbit hole, walking down a spiral staircase, or whatever you invent. Here is my favorite voice induction:

EXERCISE 54: THE RAINBOW: TRANCE INDUCTION*

(Begin with the Exercise 9, Relaxation. Everyone should be lying down, comfortably relaxed.)

"Breathe deep—you are floating down . . . down . . . on a beautiful red cloud, and your whole body is red—as you go drifting and floating . . . rocking gently . . . deeper . . . and deeper . . . down . . ."

> (Repeat, once each, with an orange
> yellow
> green
> blue
> and violet cloud.)

"Land very gently . . . very softly . . . in the center of a round, white pearl. See it glowing, softly, gently . . .

> "Now turn and face the East . . .
> and then the South . . .
> and then the West . . .
> and now the North.
> "Open all of your inner senses."

The first trance exercise is to create an internal Place of Power, a safe space that serves as "home base" for all trance journeys. After the induction, continue:

EXERCISE 55: PLACE OF POWER

"In a moment, you will enter into a new space, a place in which you are completely safe and protected, where you are in complete control and in touch with your deepest sources of strength. It may seem to be indoors or outdoors—it may contain anything or anyone you like. It is completely yours. Wherever you may be, whatever state of consciousness you may be in, you can return to your Place of Power, simply by visualizing it.

"Now turn and face in the direction that feels most comfortable to you. On the pearl's wall, draw an invoking pentacle. If you like, you may use a symbol of your own, that will be your own secret key into your Place of Power. See the symbol glow with a deep blue flame. Take a deep breath—inhale—exhale. See the wall open, and walk through into your Place of Power.

"You are in your Place of Power. Turn and face the East. Notice what you see and hear and feel and sense. (Pause.)

"Turn and face the South. Notice what you see and hear and feel and sense. (Pause.)

"Turn and face the West. Notice what you see and hear and feel and sense. (Pause.)

"Turn and face the North. Notice what you see and hear and feel and sense. (Pause.)

"Now take time to explore your Place of Power. (Allow at least five minutes.)

"You are about ready to leave your Place of Power. Finish whatever you need to complete.

"Now turn and face the East, and say goodbye. (Pause.)

"Turn and face the South, and say goodbye. (Pause.)

"Turn and face the West, and say goodbye. (Pause.)

"Turn and face the North, and say goodbye. (Pause.)

"Now look for your symbol. See it glow. See it open. Take a deep breath—inhale—exhale—and walk through back into the pearl."

Coming out of trance is equally as important as going in.* Take time to emerge slowly and gently, reversing every process of the induction. Facing the directions is important because it forces you to orient yourself in inner space—to *be* in the scenes, not just watch them like movies. It also reinforces the protective circle, and the repetition, with each trance, reinforces the depth of the state.

EXERCISE 56: THE RAINBOW: EMERGING*

"In the pearl, prepare to awaken. When you awake, you will feel refreshed, alert, renewed, and filled with energy. You will remember all that you have experienced.

Now turn and face the East then the South . . . then the West . . . then the North. Take a deep breath . . . inhale . . . exhale . . .

"You are floating up . . . up . . . on a beautiful violet cloud, and your whole body is violet as you drift gently upward . . .

"On a beautiful blue cloud . . . up . . . up . . . and your whole body is blue and you are beginning to awaken gently and you drift gently up . . .

"On a beautiful green cloud . . . and your whole body is green . . . as you drift gently . . . up . . . up . . .

"On a beautiful yellow cloud . . . getting more and more awake . . . your whole body is yellow . . . as you drift gently . . . up . . . up . . .

"On a beautiful orange cloud . . . filled with energy and vitality . . . your body is orange . . . as you float up gently . . .

"On a beautiful red cloud . . . almost fully awake now . . . and your whole body is red as you float gently . . . remembering fully . . .

"And in a moment you will count to three and awaken fully and come to feeling refreshed, renewed, and filled with energy . . . take a deep breath . . . inhale . . . and exhale . . . one . . . two . . . three . . .

"Open your eyes, and awake."

Occasionally subjects do not come out of trance. This is nothing to be alarmed about—it simply means they have drifted from trance into sleep. Awaken them gently by touching them or by calling their name.

Scrying involves concentrating on an object: a crystal ball, a bowl of ink or a dark bowl filled with water, or a mirror with a black-painted surface in order to see psychically.

EXERCISE 57: SCRYING

Cast a circle. Ground and center. Sit in a comfortable position, and gaze at your crystal or focusing object. Some people prefer to have the room completely dark; others light a candle. Lighting should never be bright.

Relax, and wait peacefully. Do not force anything to come. Many people feel fear and insecurity—"It won't work for me"—"I'm not doing it right." Acknowledge the fears, relax into them, and let them dissolve.

After a time—and it may require regular practice over several sessions—the surface of the crystal may "cloud over" with *raith* energy. For some people, the clouds clear, and images appear in the crystal. Others find themselves closing their eyes, and seeing the images with the inner eye. Both methods are valid—choose the one that comes most easily.

To end, let the clouds return, then disperse. See the crystal as the solid object it is. Cover it, and open the circle.

EXERCISE 58: SUGGESTION

Because suggestion works through Younger Self, it is most effective with language of symbols and imagery. Suggestion can be incorporated into trance. Instead of verbal assertions, create a mental scene showing the results that you want. If you want to overcome shyness, see yourself at a large party behaving with poise and charm. If you want to be richer, see yourself earning money. If you want to be healed, see yourself healthy and active.

Cast a circle, go into trance, and go into your Place of Power. Orient yourself to the four directions.

Create your suggestion in your Place of Power. Make it as vivid, as real, as sensual, as you can. Take as much time as you need to do so.

Leave your suggestion in your Place of Power. It will take root and grow, and become your reality.

Bid farewell to the four directions, and come out of trance.

EXERCISE 59: MEMORY

Cast a circle, go into trance, and orient yourself in your Place of Power. Face in the direction that feels most comfortable to you.

In front of you, you see a path. Search for the path, and find it. Now follow it, looking around you, noticing what you see and hear and feel and sense. Follow it along, further and further.

The path leads over a ridge. Climb the ridge, and begin to descend, going down . . . down . . . down . . . circling down the hillside.

On your way down, you will see the entrance to a cave that leads deep . . . deep into the hill. Find the cave, and stand before the entrance.

Within the cave are all of your memories, from this life, and from all previous lifetimes. In a moment, you will enter the cave. You will be able to go as deep as you wish, to explore any branching tunnel, any cavern that you wish. If you have a particular memory you want to experience, hold it in your mind, and you will be led to the proper place. If there is a memory you are not ready to face, the path to it will be blocked.

Take a deep breath, inhale, exhale, and, as you count to three, enter the cave of your memories. Take as much time as you need to explore. (Allow at least ten minutes.)

Now prepare to come back from your memory. Take time to end it. Come back to the entrance of the cave.

Take a deep breath—inhale, and as you exhale count to three and come out of the cave. Exhale—count one, two, three.

Come out of the cave, and climb back up the hillside. Return up the hill, over the ridge, following the path back to your own Place of Power.

Bid farewell to the four directions, and come out of trance.

EXERCISE 60: TRANCE INTO A DREAM

Cast a circle, go into trance, and orient yourself in your Place of Power. Face in the direction that feels most comfortable to you.

You see a new path—a winding, secret path that leads down to a river. Look for the path, and find it. Follow it. Look around you, noticing what you see and hear and feel and sense along the way.

Stop on the riverbank. Across the river is the dream realm. When you enter it, you can explore or change your dreams at will. You can confront and defeat your enemies, and can learn from your friends. Now picture the dream you wish to enter, and see its landscape form across the river.

Take a deep breath. Inhale. As you exhale, step down into the river. Feel the cold water on your feet, and notice it moving and sparkling.

Take another deep breath. Inhale. As you exhale, wade across the river. Feel the stones under your feet; hear the river.

Take another deep breath. Inhale. As you exhale, step up on the far shore, into the dream realm. Exhale. Feel the firm ground under your feet again.

You are now in the dream realm. Take as much time as you need to explore, change, and discover your dreams.

Now prepare to leave the dream realm. Say farewell to any beings you have met, and complete your exploration. Come back to the river.

Again, taking three deep breaths, and three steps, cross the river. Step down into it, wade across, and emerge on the other side. Feel the stones under your feet; hear and see the water.

Follow the path back into your own Place of Power. Bid farewell to the four directions, and come out of trance.

Dreams can also be explored through scrying. A group can visualize a dream image in a crystal or water bowl and can explore it. For example, here is a partial record of a group trance into an image from Holly's dream, in which a group of old women were looking at a picture of a seal in a newspaper, and one said, "The seal will bring perpetual youth."

We are on a beach—waves—faint music plays from a carnival merry-go-round—Holly is in the lake—her father says she swims like a fish. . . .

Now there is a lighthouse—a foghorn, foam sprays on rocks—the sound of seals. . . .

Holly is in the water, her hair floating behind like a mermaid's hair—we are all swimming under the rocks, the water is crystal blue—the rocks are made of crystal.

There is a cave under the rocks—Valerie recognizes it from a dream she had long ago—there were people who wanted to dive into the cave; she warned them not to go, but they did. They couldn't get out. The cave is filled with bones.

We move through it and emerge into a city of glass. Towers and turrets of shining crystal rise under the sea . . . colored fish swim in the clear glass walls . . . we move down a long corridor, through Gothic halls with clear arches. . . .

The city is spinning—we are flung with it, spun around, spun back into the cave.

In the cave is a seal. The seal guards a fountain. "The seal will bring perpetual youth." We drink from the fountain.

Once you become familiar with trance techniques, you can create your own imagery and use the trance state for many kinds of experience. You can call up a negative part of yourself, as Valerie did at the opening of this chapter, or you can call your Deep Self into your Place of Power and receive help, teaching, and advice. You can search for answers to questions, drink from the fountain of inspiration, die, and be reborn.

In rituals, all elements of trance induction (excepting, hopefully, boredom) are present. The release of energy with the Cone of Power creates relaxation. The space is dark, and attention can be focused on candle flames or a central cauldron. Chants, invocations, and movements are rhythmic and repetitive. Trance inductions are a natural and beautiful element of the ritual itself. Often they involve multiple voices, an effect difficult to reproduce on the printed page. In the following, imagine the grouped lines read simultaneously, like a musical score.

EXERCISE 61: RITUAL INDUCTION

1st Voice: Your fingers are dissolving into water, and your
2nd Voice: (Pause) Your fingers are dissolving into
3rd Voice: Sle-eee-ee-eep Dee-ee-eee-ee-eep, and

1st Voice: toes are dissolving into water, and your wrists
2nd Voice: water, and your toes are dissolving into water,
3rd Voice: drea—ea—ea—eam of becoming,

1st Voice: are dissolving into water, and your ankles are
2nd Voice: and your wrists are dissolving into water, and
3rd Voice: drea—ea—eam deee-ee-ee-ee-eep,

1st Voice: dissolving into water, and your hands are dissolving
2nd Voice: your ankles are dissolving into water, and your
3rd Voice: and slee-eee-ee-ee-eep,

1st Voice: into water, and your feet are dissolving into water,
2nd Voice: hands are dissolving into water, and your feet are
3rd Voice: Slee-eee-eeee-ee-p dee-ee-ee-eep, and

1st Voice: and your forearms are dissolving into water, and
2nd Voice: dissolving into water, and your forearms are dis-
3rd Voice: drea—ea-ea-eam of becoming,

1st Voice: your calves are dissolving into water, and your
2nd Voice: solving into water, and your calves are dissolving
3rd Voice: Brea—the dee-ee-ee-ee-p,

1st Voice: elbows are dissolving into water, and your knees
2nd Voice: into water, and your elbows are dissolving into
3rd Voice: and slee—ee—ee—ee—eep.

Continue on with this induction until the whole body is relaxed. Another voice may then pick up and continue to guide the trance and later reawaken members. When coveners are comfortable working together, the guiding can also be shared by several members, who may each create part of the imagery.

Mystery rituals, such as those of Witchcraft, follow a pattern of induction and revelation. The Mysteries are teachings that cannot be grasped by the intellect alone, but only by the deep mind made accessible in trance. They may be conveyed by an object—a shaft of wheat, as in the Eleusinian Mysteries—by a key phrase, or symbol. The secret itself may be meaningless when out of context: only within the framework of the ritual does it take on its illuminating power.

Divination, through palmistry, Tarot cards, astrology, and reading oracles, is another method of awakening the deep mind. I don't have space to even begin a discussion that would do justice to such a vast practice, except to point out that all divinatory techniques work essentially to focus awareness and engage the heightened intuition and perception that are possible in trance. Today, these techniques are used not for "fortunetelling," but as methods of spiritual and psychological counseling.

Feasting*

After trance, the process of returning to the world and ending the ritual begins with the sharing of food. This may actually be anything from juice and barley-flour crescents to cookies and milk. Sometimes a full meal is shared; at other times a coven will prefer organic fruit and apple juice, or champagne and caviar. The tastes and resources of members are the only limitations.

The Priestess and Priest (or other members) hold up a plate of food and a goblet, and say a blessing that is simple and often spontaneous:

> BLESSING OVER CAKES AND WINE
>
> All life is your own,
> All fruits of the earth
> Are fruits of your womb,
> Your union, your dance.
> Goddess (and God)
> We thank you for blessings and abundance.
> Join with us, Feast with us, Enjoy with us!
> Blessed be.

A small libation may be poured into the fire or cauldron. The goblet is passed around the circle, and each member gives thanks for good things that have happened since the previous meeting. While eating, members relax, laugh, joke, and socialize, or talk about the ritual and plan future meetings. The social aspect of ritual is an integral part of strengthening and maintaining the group bond. Sharing food is sharing a tangible symbol of love and caring. It is important that this part of the ritual be fun—a reward to Younger Self for undergoing all the serious work of ritual and magic.

It is vitally important to formally end the meeting, and break the circle. Having stepped between the worlds when we began the ritual, we must deliberately and consciously step back out into ordinary space and time. Only thus can we preserve the integrity of the ritual space and time. People should never be allowed to drift away before the circle is opened, and the transition back to ordinary consciousness is complete.

Farewell to the Goddess and God*

The power of the ritual should be grounded, if this has not already been done. The Priestess (or whoever performed the invocations) goes to the altar, and stands facing the coven in pentacle position. She says,

> Goddess and God
> We thank you
> For your presence,
> For your circle,
> For light and love,
> For night and change,
> We ask for your blessing
> As you depart.
> Hail and farewell! Blessed be.

Opening the Circle*

The Priestess goes to each of the four directions in turn, and draws a Banishing Pentacle (see illustration, page 76), saying,

> Guardians of the East (South, West, North), Powers of Air (Fire,
>   Water, Earth), we thank you
> For joining in our circle
> And we ask for your blessing
> As you depart.
> May there be peace between us
> Now and forever. Blessed be.

She raises her *athame* to the sky and touches it to the earth, then opens her arms and says,

> The circle is open, but unbroken,
> May the peace of the Goddess
> Go in our hearts,
> Merry meet, and merry part.
> And merry meet again. Blessed be.

Notes

1. Barbara Brown, *New Mind, New Body* (New York: Harper & Row, 1974), p. 17.
2. John C. Lilly, *The Center of the Cyclone* (New York: Julian Press, 1972), p. 49.
3. Lilly, p. 39.
4. Dion Fortune, *Moon Magic* (New York: Weiser, 1972), pp. 81–82.
5. Carlos Castaneda, *The Teachings of Don Juan: A Yaqui Way of Knowledge* (New York: Ballantine Books, 1968), p. 79.
6. Fortune, p. 76.
7. For a further exploration of dreamwork, see Patricia Garfield, *Creative Dreaming* (New York: Simon & Schuster, 1975).
8. Robert Ornstein, *The Psychology of Consciousness* (San Francisco: W. H. Freeman, 1972), p. 126.
9. The traditional view of trance and hypnosis is that the subject forgets the experience, presumably so that the doctor or psychiatrist in charge can elicit information from the unconscious that the patient may not be ready to face. Trance work in the Craft, however, is aimed at teaching the subject to control her own state of consciousness, and so memory becomes vitally important. If she is not ready to face certain information, she will not contact it. It is considered a misuse of the trance state to pry into each other's secrets.

CHAPTER 10

Initiation* *and* **

Between the Worlds

THE GODDESS IN THE KINGDOM OF DEATH*

In this world, the Goddess is seen in the moon, the light that shines in darkness, the rain bringer, mover of the tides, Mistress of mysteries. And as the moon waxes and wanes, and walks three nights of its cycle in darkness, so, it is said, the Goddess once spent three nights in the Kingdom of Death.

For in love She ever seeks her other Self, and once, in the winter of the year, when He had disappeared from the green earth, She followed Him and came at last to the gates beyond which the living do not go.

The Guardian of the Gate challenged Her, and She stripped Herself of her clothing and jewels, for nothing may be brought into that land. For love, She was bound as all who enter there must be and brought before Death Himself.

He loved Her, and knelt at her feet, laying before Her his sword and crown, and gave Her the fivefold kiss, and said,

"Do not return to the living world, but stay here with Me, and have peace and rest and comfort."

But She answered, "Why do you cause all things I love and delight in to die and wither away?"

"Lady," He said, "it is the fate of all that lives to die. Everything passes; all fades away. I bring comfort and consolation to those who pass the gates, that they may grow young again. But You are my heart's desire—return not, but stay here with Me."

And She remained with him three days and three nights, and at the end of the third night She took up his crown, and it became a circlet that She placed around her neck, saying:

"Here is the circle of rebirth. Through You all passes out of life, but through Me all may be born again. Everything passes; everything changes. Even death is not eternal. Mine is the mystery of the womb, that is the cauldron of rebirth. Enter into Me and know Me, and You will be free of all fear. For as life is but a journey into death, so death is but a passage back to life, and in Me the circle is ever turning."

In love, He entered into Her, and so was reborn into life. Yet is He known as Lord of Shadows, the comforter and consoler, opener of the gates, King of the Land of Youth, the giver of peace and rest. But She is the gracious mother of all life; from Her all things proceed and to Her they return again. In Her are the mysteries of death and birth; in Her is the fulfillment of all love.

Traditional Craft Myth

An initiation is a symbolic death and rebirth, a rite of passage that transforms each person who experiences it. In the Craft, it marks acceptance into a coven, and a deep, personal commitment to the Goddess. It is a gift of power and love that coveners give each other: the experience of those inner secrets that cannot be told because they go beyond words. For the individual, it becomes a change that causes revelation and understanding and sparks further growth and change.

The timing of an initiation is important. Traditionally, apprentice Witches were required to study for "a year and a day" before they could be initiated. This rule is not always followed in present-day covens, but it is a good one. Magical training cannot take place overnight. It is, as we have said, a process of neurological repatterning, which requires time. Unless an initiate can, at least to some extent, channel energy and move into altered states of awareness, she will not benefit deeply from the ritual.

There is another, more subtle aspect to timing. Initiation also means "beginning," and what is begun is the process of confronting the Guardian of the Threshold. A new initiate may not yet have faced the Shadow, but she[†] must be committed to doing so. The Guardian's injunction—"Better to fall upon my blade and perish than to make the attempt with fear in thy heart"— does not mean she must be fearless, but that she is willing, in spite of fear, to go on, not to run away, to face her defenses even though the process may be painful. "Are you willing to suffer to learn?" she is asked, because learning and growth always involve pain.

[†]An initiate may be female or male—in this and following chapters I use "she" inclusively to simplify questions of grammar.

When an apprentice is able to confront other people in the group, face issues, take responsibility for her own feelings and actions, and both expects and desires to influence the course of the group, she is probably ready for initiation. She must ask for initiation, because she is not ready until she realizes that she, and no one else, controls the course of her progress in the Craft. An initiation creates a strong emotional bond and a deep, astral tie between coven members, so consider very carefully whom you initiate.

Death and rebirth are the theme of initiation. Death is the root of our deepest fears, and the true face of the Shadow. It is the terror behind vulnerability, the horror of annihilation that we fear our anger or our power will provoke. As in the myth, what pulls us to risk that confrontation is desire and longing, for those split-off parts of ourselves that lie on the other side of the abyss, which alone can complete us and free us to love. Because where there is no courage, there is no love: Love demands honesty, which is frightening, or it is only pretense. It demands vulnerability, or it is hollow. It engages our deepest power, or it lacks force. It brings us to confront sorrow, loss, and death.

And so we learn the Mystery: the feared Shadow, the Guardian of the Threshold, is none other than the God, who is named Guardian of the Gates, in his aspect of Death.

We must strip ourselves of our defenses, pretensions, masks, roles, of our "clothing and jewels," all that we assume and put on, in order to cross that threshold and enter the inner kingdom. The door opens only to the naked body of truth, bound by the cords, our recognition of mortality.

Death is seductive, for once the frightening threshold is crossed there is no more fear. Fear and hope are both dissolved; all that is left are rest, repose, relief, blessed nothingness, the void. But just as the void, to physicists, is the "mother state," so the crown of death becomes the circlet of rebirth, and the cords of binding become the umbilical link to life. Death is subsumed to life, and we learn the Great Mystery—not as a doctrine, not as a philosophy, but as an experience: There is no annihilation.

Traditionally, initiation rituals are secret—if for no other reason than to preserve the element of surprise. I have somewhat mixed feelings about publishing one of our initiations, but I feel the book would not be complete without it. I have omitted secret Faery material and concentrated on many of the creative elements of the ritual, which we generally write anew for each new member. The following should not be seen as an unchangeable script, but as a blueprint for creating your own rituals.

An initiation begins with a death cycle—an enacted dissolution, symbolic annihilation, and purification. An element of testing is sometimes involved. In the country, an apprentice might be taken to an unknown path and told to find her way along it. At intervals, guides will reveal secrets, or point out the direction. At the beach, a blindfolded apprentice might be asked to find her way by scent, by sound, and finally to let go of fear and walk trustingly into the waves, where protective hands will pull her back. Indoors, an apprentice might be told to keep solemn silence and lie quietly, while a plaster face-mask is made, and then left to meditate while it dries. At Paul's initiation, he was told to close his eyes and led into the garden. At intervals, he was allowed to open his eyes; a light was flashed and revelations were made; for example, he was shown an ear of corn, and told, "Behold Kore, the Maiden." He was shown a rose, and told, "Feel the blossom and the thorn." He was shown a lacy, insect-eaten leaf, and told, "See how life feeds on life."

He was then left to meditate on the sky, while the rest of us went indoors, cast the circle, and prepared the ritual bath.

The ocean, or a running stream, is an ideal location for a ritual bath, but most of them are held in an ordinary tub. Coveners perform their Salt-Water Purification; salt is added to the bath water and it is charged with the power to cleanse and make new. Appropriate herbs and oils are added: I use rose petals, bay leaves, mistletoe, vervain, rue, a few drops of Priestess or Goddess oil, and Delphi water.** Incense and candles are lit. The blindfolded apprentice is helped into the tub, washed by other coveners, and chanted over. She is told to meditate, purify herself, resolve any doubts, and look for a new name. She is then left alone.

Coveners finish any last preparations for the ritual, and invoke the Goddess, God, and Mighty Ones of the Craft. One covener, who acts as the sponsor for the apprentice, returns to her, dries her, and makes sure she is ready to enter the circle. She ties a thin cotton cord loosely around the apprentice's wrists, saying, "And She was bound as all living must be, who would enter the Kingdom of Death." She ties the cord also around one ankle, saying, "Feet neither bound nor free," recognizing that entrance into the Craft is a free choice, but that once a person steps on the path, they have set in motion currents that will impel them forward. The sponsor asks the apprentice her new name and leads her to the circle, where a gate has been cut in the east.

A covener chosen to be the Challenger steps forward with sword or *athame* and says, "Who comes to the gate?"

The apprentice, coached beforehand, answers, "It is I, _____ (her new name), child of earth and starry heaven."

Challenger: "Who speaks for you?"

Sponsor: "It is I, _____, who vouches for her." The Challenger holds the point of the blade up to the apprentice's heart, and says,

"You are about to enter a vortex of power, a place beyond imagining, where birth and death, dark and light, joy and pain, meet and make one. You are about to step between the worlds, beyond time, outside the realm of your human life.

"You who stand on the threshold of the dread Mighty Ones, have you the courage to make the essay? For know that it is better to fall on my blade and perish than to make the attempt with fear in thy heart!"

The apprentice answers, "I enter the circle with perfect love and perfect trust."

The Challenger grounds the point of her blade to earth, kisses her, and draws her into the circle, saying, "Thus are all first brought into the circle."

The Priestess and/or Priest now lead the apprentice to each of the four quarters, sunwise, saying:

"Hail, Guardians of the Watchtowers of the East (South, West, North) and all the Mighty Ones of the Craft. Behold _____ (new name), who will now be made Priestess and Witch."

The apprentice is brought back to the altar. The Priestess kneels, and gives her the fivefold kiss, on the parts of the body named, saying:

> Blessed are your feet, that have brought you in these ways.
> Blessed are your knees, that kneel at the sacred altar.
> Blessed is your sex, without which we would not be.
> Blessed are your breasts, formed in strength and beauty.
> Blessed are your lips, which shall speak the sacred names.

The apprentice is then measured with thin cord, from head to toe. The cord is cut; she is measured around the head and chest. Knots are tied to mark the measurements. The Priestess rolls up the cord, and asks the apprentice, "Are you willing to swear the oath?"

Apprentice: "I am."

Priestess: "Are you willing to suffer to learn?"

Apprentice: "Yes."

The Priestess takes the apprentice's hand, and, with a needle properly purified by fire and water (that is, sterilized), pricks her finger, squeezing a few drops of blood onto the measure.

Priestess: "Repeat after me:

"'I, _____, do of my own free will most solemnly swear to protect, help, and defend my sisters and brothers of the Art.

"'I always will keep secret all that must not be revealed.

"'This do I swear on my mother's womb and my hopes of future lives, mindful that my measure has been taken, and in the presence of the Mighty Ones.'"

The apprentice is then told to kneel, place one hand on her head and the other beneath her heel; she says,

"All between my two hands belongs to the Goddess."

Coven: "So mote it be!"

Coven members grab her suddenly, lift her up (if possible), and carry her three times around the circle, laughing and shrieking. They lay her face down before the altar and press her into the ground. Gradually, the pressing changes to stroking. They chant her new name, raising a Cone of Power over her, giving her power to open her awareness and work magic. The blindfold is removed, and she is told,

"Know that the hands that have touched you are the hands of love."

The Charge of the Goddess is spoken, and other myths, mysteries, and secrets are revealed. Generally, the new initiate is given time to scry in a crystal, to find her own personal sources of power and inspiration. She is told the coven names of other members, the inner name and symbols of the coven.

The sponsor consecrates her on breasts and forehead with oil, with a coven symbol. The Priestess returns her measure, saying:

"In the Burning Times, when each member of the coven held the lives of the others in her hand, this would have been kept, and used against you should you endanger others. But in these more fortunate times, love and trust prevail, so take this, keep it or burn it, and be free to go or stay as your heart leads you."

The new initiate is then given a set of tools, which other coveners have made or collected for her. One by one, they are handed to her, their use is explained, and they are consecrated and charged. (See Exercise 36—although the process is often shortened within the initiation ritual.)

Food and drink are shared, and coveners relax and party. An initiation is a joyful occasion.

Before the circle is opened, the new initiate is taken around to the four quarters for a final time. The Priestess says,

"Guardians of the East (South, West, North), and Mighty Ones of the Craft, behold _____, who has now been made Priestess and Witch, and member of the _____ coven."

Goddess, God, and Guardians are thanked and dismissed, and the circle is opened.

CHAPTER 11

Moon Rituals*

Between the Worlds

ESBATS

The coven meets in moontime, new, full, or dark. The rituals are healing rituals, magical workings, times of growth, inspiration, insight. They change constantly, are never static. We make them anew, rewrite them, re-create them, but always on the same pattern: the creation of the sacred space, the invocations, the use of magical symbols, the raising of the Cone of Power, trance, sharing of food and drink and laughter, and the formal return to ordinary space and time. The ritual may be formal or informal; scripted or spontaneous; structured or loose—as long as it is alive. As long as it sings.

> *"The first and most important effect of a living mythological symbol is to waken and give guidance to the energies of life."*
>
> Joseph Campbell[1]

The rituals that follow in this chapter and the next are scripts meant to be changed, reworked, improved on, or used as they are. If you use written words, they should be memorized rather than read aloud. Speaking memorized words may itself create a trance state; reading entraps us in the left-brain, flashlight mind. If you cannot memorize, improvise. Don't worry about literary quality— simply say what you feel. Or better yet—let your rituals be wordless.

WAXING MOON RITUAL

(To be performed after the first visible crescent has appeared.)

On the altar, place a bowl of seeds. Fill the central cauldron with earth, and place a candle in the center.

When the coven gathers, begin with a breathing meditation. A Priestess says,

"This is the time of beginning, the seed time of creation, the awakening after sleep. Now the moon emerges, a crescent out of the dark; the Birthgiver returns from Death. The tide turns; all is transformed. Tonight we are touched by the Maiden who yields to all and yet is penetrated by none. She changes everything She touches; may She open us to change and growth. Merry meet."

Purify, cast the circle, and invoke the Goddess and God.

A covener chosen to act as Seed Priestess takes the bowl of grain from the altar, saying,

"Blessed be, creature of earth, moon seed of change, bright beginning of a new circle of time. Power to start, power to grow, power to make new be in this seed. Blessed be."

Going sunwise around the circle, she offers the bowl to each person, asking, "What will you plant with the moon?" Each person replies with what she plans to begin, or hopes will grow, in the month to come. "The blessing of the new moon be upon it," the Priestess answers.

Each person visualizes a clear image of what they want to grow, charging the seeds with the image. One by one, they plant the seeds in the earth in the central cauldron.

Together, they raise a Cone of Power to charge the seeds and earth with energy, and empower the projects they represent. The Cone is grounded into the cauldron.

Trance work or scrying may focus on clarity of vision for the projects now begun.

Feast, and open the circle.

FULL MOON RITUAL**

(To be performed on the eve of the Full Moon.)

The circle gathers, does a breathing meditation, and a Priestess says,

"This is the time of fullness, the flood tide of power, when the Lady in full circle of brightness rides across the night sky, arising with the coming of dark. This is the time of the bearing of fruits, of change realized. The Great Mother, Nurturer of the world, which is Herself, pours out her love and her gifts in abundance. The Hunter draws near to the Brilliant One, She who awakens yearning in the heart and who is the end of desire. We who look on her shining face are filled with love. Merry meet."

Purify, cast the circle, and invoke the Goddess and God.

One covener moves into the center of the circle, and speaks her name. The others repeat it, and chant it, raising a Cone of Power as they touch her, earthing it into her and filling her with the power and light of the moon. She returns to the circle, and another covener takes her place, until each in turn has been the focus of the power. While chanting, other coveners come to recognize that each individual is, in truth, Goddess/God.

A final Cone can be raised for the coven as a whole. Earth the power, trance or scry, then feast and open the circle.

DARK MOON RITUAL

(To be performed on the waning moon. A gazing crystal or scrying bowl should be placed in the center of the circle.)

Gather, and meditate on a group breath. A Priestess says,

"This is the ending before the beginning, the death before new life. Now on the ebb tide the secrets of the shoreline are uncovered by the retreating waves. The moon is hidden, but the faintest of stars are revealed and those who have eyes to see may read the fates and know the mysteries. The Goddess, whose name cannot be spoken, naked enters the Kingdom of Death. In the most vast silence and stillness, all is possible. We meet in the time of the Crone, to touch the deep power of the dark."

Purify and cast the circle, but do not light the altar candle. Invoke the Goddess and God.

The leader begins an *antiphon* chant: a repeated bass line, with spontaneous lines interjected between.

Leader: "She lies under all, She covers all."

All: "She lies under all, She covers all." (Repeat several times.)

Covener: "She is the teacher of mysteries."

All: "She lies under all, She covers all."

Covener: "She is the motion behind form."

All: "She lies under all, She covers all."

Covener: (Improvised line)

All: "She lies under all, She covers all."

Continue as long as there are energy and inspiration. (This type of chanting requires sensitivity and openness, both to personal inspiration and to others. While at first there may be some hesitations, silences, and collisions, in a cohesive group it will soon flow naturally. It is a powerful way of opening the inner voice.)

Build into a wordless power chant, and earth the cone into the scrying bowl or gazing crystal. Scry together, sharing what you see.

Feast, and open the circle.

Note

1. Joseph Campbell, *Myths to Live By* (New York: Bantam Books: 1973), p. 89.

CHAPTER 12

The Wheel of the Year

Between the Worlds

THE SABBATS[1] * and **

Winter, Spring, Summer, Autumn—birth, growth, fading, death—the Wheel turns, on and on. Ideas are born; projects are consummated; plans prove impractical and die. We fall in love; we suffer loss; we consummate relationships; we give birth; we grow old; we decay.

The Sabbats are the eight points at which we connect the inner and the outer cycles: the interstices where the seasonal, the celestial, the communal, the creative, and the personal all meet. As we enact each drama in its time, we transform ourselves. We are renewed; we are reborn even as we decay and die. We are not separate from each other, from the broader world around us; we are one with the Goddess, with the God. As the Cone of Power rises, as the season changes, we arouse the power from within, the power to heal, the power to change our society, the power to renew the earth.

Yule (Winter Solstice, December 20–23)[2] * and **

The altar is decorated with mistletoe and holly. A fire of oak roots is laid, but not lit. The room is dark.

The circle gathers. All meditate together, linking breaths. The Priestess[†] says,

---

[†] Parts may be taken by any coveners: Priestess and Priest are given here for simplicity.

"This is the night of Solstice, the longest night of the year. Now darkness triumphs; and yet, gives way and changes into light. The breath of nature is suspended: all waits while within the Cauldron, the Dark King is transformed into the Infant Light. We watch for the coming of dawn, when the Great Mother again gives birth to the Divine Child Sun, who is bringer of hope and the promise of summer. This is the stillness behind motion, when time itself stops; the center which is also the circumference of all. We are awake in the night. We turn the Wheel to bring the light. We call the sun from the womb of night. Blessed be!"

Purify, cast the circle, but do not light the candles. Invoke the Goddess and God. All sit down, and begin an antiphonal chant.

> ALL: To die and be reborn,
> The Wheel is turning,
> What must you lose to the night? (Repeat.)

> COVENER: "Fear."

> ALL: Fear is lost to the night.
> Fear is lost to the night.
> To die and be reborn,
> The Wheel is turning,
> What must you lose to the night?

Continue interjecting lines and echoing each other, until the energy dies away. Stand up, and link hands. The Priest stands before the altar, holding an animal skull filled with salt. The Priestess leads a slow, spiral procession, which first snakes outward so that each member is brought to face the Priest. They are chanting,

> The light was born,
> And the light has died. (Continue repeating.)

Another Priestess whispers,

> Everything passes,
> All fades away.

The Priest places a pinch of salt on each member's tongue, saying,

> My body is salt,
> Taste the breath of death.

The Priestess leads the spiral inward, until the members are huddled together. She leads an improvised trance induction, slowly suggesting that they crumble to the earth and sleep. As all lie down, they are sent into a deeper trance with a multivoiced induction. As it fades out, they are told,

"You are entering a space of perfect freedom."

Time is allowed for trance in the state of suspension before birth.

The Priestess approaches one of the coveners, stands by her head with her legs apart, and pulls her through, symbolically giving her birth. She becomes part of the birth canal; they continue the process with the other coveners, the birth canal growing longer. One member of the coven takes the newborns one by one and lays them back down to sleep, telling them,

"Sleep the sleep of the newborn."

As all sink back into trance, they are guided into a visualization of their hopes for their new life to come. Priestesses smear honey on their tongues, one by one, saying,

"Taste the sweetness of life."

A new chant begins softly, builds in power as it gradually wakes the sleep-ers, who join in on repeating lines:

> Set sail, set sail,
> Follow the twilight to the West,
> Where you may rest, where you may rest.
>
> Set sail, set sail,
> Turn your face where the sun grows dim,
> Beyond the rim, beyond the rim.
>
> Set sail, set sail,
> One thing becomes another,
> In the Mother, in the Mother.
>
> Set sail, set sail,
> Make of your heart a burning fire,
> Build it higher, build it higher.
>
> Set sail, set sail,
> Pass in an instant through the open gate,
> It will not wait, it will not wait.
>
> Set sail, set sail,
> Over the dark of the sunless sea,
> You are free, you are free.

Set sail, set sail,
Guiding the ship of the rising sun,
You are the one, you are the one.

Set sail, set sail,
Into the raging wind and storm,
To be reborn, to be reborn.

Set sail, set sail,
Over the waves where the spray blows white,
To bring the light, to bring the light.

ALL: We are awake in the night!
We turn the Wheel, to bring the light!
We call the sun from the womb of night!

PRIESTESS: He sets his face to the West, but in the East arises!
ALL: Who is that?
P: Who goes down in darkness?
A: Who is that?
P: Who sails?
A: Who is that?
P: The Renewer.
A: Who is that?
P: Who brings the golden fruit.
A: Who is that?
P: Unstained.
A: Who is that?
P: Whose hands are open?
A: Who is that?
P: Whose eyes are bright!
A: Who is that?
P: Whose face is shining?
A: Who is that?
P: Morning's hope!
A: Who is that?
P: Who passes the gate?
A: Who is that?
P: Who returns in light?
A: Who is that?
P: A glow between twin pillars.

A: Who is that?
P: A cry between thighs!

ALL: "Io! Evohe! Io! Evohe! Io! Evohe!"

PRIESTESS (leading, repeated by all):

> Queen of the sun!
> Queen of the moon!
> Queen of the horns!
> Queen of the fires!
> Bring to us the Child of promise!
>
> It is the Great Mother
> Who gives birth to Him,
> It is the Lord of Life,
> Who is born again!
> Darkness and tears
> Are set aside,
> When the sun comes up again!
>
> Golden sun,
> Of hill and field,
> Light the earth!
> Light the skies!
> Light the waters!
> Light the fires!
> (*Traditional chant.*)

ALL: "Io! Evohe! Io! Evohe! Io! Evohe!"

The Priest lights the fire and point candles, and all begin chanting:

> I who have died am alive again today,
> And this is the sun's birthday! (Repeat.)
>
> This is the birthday of life and love and wings,
> And the gay great happening illimitably earth.[3]
>
> We are born again, we shall live again![4] (Repeat.)
>
> The Sun Child, the Winter-born King!

Build a Power Chant, focused on reawakening life. Share feasting, and friendship, ideally, until dawn. Before ending, the Priestess says,

> The Dark God has passed the Gate,
> He has been reborn through the Mother,
> With Him we are each reborn!

> ALL: The tide has turned!
> The light will come again!
> In a new dawn, in a new day,
> The sun is rising!
> Io! Evohe! Blessed be!

Open the circle.

Brigid (Candlemas, February 2)* and **

This ritual is dedicated to Brigid, the Goddess of fire and inspiration; in Ireland, the Triple Goddess of poetry, smithcraft, and healing.

The central cauldron is filled with earth. Unlit candles—one for each covener and guest—are piled beside it. One candle stands upright in the center.

The circle gathers and does the breath meditation. The Priestess says,

"This is the feast of the waxing light. What was born at the Solstice begins to manifest, and we who were midwives to the infant year now see the Child Sun grow strong as the days grow visibly longer. This is the time of individuation: Within the measures of the spiral, we each light our own light, and become uniquely ourselves. It is the time of initiation, of beginning, when seeds that will later sprout and grow begin to stir from their dark sleep. We meet to share the light of inspiration, which will grow with the growing year."

Purify, cast the circle, and invoke the Goddess and God. The Priestess leads a call and response chant:

> Fire of the heart,
> Fire of the mind,
> Fire of the hearth,
> Fire of the wind,
> Fire of the Art,
> Fire out of time!

All: "She shines for all, She burns in all!"

(Repeat. Spontaneous lines can be interjected.)

When power has been raised, light the central candle. Begin the Spiral Dance, singing,

> I circle around, I circle around,
> The boundaries of the earth.
> Wearing my long wing feathers as I fly.[5]

(The Spiral Dance: All face out. The leader begins moving counterclockwise, with a simple grapevine step. As the circle unwinds, she whips around, facing the person next to her, and leads the spiral inward, clockwise. As coveners pass, face to face, they look into each other's eyes.)* *and* **

When the dance unwinds back into a circle, drummers break away and begin a stronger, wilder beat. One by one, each covener breaks out of the circle, takes a candle and lights it from the center, and then dances with the lit candle, raising power and focusing on the inspiration and creativity they wish in the coming season. Then, one by one, they place their candles in the central cauldron of earth. A Cone of Power is raised, and grounded into the cauldron.

Allow time for trance, opening to inspiration.

Share cakes and drink. Coveners share their creative work—poetry, songs, art works, stories, crafts. Those who are not artistic might share something about their work—a plan that materialized, a good idea, a special accomplishment. The Goddess is thanked for her inspiration.

Open the circle.

Each covener takes home some earth to sprinkle on her garden or keep on her altar for grounding.

Eostar Ritual (Spring Equinox, March 20–23)* *and* **

Decorate the altar with spring flowers. Place the appropriate element at each of the four points: earth at the North, smoking incense at the East, fire at the South, and a bowl of water at the West. Also place flowers of an appropriate color at each point.

Gather and do a breath meditation. The Priestess says,

"This is the time of spring's return; the joyful time, the seed time, when life bursts forth from the earth and the chains of winter are broken. Light and dark are equal: It is a time of balance, when all the elements within us must be brought into a new harmony. The Prince of the Sun stretches out his hand, and Kore, the Dark Maiden, returns from the Land of the Dead, cloaked in the fresh rain, with the sweet scent of desire on her breath. Where They step, the wild flowers appear; as They dance, despair turns to hope, sorrow to joy, want to abundance. May our hearts open with the spring! Blessed be!"

Purify, cast the circle, and invoke the Goddess and the God.

The Priest takes a skein of black wool and goes to each covener in turn. He asks them: "What binds you?"

When they reply—saying, for example, "guilt"—he binds their wrists lightly, repeating, "Guilt binds you; guilt binds you."

Other initiates begin the Kore Chant.[†] All softly repeat:

> She changes everything She touches,
> And everything She touches, changes.

The Priestess, following the Priest, asks each bound covener "Where must you go to be free?" Each replies with one of the four directions—which embodies the quality she feels she most lacks: for example, the East. The Priestess replies: "Go to the East, and free your mind." (Continue, using spirit for the South, emotions for the West, body for the North.)

Each covener goes to the appropriate direction, meditates on its quality (still chanting softly), and passes the bindings through smoke, flame, water, or earth.

The chant slowly builds into a wordless Cone of Power. At its peak, the Priestess cries out, "Now!" All break the bindings, shouting out, and begin dancing freely, singing, chanting, or whatever they are inspired to do.

When all is quiet, and the circle has formed again, time is allowed for trance and meditation. Priest and Priestess gather the flowers from the points and go around to each covener, saying, "Take what you need."

Each takes the color or colors of the direction they feel most in need of.

Share cakes and drink, and open the circle.

Beltane: May Eve* *and* **

A Maypole, crowned with flowers and hung with multicolored ribbons, is set up in an outdoor clearing. Fruits, flowers, round breads, cookies, and dough-nuts are hung from bushes and tree branches. A fire is built in the South, well within the boundaries of the circle.

Gather, and breathe together. The Priestess says,

[†] See pages 114–15.

"This is the time when sweet desire weds wild delight. The Maiden of Spring and the Lord of the Waxing Year meet in the greening fields and rejoice together under the warm sun. The shaft of life is twined in a spiral web and all of nature is renewed. We meet in the time of flowering, to dance the dance of life."

Purify, cast the circle, and invoke the God and Goddess.

One by one, each covener chooses a ribbon of the appropriate color, saying aloud what it is for:

"I choose the red of blood, for my health."

"I choose the sky-blue, for flights of imagination."

"I choose green, for growth." (Etc.)

The music begins (if you don't have musicians in the coven, teach the group a simple folk tune they can all sing together). Coveners dance the Maypole dance, weaving in and out, concentrating on weaving what they have chosen into their lives. As the ribbons wind tighter, the power grows, until it becomes a wordless Cone of Power. When the cone is released, coveners may continue dancing, and leap over the bonfire, calling out loudly their particular wish each time they leap. Jumping the flames is an act of purification and brings luck. Lovers can leap the bonfire together, to cleanse their relationship of petty disharmonies. Those who want to get rid of something—insecurity, for example—can jump, calling out, "I leave my insecurity in the flames!"

When the excitement dies down, raise a quieter, more solemn cone for healing, for members, or for friends not present. Bless cakes and drink, and open the circle.

Feast on the fruits and food that have been hung in the trees.

Litha (Summer Solstice, June 20–23)* *and* **

The altar and circle are decorated with roses and other summer flowers. A bonfire is lit in the center of the circle. The Priest carries a God figure made of woven sticks. A loaf of bread (carefully wrapped in many layers of tin foil) is concealed in its center. A wreath of roses and wildflowers lies on the altar. Coveners and guests also wear flowers.

Gather, do a breathing meditation, and light the fire. The Priestess says,

"This is the time of the rose, blossom and thorn, fragrance and blood. Now on this longest day, light triumphs, and yet begins the decline into dark. The Sun King grown embraces the Queen of Summer in the love that is death because it is so complete that all dissolves into the single song of ecstasy that moves the worlds. So the Lord of Light dies to Himself, and sets sail across the dark seas of time, searching for the isle of light that is rebirth. We turn the

Wheel and share his fate, for we have planted the seeds of our own changes, and to grow we must accept even the passing of the sun."

Purify, cast the circle, and invoke the Goddess and God.

Dance the Spiral Dance, singing,

> She is luminous
> She is white
> She is shining
> Crowned with light!
> He is radiant
> He is bright
> He is rising
> He takes flight!

As power is raised, the chant gradually changes. (The following lines are chanted over and over again; different coveners chant different lines simultaneously:)

> SHE who is at CENter, SHE WHO BLOOMS!
> The LEAFy One The GREEN One The LEAFy One The GREEN One . . .
> She who is CROWNED, She who EmBRACes!

The Priest dances with the God figure in the center of the circle. Still chanting, coveners place flowers on the figure, twining them into the sticks, until, as the power grows, the figure is covered with blossoms. The circle opens out: The chant becomes a wordless Cone of Power, as Priest and Priestess dance closer to the fire. As the Cone peaks, the Priestess opens her arms and calls out: "To me! To me!"

The Priest tosses the figure onto the flames. All are silent, meditating on the withering and burning blossoms.

As the blossoms die away, coveners may softly chant, "Set Sail" (see the ritual for the Winter Solstice). A covener carries the wreath around the circle, holding it up to each person's face so that they can see the flames through it. She says, "See with clear sight."

She holds the wreath aloft, and says, "And know the mystery of the unbroken circle!"

Priest and Priestess remove the bread from the fire and break it open. The Priestess holds it up.

Priestess: "Behold, the God has gone into the grain!"

All: "He will feed us!"

Priestess: "The sun is on the water!"

All: "He will quench our thirst!"
Priestess: "The God is in the corn!"
All: "It will grow high!"
Priestess: "The God is on tree and vine!"
All: "He will ripen in season!"
Priestess: "The sun is not lost!"
All: "It will rise again!"
Priestess: "The sun is within us!"
All: "See how we shine!"

All chant, "See how we shine!" as bread and drink are passed around the circle.

Share food, and open the circle.

Lughnasad (August 1)* *and* **

Decorate the altar with sheafs of wheat and grain. A large cornbread God figure lies on the altar, and small bread men and women are piled in baskets. Other baskets hold star-shaped cakes or cookies. A fire is lit in the center of the circle.

Gather, meditate, and breathe together. The Priestess says,

"This is the wake of Lugh, the Sun King who dies with the waning year, the Corn King who dies when the grain is reaped. We stand now between hope and fear, in the time of waiting. In the fields, the grain is ripe but not yet harvested. We have worked hard to bring many things to fruition, but the rewards are not yet certain. Now the Mother becomes the Reaper, the Implacable One who feeds on life that new life may grow. Light diminishes, the days shorten, summer passes. We gather to turn the Wheel, knowing that to harvest we must sacrifice, and warmth and light must pass into winter."

Purify, cast the circle, and invoke the Goddess and God.

The Priestess carries the baskets of bread figures to each covener, asking, "What do you fear?" The covener answers, saying, for example, "Failure." The Priestess repeats the answer, encouraging the covener to chant it: "Failure, failure, failure . . ." A chant emerges out of all the collective fears, as they are channeled into the bread figures.

As the chant grows stronger, the Priestess leads a chain-procession dance in a snake, going against the sun, and passing the fire. Each person tosses their bread figure into the fire, concentrating on freeing themselves from their fear. The Priestess chants,

> In this fire, may it pass from me and mine!
> May it pass, may it pass,

> May it pass on the outflowing tide
> And burn with the red sun
> As the year dies
> And fade
> As everything fades,
> As everything passes,
> All fades away. . . . (Repeat the last two lines.)

When all have passed the fire, a wordless Cone is raised to purify the group of their fears. Coveners now carry around the baskets of stars, giving one to each person and asking,

"What do you hope to harvest?"

A chant is built from the responses, and a new Cone is raised to charge the stars with the power to make hope manifest. When the power is earthed, the Priestess holds up a star, saying,

"May the star of hope be in us always."

All eat the stars.

The Priest holds up the bread God, saying, "Behold the grain of life!"

He carries it to each person, and, as each breaks off a piece and eats it, he says, "Eat of the life that ever dies and is reborn."

Feast, and open the circle.

Mabon (Fall Equinox, September 20–23)* *and* **

Decorate the altar with fall fruits, flowers, and grain. Coveners should bring thank offerings of sprouts, grain, or cloth. Baskets of yarn, seed pods, shells, feathers, and small pine cones are set by the altar. A fire is lit.

Gather, do a breathing meditation. The Priestess says,

"This is the time of harvest, of thanksgiving and joy, of leave-taking and sorrow. Now day and night are equal, in perfect balance, and we give thought to the balance and flow within our own lives. The Sun King has become the Lord of Shadows, sailing West: we follow Him into the dark. Life declines; the season of barrenness is on us, yet we give thanks for that which we have reaped and gathered. We meet to turn the Wheel and weave the cord of life that will sustain us through the dark."

Purify and cast the circle. Invoke the Goddess and God.

Begin with a Banishing Dance, moving counterclockwise. One person shouts out a phrase, something that has hurt her or held her back, kept her from being more than she could be. The others take it up and echo it until its power dies away. Then someone else shouts out a phrase, which is picked up by the rest. Continue until a banishing, purifying Cone can be raised and earthed.

All sit in the circle, and baskets of cord, seeds, shells, and so on are passed around. Each person braids or weaves a cord, twined with natural symbols, concentrating on what she wants to weave into her life. While the work goes on, all chant the Kore Chant.[†]

When the cords are woven, the Priestess knots each around the neck of its creator, saying,

> Behold the circle of rebirth,
> The cord of life.
> You will never fade away.

A Cone is raised to charge the cords. Time is allowed for trance and meditation. Then the Priest steps forward, holds up a sheaf of wheat, and says, "Autumn's grain is spring's seed."

He tosses it into the fire and pours out a libation of water, saying,

> Blessed be the Mother of all life.
> Blessed be the life that comes from Her and returns to Her.

He gives the cup to the Priestess, who says,

> We have sown, We have tended,
> We have grown, We have gathered,
> We have reaped a good harvest.
> Goddess, we thank you for your gifts.
> God, we thank you for your bounty.
> I thank you for _____. (Something personal.)

She pours a libation and tosses her offering into the fire. As the cup goes around, each person gives thanks for something and burns her offering.

Share food and drink, and open the circle.

Samhain (Halloween, October 31)* _and_ **

(The ending of the year at Halloween is the Witches' New Year. And so we end in the beginning, as we should, and the Wheel turns on.)

[†]See pages 114–15.

Before leaving home for the ritual, each covener sets out a plate with cakes and drink and a lighted candle, as an offering to their own beloved dead, and spends some time recalling the memory of friends and relatives who are gone.

The altar is decorated with fall leaves. An apple and pomegranate sit on the altar, and in the center of the circle is a gazing crystal or scrying bowl.

The circle gathers, does a breathing meditation, and the Priestess says,

"This is the night when the veil is thin that divides the worlds. It is the New Year in the time of the year's death, when the harvest is gathered and the fields lie fallow. For tonight the King of the Waning Year has sailed over the sunless sea that is the womb of the Mother, and steps ashore on the Shining Isle, the luminous world egg, becoming the seed of his own rebirth. The gates of life and death are opened; the Sun Child is conceived; the dead walk, and to the living is revealed the Mystery: that every ending is but a new beginning. We meet in time out of time, everywhere and nowhere, here and there, to greet the Lord of Death who is Lord of Life, and the Triple Goddess who is the circle of rebirth."

Purify, cast the circle, and invoke the Goddess and God.

All take hands, and begin an antiphonal chant:

> It is the great cold of the night, it is the dark.[6] (Repeat.)
> The woman lives, she passes, she dies.
> It is the great cold of the night, it is the dark.
> Fear lives, it passes, it dies.
> It is the great cold of the night, it is the dark.
> (Continue with improvised lines.)

As the chanting goes on the Priest and Priestess blindfold each member. One by one, they are taken out of the circle, spun around, and formed into a "ship"—aligned in a long triangle, with hands on each other's shoulders, swaying and rocking back and forth. The Priest winds a cord around their wrists, binding them together. Coveners are softly chanting,

> Weaving the silver ship's thread
> of the milk-white
> sail the waves
> of the sunless sea are
> weaving (Etc.; repeat.)

As each person boards the "ship," they are given one word or phrase to repeat: "weaving, weaving, weaving," or "Sail the waves, sail the waves," for example, so that a complex, hypnotic rhythm is built up. Continue until coveners begin to trance—then the chant changes to:

> Pearl-gray warrior, ghostly quest;
> Prince of twilight, sailing West!

Build power, wait for silence. The Priest steps forward, and says,

> We are in sight of the far shore.
> See the light on the waves, a shroud,
> A track to follow.
> Step into the surf, step ashore.
> Cast off your bonds, and be free!

Coveners break bindings.

> For here there is no binding.
> Cast off the veils that cloud your sight!

Coveners remove blindfolds.

> For here all eyes are opened!
> You warriors—here your battles are over.
> You workers—here your tasks are done!
> You who have been hurt, here find healing!
> You who are weary, here find rest.
> You who are old, here grow young again!
> For this is the Land of Youth,
> The Shining Land, the Isle of Apples.
> Here woods never fail; here there is a tree, the heart of light,
> And a well of silence.
> Sink down, sink to sleep, beside that deep, green well.

Coveners lie down, looking at the gazing crystal. They begin a multivoiced trance induction while the Priest continues:

> And follow Him—He is here—
> The Comforter, the Consoler,
> Heart's Ease, and Sorrow's End.
> He is the Guide: the Gate is open.
> He is the Guide: the way is clear.
> He is the Guide: Death is no barrier—
> For He is Lord of the Dance of Shadows—
> King in the realm of dreams.

All scry together, either silently, or saying what they see. Allow a long time: This is the best night for scrying in the year.

When all have returned, the Priest and Priestess go to the altar. She takes the pomegranate and holds it up, saying, "Behold the fruit of life . . ."

He plunges his *athame* into it and splits it open, saying, "Which is death!"

They feed each other and the coveners seeds, saying, "Taste the seeds of death."

He holds up the apple, saying, "Behold the fruit of death . . ."

She cuts it crosswise, saying, "Which is life!" She holds it up to show the pentacle formed by the seeds, and says, "Behold the fivefold star of rebirth!"

Everyone is given a taste of apple and a sip of drink, as they say, "Taste the fruit of rebirth, and sip the cup of the drink of life."

All take hands, and hold them up. The Priestess says,

"Here is the circle of rebirth. Through you (to the Priest) all passes out of life, but through Me all may be born again. Everything passes, changes. Seed becomes fruit; fruit becomes seed. In birth, we die; on death, we feed. Know Me, and be free of all fear. For My womb is the cauldron of rebirth, in Me, the circle is ever turning."

All: "Blessed be!"

Feast, and open the circle.

Notes

1. The rituals of our tradition are constantly changing and evolving. We rewrite them and re-create them every year, keeping the elements we like the best and adding new aspects that grow out of the underlying myth and season. Some festivals seem to evoke words, chanting, and liturgy; others cry out for action and concrete symbolism. The rituals given here are necessarily condensed, a skeletal framework on which new ceremonies can be built. Readers may be moved to enact the rituals as written, but should also feel free to change them, discard parts of them, and add to them.

   Generally, people are present who are unfamiliar with the structure of the ritual and the responses to be made. We run through the outline of the ritual with guests and coveners first. In a complicated ritual such as that for the Winter Solstice, we teach them simple responses linked to cue words: for example, "Follow!" might mean "Repeat the lines after me"; "Now!" might be the cue to shout "Io! Evohe!" etc. Initiates may memorize the more complicated responses beforehand, and others join in as they pick it up. For the antiphonal chants, we generally prepare some "spontaneous" lines ahead, enough to get the process started, so that genuine spontaneity can take over.

   Some people dislike "wordy" rituals and memorization—they should feel free to ignore the "set" chants and speeches and should improvise their own. Although the rituals are written, for the sake of simplicity, as being performed by the Priestess and Priest, different coveners may each lead a section of the ritual—which cuts down considerably on the amount of memorization necessary.

2. The dates of solstices and equinoxes vary from year to year. Check them with an ephemeris or astrological calendar.

3. e. e. cummings, from "i thank you God," *Poems 1923–1954* (New York: Harcourt Brace Jovanovich, 1954).

4. Native American Ghost Dance song, Jerome Rothenberg, ed. in *Technicians of the Sacred* (New York: Doubleday, 1969), p. 99.

5. Native American Ghost Dance, in Rothenberg, p. 99.

6. Adapted from the Gabon Pygmy, "Death Rites II," in Rothenberg, p. 171.

CHAPTER 13

Creating Religion:
Toward the Future

Between the Worlds

SAMHAIN, DAWN

The women climb Twin Peaks, which rise like uplifted breasts above San Francisco Bay. They form circles. Their voices ride the wind. On the summit, they leave gifts for the Goddess: a feather, a shell, a bird's nest.

They are reclaiming the heights.

NIGHT

The speakers at the Conference on Violence and Pornography stand before an image of the Goddess of Night, with her hands upraised and her hair streaming.

Three thousand women march through the streets where the topless bars and sex shows blare a constant, neon assault. At the park where they finish, they chant, dance, sprinkle each other with purifying salt water:

"Wipe the slate clean; dream your own dream!"

"Our bodies are sacred; our breasts are sacred."

"Take back the night; the night is ours!"

They are reclaiming the night.

NOVEMBER 1978

It is the ebb tide of the year, the waning moon before the Winter Solstice. I am writing this final chapter. The newspapers are filled with corpses; mass "suicides," sudden death. Murder at City Hall—the gun held to the back of the head, fired deliberately. In Guyana, we hear, mothers held the cup of poison to their children's lips. Horror follows horror. One by one, species abandon the earth. The sacred places are strip-mined. Consider: pesticides in breast milk; the neutron bomb. Consider: I am trying to write about things for which there are no longer words in the language, and the meanings of the words I use have been twisted, and may twist my meanings. Religion has come to mean placing our trust outside of ourselves, remaining like children following a long succession of father figures, teachers, preachers, politicians. And how do we know, once we have ceased to trust ourselves, whether they are Gods or psychopaths?

Are we, as a species, lined up to drink a poisoned brew?

Witch—Wicca— from wic—"to bend." Can we bend the meanings of the words back? Can we make "religion" mean "re-linking"? And can we make "spirituality" refer to the human spirit?

"The Goddess is reawakening," I say to Laurel, in a moment of probably lunatic optimism. "What do you mean by that?" she asks.

I say, "A mode of consciousness that has been dormant for thousands of years is now coming to the fore; we are beginning to see holistically; our model of the cosmos has been changed; we are beginning to value the feminine, the life-generative principle, to value humanness, and the existing world."

I look at what I have written,

"In circles, in cities, in groves, in streams, in waking and sleeping dreams, in words, in motion, in a flow of music, in poetry, in an opening art, in a day and a night, in struggle, in hunger, in joy, in quickening, in milk, in wine, in the blink of an eye, in a breath, in love, a seed is planted."

But I am forced to consider the question, "Will it have time to take root and grow?"

At first I think of it in terms of faith—that the credo qui absurdum, *the "I believe because it is absurd" of Witchcraft is belief in the continuance of life, and the possibility of a truly life-serving culture.*

The dogs scratch to go out. I take them across the street to the empty lot, and watch them play fight, rolling in the mud belly-up, their teeth clicking together like glasses of champagne. I realize suddenly that it is not a question of faith, but of will. I will life to go on.

We have collectively created the death cults. We can collectively create a culture of life.

But to do so, we must be willing to step out of line, to forgo the comfort of leaving decisions up to somebody else. To will is to make our own decisions, guide our own lives, commit ourselves, our time, our work, our energy, to act in the service of life.

To will is to reclaim our power, our power to reclaim the future.

From my Book of Shadows

"We tell you this: We are doing the impossible. We are teaching ourselves to be human."

Martha Courtot[1]

and when we have won clear
we must return to the circle

Return
the hunt
to the measure of the dance.

Diane Di Prima[2]

Kevyn, one of my coveners, recently had a dream in which a powerful woman figure appeared to her and said, "When a Witch acquires the acrostic eye, she changes." We both thought a lot about the meaning of "the acrostic eye." An acrostic, of course, is a form of crossword puzzle, in which everything has many meanings. Looked at as we normally do, horizontally, the letters form certain words—but if we shift our vision to right angles, it all changes. The essence of Witchcraft, and of political feminism, is acrostic vision: We look at our culture and our conditioning from another angle, and read an entirely different message. Acrostic vision is uncomfortable; it sets us at odds with everything we have been taught. We are forced to validate our own experience, since no external authority will do it for us.

In thinking about the future of religion and of culture, we need to look at the present through the acrostic eye. That slightly skewed vision reveals those underlying mind-sets I think of as the scabies of consciousness—because they cause us extreme discomfort and yet we can't ordinarily see them. They are embedded in us, under the skin. In this chapter, I want to examine the destructive forces, as well as the creative forces that are influencing the direction of our evolution as a society. Only when we understand the currents of the present can we clearly envision the future.

If we accept the responsibility of claiming the future for life, than we must engage in the demanding task of re-creating culture. A deep and profound change is needed in our attitude toward the world and the life on it, toward each other, and in our conceptions of what is human. Somehow, we must win clear of the roles we have been taught, of strictures on mind and self that are learned before speech and are buried so deep that they cannot be seen. Today women are creating new myths, singing a new liturgy, painting our own icons, and drawing strength from the new-old symbols of the Goddess, of the "legitimacy and beneficence of female power."[3]

A change in symbols, however, is not enough. We must also change the context in which we respond to symbols and the ways in which they are used. If female images are merely plugged into old structures, they too will function as agents of oppression, and this prospect is doubly frightening because they would then be robbed of the liberating power with which they are imbued today.**

Witchcraft is indeed the Old Religion, but it is undergoing so much change and development at present that, in essence, it is being re-created rather than revived. The feminist religion of the future is presently being formed. Those of us who are involved in this re-formation must look closely at the cultural context in which our own ideas about religion were formed, and examine the many regressive tendencies present in society today. Otherwise, the new incarnation of the Goddess will be subtly molded on the very forms we are working to transcend.

One regressive tendency is what I call *absolutism*, which stems from an intolerance of ambiguity. Our culture is highly symbol-bound, and we carry the unconscious assumption that symbolic systems *are* the realities they describe. If the description *is* the reality, and descriptions differ, only one can be true. *Either* God created Adam and Eve, *or* they evolved a la Darwin. *Either* unresolved unconscious conflicts are the final cause of our unhappiness, *or* economic and material conditions. We may change ideologies, but we do not examine the underlying idea that there is One Right, True, and Only Way— Ours!—and everybody else is wrong.

Absolutism is divisive. It sets up false conflicts—for example, between politics and spirituality. In an article entitled "Radical Feminism and Women's Spirituality: Looking Before You Leap," Marsha Lichtenstein writes, "the contradiction which is the seed of the distance and distrust between spirituality and politics is that each perceives consciousness in *antithetical* [italics mine] ways. An analysis of consciousness growing from spirituality seeks final causes in a priori categories of thought, as in the discovery of archetypes, as in the mythology of Eve as the repository of evil. . . . processes of change emphasize an inward journey. . . . Radical feminism analyzes the historical material conditions under which women's consciousness has developed. . . . the orientation toward social change is outer-directed, directed at transforming those societal conditions which shape our lives."[4]**

The key word in this passage is *antithetical*. A feminist spirituality based on the Goddess immanent in the world will see these analyses as complementary, rather than in opposition. They are both true. *Of course,* a priori categories of thought influence consciousness—and, *of course,* material conditions affect our ability to be whole. We need both inner and outer change—either one alone is not enough.

The Judeo-Christian heritage has left us with the view of a universe composed of warring opposites, which are valued as either good or evil. They cannot coexist. A valuable insight of Witchcraft, shared by many earth-based religions, is that polarities are in balance, not at war. Energy moves in cycles. At times, it flows outward, pushing us to change the world; at other times, it flows inward, transforming ourselves. It cannot be indefinitely exerted exclusively in one direction; it must always turn and return, push and pull, and so be renewed. If we label either end of the cycle as "wrong" or unnecessary, we cut ourselves off from any possibility for renewal or for the exercise of sustained power. We must win clear of the tendency to associate religion and spirituality with withdrawal from the world and the field of action. The Goddess is ourselves *and* the world—to link with Her is to engage actively with the world and all its problems.**

Dualism** slides over into what I call the "Righteousness Syndrome." When there is One Right True and Only Way—Ours!—and everybody else is wrong, then those who are wrong are damned, and the damned are evil. We are excused from recognizing their humanness and from treating them according to the ethics with which we treat each other. Generally, the Righteous set about the task of purifying themselves from any contact with the carriers of evil. When they are in power, they institute inquisitions, Witch-hunts, pogroms, executions, censorship, and concentration camps.

Oppressed and powerless groups may also tend to see themselves as the Righteous.* Since they are not in a position to weed out undesirables from society, they can be "pure" only by removing themselves from the larger community. In the women's movement, this has given birth to separatism.

I distinguish between separation and separatism. Women need women's spaces, especially at this point in history when many of us are recovering from hurts inflicted by men. There is a special intensity in women's mysteries and an unequaled intimacy in women's covens. Women who love other women, or who live Virgin, belonging to themselves alone, attain a very special power. But it is not the *only* form of power inherent in feminist spirituality, nor is it the best form for everyone. The Goddess is Mother, Crone, Lover, as well as Virgin; She is bound up with the birth, love, and death of men as well as of women. If She is immanent in women, and in the world, then She is also immanent in men.

A matrifocal culture, based on nature, celebrates diversity, because diversity assures survival and continuing evolution. Nature creates thousands of species, not just one; and each is different, fitted for a different ecological niche. When a species becomes overspecialized, too narrow in its range of adaptations, it is more likely to become extinct. When political and spiritual movements become too narrow, they are also likely to die out. The strength of the women's movement lies in its diversity, as old and young women, lesbian and straight, welfare mothers and aspiring bank presidents discover common interests, common needs, and common sisterhood. If our culture as a whole is to evolve toward life, we need to foster diversity, to create and maintain a wide range of differences in lifestyle, theory, and tactics. We need to win clear of the self-righteousness that comes from seeing ourselves as Chosen People, and need to create a religion of heretics, who refuse to toe any ideological lines or give their allegiance to any doctrines of exclusivity.

Another spurious conflict created by absolutism is that between religion and science.* When God is felt to be separate from the physical world, religion can be split off from science, and limited to the realm of things having to do with God. But the Goddess is manifest in the physical world, and the more we understand its workings, the better we know Her. Science and religion are both quests for truth—they differ only in their methodology and the set of symbols they use to describe their findings. The field of inquiry is the same.

"Understanding a thing is to arrive at a metaphor for that thing by substituting something more familiar to us," write Julian Jaynes (in *The Origin of Consciousness in the Breakdown of the Bicameral Mind*).[5] "We say we understand an aspect of nature when we can say it is similar to some familiar theoretical model."[6] Scientific knowledge, like religious knowledge, is a set of metaphors for a reality that can never be completely described or comprehended. Religion becomes dogmatic when it confuses the metaphor with the thing itself. Metaphors themselves are not contradictory or antithetical; many can be true at once. They point to something beyond themselves; they are separate lights beaming at the same spot.

Scientific metaphors strive to be consistent and testable. They are expected to conform to objective reality. The myths and symbols of nature-oriented religions also began as metaphors for observed reality: for the movement of sun and moon, plant growth and decay, animal behavior and seasonal changes. They resonate on many levels, engaging both our verbal-analytical awareness and our holistic-imagistic awareness. They touch our emotions, determining not only what we know but also how we feel about nature. If we describe the vagina as a flower, we feel differently about it than if we call it "a piece of meat" or a "genital orifice." If we call the ocean "our Mother, the womb of life," we may take more care not to pump Her full of poisons than if we see the ocean merely as "a mass of H_2O."

I would like to see the Goddess religion of the future be firmly grounded in science, in what we can observe in the physical world.** Observation is meditation, as the builders of Stonehenge—temple, astronomical observatory, calendar, and calculator—knew well. Witchcraft has always been an empirical religion; herbs, spells, and practices were constantly tested, and results compared at gatherings of the covens. Today, when we introduce a new ritual, exercise, or invocation, the question is always "Does it work?" The tests are more subjective than those of science: Did we feel anything? Were we changed? Did we get the results we expected? Were we excited? Ecstatic? Anxious? Bored? Why?

The old symbols were drawn from observation of recurring patterns in nature. Some have merely been deepened by our expanded knowledge of those patterns. For example, the spiral was the ancient symbol of death and rebirth. We now recognize it as the shape of the DNA molecule, which sets the pattern for an organism's growth, and so it takes on another level of meaning. The galaxy is a spiral; "as above, so below."

Other myths and symbols may change to reflect new knowledge. Many of the old seasonal myths are based on the experiential perception that the sun moves around the earth. Even our language reflects this misconception; we say "the sun rises," although we know intellectually that it does not and never has; instead, the earth turns. Because our physiology and psychology evolved under the apparently-rising-and-setting sun, the old myths "work" to connect our internal cycles with those of the outer world and cannot just be discarded. Yet perhaps there is an esoteric meaning in the earth's motion, too: We do not just await the light; we journey toward it.

In future or contemporary Goddess religion, a photograph of the earth as seen from space might be our mandala. We might meditate on the structure of the atom as well as icons of ancient Goddesses; and see the years Jane Goodall spent observing chimpanzees in the light of a spiritual discipline. Physics, mathematics, ecology, and biochemistry more and more approach the mystical. New myths can take their concepts and make them numinous, so that they infuse our attitudes and actions with wonder at the richness of life.

Spirituality leaps where science cannot yet follow, because science must always test and measure, and much of reality and human experience is immeasurable. Without discarding science, we can recognize its limitations. There are many modes of consciousness that have not been validated by Western scientific rationalism, in particular what I call "starlight awareness," the holistic, intuitive mode of perception of the right hemisphere of our brains. As a culture, we are experiencing a turn toward the intuitive, the psychic, which have been denied for so long. Astrology, Tarot, palmistry—all the ancient forms of divination are undergoing a revival. People seek expanded consciousness in everything from yoga to drugs to expensive weekend seminars, and they see no value in a religion that is merely a set of doctrines or a dull Sunday morning's entertainment. Any viable religion developing today will inevitably be concerned with some form of magic, defined as "the art of changing consciousness at will."

Magic has always been an element of Witchcraft, but in the Craft its techniques were practiced within a context of community and connection. They were means of ecstatic union with the Goddess Self—not ends in themselves. Fascination with the psychic—or the psychological—can be a dangerous sidetrack on any spiritual path. When inner visions become a way of escaping contact with others, we are better off simply watching television. When "expanded consciousness" does not deepen our bonds with people and with life, it is worse than useless: It is spiritual self-destruction.**

If Goddess religion is not to become mindless idiocy, we must win clear of the tendency of magic to become superstition. Magic—and among its branches I include psychology as it purports to describe and change consciousness—is an art. Like other arts, its efficacy depends far more on who is practicing it than on what theory they base their practice. Egyptian tomb painting is organized on quite different structural principles than twentieth-century Surrealism—yet both schools produced powerful paintings. Balinese music has a different scale and rhythmic structure from Western music, but it is no less beautiful. The concepts of Freud, Jung, Melanie Klein, and Siberian shamanism can all aid healing or perpetuate sickness, depending on how they are applied.

Magical systems are highly elaborated metaphors, not truths. When we say, "There are twelve signs in the Zodiac," what we really mean is "we will view the infinite variety of human characteristics through this mental screen, because with it we can gain insights"; just as when we say, "There are eight notes in the musical scale," we mean that out of all the possible range and variations of sounds, we will focus on those that fall into these particular relationships, because by doing so we can make music. But when we forget that the signs are arbitrary groupings of stars, and start believing that there are large lions, scorpions, and crabs up in the sky, we are in trouble. The value of magical metaphors is that through them we identify ourselves and connect with larger forces; we partake of the elements, the cosmic process, the movements of the stars. But if we use them for glib explanations and cheap categorizations, they narrow the mind instead of expanding it and reduce experience to a set of formulas that separate us from each other and our own power.

The longing for expanded consciousness has taken many of us on a spiritual "journey to the East," and Hindu, Taoist, and Buddhist concepts are infusing

Western culture with new understandings.* The East-West dialogue has become a major influence on the evolution of a new world view. Eastern religions offer a radically different approach to spirituality than Judeo-Christian traditions. They are experiential rather than intellectual; they offer exercises, practices, and meditations, rather than catechisms. The image of God is not the anthropomorphic, bearded God-Father in the sky—but the abstract, unknowable ground of consciousness itself, the void, the Tao, the flow. Their goal is not to *know* God, but to *be* God. In many ways, their philosophies are very close to that of Witchcraft.

As women, however, we need to look very closely at these philosophies and ask ourselves the hard-headed, critical question "What's in it for *me?* What does this spiritual system do for women?" Of course, the gurus, teachers, and ascended masters will tell us that, even by asking such a question, we are merely continuing in our enslavement to the Lords of Mind; that it is simply another dodge of the ego as it resists dissolution in the All. The truth is that while men, in our society, are encouraged to have strong egos and to function in competitive, aggressive, intellectualized modes that may indeed cause them pain, for most women the ego is like a fragile African violet, grown in secret from a seed, carefully nursed and fertilized and sheltered from too much sun. Before I toss mine out into the collective garbage heap, I want to be sure I'm getting something in return. I don't feel qualified to discuss the way Eastern religions function within their own cultures. But if we look at women in the West who have embraced these cults, by and large we find them in bondage. An ecstatic bondage, perhaps, but bondage nevertheless.

Eastern religions may help men become more whole, in touch with the intuitive, receptive, gentle feelings they have been conditioned to ignore. But women cannot become whole by being yet more passive, gentle, and submissive than we already are. We become whole through knowing our strength and creativity, our aggression, our sexuality, by affirming the Self, not by denying it. We cannot achieve enlightenment through identifying with Buddha's wife or Krishna's gopi groupies. While India has strong Goddess traditions—of tantra, of Kali worship—these are less easily popularized in the West, because they do not fit our cultural expectation that truth is purveyed through male images, by charismatic males. If we look closely at the symbols, the hierarchical structure, the denial of sexuality and emotion purveyed by the gurus who do attract popular cults in the West, we can only conclude that, while they may be using different instruments, they are playing the same old song.

Another dimension of absolutism is our tendency to think that truth is somehow more true if it is expressed in extremes; that a theory, to be valid, must explain everything. For example, a psychologist discovers that rats can be conditioned to respond to certain stimuli in predictable ways and concludes that all learning is nothing more than conditioned responses. This makes for ringing pronouncements and endless arguments in professional journals—after all, how do we *prove* what we innately feel—that somewhere in the gap between the rat in its maze, and Makarova learning to dance, some other factor enters in? But were the psychologist to say simply "*some* learning is a matter of conditioning," who would listen? A statement like that is not impressive; it doesn't sound new or original; it furnishes no grounds for starting experimental utopian communities, and leads to no international recognition or lucrative lecture tours. It sounds flat, obvious. Its sole virtue is that it is true, which the fine-sounding generalization is not.

Absolutist statements are often extremely appealing. Something in us wants life to be neatly organized around clear principles, with no loose ends left hanging. We desperately wish all problems in long division would work out to whole numbers, not fractions. But if we are interested in solving problems rather than manipulating pretty patterns, we have to accept that they don't. Only when we are ready to confront the muddiness and unclarity of reality can we hope to transform it.

In the past few years, a spate of secular gurus have traded heavily on our cultural longing for simple organizing principles around which to base our lives. The basis of many of the "growth" movements and human potential movements is the absolutist concept "I create my own reality."** It is in some ways comforting to believe this; in other ways, it is a terrifying thought. It seems to be true that we do create more of our lives, our opportunities, our physical health, than we ordinarily take responsibility for. If I blame my unhappiness on my mother, on the "system," on bad luck, I will continue being unhappy rather than taking action to change my situation. It is up to no one but me to create for myself meaningful work, money to live on, and important relationships, and nothing outside of myself stops me from having them all. I am, of course, like most members of these movements, white and middle-class. If my skin were another color, if I were mentally retarded because of early malnutrition, or disabled, I doubt that I would be quite so sublime about my ability to create reality. Does the rape victim create the assault? Did the children of Vietnam create napalm? Obviously, no.

Much of reality—the welfare system, war, the social roles ordained for women and men—is created collectively and can only be changed collectively. One of the clearest insights of feminism is that our struggles are *not* just individual, and our pain is not private pain; it is created by ways in which our culture treats women as a class. Sexism, racism, poverty, and blind accident do shape people's lives, and they are not created by their victims. If spirituality is to be truly life serving, it must stress that we are all responsible for each other.

Its focus should not be individual enlightenment, but recognition of our inter-connectedness and commitment to each other.

Feminist religion does not make false promises. It does not set people up for the pain and disillusionment that come when the growth groupie bumps up against a reality that can't be changed. Night will follow day, and there's not a damn thing you or I or Werner can do about it.

The paradox, of course, is that we are the Goddess: We are each a part of the interpenetrating, interconnecting reality that is All. And, while we can't stop the earth from turning, we can choose to experience each revolution so deeply and completely that even the dark becomes luminous. To *will* does not mean that the world will conform to our desires—it means that *we* will: We will make our own choices and act so as to bring them about, even knowing we may fail. Feminist spirituality values the courage to take risks, to make mistakes, to be our own authorities.

We need to win clear of the belief that only a few individuals in history have had a direct line on truth; that Jesus or Buddha or Mohammed or Moses or Freud or Werner Erhard know more about our souls than we do. Certainly, we can learn from teachers, but we cannot afford to give over our power to direct our lives. A feminist religion needs no messiahs, no martyrs, no saints to lead the way.** Instead, it must validate us in discovering and sharing our experiences, inner and outer. Its goal should be that impossible task of teaching ourselves—because we have no models and no teachers who can show us the way—to become human, fully alive with all the human passions and desires, faults and limitations, and infinite possibilities.

Many forces today are shaping the genesis of new myths. I have discussed the changes science has brought to religion, and the impact of the East-West dialogue. Our growing awareness of ecology, the impending environmental apocalypse, has forced on us a realization of our interconnectedness with all forms of life, which is the basis of Goddess religion. Our changing cultural attitude toward sexuality is also influencing our spirituality.

Feminists have quite rightly pointed out that the so-called sexual revolution has too often meant the open marketing of women's bodies and the objectification of women. But this is because we are not yet sexually free. Pornography, rape, prostitution, sadomasochism simply bring out into the open the theme that underlies asceticism, celibacy, and Christian chastity—that sex is dirty and evil, and by extension, so are women. Under patriarchy, sexuality provides the rationale for violence against women—the stoning of adulteresses, the burning of Witches, the snickering probe into the conduct of rape victims.

Goddess religion identifies sexuality as the expression of the creative life force of the universe. It is not dirty, nor is it merely "normal"; it is sacred, the manifestation of the Goddess. Fortunately, this does not mean you have to be ordained before you can do it. In feminist spirituality, a thing that is sacred can also be affectionate, joyful, pleasurable, passionate, funny, or purely animal. "All acts of love and pleasure are My rituals," says the Goddess. Sexuality is sacred because it is a sharing of energy, in passionate surrender to the power of the Goddess, immanent in our desire. In orgasm, we share in the force that moves the stars.

The strongest mythogenic force at work today, however, is feminism. Women have dared to look through the acrostic eye, and the molds have shattered. The process of cultural change is a long and difficult one. The laws, the language, the economic and social system do not yet reflect our vision. We are discovering and creating myths and symbols and rituals that do. We need images that move us beyond language, law, and custom; that hurl us beyond the boundaries of our lives to that space between the worlds, where we can see clear.

The feminist movement is a magicospiritual movement as well as a political movement. It is spiritual because it is addressed to the liberation of the human spirit, to healing our fragmentation, to becoming whole. It is magical because it changes consciousness, it expands our awareness and gives us a new vision. It is also magic by another definition: "the art of causing change in accordance with will."

If we are to reclaim our culture, we cannot afford narrow definitions.

And when we have won clear, "we must return to the circle." The circle is the ecological circle, the circle of the interdependence of all living organisms. Civilization must return to harmony with nature.

The circle is also the circle of community.* The old family structures, the networks of support and caring are breaking down. Religion has always been a prime source of community, and a vital function of feminist spirituality is to create new networks of involvement. Community also implies broader issues of how equitably power, wealth, and opportunities are shared among different groups, and the issues of who cares for children, the aged, the sick, and the disabled. When the Divine becomes immanent in the world, these are all areas of spiritual concern.

The circle is also the circle of Self. Our view of the Self—what it is, how it perceives, in what modes it functions—has changed greatly. Feminist spirituality is also an inner journey, a personal vision quest, a process of self-healing and self-exploration.

To return to the circle does not necessarily mean to embrace Witchcraft specifically. I hope the religion of the future will be multifaceted, growing out of many traditions. Perhaps we will see a new cult of the Virgin Mary and a revival of the ancient Hebrew Goddess.** Native American traditions and Afro-

American traditions may flourish in an atmosphere in which they are given the respect they deserve. Eastern religions will inevitably change as they grow in the West—and part of that change may be in the roles they assign women.

But there are valuable underlying concepts in Witchcraft, on which other feminist traditions can draw. The most important is the understanding of the Goddess, the divine, as immanent in the world, manifest in nature, in human beings, in human community. The All-That-Is-One is not now and never has been separate from this existing physical world. She is here, now, *is* each of us in the eternal changing present; is no one but you, is nowhere but where you are—and yet is everyone. To worship Her is to assert, even in the face of suffering and often against all reason, that life is good, a great gift, a constant opportunity for ecstasy. If we see it become a burden of misery for others, we have the responsibility to change it.

Because the Goddess is manifest in human beings, we do not try to escape our humanness, but seek to become fully human. The task of feminist religion is to help us learn those things that seem so simple, yet are far more demanding than the most extreme patriarchal disciplines. It is easier to be celibate than to be fully alive sexually. It is easier to withdraw from the world than to live in it; easier to be a hermit than to raise a child; easier to repress emotions than to feel them and express them; easier to meditate in solitude than to communicate in a group; easier to submit to another's authority than place trust in oneself.** It is not easy to be a Witch, a bender, a shaper, one of the Wise; nor is it safe, comfortable, "laid back," mellow, uplifting, or a guarantee of peace of mind. It requires openness, vulnerability, courage, and work. It gives no answers: only tasks to be done, and questions to consider. In order to truly transform our culture, we need that orientation toward life, toward the body, toward sexuality, ego, will, toward all the muckiness and adventure of being human.

Witchcraft offers the model of a religion of poetry, not theology. It presents metaphors, not doctrines, and leaves open the possibility of reconciliation of science and religion, of many ways of knowing. It functions in those deeper ways of knowing which our culture has denied and for which we hunger.

The world view of Witchcraft is cyclical, spiral. It dissolves dualities and sees opposites as complements. Diversity is valued; both poles of any duality are always valued because between them flows the on-off pulse of polar energy that sustains life. That cycle is the rhythm of the dance, to which the Hunter, the seeker, is always drawn back.

Finally, the Craft provides a structural model: the coven, the circle of friends, in which there is leadership, but no hierarchy, small enough to create community without loss of individuality. The form of ritual is circular: We face each other, not an altar or a podium or a sacred shrine, because it is in each other that the Goddess is found. Every Witch is Priestess or Priest: there are no hierophants, no messiahs, no avatars, no gurus. The Goddess says, "If that which you seek, you find not within yourself, you will never find it without. For I have been with you from the beginning."

When we return to the circle, when we win clear, what will we be? I have snatches of visions; perhaps they are the memories of future lives:

> The children awaken in the middle of the night, to watch the moon rise. They are taught nothing about the moon until they have lived with her for a cycle, arising with her rising, sleeping when she sets. They are not taught about the sun until they have watched it for a year, following its movements along the horizon. Their teachers encourage them to make pictures, stories, and songs about the moon and sun.
>
> When they are older, they are shown a model of the solar system. They are not told about it, they are simply left with it for a time each day, to observe it, with an open mind. For some of them, understanding will come in a moment's illumination. For others, it will not. It doesn't matter. After a time, they are encouraged to ask questions. After a time, they are answered.
>
> When they are older yet, they may make a pilgrimage to the moon. Some may live for a time in the Shrine of the Bright Face, watching the earth wax and wane. Some may prefer the Dark Shrine, which always faces the stars.

> The path is sometimes steep, but not hard to follow. Aradia knows her uneasiness comes only from being alone. Like all the other children, she has hiked and camped in these mountains many times. But never before alone.
>
> She stops for a moment in a high meadow, to soak up the sun. Three days. She will live off the land, or fast. Already the Feast of First Blood, the celebration, the ceremonial dishes of red food, the gifts wrapped in red paper that she will not use for a year, are memories of a past life. Now she is passing. She has given away her dolls and toys. Along the high ridge, she follows the trail to the Lake of Women.

> Anna waits by the lake. It lies cupped in the hollow of the mountains like a teardrop in the hand. She drinks the silence: after all the years of noise, children, work, demands. After years of drawing plans for buildings, it is good to look at trees and rocks, to take her Year of Repose. When the young girls come, she and the other women teach them things about their bodies, about wind and rock, fire and water. They learn to spin and weave, to bring flame without matches, to understand the speech of animals. At night, they are taught the mysteries and songs that women remember. And they work magic. . . .

It is the night of the Winter Solstice. In San Francisco, there are bonfires everywhere: strung along the beaches, blazing on Twin Peaks, on all the high places. In the parks and on rooftops, small groups gather around cauldrons. There are no mass meetings, only circles.

They begin with a very old custom: walking the land and searching for papers or foreign objects. The Elders have debated discontinuing the custom: It is outdated. There is never any trash to find. Nothing is made to be idly tossed away; nothing is wasted.

From the hilltops, the city is a colored mosaic set in green. Everywhere are gardens. The last rays of the sun gleam rose in a thousand solar collectors.

The Witches take hands around the fire. The wind rises, rattling the eucalyptus branches. Across the city, thousands of gaily painted windmills spin to life, flashing the colored lights with which they are decorated at Midwinter. Candles are blown out; altars topple over. No one minds. They have all they need to make magic: their voices, their breath, each other.

Through the long night, they chant each other's names. They sing hymns to the newborn sun, to the eternally revolving Goddess. They pour libations and give thanks—especially the very old ones, who remember when it was different:

"I am thankful that in this city, no one goes hungry."

"I am thankful that in this city, no one is left to die alone."

"I give thanks that I can walk the dark streets without fearing violence."

"I give thanks that the air is clean, that life has returned to the waters of the bay, that we are at peace."

"I give thanks that everyone has work to do."

In the morning, there are parades down Market Street, and the neighborhood groups and unions present their elaborate floats, the creation of the city's finest artists. Gorgeously arrayed figures of the Virgin arrive from the Mission District, followed by a glittering Wheel of Lights from the Electrical Worker's Union, and a Sun Child made of yellow flowers from the Midwives' Guild. There are clowns, jugglers, marching bands—people pour out of their houses to dance in the streets. Later, there will be concerts, parties, masquerade balls, and special theater performances.

The last day of celebration is quiet and peaceful. People visit in each other's homes, exchanging food and simple gifts. Families and covens eat together.

At night, they return to the hillsides and rekindle the fires. They join together to earth the power of the season, and slip between the worlds. Beyond time, in touch with past and future both, with all possibilities, they speak to us. We can hear them. They say to each one of us,

"Wake up! You are it. You are a part of the circle of the Wise. There is no mystery that has not already been revealed to you. There is no power you do not already have. You share in all the love that is."

"When we return to the circle
we have won clear.
Return the dance to the pulses of the Hunt."[7]

The Goddess awakens in infinite forms and a thousand disguises. She is found where She is least expected, appears out of nowhere and everywhere to illumine the open heart. She is singing, crying, moaning, wailing, shrieking, crooning to us: to be awake, to commit ourselves to life, to be a lover in the world and of the world, to join our voices in the single song of constant change and creation. For Her law is love unto all beings, and She is the cup of the drink of life.

May life thrive, now and always!
The circle is ever open, ever unbroken.
May the Goddess awaken in each of our hearts.
Merry meet, and merry part. And blessed be.

Notes

1. Martha Courtot, "Tribes," *Lady-Unique-Inclination-of-the-Night*, Cycle 2, Summer 1977, p. 13.
2. Diane Di Prima, "Now Born in Uniqueness, Join the Common Quest," in *Loba* (Berkeley: Wingbow Press, 1978), p. 188.
3. Carol P. Christ, "Why Women Need the Goddess," in Carol P. Christ and Judith Plaskow, eds., *Womanspirit Rising* (San Francisco: Harper & Row, 1979), p. 278.
4. Marsha Lichtenstein, "Radical Feminism and Women's Spirituality: Looking Before You Leap," *Lady-Unique*, Cycle 2, Summer 1977, pp. 37–38.
5. Julian Jaynes, *The Origin of Consciousness in the Breakdown of the Bicameral Mind* (Boston: Houghton Mifflin, 1976), p. 52.
6. Jaynes, p. 53.
7. Di Prima, p. 189.

Ten Years Later: Commentary on Chapters One through Thirteen

Notes on Chapter One

Page 26 When I originally wrote *The Spiral Dance*, my covens always invoked both the Goddess and the God. In the intervening decade, the covens I work with have become more fluid in our interpretation of our relationship to images of divinity, or perhaps more frank in our understanding that these things are mysteries that we cannot ever fully understand. Now we invoke whatever aspects of deity we feel are appropriate or hovering around us at any given time. Almost always we invoke some form of the Goddess, although not always as a specific, named aspect. For example, if we are doing a ritual with people who are not Pagans, perhaps during a political action, we might simply invoke the elements or call the God/dess by the names of people present. If we feel some aspect of the God demanding our attention, we invoke him.

Pages 27–32 The history presented here is a mixture of oral tradition, interpretations of physical evidence, and standard scholarship. A complete, documented, and footnoted presentation of this material would require volumes—many of which have already been written by other people. In *Truth or Dare*, I explored more fully the history of the Middle East and the transition to patriarchy. In the Appendix to *Dreaming the Dark*, I give a much more developed account of the European Witch persecutions. A wealth of Goddess scholarship is available today that was not yet published ten years ago. See the Suggested Reading for references.

Rereading this history, I am struck by its Eurocentric character. Of course, I am tracing the history of a European tradition; however, it is important to know that matrifocal, Goddess-centered traditions also underlie the rich cultures of Asia, the Americas, Africa, and Polynesia. African and Asian roots also fed the European tradition. In many areas these traditions survive today. The works of Paula Gunn Allen and Luisa Teish, as well as Carl Olsen's anthology, are good starting points for exploring other traditions.

Shamanism has become a trendy word over the past ten years. The interest in spiritual traditions that offer direct encounters with dimensions beyond the everyday has grown enormously, spawning a minor industry in workshops and exotic tours. But real spiritual growth takes place in the context of a culture. People of European heritage, out of hunger for what that culture lacks, may unwittingly become spiritual strip miners, damaging other cultures in superficial attempts to uncover their mystical treasures.

Understanding the suppression and grounding ourselves in the surviving knowledge of the European traditions can help people with European ancestors avoid flocking to the sad tribe of "Wannabees"—want to be Indians, want to be Africans, want to be anything but what we are. And, of course, any real spiritual power we gain from any tradition carries with it responsibility. If we learn from African drum rhythms or the Lakota sweat lodge, we have incurred an obligation to not romanticize the people we have learned from but to participate in the very real struggles being waged for liberation, land, and cultural survival.

Readers whose own heritage preserves a living, earth-based spirituality may find here interesting parallels and comparisons.

Page 28 "In the lands once covered . . ." The power of the ley lines and standing stones was perhaps not newly discovered, nor was Northern Europe necessarily its place of discovery. Similar stones and alignments are found all around the world, from the medicine wheels of North America to the monoliths of Easter Island.

Page 30 ". . . an estimated nine million Witches . . ." Actually, estimates range between a low of one hundred thousand and this figure, which is probably high. The truth, clearly, is that nobody knows exactly how many people died in the persecutions. Many died in prison who were not counted in the executioners' tallies. But the effect of the persecutions on the psyche of Europe, and especially on women, was that of a collective trauma. In the Appendix of *Dreaming the Dark*, I explore this whole question more fully than I can here.

Page 34 "Because women give birth to males . . ." I am no longer so sure that there is a "feminine side" to a man's nature or a "masculine side" to a woman's nature. Today I find it more useful to think of the whole range of human possibilities—aggression, nurture, compassion, cruelty, creativity, passivity, etc.—as available to us all, not divided by gender, either outer or inner.

Page 35 "Modern Witchcraft . . ." The Craft has grown enormously in the last ten years, and probably its greatest growth has been among groups that are self-started, cooperatively run, mostly self-trained, and eclectic.

Page 38 "Witchcraft is not a religion of masses . . ." Besides covens, there are many Witches who are solitaries, who choose to practice alone, either because they cannot find companions in their area or because they prefer it that way, just as some people prefer to live alone.

Notes on Chapter Two

Page 42 "Our fellow men are the black magicians . . ." Today, I would not use this quote, as I feel the use of the "black" and "dark" to mean "evil" perpetuates racism. Also, in the intervening years Castaneda's work has come to be viewed more as fiction than as anthropology. However, it still contains valuable magical insights.

Page 43 "Perhaps the most convincing way . . ." The left- and right-hemisphere brain research, so exciting in the late seventies, today leaves me less enthusiastic. Other cultures have always known there are many different states of consciousness and have valued them. Only in the last few hundred years of Western culture have we so denied any mode of consciousness other than the linear and rational that we need an elaborate scientific metaphor as "proof" that something else exists. Once we accept that consciousness has many dimensions, knowing exactly where in the brain they are located seems only mildly relevant unless one has suffered a head injury or plans to practice neurosurgery.

Pages 45–46 Discussion of the three selves. I have eliminated from this discussion comparisons with Freudian, Jungian, and Transactional Analysis terms such as id, ego, collective unconscious, Parent, Child, etc. None of the Selves, as discussed here, corresponds exactly with any of these terms, and making the comparisons is, I believe now, more misleading than clarifying.

Originally, I called the Deep Self the "High Self." I have changed the term here to make it consistent with the terms I have used in later writings, as I came to believe that the "high/low" metaphor for good/evil, advanced/primitive, evolved/unevolved, and the like perpetuated an underlying denigration of the earth, the body, and the material world, which seemed inappropriate for a thealogy of immanence.

Pages 48–52 The creation myth and the question of polarity. The Creation myth that opens this chapter and on which this discussion is based was taught to me as an oral teaching of Faery tradition Wicca by Victor Anderson. In the Craft myths are not seen as dogma. Each reveals to us another facet of understanding, but no one myth reveals the whole and only truth. The test of a true myth is that each time you return to it, new insights and interpretations arise.

Earlier, I saw this myth as a teaching about *polarity*, the magnetic attraction of opposites, the dynamic tension of differentiation, and I saw the primary differentiation as female/male. The unexamined model in my mind at the time, I believe now, was of erotic attraction between women and men as the basic pattern for understanding the energy dynamics of the universe.

Polarity can exist between women and men, female and male, and when it does it is a powerful force. Many Craft traditions, and spiritual traditions outside the Craft, tap this force and work with it. It is one valid way to understand energy—but it is only one way.

Now, I see the myth as teaching something else—that what we call "female" and "male" are sort of arbitrary designations of points along a continuum, stations on a wheel. Polarity, desire, attraction might arise between and among any combination of them. Polarity is not merely a straight line between two poles; it is a net of forces between a multiplicity of nodes in a sphere, each of which contains its own opposite.

If this discussion is getting so mystical as to become incomprehensible, draw two points and connect them with a straight line. Picture it as a line of reverberating force flowing both backward and forward at once, and you can well imagine how power can be generated. Now draw a larger circle and mark a number of points—say, five, one for each character in the story: the Primary Goddess, Miria, the Blue God, the Green God, and the Horned God. Now connect them with lines in every way you can. You will find yourself drawing the pentacle inside the circle: symbol of the Craft, and of magic, a power that is subtle and complex in its interactions.

Now consider that the Horned God, the most "male" (or perhaps we should say "butch") aspect of the God, is now closest to the Prime Goddess on this continuum. Consider that if he is Death, he is also Life—the animal that feeds the tribe, the desire to seek and find and know. Consider that if the Primary Goddess is the Creatrix, she is also the Destroyer, for any act of Creation undoes what was before. Consider that love generates creation but also loss of the beloved, who is swept away and undergoes a sex change right before the Goddess's eyes.

Something is going on here that is far more complicated than "woman needs man, and man must have his mate." The myth now seems to be saying that desire, the erotic glue that holds the worlds together, is not dependent on gender differentiation, that it arises in unique ways among and between any and all beings who are whole in themselves, meaning willing to integrate a wide spectrum of qualities that range from birth to death and back again. Interpreted in this way, the myth opens up far more diverse and interesting possibilities of power and provides a model that gives cosmic validity to all sexual preferences.

Today we also have Creation myths as told to us by scientists investigating the origins of the universe. These do not necessarily conflict with our mythic retellings—in the opening story of *Truth or Dare*, I experimented with writing a mythic version of the scientists' truth as I have heard it told by physicist Brian Swimme, my colleague at the Institute for Culture and Creation Spirituality. The Creation myth given here could also be interpreted as a poetic retelling of the story of the original fireball exploding into galaxies and stars.

Pages 52–56 The Wheel of the Year myth. Myths in the Craft are not graven in stone. The traditional tales have much to teach us, and we should be wary of changing them. But as we work with them and reflect on them, we may understand them in new images and language that reflect our own changes.

Today, many people are working with the myth of the Wheel. Within my own extended community, several groups and individuals have been reworking the myth to reflect other models of the cycle of change besides heterosexual love. Not that there's anything wrong with desire between women and men, but it seems a rather limited blueprint for a community, and a universe, that also contains life-generating and renewing desire between women and women and men and men, as well as energy that is erotic in the broadest sense between human beings and trees, rocks, flowers, and mountains.

In part, the regeneration of the Craft as a living religion is linked to a broader attempt to create a culture of life. In that endeavor, in a time in which gender politics and sexual politics are hotly debated, we cannot just accept the assignment of certain roles or aspects of the cosmos as "male" or "female." In fact, almost any image of power we might care to name has been seen as female in some cultures and male in others.

At the same time, the Goddess, the Gods, are real—that is, meditate on the Horned God and something begins to happen that is very different from what happens when you meditate on the Great Mother. Each is a doorway or pipeline to power. And we cannot simply reconstruct them according to the political fashions of the moment. Part of the purpose of a living spirituality is to make us stretch our imagination and our perceptions beyond what we think is correct.

What we can do is to meditate deeply on the myth, to listen to our intuition and our emotions and to what we can learn about the real events the myth represents. What does happen as the year progresses from winter to summer and back again? What changes, within us and around us?

Myth is not created merely to furnish material for psychologists to ponder. Myth is the telling of the collective story about what really happens in the spiritual counterpart of the physical world. When we enter into a myth, through ritual, then similar processes unfold in us. Our link with the processes of the universe and our connection to the community are strengthened.

So here is my own meditation on the Wheel of the Year as a journey from what is potential through promise and desire to realization, and from the realization that is consumed in its culmination through descent and dissolution to renewal.

THE WHEEL OF THE YEAR

Birth, growth, death, rebirth: the turning of the Wheel is a circle as the year is a circular journey we make around the sun.

Begin in the dark of the year, when there comes a crack in time, a moment when the veil is thin and those who have gone before us and those who will come after us are not separate from us. In that fertile moment, when present, past, and future meet, the Year Child is conceived. What is conceived is All Possibility, for the Child is as yet unformed.

We say the night sky is the Womb of the Goddess, because it is dark like the womb and encloses us, and within it the billion living stars are points of light, like the souls of the dead swimming in the dark cauldron womb toward rebirth. We say that on the Winter Solstice, the Great Mother gives birth to the Sun. But what is really born? Not the physical sun, that blazing ball of gas. It is Spirit Sun that is born out of Spirit Night. It is the Child of Promise who awakens within us, reminding us that we can be more than we are. And as the year waxes, the unformed Child begins to take on personality, to grow into the form and face that this year shows, to ask from us the promise of what this year demands.

What is potential takes root, sends up shoots, and puts forth leaves. The spirit of the Sun enters into the seeds of spring. Call the Seed Daughter of the Sun, for she will grow to ripen, swell, and give birth to herself. Call the Seed Son of the Sun, for he will rise and spill himself out and fall again. Or call the Seed the Child of Balance, for in it meet all opposites. Darkness and light, fire and water, earth and air, day and night are necessary for its growth.

Where there is balance, there are both difference and sameness, and out of difference and sameness desire is born. Desire rises straight as the shaft of the Maypole, and desire twines, dances, in a rainbow of colors like hanging ribbons, and desire flickers and gives off heat that rises and falls like the cauldron flames. And when we give ourselves to the rising tides of life, they carry us on the crest of the wave—the Child matures; the Potential is realized; the Seed sprouts its trunk and branches and gives forth fruit, which must fall.

The Wheel turns. We say that the Summer Solstice is the Give-Away time of the Sun. Call Sun our Mother, for she feeds us from her own body. Call Sun the God Who Gives Himself Away, for he consumes himself to generate heat and light. Call the Sun Time.

What rises must fall to spill its seed. What ripens must drop to earth and decay. So the Sun becomes the Journeyer, the One Who Descends, the One Who Knows the Other Side and so brings us to a new balance in the time of harvest, when to live we must become the reaper of life. Call the harvest Daughter of the Sun, for each ripe fruit and grain is a new womb. Call the harvest Son of the Sun, for the seed that spills from the shaft.

Go down, as the seed goes down to ground. Enter the Underworld, the Dreamtime, the spirit world. Call the spirit of the Sun your Ship and set sail over oceans that are immune to sunlight and moonlight, absolved from time. In the distance something shines. It is a point of light; it is a single island where present, past, and future meet.

Carry with you the cargo of the past until you reach the hinge of the spiral where death and life are one, where what has been consumed can be renewed, and All Possibility is quickened to new life by what has been. The cycle ends and begins again, and the Wheel of the Year turns, on and on.

Page 54 ". . . Robert Graves . . ." I wouldn't say any longer that Graves has been the greatest force for the revival of interest in the Goddess. That honor would have to go to the feminist movement as a whole, which has led many women and men to seek new dimensions of their spirituality. Graves was one of the earliest and most influential authors to provide information on the early Goddesses, the one recommended to me when I began studying the Craft twenty years ago. The last ten years have fortunately seen a flourishing of scholarship and writings about the Goddess and feminist spirituality.

Notes on Chapter Three

Page 59 Coven structure. Today, many groups that are starting out form *circles* rather than covens. In fact, a *circle*, a looser-knit group of people who practice ritual together, is the only way a new coven can really begin. The coven bond is powerful and karmic, not to be entered into lightly or hastily. We often need to work in a circle with new people for a long time, at the very least for a year and a day, before we know whether or not that bond is appropriate.

By "karmic" I mean several things—that the connection established has repercussions that go beyond the immediate circumstances, that it remains on some level even when personal relationships deteriorate, that coven relationships tend to bring up for us those aspects of ourselves that we need most to transform. This means that covens are not always havens of peace and support. They generate conflict and confrontation, as do any truly intimate relations. In covens as in families, we tend to play out different roles and manifest each other's fears. Over the years, as the work of the coven deepens and intensifies, people may reach thresholds of change at different rates. Some groups, like some relationships, seem to have an innate life span, carrying members through until the group as a whole reaches the limits of its ability to grow together. Others endure for years and lifetimes.

Besides covens and circles, other sorts of groups may develop. For example, in San Francisco I work with a group called Reclaiming, a collective of women and men from several covens (and a few solitary Witches), which began when several of us from my women's coven started teaching together. Today, Reclaiming offers classes in Goddess religion, public rituals, workshops, and summer intensives and publishes a quarterly magazine. (See Resources.) It also serves as the core of a looser network or community of people involved in earth-based spirituality and work for political and social change.

In other parts of the country similar groups organize festivals, run training programs, put out newsletters, and do Pagan networking or similar projects. As the Pagan community grows, we need more and more of these working groups to develop the resources and services that can sustain our movement.

Witches also have legally incorporated as recognized churches. Probably the most extensive such group is the Covenant of the Goddess, a league of covens from many different Wiccan traditions, with local councils in many areas of this country, Canada, and England. More recently, among the Unitarian churches a Covenant of Unitarian Universalist Pagans has been formed, which serves as a forum for interested people to meet and explore Pagan ritual within the Unitarian church. (See Resources.)

Page 60 ". . . few all-male covens . . ." Today, more men seem to be interested in men's covens, ritual circles, or similar groups stemming from other traditions such as Native American. Such groups can be a source of support and of exploration of the particular energy men can generate together. They also give the men somewhere to go while the women are at their women's groups.

In the loose community around Reclaiming, individual covens, whether for women, for men, or mixed, often meet for full moons or for regular weekly or bimonthly meetings. On the Sabbats, the eight major holidays, we generally have larger gatherings in which many covens come together and celebrate. This rhythm allows intense and intimate work in our small circles and a sense of festivity and general celebration for the seasonal holidays.

Pages 63–65 Compost and Honeysuckle. While the original members of Compost went separate ways in the early eighties, the coven itself continued (and still does) under Valerie's leadership. Recently, most of the founders got together for a thirteenth anniversary reunion. Even though some of us had been out of contact for years, as soon as we cast the circle we immediately felt the strong power we remembered, as if the *raith* form of our collective power had never dissolved but remained waiting for us until we were ready to step back in. We were a coven still. Several of us remain close friends or have been able to reestablish connections.

Honeysuckle, after several name changes and transformations, also dissolved in the mideighties when members' lives took them into new directions and faraway places. In retrospect, when we began in Honeysuckle, all of us were in places of transition in our lives, struggling to establish ourselves in the world. We were a coven of Maidens, supporting each other in finding our power and learning to put it out into the world. In doing so, we gave birth to Reclaiming and to individual work directions. Now, all of us are in the Mother phase of life—the time of using, sharing, and teaching our skills, of nurturing creative projects and healing endeavors, and, in at least two cases, gestating children. We still maintain connection and involvement in each other's lives.

My current coven, the Wind Hags, grew out of a Reclaiming class taught by members of Honeysuckle. We have, at various times, worked together, taught together, organized public rituals and political actions, gone to jail together or supported each other in actions; celebrated births, marriages, and rites of passage; and shared the mourning of deaths and the acknowledgment of growth and achievements. Two of us live together as part of a larger collective. (At one time four of us lived together. We hated it. We nearly grew to hate each other. When we had sense enough to move out, we could renew our friendship at a much deeper level. And the moral here is that not all relationships are appropriate with everybody at all times.)

Page 65 Finding a coven. The suggestions here are all good. In addition, many people today offer classes, workshops, and public programs from which circles may form. Use the Resources at the back of the book (but *don't* write to me or to Reclaiming for coven contacts, please, because we don't have the resources to handle national networking. Write to Circle, or try CUUPS. And please don't call my ex-husband—we're divorced now, and while he's extremely good-natured, he'll simply tell you to write to me care of Harper & Row).

Pages 68–69 Tree of Life and grounding exercises. The Tree of Life is still the most basic magical discipline I practice, the exercise I use to begin every ritual. Much can be added to the simple framework given here. For example, once I have extended my "branches," I usually draw in sky energy, from the sun or from the moon or starlight during the dark of the moon. The branches themselves are a symbolic way of seeing the body's aura, or energy field. They can be made thicker to create a shield or filter when we need protection, or thinned out and extended further when we feel isolated. I encourage people to play with this exercise, experiment, and improvise.

The term *grounding* means to create an energy connection with the earth. It is used to describe what we do at the beginning of a ritual with the Tree of Life exercise or something similar—to link our own energy field to that of the earth, to connect the group together, and to establish a flow of power running through us, up from the earth, down from the sky, and back again.

Grounding is also used to describe what we do after we have raised power in a ritual, giving it back to the earth, letting it flow down through our bodies, and releasing it, often by placing the palms of our hands on the ground or by lying down.

Page 70 Group conflict. Volumes could be written about group conflict, and I have written more about it in both *Dreaming the Dark* and *Truth or Dare*. But no book can tell you how to handle conflict when it arises. Some guidelines I find helpful are:

- to look at conflict not as a failure but as a challenge; to find new ways to grow and communicate
- to remember that speaking the truth, getting the dirt out, and making the invisible visible are the only ways to really resolve conflict
- to stop when I find myself feeling self-righteous and blaming and ask, "What is my part here?"
- to remember that we cannot fix each other, change each other, or make everything all right all the time; to let go
- to accept people's feelings as valid, even when we can't accept their actions, behavior, or words
- to name power relations openly and honestly

Although this discussion refers to the coven leader as *she*, leaders of circles and covens can also be men, and leadership itself may (and should) shift between many members of a circle. When I wrote this section, my covens were working on the model of one person's having primary responsibility as leader. Today, we work collectively: The "leader" may change every few moments in the course of a ritual.

Page 70 ". . . the group may need to cast lots . . ." We often use divination, with Tarot cards or some other form of oracle, to help us make decisions that we cannot otherwise seem to make. This technique is especially useful when we don't have adequate information for decision making—for example, trying to plan for an outdoor ritual when we don't know what the weather will be like.

My coven sister Rose May Dance says that sometimes divination simply clarifies what you really want. You say, "We'll flip a coin—heads, Joan stays; tails, Jane stays." The coin comes up tails, and suddenly you realize that you actually want to work with Joan, not Jane. That's part of the process, and it's better to acknowledge it openly and continue struggling toward a decision than to accept a judgment with which you feel uncomfortable.

I would add the caution, however, that if you ask an oracle a question, if you read the cards or consult the runes or the *I Ching*, and you get a clear answer, you do well to listen to it. If you already have a solution secretly in mind, state it openly rather than waiting for the Goddess to magically confirm it.

Page 77 Taking on new members. When a circle develops into a close-knit coven, it often needs to close its membership so that those in the group can develop a stronger sense of intimacy. At their largest, covens are necessarily small. Today, many more people are interested in practicing the Craft than existing covens can accommodate. We teach regular classes and encourage students to form their own circles.

Pages 78–79 Daily discipline. Okay, now comes the moment for honest confession— have I maintained this discipline myself over the last decade? Well—yes and no.

As far as exercise goes, I've had good years and bad years. Right now, in a good year, I'm more than ever convinced of its importance in staying grounded, healthy, and able to move energy.

At times I've felt a need for regular meditation or visualization practice. At other times these needs are served by the demands of writing and teaching ritual. Years of magical practice have definitely improved my concentration as a writer.

I regret to say that I have not kept a consistent Book of Shadows and recorded all the rituals I've done and exercises, meditations, trances, and so on that I've participated in. If I had, it would be an invaluable document of the development of a changing tradition. So, in this case, do as I say, not as I do.

Notes on Chapter Four

Pages 80–82 Description of Circle Casting. These pages describe a very formal ceremony for casting the circle, or creating the sacred space. The circle can also be created informally. Here are a few suggestions:

- Think of your favorite color. Imagine it as a ribbon of light enclosing the circle. Imagine all the colors we are each visualizing twining together into a rainbow braid.
- Think of a time you have felt safe and a place that feels safe to you. Pick a color or a sound or an image that reminds you of that place and imagine it encircling us.
- Walk around the circle and draw it with a wand, or with salt, or by sprinkling salt water.
- Make up your own method.

We sometimes also use what we call "short-form" circle casting—an invocation I learned from Victor Anderson:

> By the earth that is Her body
> And by the air that is Her breath
> And by the fire of Her bright spirit
> And by the living waters of her womb,
> The circle is cast.

(As Victor originally taught it to me, it went: "By the waters of Her living womb." Unfortunately, the warped minds of Reclaiming continually changed this to "By the waters of Her living room." A bad joke is funny once, but repeated too many times it becomes merely distracting, so I changed the invocation.)

Or we might call the elements simply by chanting and/or dancing. Some of the chants we use can be found on the Reclaiming tapes—see Resources.

Page 84 Group salt-water purification. Of course, the most powerful salt-water purification is a plunge in the ocean. If you don't live near the ocean, a running stream, clear pool, lake, bay, or pond will substitute. (If necessary, sprinkle in a few grains of salt.) We plunge together at sunset on the eve of the Winter Solstice (in our climate, cold enough to be purifying without being fatal). We also sometimes plunge at other Sabbats and before initiations, and individuals may plunge whenever they need to be cleansed spiritually. Go to the body of water, take time to meditate on what you are releasing or cleansing, take off your clothes, and jump in. Sing appropriate chants and immerse yourself as many times as you need to to feel complete. When you emerge, thank the ocean (pond, lake, etc.) and bless yourself. Have warm clothes ready and perhaps a warm fire.

Page 85 Invocations. The ending of these invocations was originally

> By the power of the Mother of all Life,
> And her lover the Horned God,
> So mote it be.

Today, I prefer the less anthropomorphic and heterosexist terms "life, death, and rebirth."

Page 86 "The concept of the quartered circle . . ." This concept is common to Native American, African, East Indian, Tibetan, and many other spiritual systems, as are the four elements of air, fire, water, and earth. Of course, we know that these are not elements in the same sense as are hydrogen, helium, and carbon, but they are the basic necessities for sustaining life. Without air to breathe, without the radiant energy of the sun and water to drink, without earth to produce food and sustenance, we could not live. In times like the present, when the air, the waters, and the earth are under assault and the element of fire has given us destructive weapons of unimaginable power, we need to remember what truly sustains our lives.

Different systems do not necessarily agree on which element goes with which direction, even among differing traditions of the Craft. Correspondences differ because they originate from the qualities of differing places. In western Scotland the west wind will be moist and bring rain, and the quality of the West will be identified with water. On the Great Plains the west wind may be dry, and when we look to the West, the Rocky Mountains will loom up, mysterious and wild. We might feel the West as earth.

In this book I present the system of correspondences I learned and still work with, as they fit very well the climate on the West Coast of California, where I live. Familiarity with them can give you the sense of how an intact system works. But you might want to adapt them to the conditions of the land in your own area or to use a set of correspondences that originated where you live.

Pages 87–90 Meditation on the elements. The best way to meditate on any of the elements is to contact them in reality. Jump in the ocean, sit by a stream, lie down on the grass or freshly turned earth, touch a tree, bask in the sunlight, stare into a fire, let the wind whip through your hair. While meditating, consider what we might do to preserve the life of the earth, the air, the waters, and the biosphere.

Then do it.

Page 88 *Athame* or sword meditation. Many people dislike the imagery of the sword, seeing it as warlike and violent. Personally, I don't own one, and we rarely use one in our circles.

To me the symbolism of the *athame* or knife is very different from that of the sword. The sword is necessarily a weapon. Its use may have come into the Craft at a time when people felt we needed weapons to protect ourselves, or it may have been adopted through exposure to Freemasonry or ceremonial magic.

A knife, however, an edged blade, is one of the oldest and most necessary tools of culture, going all the way back to the stone axes of the Paleolithic. The knife may be a bread knife, a digging trowel, a grafting knife, a knife that prepares skins and cuts cloth and lances wounds, a cooking knife, a penknife or pencil sharpener, a pruning knife, or a midwife's knife that cuts the umbilical cord.

Beware of giving a knife as a gift, even a ritual knife. A folk saying is that giving someone a knife will cut the friendship. If you wish to give someone an *athame*, have your friend pay you for it, with a symbolic penny, to remove the bad luck.

Page 91 The tree alphabet. You might want to research trees of your local area to find those that would best correspond to the symbolic meanings of these natives of the British Isles. Earth religions are rooted in specific places on the earth, and to take root here they must reflect the real powers of the land, the plants, the trees, and the particular climatic manifestation of the cycles of birth, growth, death and decay, and regeneration.

Page 91 Sex and polarity. See my discussion of this issue in the notes to Chapter Two. Sex and polarity, of course, arise in many different ways among those who are like us and unlike us in many ways—gender being only one of them. Perhaps instead of "polarity" I might today say that "the manifestation of the driving life force of the universe" is *desire*, attraction, the pull toward pleasure and connection and union.

Page 95 Additional tools. I'm surprised to realize that in this discussion I didn't even mention the tool that now is more useful and central to my work than any of those described above. That is, of course, the drum.

The drum brings together the energy of a group and is especially important for unifying a large group. Rhythm alters consciousness. A drumbeat can induce a trance or arouse us to dancing frenzy. It helps a circle get loose and wild and provides the pulse of the ritual. The drum lets us hear the heartbeat of the earth.

The drum I use is a Middle Eastern hourglass-shaped drum called a *doumbec*. It is played with both hands, produces a variety of tones, and with a strap attached can easily be carried in ritual. It is a very ancient form of drum, originally made of clay, today often made of metal—more practical for traveling Witches. It is the drum Miriam played on the shores of the Red Sea and was also, most probably, played by the ancient Priestesses of the Goddess.

Besides the *doumbec*, I use the tar, a round hand drum that may be the most ancient form of sacred drum. I especially like its softer, hypnotic tones for trance.

After playing intuitively for four or five years, I have finally found a teacher who has introduced me to the rich world of Middle Eastern rhythm and music. For information on her books and tapes, see Resources.

Many people also like round, flat stick drums, which lend themselves well to steady beats.

The art of drumming for ritual is primarily the art of listening. Learn to listen to the rhythm of the chants and the energy of the circle. Follow the energy; don't try to control it or lead it. Begin by learning to keep a simple, steady beat in time to the chants. Later, when your sense of rhythm becomes solid and unshakable, more complex patterns will suggest themselves.

It's helpful to have more than one person in a circle who can drum. Two or more drummers can play against each other and can generate more excitement. And one drummer alone can control the energy of the group to an unfair extent. Share the power. And don't forget to allow quiet times in the ritual.

Notes on Chapter Five

THE GODDESS—HOW I SEE HER TODAY

The core thealogy of Goddess religion centers around the cycle of birth, growth, death, decay, and regeneration revealed in every aspect of a dynamic, conscious universe. The Goddess is the living body of a living cosmos, the awareness that infuses matter and the energy that produces change. She is life eternally attempting to maintain itself, reproduce itself, diversify, evolve, and breed more life; a force far more implacable than death, although death itself is an aspect of life.

When I'm in an anthropomorphic mood, I like to think the Goddess is eternally trying to amuse herself by creating moments of beauty, pleasure, humor, and drama. To aid her in this project she evolved human beings, perhaps her most complex and weird children, at least on this planet. Like all children, we do things she would never have thought of and might not necessarily approve of. We are endowed with freedom, which means the capacity to make mistakes, even on a global scale. We are ourselves aspects of the Goddess, cocreators, and therefore responsible for cleaning up the messes we've made and tending our part of the whole.

So far I have been speaking of *the Goddess* as the whole, the underlying unity of which all things are aspects. But there are also *Goddesses*, specific ways to imagine and experience that whole, different roads to the center. They are each real, in the sense that they are powerful forces and distinct paths. Start to work with one, and changes will happen to you in ways that are different than what happens if you choose another. Some of those aspects may also be male images, Gods.

The Goddess, the whole, of course has no genitalia (or is all genitalia). But I prefer using a female-gendered word for a number of reasons. One is simply that, at this time in history, I think we still subconsciously perceive a word of neutral gender as male. *Goddess* breaks our expectations and reminds us that we are talking about something different from the patriarchal Godfather.

The female image also reminds us that what we call sacred is immanent in the world, embodied (and hence perceivable through the body, through the senses, through real contact with real things, and through metaphors that are body based). What we value is life brought into the world, nurtured, sustained, replicated, and regenerated. Matter itself is sacred.

So *the Goddess* reminds us that our spirituality does not take us out of the world but brings us fully into it, and our goal is to live in it, preserve it, protect it, fight against its destruction, enjoy it, transform it, get our hands dirty, and dig our toes into the mud.

Pages 102–3 The Charge of the Goddess. When *The Spiral Dance* was written, I did not know where the Charge originated. Since then I have learned that it was written by Doreen Valiente, author of many books on the Craft and a colleague of Gerald Gardner. In the summer of 1987, I had the pleasure, with my friend Lauren, of visiting her in her home in England. Like many Witches, she lives surrounded by shelves, stacks, and piles of books. She served us tea and sandwiches and showed us, among other treasures, the original drafts of the Charge of the Goddess. She wrote a verse version and a prose version. She liked the verse—her coven liked the prose and sent her back to rework it into its present form. I took the liberty of modernizing the language, as the archaic "thou" forms in which she wrote it sound too self-conscious to the American ear.

When I first met Witches in the late 1960s, they read us the Charge. I felt that I was hearing a clear expression of what I had always intuitively believed, and from that moment felt committed to the Craft as my spiritual direction. The Charge is still my favorite Craft liturgy.

Page 111 "For a man, the Goddess . . . is his own, hidden, female self . . ." I no longer believe we each have a female self or a male self. Instead, I would say that we each have a complex and multifaceted self that embraces the possibilities inherent in many different forms, including that of gender. We have animal selves and spirit selves and, for all I know, vegetable and mineral selves. Why should our imagination be limited by the shape of our genitalia? If a man invokes the Goddess, something powerful will happen for him.

Notes on Chapter Six
HOW I SEE THE GOD TODAY

The God is a much more problematic figure than the Goddess. Male images of the sacred have been severely distorted by patriarchal culture. The nurturing qualities of maleness are subsumed by the authoritarian father God. Wildness, exuberance, erotic and animal energy have been twisted into images of the Devil and identified with evil. Patriarchal culture offers men many avenues to power-over and few models of strength based on power-from-within.

Reclaiming and reenvisioning the ways power-from-within might reveal itself to us in male forms is an important task as we try to reshape culture. But not everyone is called to that task. For some the Goddess is enough, complete within herself. For others male power has been too deeply tainted by the culture of domination.

When talking about the Goddess and the God, we tend to view them as cosmic role models. We look to them to show us how to be as women and as men, because our traditional cultural roles are unworkable and uncomfortable and the task of developing new ones is awesome. But in indigenous cultures, people knew how they were expected to behave and what roles they were expected to play. (How satisfied they were by them, we can only speculate.) They weren't necessarily looking to their God/desses as behavioral models. On the contrary, sacred beings were often seen as delineating the forces that played beyond the boundaries of acceptable human behavior.

So, in the Sumerian myth, when Ereshkigal, Queen of Death, flays the skin of her own sister/Goddess Inanna, who has challenged her power, she is not teaching us how to be a good sister, or even how to be female; she is teaching us something about how death operates in the world. When Raven, Trickster/Creator of the Native Americans of the Pacific Northwest, behaves with greed and gluttony, he is not telling men of the tribe how they are supposed to act but that the wild force in nature that breaks the patterns is in itself a creative force. In such societies, the task of human beings is not to emulate the God/desses, but to hold the patterns firm, to maintain the order through which the mysteries can move.

So the God is not just about maleness, although he can open up for us expanded visions of what men can be. Nor is the Goddess just about femaleness, although she can provide us with imagery empowering to women. The heart of the mysteries of our tradition is that each Goddess, each God, is another way to know and experience that cycle of birth, growth, death, and rebirth. And any quality or aspect assigned to the God or the Goddess does not take that quality away from the other one. If the God is seen as nurturing, it doesn't diminish the Goddess's nurturing power but expands our vision of what nurturing can be. If the Goddess is strong, the God does not have to be weak in response; rather, our understanding of strength is augmented.

Often the God is seen as the one who goes through the cycle of rebirth, as seed that grows, is cut, buried, and grows again, as animal that is hunted so that other life can go on. The God can be praised as the Good Provider and the one who gives abundance. And often the God is the Trickster, the Raven, the Fool of the Tarot, Elegba of the Yoruba who opens the gate, Br'er Rabbit, Coyote of the Southwest whose tricks bring many gifts to the people.

The Trickster represents the quality of randomness and chance in the universe, without which there could be no freedom. In the Craft the Goddess is not omnipotent. The cosmos is interesting rather than perfect, and everything is not part of some greater plan, nor is all necessarily under control. Understanding this keeps us humble, able to admit that we cannot know or control or define everything.

The Trickster also represents that aspect of creation that is always a gamble. Consider this question: Why are there two sexes? What function does this arrangement serve? So that the Goddess can reshuffle the genetic deck for each new birth, increasing the variety and diversity of life. The price is that when we conceive and give birth, we don't know exactly what we'll get. If we all reproduced by cell division or parthenogenesis, we would all (except for the mutants among us) remain exactly like our mothers. How dull—and dangerous, for our ability to respond in diverse ways to changes in our environment would be severely restricted, compromising our survival as a species.

What holds true for physical conception and birth is also true for other creative endeavors. Any creative work that is truly alive is influenced by a thousand chance factors in its generation. These notes are shaped by conversations I had yesterday, the papers my students decided to write this quarter, the movie we rented for the VCR. Thus they remain alive for me—and also, I hope, for you. The God as Trickster teaches us this truth.

The God is also the one who gives himself away, the sacrifice. He is food. We live in bodies that must constantly take in parts of the world around us, transform them, shit them back out. We cannot exist separate from other life, which must give itself away to sustain us.

The Craft does not glorify sacrifice, nor does the Goddess demand it, except in that each of us must ultimately die and give back our lives. What the God is teaching us, over and over again, is that letting go brings rebirth, regeneration, renewal in some new form. The God is that force within us that chooses to surrender itself to the cycle, to ride the Wheel. So he becomes also the nurturer, the good provider, meat, grain, fruit to feed our continuing life.

Page 121 "A common practice . . ." Actually, these accounts seem to indicate the practice of trance possession by the Goddesses and Gods, similar to the way initiates of the Yoruba-based Afro-Caribbean traditions are "ridden" by the *orishas*. Power is not just dramatized, but manifested.

Page 121 "In the women's movement, Dianic/separatist Witchcraft has become the fashion . . ." This statement was true at the time, but today the feminist movement has birthed a broad variety of approaches to Wicca and other spiritual traditions. Some are for women only; some include men or encourage men to form their own circles.

As far as worshipping the God goes, today I would say that images of the God can open up sources of power to women as well as men, but there is no reason why any woman should feel obligated to tap those particular sources unless she is moved to do so.

Pages 121–22 "The Goddess is the Encircler . . ." This paragraph tells a story that works, but it can also be told differently. For the Goddess also has aspects in which she is the hero/hera of her own journey. She is Inanna who descends to the underworld and Kore who goes down to hell and arises again to bring us a single shaft of grain. She is not just ground but protagonist of her own story.

And the God himself has aspects in which he is earth, he is sky or moon to her flaming sun. The story we tell is one of birth, growth, death, and regeneration, but it can be told in an infinite number of ways, and each will reveal some new facet of truth, which we may need at different times.

Page 122 "In our culture . . ." This discussion of men, masculinity, and power-over is extended in *Truth or Dare: Encounters with Power, Authority and Mystery*.

Page 123 "He has no father; He is his own father . . ." In this discussion of the God, I was deliberately trying to break the association of God and Father, which is so central to patriarchy and in which the Father inevitably becomes the authoritarian father. I felt that until women were fully empowered, spiritually, economically, and politically, we could not truly reenvision the fatherhood of God outside of a context of power-over. I still feel that way.

I have, however, had glimpses of what that vision might be. I remember one Summer Solstice at the beach, watching Robin, a man in the Reclaiming community, invoke the God while wearing his infant daughter in a pack on his chest. Because I know the time and care he gives, not just to his own daughter but to his partner's older children, I felt a power come through that I could name as *fathering,* and trust.

My housemate Brook, himself a caring and devoted new father, feels that reclaiming the God as father (distinct from God the Father) is vitally important. He suggests looking at the nurturing roles men can play. Perhaps we could begin by invoking He Who Changes the Dirty Diapers, or He Who Makes Up Silly Games, or He Who Teaches Through Play.

I don't have a clear answer to offer here, but I do think this discussion is an important one for circles and families to consider. As I said earlier, the God/desses are not just role models. On the contrary, in some ways we ourselves are role models for the God/desses—in that as we live in certain ways we become capable of evoking and bringing into being new powers.

When power relations of domination are no longer the norm in society, and when men assume truly equal shares of all aspects of child-rearing, perhaps we will be able to fully reclaim the nurturing father aspects of the God. Until then, let us hope some men will begin this process by the way they live their lives.

Page 123 ". . . love includes sexuality, which is also wild and untamed as well as gentle and tender." One of the great disservices a culture of domination has done to all of us is to confuse the erotic with domination and violence. The God is wild, but his is the wildness of connection, not of domination. Wildness is not the same as violence. Gentleness and tenderness do not translate into wimpiness. When men—or women, for that matter—begin to unleash what is untamed in us, we need to remember that the first images and impulses we encounter will often be the stereotyped paths of power we have learned in a culture of domination. To become truly wild, we must not be sidetracked by the dramas of power-over, the seduction of addictions, or the thrill of control. We must go deeper.

Men in patriarchal cultures are taught to worship the erect phallus, firm and hard. But an eternally hard penis would be awkward to live with, uncomfortable, and unsatisfying. A real, living penis is soft more often than it is hard. The magic quality of the penis is that it moves from soft to hard and back again, that it embodies the cycle of birth, growth, death, and rebirth as it rises, swells, spurts, and falls, hopefully to rise again. That is why the Gods so often are dying and reviving Gods.

To worship the frozen phallus of patriarchy cuts us off from the possibility of knowing the real power inherent in maleness. It is to glorify a plaster cast instead of the real thing. Real male power is rooted in the cycle of birth, death, and rebirth, as manifested in the male body. To find it, we must keep moving around the full circle.

Page 124 "For women raised in our culture . . ." This discussion of how women might work with the God was, of course, based on my own experiences at the time. At first images of the God did allow me to own and integrate qualities that the culture has defined as male—my own aggression, physical power, and ability to pursue my own goals. However, as these qualities became mine, I ceased to identify them as male. They became simply qualities, which I as a woman had as much access to as any man. The God can be seen as the creation-that-is-not-oneself, but a daughter is as separate, and possibly different, as a son.

So today I would say that, for a woman, the God is whatever begins to happen when you invoke him, should you care to do so.

Page 125 ". . . in a culture of hunters the hunt meant *life* . . ." A culture of hunters was actually mostly a culture of gatherers. In most such cultures the vegetable food gathered by women provides the main, sustaining diet. Meat, however, often has a symbolic as well as nutritional value and was certainly seen as an important source of life.

Pages 125–26 "The Sun Child is born . . ." For an alternative version of the myth of the Wheel of the Year, see the notes on Chapter Two and Chapter Twelve.

Page 127 "A man must also know . . . his own, inner, female self . . ." Again, I no longer find useful the Jungian concept of inner female and male counterpart selves. Today I might rephrase this to say: "A man must know within himself the human possibility to generate those qualities of caring and nurturing that a patriarchal society has assigned to women, so that he can nurture and care for himself and others and not only demand nurturing from others."

Page 131 "Invocation to the Ground of Being." My ex-husband and I wrote this for our wedding in 1977, as an attempt to synthesize my Wiccan tradition with his yoga practice and at the same time not offend my Jewish or his German Lutheran relatives. If you're ever in a similar dilemma, feel free to adapt it.

Notes on Chapter Seven

I'm surprised, rereading this chapter, that I can find almost nothing to change or disagree with. Of course, I could add much material, but the point of this chapter is that once you understand the basics of magical practice, you can create your own spells, charms, and rituals. If you want more examples, see *Truth or Dare* for many spells and rituals of personal and political transformation.

In the Indrinking Spell, I did change my original suggestion of wine to juice in keeping with my decision not to suggest ritual use of substances that might perpetuate addictions. But you are, of course, free to change it back to wine should that feel right for you.

The other major change I have made here, and in the Tables of Correspondences in the back of the book, is a change in terms. Earlier, I followed Z. Budapest's feminization of High John the Conqueror root and St. John's Wort into High Joan the Conqueress and St. Joan's wort—honoring Joan of Arc, widely believed by Witches to have been a real Witch, a priestess of the Goddess. "John the Conqueror" sounded militaristic and masculinist.

When I made the change, however, I was shamefully ignorant of African-American culture and the real lore surrounding John the Conqueror. For John the Conqueror was the bringer of hope and laughter to those who suffered under the lash of slavery. In Zora Neale Hurston's beautiful essay *The Sanctified Church* she describes his power as follows:

"High John de Conqueror came to be a man, and a mighty man at that. But he was not a natural man in the beginning. First off, he was a whisper, a will to hope, a wish to find something worthy of laughter and song. Then the whisper put on flesh. . . . The sign of this man was a laugh, and his singing-symbol was a drum-beat. No parading drum-shout like soldiers out for show. . . . It was an inside thing to live by. It was sure to be heard when and where the work was the hardest, and the lot the most cruel. It helped the slaves endure. . . . He walked on the winds and moved fast. Maybe he was in Texas when the lash fell on a slave in Alabama, but before the blood was dry on the back he was there. . . .

"The thousands upon thousands of humble people who still believe in him, that is, in the power of love and laughter to win by their subtle power, do John reverence by getting the root of the plant in which he has take up his secret dwelling, and 'dressing' it with perfume, and keeping it on their person, or in their houses in a secret place. It is there to help them overcome things they feel that they could not beat otherwise, and to bring them the laugh of the day. John will never forsake the weak and helpless, nor fail to bring hope to the hopeless."[1]

St. John became associated with the summer solstice, the time of year when the golden flowers of St. John's Wort open. But the main reason I've changed this term back is because for ten years, I've been receiving letters saying, "I tried to do the spells in your book, but I can't find St. Joan's Wort anywhere. Help!"

Page 139 "Emotion is a strobe light . . ." I might add a little word of caution to this paragraph. We need to fully feel and express our emotions without worrying that they are likely to cause harm to another. But intensely and obsessively brooding on one's anger or resentment is not a good thing to do. We do better to find a way to move the energy through us into some change we need to make, into protective energy or directed action.

Note
1. Zora Neale Hurston, *The Sanctified Church* (Berkeley: Turtle Island Foundation, 1984), pp. 69–79 (Turtle Island Foundation, 2845 Buena Vista Way, Berkeley, CA 94708).

Notes on Chapter Eight

Pages 156–58 Political rituals. Over the past decade I have done many more political rituals, some of which are described in *Dreaming the Dark* and *Truth or Dare*. Hallie Iglehart has also written about this ritual in her own book: *Womanspirit: A Guide to Women's Wisdom* (San Francisco: Harper & Row, 1983).

Page 159 The cone of power. This is one of the few places in this book where I have actually changed the text. Originally, I described the Priestess (or a leader) as "calling the drop": directing the coven to let go of the cone. It read as follows:

"The High Priestess (or whoever directs the cone) senses the movement of energy. She holds the visualized image, the object of the working, clearly in mind. When the power reaches its peak, she cries out, 'Now!'

"(This requires great sensitivity and practice. It can only be learned by experience—which of necessity implies many mistakes along the way. If the High Priestess is afraid of power, she will ground the cone too quickly. If she is indecisive, she will let it go on too long, so that its full force is dissipated. The best course is to relax into the power and not think about when to ground it. When the right time comes, a sensitive High Priestess will find herself calling the drop, out of intuition, not conscious decision.)"

The truth is, nobody ever really got it right, including myself. What we learned over the years is that the energy has a form and shape of its own. When a group works together collectively, everyone seems to intuitively follow the energy and to know when it has begun to fall.

In large groups, even when many people are new to ritual, a few people who know how to channel energy can shape the cone by visualizing a form for it. Even one strong person can sometimes do this. But shaping the cone is not the same as controlling it.

In large groups, when energy rises high, people will often scream, yell, and cheer at the peak of the cone, which dissipates the power instead of focusing it. That's not necessarily bad, but if you want to focus the energy, try holding a clear, steady tone yourself while clearly visualizing the cone and the symbol of your intention. Hold on when the screaming stops—and it may shift into a powerful moment that will surprise you. Or—you may end up singing all alone, hideously embarrassed. But those are the risks we take when we work magic.

The cone of power sets in motion energies and forces that begin to bring about our intentions. Today, I always work with a visualized or physical image of that intent, even something as simple as saying to a group, "When we raise energy, imagine it as a fountain of healing power we can draw on." A group that is raising power together should always be made aware of each person's intention and imagery. To use the power of a group for a private, unacknowledged end—even a positive one—is manipulative.

Notes on Chapter Nine

Pages 172–73 Facing the Shadow. By using the term *Shadow*, I do not mean to imply that "dark" is synonymous with "bad" or "dangerous." I have kept the term because of its imagery of what is unseen, the silhouette of what *is* us that is projected from us.

In *Truth or Dare* I explore further the question of what we encounter in the underworld. In that work, I describe the Self-Hater and name five aspects in which it often appears: the Conqueror, the Judge, the Orderer, the Censor, and the Master of Servants.

The Self-Hater is not exactly the same as the Shadow, although they are related. The Self-Hater is an entity we internalize from a culture based on power-over. It splits us down the middle, into Self and Shadow. Neither Talking Self nor Younger Self, it draws on the energy of both and often sets one against the other. We are possessed by it in its varying forms.

Let's look at them one at a time:

The Conqueror, whose core issue is safety, splits us into Conqueror and Enemy/Victim, tells us, "Don't trust!" and generates fear, paranoia, distortions of reality, and the need to annihilate enemies. The Conqueror seduces us by making us feel special, sometimes grandiose and self-righteous, sometimes especially weak and victimized.

The Judge, whose core issue is our sense of self-worth and value, splits us into Judge and Subject to be Judged. When possessed by the Judge, we live in a world of comparisons, competition, and punishment, constantly rate ourselves and others, feel jealousy and guilt. The Judge seduces us with the false promise that we can gain value if we obey, perform, produce.

The Orderer, whose core issue is control, splits us into Controller and Out-of-Control selves, tells us, "Don't feel," and generates anxiety, rigidity, and addictions. The Orderer seduces us with the belief that order can be imposed from without, that the answer to chaos is a more rigid order.

The Censor, whose core issue is isolation and connection, splits us into Silencer and Secret-to-be-kept, tells us, "Don't speak of it; don't see it; you're the only one who ever felt that." Possessed by the Censor, we feel shame, confusion, and blame, often for the victim, or we live in denial. The Censor deludes us with the belief that the pain we are in will go away if we don't name it or speak of it.

The Master of Servants, whose core issue is need, splits us into Master and Servant, tells us, "Others only exist to meet my needs," or, "I have no needs—I only exist to meet the needs of others." In the Master's grip, our sense of worth is both inflated and lost. We are seduced by the promise that we will be taken care of without having to take care of ourselves or admit our needs.

Antidotes to the toxic structures of power-over can be embedded in the actual structure of a circle. To counter the Conqueror, a group must provide real safety: clear boundaries, open lines of communication and power, open conflict, and solidarity in the face of outside dangers. To counter the Judge, we must create situations that are not judgmental, not built on lines of competition and punishment, but on rituals and decision-making processes that affirm our immanent value. To counter the Orderer, a group can remain open to mystery, remembering that spirituality is about wonder and unanswerable questions, not answers. To counter the Censor, the group can encourage members to tell their stories, share experiences, speak the unspeakable, and use decision-making processes such as consensus that encourage each person's voice. To counter the Master, we can do away with hierarchies, share group resources and rewards equitably, avoid overextending ourselves, and create sustainable ways to meet needs.

These principles can help us face what we encounter when we drop the veil between the worlds and can also help us keep our circles functioning in a healthy way generally.

Working in trance and working at the close levels of intimacy circles develop as they do trancework together often bring us into encounters with the Self-Hater. When conflict erupts in groups, we may find ourselves literally enacting each other's Shadows.

Conflicts, encounters, can further our growth or entrench us deeper in patterns of power-over. Each of us has a choice, when faced with conflict, and so does the group as a whole. No set of rules can tell us how best to come through conflicts that arise when we face our shadows. The suggestions in Chapter Three may be helpful, and some additional principles I like to remember follow:

- All groups eventually face conflict. It is not a sign of failure but of change and potential growth.
- Name the Shadow; name the conflict; speak the truth.
- Own your own Shadow; ask, "What is my part? What is my responsibility?"
- Resist the temptation to try to make someone else own *their* Shadow or take the responsibility you think *they* should take. Let them be where they are—even if they are stuck. (You might choose, however, not to work with this person for a while, or permanently. It's always sad when a group finds members can no longer work together, but it is not necessarily tragic. Group members may simply be growing in different ways.)
- Don't try to fix the conflict, or others. Instead, take responsibility for your own part. If you truly have no part in perpetuating it, then let go. If you didn't create it, you can't fix it.
- If you've made mistakes, if you've hurt someone, admit it. Make appropriate amends. Feel the pain, the hurt, the shame, the guilt, go through it, and grow from it. This is hard at the time but feels better in the long run than avoiding the pain by blaming someone else, defending yourself, or identifying with some aspect of the Self-Hater.

There is no space here to elaborate further on this subject, which could well fill volumes. Besides the material in *Truth or Dare*, other helpful approaches can be found in material from the Twelve-Step Programs.

Page 173 "Valerie . . . is now Priestess of Compost." When I wrote this, we were still using the term "High Priestess" and still designating one person as official leader of a coven, although we had recognized the need to pass that role around. Now the covens I am in work by consensus, and no one has that formal role.

Long after most of the original members of Compost went our separate ways, Valerie continued as leader, training many new people over the years and passing the wand many times. Like a boomerang, however, it tends to revert back to her.

Page 174 Drugs and magic. If anything, I feel even more strongly about this issue now than I did ten years ago. We need to confront the widespread addictive patterns in our culture and change them before we can safely use consciousness-altering substances in magic. And we need circles that are safe places for those who are in recovery from addictions and codependence.

Page 176 Rhythm, drums, and trance. As I mentioned in the notes to Chapter Four, the drum is the one tool that is presently most important to me in ritual. A sustained drumbeat does, indeed, induce trance and substitutes for some of the more elaborate inductions given later in this chapter. The drum opens up the possibility of more fluid combinations of imagery, chanting, movement, and sound that open up deepened states of consciousness.

The rhythm I use (because it seems to come naturally to me) is a syncopated eight-beat rhythm as a base, which works with most of our chants, as they tend to have either four- or eight-beat rhythms. Other cultures use different styles of drumming. Native American rhythms tend to be very steady and nonsyncopated. African rhythms for rituals often have six beats, creating a rocking, hypnotic feel. Experiment to find what works for you.

Drumming and talking at the same time take some practice, but the tasks can also be divided—some can drum while others guide imagery or sing chants.

Page 176 Cautions about cautions. I've actually given up using these cautions, because what they seem to do is implant in us the idea that we're about to do something dangerous. Younger Self is perverse and rebellious, and often telling it something immediately produces the opposite reaction. Also, no matter how often we tell ourselves we will remember everything, some of us do, and some don't. In ten years of guiding thousands of people through trance, I've never had anyone not come out—although I've had a few fall asleep and one or two fake it. Sometimes people don't come fully out and remain somewhat sleepy or spacey. In that case, grounding, eating, or physical exertion helps put the person fully back in her or his body.

Page 177 Trance induction. Over the years I've also learned that people do not need to lie down in trance. Many people, especially those who tend to experience kinesthetically more than visually, find it helpful to stand up, to move through the journey, walking or dancing. When people are up and moving, they feel more in control and less vulnerable than when they are lying down. People can also sing, make sounds, and even talk in trance. In fact, I don't always use a formal induction but let the trance evolve as an enacted story that flows out of the ritual.

However, a formal induction is a good tool to practice and an important safeguard, especially in groups in which everyone is relatively inexperienced. Too much fluidity can blur the boundaries between the worlds, and as Witches our task is to know the gates in that boundary and move back and forth at will. When beginning, the clear demarcation of a formal induction is useful.

Page 178 Emerging from trance. There are three other simple things I do to help people come fully out of trance. One is to ask them to pat the boundaries of their physical bodies. The second is to say their own names out loud. And the third is to clap their hands three times.

Page 184 Feasting. This section was originally called "Cakes and Wine," which is the old traditional term for this part of the ritual, although one does wonder if even the dedicated worshippers of ancient times really liked wine and cake together. Today, in keeping with our deeper awareness of the addictive patterns so many people are struggling with, I have changed it to "Feasting." There's no reason why a group shouldn't share wine, provided nobody has a problem with it. But if it makes the ritual circle an unsafe place for someone, it's better to substitute something else. If that seriously interferes with your enjoyment of the ritual, you might need to look more closely at your own dependence on alcohol.

Page 185 Farewell. The group often says farewell separately to each Goddess and God invoked. We sometimes call this "devoking."

Page 185 Opening the circle. The circle can also be opened with the "short-form" ending, the first part of which, like the "short-form" circle casting, I learned from Victor Anderson:

> By the earth that is her body
> And by the air that is her breath
> And by the fire of her bright spirit
> And by the living waters of her womb,
> The circle is open, but unbroken
> May the Goddess awaken
> In our hearts
> Merry meet, and merry part
> And merry meet again.

Notes on Chapter Ten
GENERAL THOUGHTS ON INITIATION

Over the last ten years, initiations in our community have become a longer, more sustained process of individual growth for which the ritual is only the culmination. Someone who wants to be initiated needs to have practiced the Craft long enough to be sure that this is the right path for her or him. Generally, this means at least a year and a day: at least once around the full Wheel of the Year.

Suppose you wanted to be initiated. You would choose the people you want to ask for initiation, and they should be initiated Witches whom you respect and feel close to, who have some sort of knowledge, wisdom, personal power, or qualities you yourself want to have. An initiation creates a strong bond and a karmic tie, so they should be people within your community you feel close to, not strangers or figures you admire from a distance.

Each person you've asked would then give you a challenge. This might be something educational: "Read five books on the Craft" or "Attend five rituals of Craft groups outside our own." It might be something personal: "Exercise every day for twenty minutes" or "Learn to drive." It might be a magical challenge: "Create your own Place of Power in the underworld."

Someone who is asked for challenges can also refuse or issue certain conditions: "I can't work with you toward initiation until you confront your drug use" or "I don't think you'll be ready to focus on initiation until you've finished writing your dissertation." Sometimes the initiation process takes years and requires a major change in life patterns. Often the Goddess starts throwing challenges your way, generally tougher than those given by your friends.

Groups practicing in areas in which there are no initiated Witches can create their own rituals and traditions. Personally, I feel an initiation is most valid when it comes from people with whom you have truly close ties, even if they themselves are relatively inexperienced.

Page 187 The Goddess in the Kingdom of Death. This retelling of a traditional myth has obvious affinities to all the myths of descent and return: the Inanna myth, the myth of Persephone, the myth of Osiris, etc. If we look at these varying myths as a whole, we see that sometimes the one who descends is female, sometimes male. The Ruler of the Land Below may also be either female: Ereshkigal, Inanna's sister; or male: Hades.

In their essence, all these stories are about the process of shamanic initiation, the death to the old self and the arising of a new self. This process is not reserved for either gender, and what we face in the underworld is not determined by our genitalia.

Notes on Chapter Eleven

MOON RITUALS

The rituals described here can be used as given or can become components of more complex rituals. The truth is that we do not have a set form for moon rituals but reinvent and create them anew every month, depending on what we each need and what seasonal, astrological, and political forces are in motion around us.

Today we'd likely begin a moon ritual by going around the circle for check-in—having each person say briefly how she or he was feeling, what had happened since the last time we met, and what she or he needed from the ritual. Then we'd find a way to create what the group wanted.

Notes on Chapter Twelve

THE SABBATS

Like the moon cycle, the seasonal cycle is one of the key ways in which we see the processes of birth, growth, death, and rebirth play themselves out.

The rituals in this chapter derive from the version of the myth of the Wheel of the Year given in the original text. An alternate version can be found in the notes to Chapter Two.

Each key event in the myth is linked to one of the Sabbats. On Samhain, the Year Child of possibility is conceived. On the Winter Solstice, the Child is born. At the

Feast of Brigid, the Child becomes the Promise we make to the cauldron, which sets our challenge for the year. At the Spring Equinox, the Child of Promise becomes the Child of Balance, who grows at Beltane into the Rising Desire that culminates at Summer Solstice and passes over into its opposite, the One Who Descends, who Gives Away, the Dreamer. At Lammas we hold the wake of the dying sun, and by Fall Equinox the Dreamer becomes our Guide into the place where birth, death, and regeneration are one. And so at Samhain the cycle ends and begins anew.

We could call this the generic myth, but earth religions are not rooted in generic earth but in a specific place and climate, where the seasonal cycle reveals itself in particular forms. So, for example, here in San Francisco the Wheel of the Year might turn as follows:

Begin when the year grows dark, but the very cold of winter brings the heavy rains that renew the land. At Samhain, the Year Child is conceived, and Possibility manifests as the miracle greening of the hills. On the Winter Solstice, the Year is born in the time of gestation, and at Brigid, when fruit trees flower, bulbs blossom, and buds swell, the Promise of the Year is shown to us. The Spring Equinox is the Balance time, of day and night, of sun and rain, and at Beltane we say farewell to rain and dance with Desire as the green hills blush with silver and fade to gold. At Summer Solstice, the Year gives itself away, the grass dies and turns brown, and the land is covered with a shroud of fog. At Lammas we keep the Wake of the Year and hope for the harvest as fruits begin to ripen. And at Fall Equinox, the sun emerges from fog to beckon us into the Dreamtime of winter, which brings with it the return of the life-renewing rain. And so, at Samhain, the miracle renews itself, and even as fruits fall to earth, so new grasses sprout and cloak the land in green.

And so the Wheel turns, on and on.

This myth would be different in Minnesota, or Alabama, or even ten miles east of here across the San Francisco Bay. Try writing your own myth, for your own area. Find a tree or plant or bird to symbolize each point on the wheel.

The way we celebrate the seasonal festivals also changes over time. Some of these rituals—or some aspects of them—we still do very much as is described here. For some festivals, new traditions have evolved that are repeated year after year. For others, each year's ritual is different. Some festivals have specific children's rituals involved; others don't as yet. The opening invocations reflect the old imagery based on heterosexual polarity. Please feel free to change or adapt them. I may rewrite them someday, after a few more turns around the wheel.

Pages 197–202 Winter Solstice. Our tradition for this ritual is to meet at the beach just before sunset on the eve of the Solstice. As the sun dips down, we chant, build a fire, gather our courage, and then strip off our clothes and jump into the ocean, for cleansing. (Some who don't care to plunge simply do a salt-water meditation.) The shock of the cold water, the biting wind, and the beauty of the dying day at the end of the year are exhilarating.

We warm ourselves by the fire and have a ritual that is open to many covens, circles, and interested friends.

Then we break into smaller groups, into individual circles. Sometimes a few circles will join together. We go back to someone's house and begin our all-night vigil, which combines some of the ritual given here, with periodic eating and drinking and whatever other activities suggest themselves—dancing, crafts, reading of Tarot cards or casting of oracles, etc.

At dawn, we meet again with the larger community, to climb one of the city's hills and chant, drum, and dance until the sun comes up (or until the mist grows light, as is more often the case).

We have a children's ritual, usually the weekend before the Solstice, in which they decorate round cookies to represent the sun (or whatever they want). We give them gifts, tell them stories, and give each child a red, floating candle. On Solstice Night, they can light their candles and let them burn until morning, to keep the vigil for the children. When the children wake up, they blow the candles out.

In my house, our family altar becomes an elaborate creche (which we often call our "crush"), where instead of a Baby Jesus and Virgin Mary we ensconce a Goddess image and something to represent the Sun. Then we collect all our small animal figures, toys, plastic dinosaurs, etc., to witness this event.

Pages 202–3 Brigid. The Feast of Brigid, dedicated to the Irish Goddess of fire and water, holy well, and sacred flame, who presides over smithcraft, poetry, and healing, has become our traditional time for doing a ritual of rededication, most often with a political focus. (In *Truth or Dare* [pp. 289–95, 304–6], I describe the evolution of our political despair rituals.)

The heart of the ritual takes place around a cauldron in a well. (A small metal pot, elevated on bricks, inside a big punch bowl of water. In the pot we burn a mixture of roughly equal parts of alcohol and Epsom salts, which creates a smokeless fire. Don't let the alcohol get chilled, or it becomes hard to light, and don't refill the cauldron while it is still burning.) Throughout the year, we collect water on all our travels from sacred sites and add it to the well. We call this "waters of the world." Each person comes forward, looks into the flame, and makes a pledge for the year, a promise to Brigid. The pledge is not something we think up but something that comes to us in the moment when the ritual power is strong, and it tends to shape the year. One year, for example, my pledge was to tell the truth, and by the end of the year I had been faced with many difficult moments in which I was challenged to be honest instead of conciliatory or polite.

Page 203 The Spiral Dance. Originally the text suggested coveners kiss when passing each other. The kissing should only be done among close friends; otherwise, it feels intrusive.

The Spiral Dance can be another way to raise power. In a large group (at least thirty-five people and up to three to four hundred), begin in a circle with everyone facing in. The leader drops the hand of the person on her or his left, and begins moving in toward the center in a clockwise direction.

When the lead person nears the center of the circle, she/he turns toward her left hand, to face the person who is following her. (For simplicity's sake, let's assume the leader is a woman.) She keeps moving, always following her left hand. (1) Each person in the spiral will pass all the other people in the group.

Eventually, the leader will find herself outside the body of the spiral, facing out. She should continue about one third of the way around the outside edge and then turn again to face the person following her. She will then be leading the line around the outside of the circle, facing in. (2)

When she comes to a loop in the line, at the place where she turned, she goes inside the loop, (3) and continues until she finds herself back in the center of the circle. Then she can wind the spiral tighter, letting the energy build and the chant become a wordless sound, until the group raises and grounds a Cone of Power.

This sounds horribly complicated but is actually easy to do. Walk through it a few times first to gain confidence. Be sure to go slowly, especially in a large group, for if the leader goes too fast, the person at the tail end of the line will be jerked around dangerously.

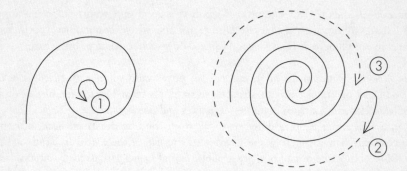

Pages 203–4 Eostar (Spring Equinox). This ritual varies greatly from year to year. Generally, we have a children's ritual. Robin and Arachne, of Reclaiming, created a basket of Story Eggs—painted to represent the Goddess, the God, and one, half black and half gold, to represent the Balance of the Equinox. We tell stories about the eggs and then have an egg hunt, with hundreds of dyed eggs.

If the opening invocation were changed so that Kore dances with her mother, Demeter, it would be more faithful to the original myth of Persephone.

Pages 204–5 Beltane. We celebrate this ritual pretty much as written. The children love jumping the cauldron, and we jump in combination with everyone with whom we have a relationship: lovers, married partners, former lovers who perhaps want to release bitterness or conflict, children, close friends, coveners, collective members, etc. The ritual usually also includes a picnic.

Over the years, the heterosexual imagery of this ritual has sparked controversy. Changing three words in the opening invocation—"Maiden" to "Promise," "Lord" to "Power," and "Shaft" to "Tree"—will make this liturgy less exclusive.

Pages 205–7 Litha (Summer Solstice). Over the years, our God figure has grown into a towering construction, far too big to carry. Instead, after he is decked with flowers, we build a fire under him and dance around him.

We've had many debates over the years about whether this figure should be specifically male, androgynous, male and female both, or an abstract representation of the sun. We have, in fact, tried it many ways, but seem to come back to making it the God.

Roy added a spectacular finish to the ritual: An archer, at the end he lights the tip of a flaming arrow from the God's fire and shoots it into the ocean. (This involved some dangerous experimentation with rags and kerosene in the dead of night in Golden Gate Park. In the end, he settled on using a sparkler tied to the arrow.)

Pages 207–8 Lughnasad. We generally celebrate this holiday, also called Lammas, much as is described here. When we meet on the beach, we sometimes mold a "corpse" of Lugh, the Celtic Sun King, out of sand. The children especially enjoy this, as they enjoy helping to build sand-castle altars for the four directions.

Pages 208–9 Mabon (Fall Equinox). Mabon is a good opportunity to celebrate an early Thanksgiving, with a Harvest Dinner for the whole community (potluck, of course). In our climate, it is also a good time to do weather magic to bring rain.

Pages 209–12 Samhain. In my house, we set up a family altar, with pictures of our Beloved Dead on it, appropriate artifacts, sugar skulls from Mexico for El Día de los Muertos, skeleton figures, and offerings of apples and pomegranates.

Our actual ritual is quite different today from the one described here, although some elements remain, such as the journey to the Isle of the Dead. In *Truth or Dare* (pp. 306–9) I describe one of our larger public Spiral Dance rituals for Samhain. For a smaller coven ritual, the important elements seem to be the public naming of our Beloved Dead, especially those who have died in the previous year, and perhaps a short story or phrase about who each of them was. Then we create a drum story, trance, or meditation in which we can feel connected to the dead, honor the ancestors, and receive help and information. At some point, we chant to name what we hope to bring into being in the coming year. Finally, we sing the names of babies who have been born during the year.

Knowing we will have our yearly Samhain becomes a comfort when someone dies, and with the rise of AIDS everyone in our community has lost someone or knows someone who is living with the disease. When we chant the names, when we sing "What is remembered, lives," we are saying that death does not sever our ties to those we love and that the community itself encompasses the circle of birth, growth, death, and renewal.

Notes on Chapter Thirteen

Page 218 "Oppressed and powerless groups . . ." I would probably write this and the following paragraph very differently today. On rereading, I find that it verges on blaming the victim, which was not my intention. I was reflecting on the ways in which even movements of liberation can be shaped by the very thought forms they seek to challenge. The decision to separate from men and devote one's time, energy, creativity, and emotional support to women is certainly a valid one. But at times the impulse toward separatism also generated an ideology that I saw and still see as false—the analysis that men are inherently violent and prone to domination, while women are inherently nurturing and cooperative. I would say that the patriarchal *system* is rooted in domination, that under it we all become dominators and dominated, with men ruling women but also men of other races and classes, and that that system must be transformed in order to change the power dynamics between women and men (and, for that matter, between women and women, men and men).

In that struggle women may need times of separation. At other times we may wish to work with men who can be allies or to confront and challenge men and women both who remain embedded in structures of domination. On some issues, we might be more effective working separately; on others, we may need broad coalitions of people who are different from us in many ways. Above all, we need flexibility and fluidity, not to be locked into any ideology but to be free to change and grow as the situation changes.

Pages 219–20 Goddess religion grounded in science. The vision of a spirituality grounded in science is also shared by Matthew Fox, head of the Institute for Culture and Creation Spirituality at Holy Names College in Oakland, where I have taught for five years. Among the faculty is Brian Swimme, an inspirational physicist, whose lectures have helped me reconceive our mythology and whose book *The Universe Is a Green Dragon* is well worth reading.

Page 222 Eastern religions. The last ten years have seen women in many of the Eastern religions challenge structures of domination and male control and research women's images and history.

Page 225 "The circle is also the circle of community." To build a true community that fosters diversity, in a country of diverse races, classes, and cultures, we must also confront the ways in which we have internalized divisions that keep us apart—our own subtle racism, our discomfort with differences, our assumptions that our style of life or use of language or level of resources is the norm for everybody and that those who differ are deviant. We need to notice ways in which our community fails to reflect the diversity around us and ask if we are subtly excluding people. And perhaps our thealogy needs an "option for the poor" as has developed in Christian liberation theology. That is, we need to ask: What are the interests of the most oppressed in this situation, and how can we serve them? For if we are all interconnected parts of the body of the Goddess, then pain in any part, no matter how small or how far away, is in some measure felt by us all.

Twenty Years Later: Commentary on Chapters One through Thirteen

Notes on Chapter One

Pages 27–32 Note that this entire section begins: "According to our legends . . . " This is a mythic history, not a Ph.D. thesis in archaeology. Months and months of reading and research went into these few pages: but they were months spent when I was in my midtwenties and was reading the sources available in the midseventies. I think it still works well as a mythic history, and I happen to believe it is basically true in outline if not in every detail.

In *Truth or Dare* (1988) I gave a more detailed account of the matrifocal roots of the Middle East, and in *Dreaming the Dark* (1982) I give an economic and social analysis of the Witch burnings.

In the sixties and seventies, when I was first exposed to the Goddess and was writing early drafts of this book, there was very little information available. Robert Graves's *The White Goddess* was recommended by the first Witches I met, and I dutifully plowed through it at age seventeen. James Mellaart's publications on Catal Hüyük were published in the late sixties. Helen Diner, Erich Neuman, and a few other Jungians talked about matriarchies, and in 1976 Merlin Stone's *When God Was a Woman* brought a feminist perspective to ancient history. Today, it is easy to look back on these books and criticize their mistakes, but at the time they were radical, illuminating works. It's hard to remember now just how mind-altering the very concept of a Goddess was in an era when there were no women priests, no women rabbis, few women ministers, and scarcely any models of women's spiritual power and leadership.

The eighties and early nineties saw a blossoming of information on the Goddess. Marija Gimbutas, the prime archaeological voice for the Goddess cultures of Old Europe, published her major works. Suddenly there were too many books to catalog them all. I consulted on director Donna Read's three films for the National Film Board of Canada, *Goddess Remembered*, *The Burning Times*, and *Full Circle*, which have been widely broadcast on public television, used in college classes and women's studies programs, and have been, for a decade, among the top ten in sales and rentals of the films offered by the Film Board.

At present, we're experiencing somewhat of a backlash against the Goddess in academic circles. As one of the projects I'm working on is a new film in collaboration with Donna Read on Gimbutas's life and work, I've become well versed in the controversy surrounding her. Gimbutas is criticized by male archaeologists and some feminist scholars, accused of leaping to conclusions and of stating her ideas too categorically. Young women are strongly discouraged from research on the Goddess if they hope to receive tenure at prestigious universities or get grants for research. While every theorist can be criticized, much of the anti-Gimbutas critique fails to look carefully at the actual evidence she presents, attributes to her formulations she never made and then knocks them down, or simply dismisses her as too "New Age," too feminist, too popular.

I don't have the space here to even begin to outline the issues and counterissues involved. I refer readers to Gimbutas's own books, and to Carol Christ's excellent book *Rebirth of the Goddess* for a fuller discussion of the Gimbutas controversy. Joan Marler's anthology *From the Realm of the Ancestors* is also an important reference. In the introduction to this edition, I address the interplay of history, myth, and experience for contemporary Goddess tradition.

Page 32 "Male images of divinity characterize both Western and Eastern religions." This section is not as true as it was twenty years ago. Today we have women priests, ministers, rabbis, and cantors, and many traditional congregations have consciously adopted neutral language or at least occasional feminine terms for God. Because of the feminist challenge to organized religions, virtually every tradition has had to at least confront this issue in the last two decades. Even the popular writer Andrew Greeley constantly refers to God as "She." However, this statement is far from untrue. I doubt that anyone, reading it, will be saying, "Boy, she couldn't be more wrong! Why, all the mainstream religions are chock-full of images of female power, there's a woman pope, women are more than equally represented at all the top levels of leadership in just about every spiritual tradition today!" Maybe if there's that fiftieth anniversary edition someday . . ."

Page 34 "Because women give birth to males . . ." I want to reaffirm the ten-year note. Today, I still dislike the "inner male" and "inner female" imagery.

Page 35 "Witchcraft can be seen as a religion of ecology." I'd say most Witches believe in this statement in theory, but we often fall short in practice. My personal direction is toward making this statement ever more true, integrating the understanding of ecology and the observation of nature with our rituals and teachings, seeing that growing food, restoring habitat, conserving energy and cleaning water are sacred acts as much as dancing and chanting. When we live closer to the land, the elements become ever more real—not just a set of symbols to invoke, but "How do I plant a windbreak on this hill? How do I take fire into account as a real threat in this area? How do I keep water from eroding this bank?"

Most Witches, like most people in general, live in cities. The elements are no less real in an urban setting, and the ecological issues concerning them are even more vital. My hope is that the lessons we can learn from rooting our spirituality in the land can also revitalize our cities.

Page 35 "The rise of Goddess religion makes some politically oriented feminists uneasy." See the introduction for my discussion of our political activism over the past two decades. Some self-defined radical or socialist feminists are still publishing critiques of the apolitical nature of Goddess tradition—which they justify by simply ignoring all the material that would contradict their prejudices. There's really no use wasting time or energy trying to debate these people.

Page 35 "My own covens are based on the Faery tradition . . ." This statement was more true in 1979, when I had studied with Victor Anderson (who now prefers the spelling "Feri Tradition" to differentiate what he teaches from many other Faery traditions of various sorts). Today, my practice is part of what we have come to call the Reclaiming tradition, the evolution of twenty years of collective creativity and experimentation that weaves together Feri material with many other sources, including our own imaginations.

Page 35 The following discussion of ethics still strikes me, twenty years later, as a sound, well-expressed, succinct discussion of our basic values. The only thing I would change if I were writing today are some of the statements about Eastern religions. With middle-aged wisdom, I would no longer presume to characterize somebody else's religious tradition, and I appreciate more the insights and truth that Eastern traditions offer.

Page 37 The Nazi issue. The whole discussion of the Nazis' relationship to Pagan ideas is still an important issue in Germany, where I have taught now for many years and where a thriving Goddess community exists. I strongly recommend Ralph Metzner's *The Well of Remembrance* for a discussion on the Goddess roots of Germanic culture. And there are, alas, self-styled Pagan groups in Germany and elsewhere that are indeed neofascist. They are neither feminist-identified nor Goddess oriented, and are not part of any tradition represented by this book.

Page 38 "'Solitaries' . . . are the exception." This statement is probably not true. Solitaries may be the norm in Witchcraft, covens the ideal. The structure of the Craft has changed greatly in twenty years. We now do have different levels of experience and commitment—Witches who devote a great deal of time and energy to providing services such as public rituals for a larger, loose "congregation" of people who draw spiritual nourishment from the gatherings but have no desire to plan them, lead them, or carry the heavy cauldron from the parking lot.

Page 38 Description of basic ritual structure. After twenty years, the structure remains. One change is that we tend to do the trance, meditation, or symbolic work first and climax with the raising of power. Especially in larger and public rituals, this orchestration of energy seems to follow more naturally. Our trance practices in larger rituals have evolved into a form we call drum trance—where the drum provides the induction and helps move the energy, the trance leader or leaders are essentially guiding the group with improvised poetic journey weaving, chanting and song are interwoven with the guiding, and the Cone of Power emerges from the flow.

Page 39 "A person blessed with imagination . . . could use [this book] as a manual to start her or his own coven." Many people have indeed done just that—used this book as a basis for coven work, training, and personal practice. Today, however, it is much easier to find opportunities for training—just do a Web search! Depending on where you live, you might need to travel for weekend workshops or summer intensives, but nobody who truly wants to learn need struggle along in isolation.

Notes on Chapter Two

Page 43 Left and right brain theory. As I said in my ten-year note, I'm still less impressed with this theory. In fact, more recent studies have called into question whether it even applies to women's brains.

Page 44 Shadow and rhythm exercises. The Shadow exercise came from my early training as an artist, and it's valuable for sharpening our powers of observation and differentiating between what we actually see—patterns of light, shadow, line, and color—and the objects we name for ourselves. I still find one of the best ways to know a place, a thing, or a person is to draw it.

Rhythm is also one of my current, regular meditation practices. I like to go out into my garden at night and simply listen to the patterns of sound, the voice of the land. That voice changes season by season, hour by hour. With a few more years of listening behind me, I hope to be able to tell you the month, the time of day, and the temperature simply by the pattern of sound.

Page 45 Younger Self/Talking Self terminology. Actually, in Faery/Feri tradition, as in the Reclaiming tradition, every teacher tends to develop their own terminology. This is the one I prefer.

Page 46 "It is not the conscious mind . . ." I find this statement a bit confusing and misleading. Obviously, we consciously communicate with the Goddess, however we perceive her. What I was trying to express is a somewhat esoteric teaching of the Feri tradition, also shared by other indigenous traditions: the idea that our verbal language needs to be "translated" to the Gods, that the actual link, the routing of the cosmic telephone cables, goes through Younger Self. I don't know if this is true or not, but I have found that clarifying an intention and embodying it in sensory images and tangible symbols as well as words makes for more powerful rituals and more effective magic.

Page 47 Over the last twenty years, our community has learned how to construct and erect a Maypole. For directions, see Starhawk, Anne Hill, and Diane Baker, *Circle Round: Raising Children in Goddess Tradition* (New York: Bantam, 1998), p. 191. However, there is always an element of chaos when we dance the dance. How those nicely trained British schoolchildren do it so neatly, I'll never know.

Page 48 Creation myth. This myth could be seen as a poetic expression of what physicists currently believe about the origins of the universe in a single event, sometimes called a "big bang." The imagery fits with our vision of cosmic origins in the big orgasm, or we might call it a she-bang as in Timothy Ferris, *The Whole Shebang* (New York: Simon and Schuster, 1997). Personally, when I want to contemplate something truly esoteric, I meditate on the periodic table of the elements.

Page 50 Female-male polarization. Again, this view of the world has been challenged by twenty years of living in the San Francisco Bay Area, with our vibrant queer, lesbian, gay, bisexual, and transsexual communities, which have played a strong role in the formation of the Reclaiming tradition.

Polarity certainly exists in nature at the atomic level, in the dance of attraction between protons and electrons—however, trying to identify one or the other as "female" or "male" seems purely silly. And that dance takes place, we now know, in a complex do-si-do with other forces: the strong force, the weak force, gravity, and undoubtedly others we don't even know of yet. Rather than a simple, bipolar universe, we might do better to conceive of a web of forces and energies holding the cosmos in dynamic tension.

Pages 50–51 "The Male and Female forces . . . are not different, in essence." I offer this statement up as proof that, even in my callow youth, I was never truly an "essentialist." Again, I now think we'd do better to simply drop the Female/Male imagery.

Page 52 "We are female and male both." Here, too, I would now prefer to simply speak of containing both aspects of creation/destruction, life/death, rather than to term them female and male.

"Sex as a polarized flow of energy." Yes, it is in the sense that electricity is a flow of electrons.

Page 52 The Male Principle is first seen as . . . the Blue God." Today, I interpret the three aspects of the God as embodying the three great strategies that life forms on this planet have developed for getting energy: fermentation, photosynthesis, and respiration.

The Green God represents the plant world, all beings that make energy from sunlight. The Horned God is the animal world, all beings whose blood contains hemoglobin, who breathe oxygen to burn food and release energy. The Green God and Horned God share breath—plants make the oxygen we red-bloods take in; we breathe out the carbon dioxide that helps sustain the plant world. And the Blue God is the third force that breaks the patterns of duality, the fermenters who release energy by breaking apart old forms, the fungi that aid in the process of decay. The myth follows the sequence of biological evolution: Fermentation is truly the oldest profession, followed by photosynthesis, then by respiration.

Page 52 The Wheel of the Year. For another version, see T. Thorn Coyle's version in Starhawk, M. Macha Nightmare, and Reclaiming, *The Pagan Book of Living and Dying* (San Francisco: HarperSanFrancisco, 1997), pp. 16–19.

Page 54 ". . . must ultimately serve the life force . . ." Witchcraft is not a religion of self-sacrifice or self-abnegation. However, as our community matures, we have learned the importance of the concept of service. When we teach, organize rituals, attend long meetings, carry the heavy cauldron, stay late and pick up the trash, we are giving service to the Goddess and the community, as we are when we work, write, change the baby's diapers, occupy a redwood tree to save it from logging, write a letter to a congressperson, compost the garbage. We do these things out of love, pride, and a sense of offering: They are the fruits we place on the altar.

Service is an especially important concept for leaders. The more influence we have in our communities, the more responsibility we have. The larger our vision, the more we are called to give.

Many years ago I spoke at a conference on a panel with a Native American woman named Inez Talamantes. She said something I've never forgotten: "People always want to have visions. They don't realize that if you have a vision of the Goddess, if you dream of her, you're obligated to work for her for the rest of your life."

You could have worse employers. The Goddess offers long hours, no unemployment, widely varying rewards, and guaranteed lack of boredom. You'll never be downsized or laid off—she'll always find something for you to do. Her service is joyful. She offers us a field in which to exercise our gifts and talents to enrich our communities, and opportunities to join with others in work, play, and mutual invention. She engages all those faculties within us that cry out to be used—our creativity, vision, and passion. And she provides great companions.

Page 55 Ritual mock death. We might suggest this to the Senate and House of Representatives as an alternative to impeachment the next time a popular president gets caught lying about his sex life.

Page 56 The media view of Witchcraft. There has been some slight improvement over the years, but not nearly enough. Many good documentaries and news programs have been done, and many people in the media are Pagan or at least sympathetic. However, in radio, films, and television we're still in the Pagan equivalent of Buckwheat, Aunt

Jemima, or Charlie Chan. We now get trivializing movies like *The Craft* along with the flat-out horror films. Occasionally a Witch shows up on a TV sitcom but is usually portrayed as a wacky, New Age type. I'm waiting for the TV Witch who happens to be an auto mechanic, an engineer, or a molecular biologist.

Notes on Chapter Three

Page 59 "To become a member of a coven, a Witch must be initiated . . ." This is not necessarily true. In practice, each coven or circle sets its own rules. See the notes on Chapter Ten for more discussion of initiation.

Page 60 ". . . coveners were the teachers . . ." This is our legend about the past. The reality, I now suspect, is that individuals and close-knit families were the keepers of traditions that ranged from ancient healing practices, herbal knowledge, and care of the land to how to properly put on the local rites. See Clark and Roberts, *Twilight of the Celtic Gods*, for a beautiful account of the survival of family traditions into this century.

Page 60 ". . . prejudice is still widespread." Unfortunately, this is still all too true, although many inroads have been made.

Page 61 "One person's power does not diminish another's . . ." I could write an entire book on power issues alone. Come to think of it, I did, a couple of them! In *Dreaming the Dark*, I differentiated power-over (domination and control) from power-from-within (creative power and ability). Power-from-within is what covens attempt to foster. In *Truth or Dare*, I explored a third type of power I called power-with: influence or social power, which especially comes into play in groups without hierarchical leadership structures. Another excellent resource is Judy Harrow's *Wicca Covens*.

Page 63 ". . . coven of elders." Hah hah hah! We were mostly in our twenties when I wrote this—who was I kidding? Actually, I was using the Covenant of the Goddess's official definition of "elder": a person capable of perpetuating her or his tradition. Yes, by that definition we were all elders, but what this sentence brings home to me now is how few true elders we had to guide us. In the seventies, people who had practiced the Craft for more than a decade were as rare as spotted owls.

Today, the Reclaiming community has been engaged in a widespread discussion of what eldership means, how it should be determined, whether age should be a criterion, and what happens when one person's elder is somebody else's crotchety old lunatic. By the time we reach some firm conclusions, I hope to be through middle age and ready to undergo a mock death and join the Council.

Page 65 ". . . the Priestess will not be driving a Mercedes . . ." Just in case this sort of thing interests you, I'm presently driving either a 1990 Toyota wagon or a pickup truck so old I've forgotten the date—hoping to nurse them both along until electric vehicles become practical and affordable.

Page 70 Group conflict. Endless volumes could not do justice to this topic But if I could add only one insight from the last twenty years, it would be this: If two people in a group have a conflict, encourage them to work it out privately. Do not use the group time to attempt to resolve it. If necessary, offer a third party as mediator. But as soon as you bring the conflict into the group, you multiply the dynamics and possible alliances, manipulations and new conflicts to infinity. Shame and humiliation also come into play. E-mail listserves and bulletin boards have illuminated this principle. People too often try to use the listserve, and by extension, the community, as a court of judgment instead of dealing directly and privately with another person. When groups are used in this way, whether they are face-to-face groups or virtual gatherings, they lose energy and rapidly lose membership.

Page 70 "Objective, constructive criticism . . ." Artist and teacher Donald Engstrom formulated what have come to be known as Donald's Three Rules of Critique.

1. Constructive critique must be specific: Not "I hated that ritual" but "For me, the meditation was very powerful for the first ten minutes or so, but when you started on the visualization of the third round of gifts and challenges, I got bored." Praise, too, must be specific: Not "I loved the invocation!" but "Your timing was right, not too long nor too short. I could hear every word and the imagery moved me."
2. The intent must be to improve the work.
3. The timing must be right. Immediately after the ritual, when everybody is still wide open emotionally and tired, is not the time to critique the priestessing or the plan. We try to leave at least an overnight or, better, twenty-four-hour moratorium on ritual critique.

To this I would add a fourth rule:
4. Private criticism can be supportive and helpful. Public criticism, especially if it has not first been given privately, can be shaming and humiliating. It's the difference between saying quietly to a friend, "Your fly is open" and shouting out to a crowded room, "Hey everybody, look at Joe—HIS FLY IS OPEN!" Again, e-mail exacerbates this issue.

Page 78 Daily practice. My current daily practice involves spending time in some natural environment simply observing what is going on around me, staying in physical reality rather than drifting into my own thoughts and images. In the city, I might spend ten minutes in my backyard. In the country, I spend an hour or two walking the land, (combining the physical exercise aspect). The more I open my eyes and ears, the more there is to see and hear.

Page 79 ". . . such information is generally xeroxed . . ." When it's not simply e-mailed or posted on a Web site.

Notes on Chapter Four

Page 84 ". . . a period of purification . . ." In practice, we often combine this with grounding, taking time to let go of anything that might interfere with our experience of the ritual, giving the blocks to the fire in the center of the earth or imagining them falling to the ground as compost for the Tree of Life.

Group purification: Sprinkling the crowd with herbs or branches dipped in salt water is one of the jobs children can easily do in ritual. Some supervision and a supply of towels are recommended.

Page 85 Banishing. Another easy way to let children participate in ritual is to provide them with pots, pans, and noisemakers and let them run widdershins (counterclockwise) around the circle, banging away and scaring off evil spirits.

Page 87 ". . . so indispensable for opening ritual wine." As I've said, we no longer use wine in our public rituals, nor generally in our private rituals, but you get the idea.

My current *athame* is my Swiss-made garden pruners. I use them daily for shaping rosebushes, pruning the apple trees, snipping plants to propagate, and for magic. I take them on trips (you never know when you're going to encounter a rosebush that needs rejuvenating!). Instead of a sword, whose symbolism I dislike, I use my extendable pole pruners. If your creative work involves an edged blade of any sort—an embroidery scissors, an exacto knife, a saw—consider it as a magical tool. For traveling, another good option is a pen—being mightier than the sword and less likely to get confiscated at the security gate.

Page 95 Additional tools. We should include the computer among the Witches' toolbox these days, as it has basically replaced the traditional Book of Shadows and is also a major tool of communication.

Notes on Chapter Five

Page 102 Today, I experience the Goddess primarily as the expression of land and place. As we begin to understand the earth as an organism, the Goddess is the consciousness of the earth being, and her various aspects are reflections of the land/climate/ecology web of a given area. So the Goddess Demeter, patroness of agriculture and barley, hailed from Eleusis, once the most fertile plain in Greece (today, alas, among the most polluted land in Greece). Her sister Athena, Goddess of the olive, which will grow on stony hillsides, hailed from the drier uplands of Athens. Goddesses and Gods embody the real relationships early peoples had with the land, the food, the animals, and the skills that sustained life and culture.

Indigenous people are keen observers of all aspects of life around them, and good communicators. They know that the earth, the plants, the animals, birds, insects, and microbial life forms that surround us and sustain us are in constant communication. To open to the Goddess is to become aware of what ethnobotanist Kat Harrison calls "the great conversation," to learn to listen and eventually, through magic, to speak.

More Goddess meditations can be found in *The Pagan Book of Living and Dying* and in *Circle Round*.

Pages 105–6 The text reflects a slight change in terminology of the pentacle, from Robert Graves's original "Birth, initiation, consummation, repose, and death" to "birth, initiation, ripening, reflection, and death." Consummation seems somehow too final—ripening expresses more the sense of process and maturation this stage represents. Now that I'm moving into the fourth stage of life, I can say from personal experience that "repose" has little to do with it. "Reflection" better expresses the gaining of wisdom from experience.

Page 105 ". . . the stage of initiation . . . for women." See *Truth or Dare* and *Circle Round* for descriptions of rites of passage for girls. *Circle Round* includes similar rites for boys as well. In the next twenty years, I hope to see our community develop more material and resources to help youth make the difficult transition from childhood to maturity.

Page 106 ". . . the final initiation, which is death." See *The Pagan Book of Living and Dying* for a full discussion of our theology, practices, liturgy, and rituals for death and dying.

Page 109 "Witches worship naked . . ." Well, I hate to admit it but as a rule we don't, at least not in cold, foggy San Francisco with its minimally heated Victorians. Nudity is welcome in our rituals, however, when privacy can be assured and conditions permit.

Page 111 "To invoke the Goddess is to awaken the Goddess within, to become, for a time, that aspect we invoke." The power of that imagined identification can vary from a mild sense of exhilaration to a deep change in perception to full trance possession. Judy Harrow and Mevlannen Beshderen have formulated four stages:

Enhancement—when your own creative powers are heightened, you play the music with greater sensitivity and passion.

Inspiration—when something is flowing through you, the music is playing you.

Integration—when you and the music/Goddess are one.

Possession—when the music/Goddess takes over and you disappear.

Many indigenous traditions such as the Yoruba-based religions and the Balinese work with full trance possession—but never without an elaborate structure of safeguards and cultural boundaries. Experimenting with trance possession is one of the few truly dangerous things you can do in ritual, and I don't recommend it. A powerful ritual that works, however, should bring participants to a state of enhancement, and even inspiration—as does any effective creative work. Identification is a bit more problematic. In one sense, of course, our core theology teaches that each of us is the Goddess. Speaking in ritual as the voice of one of her aspects, however, is likely to lead to self-inflation unless careful preparation is done. We need to have a strong sense of self, of what psychologists call "firm ego boundaries," before even attempting this work, as otherwise we may inadvertently achieve fragmentation and disintegration. Strong support, clear boundaries and safeguards, and follow-up care are needed. "Aspecting," as Reclaiming calls it, is one magical technique that really must be learned live, not from books but from personal instruction. And while it can be an illuminating and mind-altering experience for the person who does it, it's not always the most empowering form of ritual for everybody else. Information received while "aspecting" must be as carefully evaluated as any other kind of information. Even if "the Goddess says" to do something, we need to consider carefully the ethics and consequences with our conscious, rational minds. If we take the information or advice given by the aspect as Goddess Gospel, then ritual becomes disempowering and borders on a kind of Pagan fundamentalism. The vessel is not the voice, and every vessel colors the message with its own perceptions, flaws, and emotions.

Page 111 Invocations. See Resources for recordings of some of these chants and many others.

Notes on Chapter Six

Page 121 ". . . incarnate in the rites." Trance possession seems to have been a practice in what we know of early Witchcraft.

Page 123 "He has no father; he is his own father." Over the last ten years, as the Goddess tradition has matured, we have been able to focus less on the pain of patriarchal, authoritarian fathering and more on the joyful, nurturing possibilities embodied by the many Pagan fathers in our community. See *Circle Round*, page 221, for a "Father's Blessing."

Page 129 Invocations. See Resources for recordings of some of these and other God chants.

Page 131 "Song to Pan" is recorded by Aine Minogue on her CD *Circle of the Sun* (RCA Victor).

Notes on Chapter Seven

Page 137 ". . . allow the two sides of the brain to communicate . . ." Again, I am no longer enamoured with left brain, right brain theory.

Page 137 ". . . materials that feel right . . ." This is how I cast a spell today. First, I clarify my intention. I might meditate, walk a labyrinth, read Tarot cards, take whatever time I need until my intention is crystal-clear. Then I take a long walk around my land or a stroll through the garden, my *athame*/pruners in hand, snipping a bit of this or that and naming what it's for. "I'll take some rosemary, for protection, some sage for wisdom, a little of this rose for sweetness . . ." When I've collected the plants that feel right, I bind them together with raffia or natural twine, focusing on my magical image and intention, sing, chant, or breathe power into it, and then either burn it, bury it, or leave it as an offering for the elements, animals, and fungi to transform. I call this "eco-spellcasting": using nothing that can't be returned to the cycles of fertility.

Page 139 "Directing energy is not a matter of simple emoting." Clarity of intention is the key to creating a powerful spell or ritual. I'm amazed at how many ritual planning sessions I've sat through where people will go on and on for hours about which symbols to use or what chants to sing without ever stopping and saying, "What is our intention here?" Take the time to clarify your intention first, to acknowledge fears and release them, to do some form of divination, if necessary. When the intention is clear, the symbols, the acts, and objects that embody and personify it come clear.

Page 140 ". . . the moon's influence on subtle energies . . ." Gardeners also know that planting by the moon is a time-honored technique that takes advantage of these forces. Unfortunately, I mostly find myself constrained to plant when I have time to plant, moon or no moon.

Page 149 Herbal charms. Twenty years of finding little bags of dried herbs lying around in my dresser drawers or falling out of my desk have taught me to think early on about disposal. I now favor charms and spells that incorporate their disposal or decay in their construction, as in the second note for p. 137. I try not to incorporate things that can't be burned or that won't decay—unless I decide beforehand that I don't mind finding a little plastic doll in my compost pile a few years on.

I also use almost exclusively herbs I grow or gather in the wild. The relationship I have with the plant is an important part of the power it has for me. Dried leaves from the health food store just don't do it. I realize that I'm both extremely privileged and something of a snob about this—but I also think I'm right. Magic involves relationship and communication with your allies and helpers. If you live in a high-rise with no land, grow some mint in a pot and use that in your spells. Help a friend in her garden, or volunteer at a school, and in return, snip some lavender when you need it. If you do buy your herbs, know something about where they come from, and how they're grown. Most herbs we use are extremely prolific, but some herbs used in healing, such as echinacea and goldenseal, are now endangered in the wild due to overcollecting.

Notes on Chapter Eight

Page 161 "Being outdoors . . . restores vitality." There is a reason why all those old Witches lived on the edge of the village and spent a lot of time out in the woods. When running intense energy, doing healing work, even intense creative work, a strong connection to nature is a necessity. If you live in the city and do intensive psychic work, know that it is important for your physical and emotional health to spend time in a natural environment. Make that time a regular part of your personal practice, whether it is a daily walk in the park, an hour in the garden, or a weekend at a friend's cottage in the country once a month. Guard the time jealously; it is not an option, not a luxury but a necessity, like eating your green vegetables or getting enough sleep. If you find yourself feeling depleted, constantly tired, always sick, make more time for nature.

Page 161 ". . . the Overworld." I now prefer the term *Otherworld* for the energy/thought/spirit realm that infuses and shapes the physical world. For a fuller discussion, see *The Pagan Book of Living and Dying*, pp. 78–81.

Notes on Chapter Nine

Page 169 "Astral vision is always a mixture of the subjective and the objective." It is wise to remember this when dealing with visions, trance states, journeys in the Otherworld, dealings with Faery, etc. As a novelist, I know the power of my mind to create images and characters that can seem, at times, as vivid and real as my friends in the flesh. Much of what we do in magical work is similar. Both trance and fiction can bring through insights and spark personal growth and change. But they are always colored by subjectivity. A strongly imagined scene can even cover over a real memory—I've found myself answering questions about my personal history with incidents from the lives of my characters.

Page 171 "Trance states offer many possibilities . . ." Writing, playing music, dancing, making art all involve similar states to trance. Scientists, architects, gardeners, and mathematicians use visualization in their work. When we work magic, we unlock our creativity.

Page 174 Drugs and Magic. Many indigenous and tribal societies do use mind-altering plants in ritual, and it is highly likely that Witches did. However, in those cultures the shamans and Priestesses were and are using plants they had a personal relationship with. They spend long hours learning the plant, communicating with it, listening to its wisdom before imbibing it.

I still think mixing drugs and ritual is a bad idea, for all the reasons mentioned above. Reclaiming's public rituals and Witch camps are drug- and alcohol-free.

However, there is also an incredible level of hypocrisy in our society around drug use. People who themselves use alcohol (a highly destructive drug), caffeine, and nicotine (more addictive than heroin) are eager to condemn and jail those who use marijuana or who self-medicate with other drugs to relieve emotional or psychic pain. President Clinton—a man who is clearly addicted to illicit sex—refused to recognize the legalization of medical marijuana when passed by the voters of California.

I don't use mind-altering drugs now, except for caffeine, which, like most of this society, I'm addicted to, and an occasional glass of wine. But if I had never taken psychedelics, I wouldn't have become a Witch. I wouldn't have written a book like this in my twenties. On the other hand, if I had taken more drugs, I might be standing on a street corner today begging for spare change, with all my belongings in a shopping bag.

Page 176 Disco music. Rave music is also known to be trance inducing. In fact, its latest evolution is termed "trance music."

Notes on Chapter Ten

Page 187 Over the last ten years, our community has continued to practice initiation, and the power of the experience grows. Initiation is one of the few situations in which we entrust others with the power to guide us, challenge us, and direct us. We let go of control, and our friends may point us in directions we would not otherwise have gone. The experience has the potential to catalyze our growth and transformation.

But initiation loses its power when it becomes a badge, a mark of status, of who is cool and who is not. In the Reclaiming tradition, initiation is not a prerequisite for participating in ritual, or even for teaching. Some members of our community refuse to participate in initiations or to be initiated out of a belief that a ritual which potentially sets some people apart should not be part of an egalitarian tradition.

I believe initiation is a valid and important part of Craft practice, but that it should be kept separate from any external status. It should not, for example, be used as the determining factor in choosing someone to represent us on an interfaith council, or to speak at a conference, or invoke a direction, or receive licensing papers. To link it to external rewards would undercut its meaning as a heart-called commitment to the Goddess and community.

Page 190 "I use rose petals . . ." Actually, I use whatever I happen to feel like using at the time, and as I've said, only herbs and flowers I've grown or gathered. I dry rose petals throughout the summer to keep on hand for winter initiations.

Notes on Chapter Eleven

Page 194 Full moon ritual. The hands-on healing described in this ritual can be done at almost any time, for the whole group as part of a ritual, or for an individual who needs special healing.

Notes on Chapter Twelve

The Sabbats The rituals as described here have often changed greatly from what I wrote twenty years ago, when I had done most of them only a few times. However, they remain roughly the same as the rituals I described ten years ago. Of course, in the

Reclaiming tradition we encourage creativity and spontaneity, so no ritual is ever done identically twice. But the basic acts and symbolism of the seasonal cycle follow the pattern that was already set ten years ago, especially for Samhain, Yule, Brigid, Beltane, and Litha. The Spring and Fall Equinoxes and Lughnasad still seem to be somewhat fluid in form and structure.

In our larger rituals, we now generally have someone take on a role we call "anchoring" or "deep witnessing." That person or persons sits in trance throughout the ritual, simply holding the circle in the plane of her or his attention. Rituals that are anchored feel more cohesive. Large groups retain a sense of intimacy and connection, and people's attention stays more focused. For very large rituals such as our public Halloween Spiral Dance, which may have fifteen hundred people, we use teams of three or four anchors who are relieved every hour. Anchors must be fairly experienced at magical work, and they must be carefully prepared, protected, tended, and brought back afterward. Again, personal instruction and care is necessary to learn this.

For seasonal rituals tailored to children and families, including stories, crafts, and recipes, see *Circle Round*.

Pages 197–202 Winter Solstice. We still do the ritual pretty much as I described it ten years ago. Our ocean plunge now often involves two or three hundred people—and a lecture on water safety. The chant "Set sail" has migrated to our Samhain ritual.

Our home vigil continues, as well. As we age, not all of us manage to stay up all night. We have also given up trying to do arts and crafts at three A.M., especially after a couple of magical disasters with Femo and melted plastic left in the oven too long. Instead, we bake bread. We time it to rise through the night, and each take a turn kneading in our hopes and desires for the coming year. (After the year I put in a tablespoon of salt instead of a teaspoon, I learned that if you want to bake ritual bread in the middle of the night, it helps to try out the recipe a few times beforehand during the year to become familiar with it.) In the morning, we feast on fresh bread and homemade plum jam bottled on the Summer Solstice. The children participate in our ritual until they fall asleep, and I tell them the story of Mother Winter (see *Circle Round*, p. 101).

Pages 202–3 Brigid. We have developed beautiful songs and chants for this ritual. (See Resources.) The Waters of the World, the water we collect throughout the year on our travels, have become an important element of our opening rituals at every Witch camp, and remain a core part of the Brigid ritual. We also now create a beautiful Brigid doll, made of wheat, sticks, grasses, and grains, which is dressed in white and carried in procession around the circle. She presides over the well and cauldron, where we make our pledges. Each pledge is sealed by the striking of the anvil. Our community has grown. The San Francisco ritual often involves two or three hundred people, and this year Reclaiming sponsored two others in the Bay Area as well. I would never design a ritual where several hundred people each had to speak individually—but this ceremony has always had a life of its own. Making the pledge, having the community witness it, hearing the clink of the anvil, truly sets a tone for the year. At the end, we dance to raise the Cone of Power. Some years we do a Spiral Dance, other years we just dance!

Page 203 Kissing in the dance. Oh, how I hate it when people kiss in a spiral! (As this text originally suggested.) I've been known to break out of line and run around yelling at people. In a small coven or intimate group, kissing is fine, but in a large, public event, it can be intrusive and obnoxious. I think of the Spiral Dance as a metaphor for community. We are all linked, and each person's motion affects everyone down the line. When someone leans forward to kiss, or stops for a moment, a small jerk happens, which is magnified as it goes down the line, until at the end, someone's arms are getting yanked out of their sockets.

We actually dance the Spiral Dance at many different rituals throughout the year. It's a simple and effective way to connect a group and raise power.

Pages 203–4 Eostar (Spring Equinox). Our ritual often centers around an egg hunt for the children. I also like to work with the myth of Demeter and Persephone.

Pages 204–5 Beltane. The issue of how to celebrate sexuality without enshrining heterosexuality plagued our San Francisco Bay Area Reclaiming group for years. Today we invoke creativity, community, love, and sexuality without limiting ourselves to heterosexual imagery. In *Circle Round*, I wrote a story for children, "The Goddess Blesses All Forms of Love" (pp. 179–83), that explains the imagery of the Maypole ribbons as the multiple forms of love we need to make the circle whole. The book also includes instructions on building a Maypole.

Pages 205–7 Litha (Summer Solstice). Our ritual today often also involves a plunge into the ocean, which is more pleasurable if less starkly purifying than in midwinter. After several years of honoring the sacred God/Bread as a charred lump of charcoal, we learned that underbaking it and then wrapping it in a few layers of tinfoil, followed by a layer of comfrey leaves and a final few layers of tinfoil, provides just the right amount of insulation.

Pages 207–8 Lughnasad. Sacred games are also a wonderful addition to this ritual (see *Circle Round*, pp. 241, 244–45). Our traditional Lammas chant, written by Raven Moonshadow, can be found on *Chants* (see Resources).

Pages 208–9 Mabon (Fall Eqinox). The Harvest Dinner is our ongoing tradition. *Mabon* is pronounced MAH-buhn. In *Circle Round*, I include the story of Mabon, son of Modron (pp. 256–60).

Pages 209–12 Samhain. Twenty years ago, the community that was later to become Reclaiming began a tradition of celebrating a large, public Halloween ritual. As we were also celebrating the publication of this book, we called the ritual the Spiral Dance. The ritual has now evolved into an event. We rent the largest public space in San Francisco to accommodate sometimes fifteen hundred people. At least two hundred people work to put on the ritual. The invocations might be done by stiltwalkers, dancers, acrobats, aerialists descending from the rafters. A full chorus sings the body of music we've created (see Resources). We honor the babies born during the year, and read the names of those who have died during the year while participants move in silent meditation to altars to light candles. We are guided on a trance journey to the Isle of the Dead, and dance a double spiral there while singing a call and response chant that charges our vision of the future. The Cone of Power raises the roof.

With all the circus/extravaganza atmosphere, the core of the ritual is still the naming of our beloved dead and the mutual support we give each other in our grief and love. We have learned how to create an intimate space on a very large scale. In our society which offers so few opportunities for public acknowledgment of grieving, and in our community which has suffered so deeply the ravages of AIDS, we offer a healing service.

Samhain is also a time for small-scale, family and coven rituals, as described here and in *Circle Round*. In smaller groups, we can not only name our beloved dead but also tell stories about them. I like to set up an altar with pictures of my family, my grandmother's braids, which she bobbed in the twenties, and my mother's and father's books. In our household, we cook traditional foods from our family's heritage, tell tales, and look at old photos when the trick or treating is done.

Reclaiming also participates in the Latino tradition of El Día de los Muertos on November 2. In San Francisco, this involves a huge procession of thousands of people, many in costume, carrying candles. It ends at a park in the inner city where artists and youth have created fantastic walk-through altars that transform what can be a violent area into sacred space.

And then we celebrate the sacred period of postritual collapse, which can last anywhere from three days through Yule!

Notes on Chapter Thirteen

Page 217 "If female images are merely plugged into old structures . . ." Not only female symbols, when women ourselves take power in old structures, we are likely to get the Margaret Thatchers of the world. Twenty years ago I was more likely to believe that if you had the right genitalia—whether you were a human or a Goddess—I could trust you. Alas, life is not really that simple.

Page 217 Marsha Lichtenstein quote. Her article was one of the first in a long series of critiques of Goddess spirituality that eventually crystallized around the term *essentialism*—the supposed idea that women and men are different in essence. The Goddess movement is accused of being essentialist, whereas 'true' political feminists are social constructionists, believing that gender—not just our physical sexuality but the whole complex of traits, behaviors, and expectations that go with it— is formed by our social conditioning.

My own answer to Lichtenstein still stands. She, like many of the critics, is arguing about her own constructs that reflect the old patriarchal dualities, not the complexity and fluidity of thought in the Goddess movement. My own journey is clear in this book if the reader troubles to look at the notes (which I spent a lot of time writing when I could have been out looking for deadly fungi or doing other fun Witch activities). In 1979, I was still influenced by Jungian formulations and terminologies such as "inner male" and "inner female," in part because throughout the seventies virtually no one but the Jungians was addressing these issues. Nevertheless, there are many statements in the original text that are more in sympathy with social construction: By 1989, I had moved entirely away from a Jungian framework or a view of the world as female/male polarity.

The historical analyses I did in *Dreaming the Dark* and *Truth or Dare* are also firmly rooted in material and economic causes.

There is certainly a wide variation in beliefs among Goddess worshippers, and no one can presume to speak for "the movement." However, I've found that a lot of these critics simply don't bother to read the sources that might contradict their prejudices. They practice a kind of pseudoscholarship thar ignores the evidence and unfortunately seems to find a home in academia. And while they claim the political high ground, they never seem to mention what actual political work they're doing beyond writing critiques in academic journals. I could say more on the subject, but I have to go send out a petition, write three letters in defense of the redwoods, respond to a question about our El Salvador project, and prepare for a community meeting with a new winery to discuss local land use issues.

Page 218 Dualism. The end of the cold war has had a shattering affect on our dualistic cultural mind-set. We can look at much of the nineties as a blind thrashing about in the dark, hoping to encounter a new Enemy, another Evil Empire: Saddam Hussein, drug addicts, Satanists, a president afflicted with satyriasis. None of them seem to really work to capture the public imagination and wrath. Alas for the Soviet Union— such a perfect villain, inspiring us to bankrupt ourselves in pursuit of ever more powerful weaponry against the Communist Menace. What a letdown when we discovered they couldn't even feed themselves!

Page 220 ". . . firmly grounded . . . in what we can observe . . ." My personal focus today arose from a message I received a few years ago, that I was "teaching too much meditation and not enough observation." I hope over the next decades that our community can deeply integrate our spirituality with science and hands-on earth-healing work.

Page 221 "When 'expanded consciousness' does not deepen our bonds . . . [it] is spiritual self-destruction." When we don't practice observation and focus our spiritual work on our internal imagery, we may become enamored of our own visions, lost in Faery. A useful checklist for our practice is to ask, Are my connections deepening with others? Is my love for the living world growing? Is my vision rooted in compassion? Is our group isolating itself? Am I spending a lot of time feeling judgmental and self-righteous?

Pages 223–24 The "growth" movement. I've probably been as unfair in this paragraph as the critics I was earlier complaining about. Yes, there are "New Age" teachers who express simplistic philosophies, but there are also many creative, pioneering healers and teachers who have persevered with new ideas for decades.

Ironically, this book and my subsequent work put me into the New Age camp. Although most Witches don't consider ourselves "New Agers," the rest of the world does.

I think the New Age deserves more credit than it often receives. The retreat centers and workshops and forums sponsored by New Age groups function like a wide-open university for ongoing learning, and keep alive ideas and practices that are too radical for academia. They're the model of education we rallied for in the sixties— people come purely because they want to learn, they are self-responsible for their learning, there are generally no tests, exams, grades, or external rewards, and teachers can't bore their students to death if they want to continue teaching. Some of the offerings might seem trivial, flaky, or crazy, but that's the price of freedom, of not institutionalizing a canon of knowledge. The ideas and programs that have staying power tend to be those that have real value. Yes, New Age events and workshops do cost money, but every workshop center I've taught at also has some sort of scholarship or work exchange policy. Compared with the cost of university courses, most New Age workshops are cheap—and few New Age centers or teachers have endowments to fall back on. People are often under the illusion that New Age centers or teachers are raking in the big bucks. In reality, most centers struggle to survive, and most teachers work very hard without achieving anywhere near the salary or benefits of a tenured college professor, let alone a computer programmer or middle manager. One of the changes that comes with middle age is the understanding that yes, it does cost money to provide clean and pleasant accommodations for people and healthy food, not to mention answering their half dozen phone calls. And while starving for your ideals was admirable and inspirational in your twenties, it becomes downright tiresome in your forties, especially when another generation in their twenties is clamoring for you to finance their education.

I wonder now why people who are "seeking" receive such scorn, especially from those who themselves proclaim that this system isn't working. Why, then, condemn people for looking for something else? If they don't always look where you think they should, they might still find something of value that you would never have encountered. If they choose to spend their money on education and self-development, would you prefer that they bought a new car or refurnished the living room? Should they give the money to charity instead? Most of them do already contribute time and energy to causes they believe in.

True, the New Age serves a certain constituency that is predominantly white and middle-class, and much more could be done to broaden access. Still, I remember back in the sixties and seventies many writers were trumpeting "a new model of education—people will be lifelong learners!" This prediction has come true, and instead of grumbling about it, I'd rather see us celebrate and explore ways to make this feast of ideas and learning ever more available to those who most need new resources and new visions.

Page 224 "A feminist religion needs no messiahs, no martyrs, no saints to lead the way." A feminist religion does, however, need empowering leaders who can provide a different model than the old structures of domination, who lead by stepping out in front with new ideas and also by being willing to step back at the right moment and let somebody else set the direction. The model for leadership I prefer is the drum. In Reclaiming rituals, the drummers help raise the energy for the Cone of Power by setting a beat and increasing the intensity as the cone rises. But the drummers do not direct the cone or whip it up into a frenzy. Instead, when the energy is strong enough to sustain itself, the drummers subtly fade away and let the combined voices of the people carry the cone to its peak. If the drummers drop out too soon or too abruptly, the energy falters. If they carry on too long, people feel manipulated. For me, good leadership does the same. Leaders sustain an energy and a vision until it takes on a life of its own, and then fade back, ideally neither too soon nor too late, letting others take over, knowing that the vision will evolve in new directions, and to see that process take place is both the challenge and the reward of leadership.

Leaders also need support. The feminist movement on the whole has been notorious for tearing down leaders as fast as they emerge. Good leadership needs to be nurtured with love and trust, with constructive criticism (see the second note to p. 70), and with compassion for mistakes, because if you think the above-described process is easy to pull off, you haven't tried it!

Page 225 ". . . a new cult of the Virgin Mary and a revival of the ancient Hebrew Goddess." We have indeed seen such developments in both Christianity and Judaism. I have participated in the Croning Ceremony for a dear friend who is a nun, attended Yom Kippur services where Asherah was invoked, led workshops in Israel on the Hebrew Goddess, and danced with women on the shores of the Red Sea. For Judaism, I especially honor the work of Marcia Falk, whose beautiful *Book of Blessings* reconfigures the traditional prayers to be nongendered and earth honoring. It's a great resource for earth-based religions whether Jewish-based or not.

Page 226 "It is easier . . ." I've been taken to task by many people for this paragraph, and I have to admit they are right. Adopting an ascetic tradition is not an escape from engagement with life, but simply a different choice. In point of fact, I would find it a lot harder to be celibate than fully alive sexually, and extremely difficult, if not impossible, to do any of the things I termed "easier." Whereas living in the world, feeling my emotions, communicating in a group, trusting myself, helping to raise a child—hey, I do those every day. Maybe that's partly the difference between forty-eight and twenty-eight.

Tables of Correspondences

The Elements

AIR

Direction: East

Rules: The mind, all mental, intuitive, and psychic work, knowledge, abstract learning, theory, windswept hills, plains, windy beaches, high mountain peaks, high towers, wind and breath

Time: Dawn

Season: Spring

Colors: White, bright yellow, crimson, blue-white, pastels

Signs of the Zodiac: Gemini, Libra, Aquarius

Tools: Athame, sword, censer

Spirits: Sylphs, ruled by their King Paralda (many of these systems are extremely male oriented; again, I include them for interest and reference—don't use them if you don't like them)

Angel: Michael

Name of the East Wind: Eurus

Sense: Smell

Jewel: Topaz

Incense: Frankincense, Galbanum

Plants: Frankincense, myrrh, pansy, primrose, vervain, violet, yarrow

Tree: Aspen

Animals: Birds, especially the eagle and the hawk, insects

Goddesses: Aradia, Arianrhod, Cardea, Nuit, Urania

Gods: Enlil, Khephera, Mercury, Shu, Thoth

FIRE

Direction: South
Rules: Energy, spirit, heat, flame, blood, sap, life, will, healing and destroying, purification, bonfires, hearth fires, candle flames, sun, deserts, volcanoes, eruptions, explosions
Time: Noon
Season: Summer
Colors: Red, gold, crimson, orange, white (the sun's noon light)
Signs of the Zodiac: Aries, Leo, Sagittarius
Tools: Censer, wand
Spirits: Salamanders, ruled by their King Djin
Angel: Ariel
Name of the South Wind: Notus
Sense: Sight
Jewel: Fire opal
Incense: Copal, Olibanum
Plants: Garlic, hibiscus, mustard, nettle, onion, red peppers, red poppies
Tree: Almond, in flower
Animals: Fire-breathing dragons; horses, when their hooves strike sparks; lions; snakes
Goddesses: Brigit, Hestia, Pele, Vesta
Gods: Agni, Hephaetus, Horus, Prometheus, Vulcan

WATER

Direction: West
Rules: Emotions, feelings, love, courage, daring, sorrow, the ocean, the tides, lakes, pools, streams, and rivers, springs and wells, intuition, the unconscious mind, the womb, generation, fertility
Time: Twilight
Season: Autumn
Colors: Blue, blue-green, green, gray, indigo, black
Signs of the Zodiac: Cancer, Scorpio, Pisces
Tool: Cup
Spirits: Undines, ruled by their King Niksa
Angel: Raphael
Name of the West Wind: Zephyrus
Sense: Taste
Jewel: Aquamarine
Incense: Myrrh
Plants: Ferns, lotus, mosses, rushes, seaweeds, water lilies, and all water plants
Tree: Willow
Animals: Dolphins and porpoises, dragons as serpents, fish, seals and sea mammals, water-dwelling snakes, all water creatures and sea birds

Goddesses: Arhrodite, Isis, Mari, Mariamne, Tiamat, Yemaya
Gods: Dylan, Ea, Llyr, Manannan, Neptune, Osiris, Poseidon

EARTH

Direction: North
Rules: The body, growth, nature, sustenance, material gain, money, creativity, birth, death, silence, chasms, caves, caverns, groves, fields, rocks, standing stones, mountains, crystal, jewels, metal, bones, structure
Time: Midnight
Season: Winter
Colors: Black, brown, green, white
Signs of the Zodiac: Taurus, Virgo, Capricorn
Tool: Pentacle
Spirits: Gnomes, ruled by their King Ghob
Angel: Gabriel
Names of the North Wind: Boreas, Ophion
Sense: Touch
Jewels: Rock crystal, salt
Incense: Benzoin, storax
Plants: Comfrey; grains: barley, corn, oats, rice, rye, wheat; ivy
Tree: Oak
Animals: Bison, cow or bull, snakes (earth-dwelling), stag
Goddesses: Ceres, Demeter, Gaea, Mah, Nephthys, Persephone, Prithivi, Rhea, Rhiannon
Gods: Adonis, Arawn, Athos, Cernunnos, Dionysus, Marduk, Pan, Tammuz

SPIRIT/ETHER

Direction: Center and circumference, throughout and about
Rules: Transcendence, transformation, change, everywhere and nowhere, within and without, the void, immanence
Time: Beyond time, all time is one
Season: The turning wheel
Colors: Clear, white, black
Tool: Cauldron
Sense: Hearing
Incense: Mastic
Plant: Mistletoe
Tree: The flowering almond
Animal: Sphinx
Goddesses: Isis, the Secret Name of the Goddess, Shekinah
Gods: Akasha, Iao, JHVH

The Heavenly Bodies

THE MOON

Rules: Woman; cycles; birth; generation; inspiration; poetry; emotions; travel, especially by water; the sea and tides; fertility; rain; intuition; psychic ability; secrets; dreams

New or Crescent Moon—the Maiden, birth and initiation, virginity, beginnings, the hunt

Full Moon—the Mother, growth, fulfillment, sexuality, maturation, nurturing, love

Waning or Dark Moon—the Crone, the woman past menopause, old age, deep secrets, wisdom, divination, prophecy, death and resurrection, endings

Day: Monday

Element: Water

Colors:

   New—white or silver

   Full—red or green

   Waning—black

Sign of the Zodiac: Cancer

Tone: Ti

Letter: S

Number: 3 or 9

Jewels: Moonstone, pearl, quartz, rock crystal

Cabalistic sphere: 9 Yesod—Foundation

Angel: Gabriel

Incense: Ginseng, jasmine, myrtle, or poppy, sandalwood, coconut

Plants: Banana, cabbage, chamomile, chickweed, cucumber, leafy vegetables, lotus, melons, mushrooms, myrtle, opium poppy, pumpkin, purslane, sea holly, seaweed, watercress, wild rose, wintergreen

Tree: Willow

Animals: cat, elephant, hare

Goddesses: Anna, Artemis, Brizo, Ceridwen, Diana, Hathor, Hecate, Isis, Levanah, Lunah, Mari, Nimuë, Pasiphaë, Phoebe, Selene

   New—Artemis, Nimuë

   Full—Diana, Mari

   Waning—Anna, Hecate

Gods: Atlas, Khonsu, Sin

THE SUN

Rules: Joy, success, advancement, leadership, natural power, friendship, growth, healing, light, pride

Day: Sunday

Element: Fire

Colors: Gold, yellow

Sign: Leo

Tone: Re, D

Letter: B
Number: 1, 6, or 21
Metal: Gold
Jewel: Topaz, yellow diamond
Cabalistic sphere: 6 Tiphereth—Beauty
Angel: Raphael
Incense: Cinnamon, cloves, frankincense, laurel, olibanum
Plants: Acacia, angelica, bay laurel, chamomile, citrus fruits, heliotrope, honey, juniper, lovage, marigold, mistletoe, rosemary, rue, saffron, St. John's Wort, sunflower, vine
Trees: Acacia, ash, bay laurel, birch, broom
Animals: Child, eagle, lion, phoenix, sparrowhawk
Goddesses: Amaterasu, Bast, Brigit, Ilat, Sekhmet, Theia
Gods: Apollo, Helios, Hyperion, Lugh, Ra, Semesh, Vishnu-Krishna-Rama

MERCURY

Rules: Communications, intelligence, cleverness, creativity, science, memory, business transactions, thievery, trickiness
Day: Wednesday
Elements: Air, Water
Colors: Violet, mixtures of colors
Signs of the Zodiac: Gemini, Virgo
Tone: Mi, B
Letter: C
Number: 1, 4, or 8
Metals: Alloys, quicksilver
Jewels: Opal, agate
Cabalistic sphere: 8 Chod—Glory
Angel: Michael
Incense: Mace, Storax
Plants: Caraway, carrots, cascara sagrada, dill, elecampane, fennel, fenugreek, horehound, lavender, licorice, mandrake, marjoram, myrtle, parsley, pomegranate, valerian
Tree: Almond, ash, or hazel
Animal: Hermaphrodite, jackal, or twin serpents
Goddesses: Athena, Maat, Metis, Pombagira
Gods: Anubis, Coeus, Coyote, Elegba, Hermes, Lug, Mercury, Nabu, Thoth, Woden

VENUS

Rules: Love, harmony, attraction, friendship, pleasure, sexuality
Day: Friday
Elements: Earth, Water
Colors: Green, indigo, rose
Signs: Taurus, Libra
Tone: La, E

Letter: Q
Number: 5, 6, or 7
Metal: Copper
Jewels: Amber, emerald
Cabalistic sphere: 7 Netzach—Splendor
Angel: Haniel
Incense: Benzoin, jasmine, rose
Plants: Acacia flowers, almond oil, aloes, apple, birch, daffodil, damask rose, elder-berry, feverfew, fig, geranium, mint, mugwort, olive oil, pennyroyal, plantain, rasp-berry, rose, strawberry, tansy, thyme, verbena, vervain, violet
Trees: Apple, quince
Animals: Dove, lynx
Goddesses: Aphrodite, Asherah, Astarte, Beltis, Freia, Hathor, Inanna, Ishtar, Isis, Mari, Mariamne, Oshun, Tethys, Venus
Gods: Eros, Oceanus, Pan, Robin Hood

MARS

Rules: Strength, struggle, war, anger, conflict, aggression
Day: Tuesday
Element: Fire
Color: Red
Signs of the Zodiac: Aries; some authorities give Scorpio also
Tone: Do, C
Letter: T
Number: 2, 3 or 16, possibly 5
Metals: Iron, steel
Jewel: Bloodstone, garnet, or ruby
Cabalistic sphere: 5 Gevurah—Strength, severity
Angel: Kamael
Incense: Cypress, pine, or tobacco
Plants: All-Heal, aloes, asafoetida, basil, betony, capers, chiles, coriander, dragon's blood, garlic, gentian, ginger, mustard, onion, pepper, radish, sarsaparilla, tarragon
Trees: Holly, Kerm-oak
Animal: Basilisk
Goddesses: Anath, Brigit, Dione, Morrigan
Gods: Ares, Crius, Heracles, Mars, Nergal

JUPITER

Rules: Leadership, politics, power, honor, royalty, public acclaim, responsibility, wealth, business, success
Day: Thursday
Elements: Air, Fire
Colors: Deep blue, royal purple
Sign: Sagittarius

Tone: So, A
Letter: D
Number: 5 or 4
Metal: Tin
Jewel: Amethyst, chrysolite, sapphire, or turquoise
Cabalistic sphere: 4 Chesed—Mercy
Angel: Tzadkiel
Incense: Cedar, nutmeg
Plants: Agrimony, anise, ash, balm, betony, blood root, borage, cinquefoil, clover, dandelion, hyssop, juniper berries, linden, mint, mistletoe, nutmeg, sage
Tree: Oak, olive, or terebinth
Animal: Unicorn
Goddesses: Hera, Isis, Juno, Themis
Gods: Bel, Eurymedon, Jupiter, Marduk, Thor, Zeus

SATURN

Rules: Obstacles, limitations, binding, knowledge, death, buildings, history, time, structures
Day: Saturday
Elements: Water, Earth
Colors: Black, blue
Sign: Capricorn
Tone: Fa, G
Letter: F
Number: 7 or 3
Metal: Lead
Jewel: Pearl, onyx, or star sapphire
Sphere: Cabalistic sphere
Angel: Tzaphkiel
Incense: Civet, ironwood, myrrh
Plants: Aconite (monkshood or wolfbane), beets, bistort (dragonwort), comfrey, cypress, hellebore, hemlock, hemp, henbane, horsetail, mandrake, marijuana, opium poppy, nightshade, patchouli, Solomon's Seal, thyme, yew
Trees: Alder, pomegranate
Animals: Crow, raven
Goddesses: Cybele, Demeter, Hecate, Hera, Isis, Kali, Nephthys, Rhea
Gods: Bran, Cronos, Ninib, Saturn, YHVH

Aspects of Life

LOVE

Elements: Water, Earth
Planet: Venus

Best times:
> Friday or Monday
> New to Full Moon in
>> Taurus—earthy and sensual love
>> Cancer—home and family
>> Libra—idealistic
>> Scorpio—sexual!

Colors: Deep rose, green, orange for attraction
Metal: Copper or silver
Number: 5 or 7
Incense/Perfume: Benzoin, jasmine, rose; for sensual passion, civet, musk, patchouli, rose ava
Plants: All herbs of Venus, especially acacia flowers, aloes, Balm of Gilead (buds carried on your person will mend a broken heart!), cyclamen (if a potted plant is kept in the bedroom, the union will be long and happy), elecampane, gardenia, jasmine, lavender, meadowsweet, mistletoe, myrrh, myrtle, rose, tansy, tuberose, valerian, vervain, violet
Aphrodisiacs (reputed): Beth root, clover, coriander, damiana, dulse, fo-ti-tieng, ginseng, nasturtium, periwinkle, yohimbe
Goddesses: Aphrodite, Asherah, Astarte, Beltis, Branwen (can grant either union with true love or cure for the passion), Diana, Freia, Hathor, Ishtar, Isis, Maia, Mari, Mariamne, Oshun, Venus
Gods: Adonis, Cernunnos, Eros, Pan, Robin Hood

MONEY AND BUSINESS

Elements: Earth, Air
Planets: Jupiter, Mercury, the Sun
Best times:
> Thursday, Wednesday, or Sunday
> Waxing to full moon for increase in
>> *an earth sign*—for material gain
>> *an air sign*—for ideas, plans
>> *a fire sign*—for energy, growth
>> *Virgo*—for work involving detail
>> *Capricorn*—for caution, or to overcome obstacles
>> *Leo*—for solar power
>> *Sagittarius*—for expansion, travel
>> *Aries*—for beginning a new project

Colors: Green, gold, silver
Number: 1, 4, 8, or 7
Incense: Cedar, cinnamon, laurel, mace, nutmeg, or storax
Plants: Balm, borage, High John the Conqueror root, lavender, mandrake, oak leaves, saffron, sage, St. John's Wort, sunflower seeds, valerian, wintergreen
Goddesses: Demeter, Earth Goddesses, Hera, Juno
Gods: Earth Gods, Hermes, Jupiter, Lugh, Mercury, Zeus

CREATIVE WORK

Element: All
Planets: Earth, Mercury (for communication), the Moon (for inspiration), the Sun
Best times:
    Monday, Wednesday, or Sunday
        Moon waxing—for beginning
        Near the full—for inspiration
        Waning—for self-criticism, reworking
        an air sign—for mental work, especially involving words
        an earth sign—for crafts and work with the hands
        a fire sign—for creative energy
        a water sign—for emotional expressions
Colors: Gold, silver, violet, yellow, mixtures of colors
Number: 1, 3, 4, 6, or 9
Incense: Bay laurel, cinnamon, ginseng, mace, storax
Plants: Laurel, lavender, myrtle, skullcap, valerian
Goddesses: Athena or Minerva (for knowledge, wisdom), Brigit (Triple Goddess of healing, poetry, and smithcraft), Ceridwen (Keeper of the Cauldron of Inspiration), Mnemosyne (Mother of the Triple Muse)
    The Triple Muse:
        Calliope—"beautiful face"
        Erato—"beloved one"
        Urania—"heavenly one"
    The Ninefold Muse:
        Calliope—Epic poetry
        Clio—History
        Euterpe—Lyric poetry
        Melpomene—Tragedy
        Terpsichore—Choral dancing
        Erato—Erotic poetry and mime
        Polyhymnia—Sacred poetry
        Urania—Astronomy
        Thaleia—Comedy
    Any form of the Triple Goddess
Gods: Apollo (music and poetry); Orpheus (music); Ogma (poetry); Hermes, Mercury, and Thoth (knowledge and communication); Credne, Gobniu, and Hephaestus (all for crafts, smithcraft)

HEALING

Elements: All
Planets: Sun, Moon, Earth
Best times:
    Sunday or Monday

Moon waxing to full—for increased health

Moon waning or dark—to banish, drive away disease

In earth or water sign

Colors: Blue, green, gold, orange

Number: 1, 3, 7, or 9

Incense: Bay, cinnamon, eucalyptus, frankincense, sandalwood

Plants: All healing herbs

Goddesses: Artemis, Hebe, Hygeia, Moon and Earth Goddesses

Gods: Asclepius, Apollo, Diancecht

LAW AND JUSTICE

Elements: Earth, Air

Planets: Jupiter, Sun, Mercury, Saturn, Mars

Best times:

Thursday—for success, securing justice

Sunday—for freedom

Saturday—to bind a criminal, to limit someone's freedom or bring them to justice, for prosecution

Tuesday—for strength in conflict

Colors: Deep blue, royal purple, red, black, brown

Number: 4 or 8

Incense: Cedar, cypress, frankincense, pine, or sandalwood

Plants: garlic (for protection), herbs of the appropriate planetary powers, High John the Conqueror root and St. John's Wort (for invincibility), nettles or vines (for binding)

Goddesses: Aradia (to protect the poor), Athena (for mercy, especially), Maat, Nemesis (to bring justice against an offender), Themis

Gods: The Dagda, Jupiter, Osiris, Thoth, Zeus

PROTECTION

Elements: All

Planets: Moon, Sun

Best times:

Monday or Sunday

Waxing to full moon—to establish protection

Waning moon—banishing evil

Colors: Silver, white, blue

Number: 4, 5, 3, 9, or 8

Metal: Silver

Incense: Bay laurel, cinnamon, rosemary

Plants: Asafoetida, avens (Star of the Earth), basil (wards off evil), blood root, broom tops (to put in water used for aspurging and purification), burdock, cinquefoil, feverfew (protects against sickness and accidents), garlic (wear the cloves or hang on the threshold to keep evil away), High John the Conqueror root, hyssop, laurel, man-drake, motherwort, nettles (for binding), patchouli, purslane, rosemary (plant by your threshold to protect the home), rowan (especially against evil psychic forces), Solomon's Seal (used in exorcism), St. John's Wort, unicorn root, vervain (gathered with the left hand at the rise of the Dog Star, Sirius)

Goddesses: Moon Goddesses, especially Artemis (protects young children), and Aradia, Hera

Gods: Cuchulain, the Dagda, Jupiter, Thor

PSYCHIC WORK

Elements: Air, Water, Fire

Planet: Moon

Best times:

Full moon—for the height of psychic power

Dark moon—for deep, hidden secrets and mysteries

Colors: Silver, white, black

Number: 3 or 9

Incense: Cinnamon, saffron, wormwood, other appropriate plants

Plants:

Relaxation: Anise, catnip, chamomile, dandelion, hops, lavender, linden, mint, nutmeg (rub the oil on temples), parsley, red clover, sage, savory, tarragon, thyme (wild), valerian (stuff a pillow with it), vervain

Visualization: Ginseng, gota cola, mugwort, skullcap

Sleep pillow: Lavender and linden

Concentration and memory: All Heal, Eyebright, lemon balm, marjoram, nutmeg, parsley, petitgrain oil, rosemary, sage

Mental and steadiness: Celery, chamomile, and rosemary together

Energy: Ginseng, gota cola, lovage (a bath in this herb refreshes psychic powers), yerba mate

Dreams: Ash leaves, mugwort, artemisia; chamomile, mugwort, and skullcap (together in a tea, drink before sleep)

To prevent nightmares and fearful visions: Chamomile, rosemary, wood betony (place some under your pillow)

Divination and trance work: Acacia flowers, bistort (dragonwort), ginseng, laurel leaves (chewed by the Priestesses of Delphi), mugwort (drink a tea for clear vision), nutmeg, saffron (tea or incense), wormwood (incense, burned on Halloween to enable one to see the returning spirits of the Mighty Dead)

Psychedelics: Are better left alone when you are beginning to open up psychically. They tend to wrench the psychic centers open too quickly and in an uncon-trolled way—sometimes with destructive results.

Goddesses: All Moon Goddesses, Ceridwen, Cybele, Hecate (for divination and spells), Hera (for prophecy), Nephthys, Pasiphaë (for dream oracles)

Gods: Asclepius (for dream oracles that have to do with healing), Gwydion, Hermes, Math, Merddin, Thoth

Select Bibliography

Anderson, Victor. *Thorns of the Blood Rose*. San Leandro, Calif.: Cora Anderson, 1970.

Anima, An Experimental Journal, 1975, 1(2).

Bartlett, Lee. "Interview—Gary Snyder." *California Quarterly* 9 (Spring 1975): 43–50.

Besant, Annie, and C. W. Leadbeater. *Thought-Forms*. Wheaton, Ill.: Theosophical Publishing, 1969.

Blanc, Alberto C. "Some Evidence for the Ideologies of Early Man," in Sherwood L. Washburn, ed., *The Social Life of Early Man*. Chicago: Aldine Publishing Co., 1961, p. 124.

Bonewitz, P. E. I. *Real Magic*. Berkeley, Calif.: Creative Arts Books, 1979.

Braidwood, Robert J. "The Agricultural Revolution." *Scientific American* 203, no. 48 (September 1960): 130–34.

Braidwood, Robert J. *Prehistoric Men*. Glenview, Ill.: Scott, Foresman, 1964.

Breuil, Henri, and Raymond Lantier. *The Men of the Old Stone Age*. Trans. B. B. Rafter. London: Harrap, 1965.

Brown, Barbara. *New Mind, New Body*. New York: Harper & Row, 1974.

Buckland, Raymond. *Witchcraft from the Inside*. St. Paul, Minn.: Llewellyn, 1971.

Budapest, Z. *The Feminist Book of Lights and Shadows*. Venice, Calif.: Luna Publications, 1976.

Campbell, Joseph. *The Masks of God: Creative Mythology*. New York: Viking Press, 1970.

Campbell, Joseph. *The Masks of God: Oriental Mythology*. New York: Penguin Books, 1970.

Campbell, Joseph. *Myths to Live By*. New York: Bantam Books, 1973.

Campbell, Joseph. *The Masks of God: Primitive Mythology*. New York: Penguin Books, 1976.

Carruth, Hayden, ed. *The Voice That Is Great Within Us: American Poetry of the Twentieth Century*. New York: Bantam Books, 1971.

Castaneda, Carlos. *The Teachings of Don Juan: A Yaqui Way of Knowledge*. Berkeley and Los Angeles: University of California Press, 1968.

Castaneda, Carlos. *A Separate Reality: Further Conversations with Don Juan.* New York: Simon & Schuster, 1971.

Castaneda, Carlos. *Tales of Power.* New York: Simon & Schuster, 1974.

Chadwick, Nora K. *Celtic Britain.* New York: Praeger, 1963.

Chicago, Judy. *The Dinner Party: A Symbol of Our Heritage.* Garden City, N.Y.: Anchor Press/Doubleday, 1979.

Christ, Carol P., and Judith Plaskow, eds. *Womanspirit Rising.* San Francisco: Harper & Row, 1979.

Chrysalis, A Magazine of Women's Culture. Los Angeles: Winter Solstice, 1978.

Claiborne, Robert. *Climate, Man and History.* New York: Norton, 1970.

Clark, Grahame, and Stuart Piggott. *Prehistoric Societies.* London: Hutchinson & Co., 1967.

The CoEvolution Quarterly 12 (Summer 1976).

Commoner, Barry. *The Closing Circle.* New York: Knopf, 1971.

Courtot, Martha. "Tribes." *Lady-Unique-Inclination-of-the-Night.* New Brunswick, N.J.: Sowing Circle Press, 1977, Cycle 2, pp. 12–13.

Crawford, O. G. S. *The Eye Goddess.* New York: Macmillan, 1958.

Crowley, Aleister. *Magick in Theory & Practice.* New York: Dover, 1976.

Cummings, E. E. "i thank you God." *Poems 1923–1954.* New York: Harcourt Brace Jovanovich, 1954.

Daly, Mary. *Beyond God the Father: Toward a Philosophy of Women's Liberation.* Boston: Beacon Press, 1973.

Daly, Mary. *Gyn/Ecology: The Meta-Ethics of Radical Feminism.* Boston: Beacon Press, 1978.

Davis, Elizabeth Gould. *The First Sex.* New York: Putnam's, 1971.

Diner, Helen. *Mothers and Amazons.* New York: Anchor Press, 1973.

Dinnerstein, Dorothy. *The Mermaid & the Minotaur: Sexual Arrangements and Human Malaise.* New York: Harper & Row, 1976.

Di Prima, Diane. *Loba.* Berkeley: Wingbow Press, 1978.

Ehrenreich, Barbara, and Deirdre English. *Witches, Midwives, and Nurses: A History of Women Healers.* Old Westbury, N.Y.: Feminist Press, 1973.

Ehrenzweig, Anton. *The Hidden Order of Art.* London: Paladin, 1967.

Eliade, Mircea. *Rites & Symbols of Initiation.* Trans. William R. Trask. New York: Harper & Row, 1958.

Eliot, T. S. *The Waste Land and Other Poems.* New York: Harcourt Brace Jovanovich, 1958.

Eogan, George. "The Knowth Excavations." *Antiquity* 41 (December 1967): 302–4.

Evans, Arthur. *Witchcraft and the Gay Counterculture.* Boston: Fag Rag Books, 1978.

Evans-Wentz, W. Y. *The Fairy Faith in Celtic Countries.* Secaucus, N.J.: University Books, 1966.

Forfreedom, Anne, ed. *Women Out of History: A Herstory Anthology.* Venice, Calif.: Anne Forfreedom, 1972.

Fortune, Dion. *Moon Magic.* New York: Weiser, 1972.

Frazer, Sir James. *The New Golden Bough.* Ed. Theodor H. Gaster. New York: Criterion Books, 1959.

Freund, Phillip. *Myths of Creation*. New York: Washington Square Press, 1965.

Gardner, Gerald B. *Witchcraft Today*. Cavendish, Suffolk, Great Britain: Ryder, 1954.

Gardner, Gerald. *High Magic's Aid*. New York: Weiser, 1975.

Garfield, Patricia. *Creative Dreaming*. New York: Simon & Schuster, 1975.

Glass, Justine. *Witchcraft, The Sixth Sense*. North Hollywood, Calif.: Wilshire, 1965.

Goldberg, Herb. *The Hazards of Being Male*. New York: New American Library, 1977.

Goldenburg, Naomi. *The Changing of the Gods*. Boston: Beacon Press, 1979.

Graves, Robert. *The Greek Myths*. Vols. 1 and 2. London: Hazell Watson & Viney, 1955.

Graves, Robert. *Food for Centaurs*. New York: Doubleday, 1960.

Graves, Robert. *The White Goddess*. New York: Farrar, Straus & Giroux, 1966.

Gray, Louis Herbert, and George F. Moore. *The Mythology of All Races*, Vols. 1, 3, 8, and 10. New York: Cooper Square, 1964.

Grieve, M. *A Modern Herbal*. Vols. 1 and 2. New York: Dover, 1971.

Griffin, Susan. *Woman and Nature: The Roaring Inside Her*. San Francisco: Harper & Row, 1978.

Gurdjieff, G. I. *Meetings with Remarkable Men*. New York: Dutton, 1969.

Harding, M. Esther. *Women's Mysteries: Ancient and Modern*. New York: Pantheon, 1955.

Harding, M. Esther. *The Way of All Women*. New York: Harper & Row, 1975.

Harris, Marvin. *Cows, Pigs, Wars, and Witches: The Riddles of Culture*. New York: Random House, 1974.

Harrison, Jane Ellen. *Prolegomena to the Study of Greek Religion*. Cambridge, England: Cambridge University Press, 1922.

Hartley, Christine. *The Western Mystery Tradition*. London: Aquarian Press, 1968.

Hawkes, Jaquetta. *The First Great Civilizations*. New York: Knopf, 1973.

Hawkins, Gerald S. *Beyond Stonehenge*. New York: Harper & Row, 1973.

Heresies. "The Great Goddess Issue," Spring 1978 (New York).

Hitching, Francis. *Earth Magic*. New York: Morrow, 1977.

Hoyle, Fred. "Stonehenge, An Eclipse Predictor." *Nature* 211 (1966): 456–58.

Ingalls, John D. *Human Energy: The Critical Factor for Individuals and Organizations*. Reading, Mass.: Addison-Wesley, 1976.

Jaynes, Julian. *The Origin of Consciousness in the Breakdown of the Bicameral Mind*. Boston: Houghton Mifflin, 1977.

Kenyon, Kathleen. "Ancient Jericho." *Scientific American* 190, no. 22 (April 1968): 76–82.

Krippner, Stanley, and Daniel Rubin. *The Kirlian Aura: Photographing the Galaxies of Life*. New York: Doubleday, 1974.

Lady-Unique-Inclination-of-the-Night. Cycle 1. New Brunswick, N.J.: Sowing Circle Press, 1976.

Lady-Unique-Inclination-of-the-Night. Cycle 2. New Brunswick, N.J.: Sowing Circle Press, 1977.

Laming, Annette. *Lascaux*. Trans. Eleanore Frances Armstrong. Harmondworth, Middlesex: Penguin Books, 1959.

Leadbeater, C. W. *Man Visible and Invisible*. Wheaton, Ill.: Theosophical Publishing, 1971.

Leek, Sybil. *Diary of a Witch*. New York: Signet, 1968.

LeGuin, Ursula K. *A Wizard of Earthsea*. New York: Bantam Books, 1975.

Leland, Charles. *Aradia, Gospel of the Witches*. New York: Weiser, 1974.

Leroi-Gourhan, André. "The Evolution of Paleolithic Art." *Scientific American* 218, no. 17 (1968): 58–68.

Lichtenstein, Marsha. "Radical Feminism and Women's Spirituality: Looking Before You Leap." *Lady-Unique-Inclination-of-the-Night*. New Brunswick, N.J.: Sowing Circle Press, 1977, Cycle 2, pp. 36–43.

Lilly, John C. *The Center of the Cyclone*. New York: Julian Press, 1972.

Long, Max Freedom. *The Secret Science Behind Miracles*. Santa Monica, Calif.: Devorss, 1954.

Mander, Anica Vesel, and Anne Kent Rush. *Feminism as Therapy*. Berkeley, Calif.: Bookworks, 1974.

Maringer, Johannes. *The Gods of Prehistoric Man*. Trans. Mary Ilford. New York: Knopf, 1960.

Maringer, Johannes, and Hans-George Bandi. *Art in the Ice Age*. New York: Frederick A. Praeger, 1953.

Maslow, Abraham H. *Toward a Psychology of Being*. Princeton, N.J.: D. Van Nostrand, 1962.

Mathers, S. L. MacGregor. *The Greater Key of Solomon*. Chicago: De Lawrence, 1914.

Mellaart, James. "Hacilar, Neolithic Village Site." *Scientific American* 205, no. 27 (August 1961): 86–97.

Mellaart, James. *Catal Hüyük, a Neolithic Town in Anatolia*. New York: McGraw-Hill, 1967.

Millet, Kate. *Flying*. New York: Ballantine Books, 1974.

Monroe, Robert A. *Journeys Out of the Body*. New York: Doubleday, 1973.

Morgan, Robin. *Going Too Far*. New York: Random House, 1977.

Murray, Margaret A. *The God of the Witches*. New York: Oxford University Press, 1970.

Murray, Margaret A. *The Witch-Cult in Western Europe*. New York: Oxford University Press, 1971.

Noteskin, Wallace. *A History of Witchcraft in England*. New York: Crowell, 1968.

Ornstein, Robert E. *The Psychology of Consciousness*. San Francisco: W. H. Freeman, 1972.

Ostrander, Sheila, and Lynn Schroeder. *Psychic Discoveries Behind the Iron Curtain*. New York: Bantam Books, 1970.

Patai, Raphael. *The Hebrew Goddess*. Philadelphia: Ktav, 1967.

Quest: A Feminist Quarterly. (Washington, D.C.), 1, no. 4 (1975).

Rainer, Tristine. *The New Diary*. Los Angeles: Tarcher, 1978.

Renfrew, Colin. "Carbon 14 and the Prehistory of Europe." *Scientific American* 225, no. 12 (October 1971): 63–70.

Ringgren, Helmer. *Religions of the Ancient Near East*. Trans. John Sturdy. Philadelphia: Westminster Press, 1973.

Rose, Jeanne. *Herbs & Things: Jeanne Rose's Herbal.* New York: Grosset & Dunlap, 1973.

Rothenberg, Jerome, ed. *Technicians of the Sacred.* New York: Doubleday, 1969.

Rothovius, Andrew E. "The Adams Family and the Grail Tradition: The Untold Story of the Dragon Persecution." *East-West* 7, no. 5 (May 1977): 24–30.

Rothovius, Andrew E. "The Dragon Tradition in the New World." *East-West* 7, no. 8 (August 1977): 42–54.

Ruether, Rosemary R. *New Woman/New Earth: Sexist Ideologies and Human Liberation.* New York: Seabury Press, 1975.

Rush, Anne Kent. *Moon, Moon.* Berkeley, Calif.: Moon Books/Random House, 1976.

Scholem, Gershom G. *Major Trends in Jewish Mysticism.* New York: Schocken Books, 1971.

Scot, Reginald. *The Discoverie of Witchcraft.* New York: Dover, 1972.

Sheba, Lady. *The Book of Shadows.* St. Paul, Minn.: Llewellyn, 1973.

Showerman, Grant. *The Great Mother of the Gods.* Chicago: Argonaut, 1969.

Simos, Bertha. *A Time to Grieve: Loss as a Universal Human Experience.* New York: Family Service Association Press, 1979.

Spretnak, Charlene. *Lost Goddesses of Early Greece.* Berkeley, Calif.: Moon Books, 1978.

Squire, Charles. *Celtic Myth & Legend.* North Hollywood, Calif.: Newcastle, 1975.

Stern, Philip Van Doren. *Prehistoric Europe: From Stone Age Man to the Early Greeks.* New York: W. W. Norton, 1969.

Stone, Merlin. *When God Was a Woman.* New York: Dial Press, 1976.

Thom, Alexander. "Megaliths and Mathematics." *Antiquity* 40 (1966): 121–28.

Torrey, E. Fuller. *The Mind Game, Witchdoctors and Psychiatrists.* New York: Bantam Books, 1973.

Valiente, Doreen. *An ABC of Witchcraft, Past and Present.* New York: St. Martin's Press, 1973.

Von Cles–Reden, Sibylle. *The Realm of the Great Goddess.* Englewood Cliffs, N.J.: Prentice-Hall, 1962.

Waldo-Schwartz, Paul. *Art and the Occult.* New York: Braziller, 1975.

Watkins, Alfred. *The Old Straight Track.* New York: Ballantine Books, 1973.

Wedeck, Harry E. *A Treasury of Witchcraft.* Secaucus, N.J.: Stuart, 1972. *Womanspirit Magazine* (Wolf Creek, Oregon).

Suggested Reading

(The last twenty years have seen so much published on the Goddess, Witchcraft, and Feminist Spirituality that no bibliography could begin to do it justice. What follows is a very idiosyncratic selection of some of my favorites. Books marked with an asterisk include articles by me or interviews with me.)

Abbott, Franklin, ed. *New Men, New Minds: Breaking Male Tradition*. Freedom, Calif.: Crossing Press, 1987.

Abram, David. *The Spell of the Sensuous*. New York: Pantheon, 1996.

Adair, Margo. *Working Inside Out: Tools for Change*. Berkeley, Calif.: Wingbow Press, 1984.

Adler, Margot. *Drawing Down the Moon*. Boston: Beacon Press, 1986.

Allen, Paula Gunn. *The Woman Who Owned the Shadows*. San Francisco: Spinster's Ink, 1983.

Allen, Paula Gunn. *The Sacred Hoop: Recovering the Feminine in American Indian Traditions*. Boston: Beacon Press, 1986.

Allione, Tsultrim. *Women of Wisdom*. New York: Routledge & Kegan Paul, 1986.

Anderson, William. *Green Man: The Archetype of Our Oneness with the Earth*. London, San Francisco: Harper Collins, 1990.

Arthur, Elizabeth. *Binding Spell*. New York: Doubleday, 1988.

Atwood, Margaret. *The Handmaid's Tale*. Boston: Houghton Mifflin, 1986.

Ausubel, Kenny. *Seeds of Change: The Living Treasure*. San Francisco: HarperSanFrancisco, 1994.

Ausubel, Kenny. *Restoring the Earth*. Tiburon, Calif.: H. J. Kramer, 1997.

Baker, Mariam. *Woman as Divine: Tales of the Goddess*. Novato, Calif.: Crescent Heart Publishing, 1982.

Baring, Anne, and Jules Cashford. *The Myth of the Goddess: The Evolution of an Image*. New York: Viking Arkana, 1991.

Begg, Ean. *The Cult of the Black Virgin*. New York: Routledge & Kegan Paul, 1985.

Benjamins, Eso. *Dearest Goddess: Translations from Latvian Folk Poetry*. Arlington, Va.: Current Nine Publishing, 1985.

Berger, Pamela. *The Goddess Obscured: Transformation of the Grain Protectress from Goddess to Saint*. Boston: Beacon Press, 1985.

Bly, Robert. *Iron John: A Book About Men*. Reading, Mass.: Addison-Wesley, 1990.

Bolen, Jean Shinoda. *Goddesses in Everywoman: A New Psychology of Women*. New York: Harper & Row, 1984.

Bondoc, Anna, and Meg Daly, eds. *Letters of Intent: Women Cross the Generations to Talk About Family, Work, Sex, Love and the Future of Feminism*. New York: Free Press, 1999.*

Bradley, Marion Zimmer. *The Mists of Avalon*. New York: Knopf, 1983.

Broker, Ignatia. *Night Flying Woman: An Ojibway Narrative*. St. Paul: Minnesota Historical Society Press, 1983.

Budapest, Z. *The Holy Book of Women's Mysteries*. Vols. 1 and 2. Berkeley, Calif.: Wingbow Press, 1986.

Budapest, Z. *The Grandmother of Time*. San Francisco: Harper & Row, 1989.

Budapest, Z. *The Goddess in the Office*. San Francisco: HarperSanFrancisco, 1993.

Budapest, Z. *The Goddess in the Bedroom*. San Francisco: HarperSanFrancisco, 1995.

Budapest, Z. *Summoning the Fates: A Woman's Guide to Destiny*. New York: Harmony, 1998.

Cahill, Sedonia, and Joshua Halpern. *The Ceremonial Circle, Shamanic, Practice, Ritual and Renewal*. London: HarperCollins, 1991.

Caldecott, Leonie, and Stephanie Leland, eds. *Reclaim the Earth*. London: Women's Press, 1983.

Cameron, Anne. *Daughters of Copper Woman*. Vancouver: Press Gang, 1981.

Cameron, Anne. *Earth Witch*. Madeira Park, British Columbia: Harbour Publishing, 1985.

Carey, Ken. *Flat Rock Journal*. San Francisco: HarperSanFrancisco, 1994.

Carson, Anne. *Feminist Spirituality and the Feminine Divine: An Annotated Bibliography*. Freedom, Calif.: Crossing Press, 1986.

Chernin, Kim. *The Obsession: Reflections on the Tyranny of Slenderness*. New York: Harper & Row, 1981.

Chernin, Kim. *In My Mother's House*. New York: Harper & Row, 1984.

Chernin, Kim. *The Flame Bearers*. New York: Harper & Row, 1986.

Chesler, Phyllis. *Women and Madness*. New York: Avon, 1972.

Christ, Carol. *Diving Deep and Surfacing: Women Writers on Spiritual Quest*. Boston: Beacon Press, 1980.

Christ, Carol. *Laughter of Aphrodite: Reflections on a Journey to the Goddess*. San Francisco: Harper & Row, 1987.

Christ, Carol. *Odyssey with the Goddess: A Spiritual Quest in Crete*. New York: Continuum, 1995.

Christ, Carol. *Rebirth of the Goddess*. Reading, Mass.: Addison-Wesley, 1997.

Clark, David, and Andy Roberts. *Twilight of the Celtic Gods*. London: Blandford, 1996.

Clifton, Chas, ed. *Witchcraft Today: Book One: The Modern Craft Movement; Book Two: Modern Rites of Passage; Book Three: Witchcraft & Shamanism; and Book Four: Living Between Two Worlds*. Minneapolis, Minn.: Llewellyn, 1992–95.

Condren, Mary. *The Serpent and the Goddess: Women, Religion, and Power in Celtic Ireland*. San Francisco: Harper & Row, 1989.

Craighead, Menrad. *The Mother's Songs: Images of God the Mother*. Mahwah, N.J.: Paulist Press, 1986.

Curott, Phyllis. *Book of Shadows*. New York: Broadway, 1998.

Daly, Mary. *Gyn/Ecology: The Metaethics of Radical Feminism*. Boston: Beacon Press, 1978.

Daly, Mary. *Pure Lust: Elemental Feminist Philosophy*. Boston: Beacon Press, 1984.

Daly, Mary, and Jane Caputi. *Webster's First New Intergalactic WICKEDARY of the English Language*. Boston: Beacon Press, 1987.

Davis, Angela. *Women, Race and Class*. New York: Vintage, 1983.

Davis, Elizabeth, and Carol Leonard. *The Women's Wheel of Life*. New York: Viking Arkana, 1996.

De Grandis, Francesca. *Be a Goddess!* San Francisco: HarperSanFrancisco, 1998.

Demetrakopoulos, Stephanie. *Listening to Our Bodies: The Rebirth of Feminine Wisdom*. Boston: Beacon Press, 1983.

Dexter, Miriam Robbins. *Whence the Goddess: A Sourcebook*. New York: Teachers College Press, 1990.

Diamond, Irene, and Gloria Orenstein. *Reweaving the World: The Emergence of Ecofeminism*. San Francisco: Sierra Club Books, 1990.*

Di Prima, Diane. *Loba*. New York: Penguin, 1973, 1998.

Downing, Christine. *The Goddess: Mythological Images of the Feminine*. New York: Crossroad, 1981.

Dunning, Joan. *From the Redwood Forest: Ancient Trees and the Bottom Line: A Headwaters Journey*. White River Junction, Vt.: Chelsea Green Publishing, 1998.

Dunningham, Elizabeth. *The Wild Mother*. Barrytown, N.Y.; Station Hill Press, 1993.

Durdin-Robertson, Lawrence. *God the Mother: The Creatress and Giver of Life*. Ireland: Cesara Publications, 1986.

Edwards, Carolyn McVickar. *Sun Stories: Tales from Around the World to Illuminate the Days and Nights of Our Lives*. San Francisco: HarperSanFrancisco, 1995.

Eisler, Riane. *The Chalice and the Blade: Our History, Our Future*. San Francisco: Harper & Row, 1987.

Eller, Cynthia. *Living in the Lap of the Goddess*. Boston: Beacon Press, 1993, 1995.

Estes, Clarissa Pinkola. *Women Who Run with the Wolves*. New York: Ballantine, 1991.

Falk, Nancy Auer, and Rita M. Gross. *Unspoken Worlds: Women's Religious Lives in Non-Western Cultures*. San Francisco: Harper & Row, 1980.

Farrar, Janet, and Stewart Farrar. *Eight Sabbats for Witches*. London: Robert Hale, 1981.

Farrar, Janet, and Stewart Farrar. *The Witches Goddess*. Custer, Wash.: Phoenix Publications, 1987.

Fast, Suellen M. *Celebrations of Daughterhood*. Daughter Culture Publications, 1985.

Ferris, Timothy. *The Whole Shebang*. New York: Touchstone, 1997.

Fox, Matthew. *Original Blessing: A Primer in Creation Spirituality*. Santa Fe, N.M.: Bear & Co., 1983.

Fox, Matthew. *Sheer Joy: Conversations with Thomas Aquinas on Creation Spirituality.* New York: HarperCollins, 1992.

Gadon, Elinor. *The Once and Future Goddess.* San Francisco: Harper & Row, 1989.

Garcia, Jo, and Sara Maitland. *Walking on the Water: Women Talk About Spirituality.* Boston: Virago Press, 1983.

Gearhart, Sally Miller. *The Wanderground.* Boston: Alyson Publications, 1984.

Gearhart, Sally, and Susan Renne. *A Feminist Tarot.* Boston: Alyson Publications, 1981.

Genetti, Alexandra. *The Wheel of Change Tarot.* Rochester, Vt.; Destiny Books, 1997.

Gero, Joan M., and Margaret W. Conkey. *Engendering Archaeology, Women and Prehistory.* Cambridge, Mass.: Blackwell, 1991.

Giles, Mary E. *The Feminist Mystic and Other Essays on Woman and Spirituality.* New York: Crossroad, 1982.

Gilligan, Carol. *In a Different Voice.* Cambridge, Mass.: Harvard University Press, 1982.

Gimbutas, Marija. *The Goddesses and Gods of Old Europe: Myths and Cult Images.* Berkeley and Los Angeles: University of California Press, 1982.

Gimbutas, Marija. *The Language of the Goddess.* San Francisco: Harper & Row, 1989.

Gimbutas, Marija. *The Civilization of the Goddess: The World of Old Europe.* San Francisco: HarperSanFrancisco, 1991.

Gleeson, Judith. *Oya: In Praise of the Goddess.* Boston: Shambhala, 1987.

Gonzalez-Wippler, Migene. *Santeria: African Magic in Latin America.* New York: Original Products, 1984.

Gottlieb, Lynn. *She Who Dwells Within: A Feminist Vision of a Restored Judaism.* San Francisco: HarperSanFrancisco, 1995.

Grahn, Judy. *The Queen of Wands.* Freedom, Calif.: Crossing Press, 1982.

Grahn, Judy. *Another Mother Tongue: Gay Words, Gay Worlds.* Boston: Beacon Press, 1984.

Grahn, Judy. *The Queen of Swords.* Boston: Beacon Press, 1987.

Green, Rayna, ed. *That's What She Said: Contemporary Poetry and Fiction by Native American Women.* Bloomington: Indiana University Press, 1984.

Greer, Mary K. *Tarot for Yourself: A Workbook for Personal Transformation.* North Hollywood, Calif.: Newcastle, 1984.

Greer, Mary K. *Tarot Constellations.* North Hollywood, Calif.: Newcastle, 1987.

Greer, Mary K. *Tarot Mirrors: Reflections of Personal Meaning.* North Hollywood, Calif.: Newcastle, 1988.

Greer, Mary K. *Women of the Golden Dawn: Rebels and Priestesses.* Rochester, Vt.: Park Street Press, 1995.

Griffin, Susan. *Pornography and Silence: Culture's Revenge Against Nature.* New York: Harper & Row, 1981.

Griffin, Susan. *Made from This Earth.* New York: Harper & Row, 1982.

Griffin, Susan. *A Chorus of Stones.* New York: Doubleday, 1992.

Hall, Nor. *The Moon and the Virgin: Reflections on the Archetypal Feminine.* New York: Harper & Row, 1980.

Harrow, Judy. *Wicca Covens.* Secaucus, N.J.: Citadel, 1999.

Hopman, Ellen Evert, and Lawrence Bond. *People of the Earth: The New Pagans Speak Out.* Rochester, Vt.: Destiny Books, 1996.*

Hughes, K. Wind, and Linda Wolf. *Daughters of the Moon, Sisters of the Sun: Young Women and Mentors on the Transition to Womanhood*. Gabriola Island, British Columbia: New Society Publishers, 1997.*

Hurcombe, Linda. *Sex and God: Some Varieties of Women's Religious Experience*. New York: Routledge & Kegan Paul, 1987.

Hurston, Zora Neale. *Mules and Men*. Bloomington: Indiana University Press, 1978.

Hurston, Zora Neale. *Dust Tracks on a Road: An Autobiography*. Urbana: University of Illinois Press, 1984.

Hurston, Zora Neale. *The Sanctified Church*. Berkeley, Calif.: Turtle Island, 1984.

Iglehart, Hallie. *Womanspirit: A Guide to Women's Wisdom*. San Francisco: Harper & Row, 1983.

Jensen, Derrick, ed. *Listening to the Land: Conversations About Nature, Culture and Eros*. San Francisco: Sierra Club Books, 1995.*

Johnson, Buffie. *Lady of the Beasts*. San Francisco: Harper & Row, 1988.

Johnson, Elizabeth A. *She Who Is: The Mystery of God in Feminist Theological Discourse*. New York: Crossroad, 1995.

Johnson, Sonia. *Going Out of Our Minds: The Metaphysics of Liberation*. Freedom, Calif.: Crossing Press, 1987.

Judith, Anodea. *The Truth About Neo-Paganism*.

Judith, Anodea. *Wheels of Life*. St. Paul, Minn.: Llewellyn Publications, 1987.

Lacks, Roslyn. *Women and Judaism: Myth, History, and Struggle*. New York: Doubleday, 1980.

Lamb, Cynthia. *Brigid's Charge*. Corte Madera, Calif.: Bay Island Books, 1997.

Lee, Susan/Susanah Libana. *You Said, What Is This For, This Interest in Goddess, Prehistoric Religions?* Austin, Tex.: Plain View Press, 1985.

Leland, Charles. *Aradia, Or the Gospel of the Witches*. Trans. Mario Pazzaglini and Dina Pazzaglini. Blaine, Wash.: Phoenix Publishing, 1999.

Lerner, Gerda. *The Creation of Patriarchy*. New York: Oxford University Press, 1986.

Lorde, Audre. *Sister Outsider*. Freedom, Calif.: Crossing Press, 1984.

Lovelock, J. E. *Gaia: A New Look at Life on Earth*. Oxford: Oxford University Press, 1982.

Luke, Helen M. *Woman, Earth and Spirit: The Feminine in Symbol and Myth*. New York: Crossroad Publishing, 1985.

Macy, Johanna. *Despair and Personal Power in the Nuclear Age*. Philadelphia: New Society Publishers, 1993.

Marler, Joan, ed. *From the Realm of the Ancestors: An Anthology in Honor of Marija Gimbutas*. Manchester, Conn.: Knowledge, Ideas and Trends, 1997.

Matthews, Caitlín. *Sophia, Goddess of Wisdom: The Divine Feminine from Black Goddess to World-Soul*. London: Aquarian/Thorsons, 1992.

McAllister, Pam, ed. *Reweaving the Web of Life: Feminism and Nonviolence*. Philadelphia: New Society Publishers, 1982.

Metzner, Ralph. *The Well of Remembrance*. Boston and London: Shambala, 1994.

Middleton, Julie Forest, ed. *Songs for Earthlings: A Green Spirituality Songbook*. Philadelphia: Emerald Earth Publications, 1998.

Mills, Stephanie. *In Service of the Wild: Restoring and Reinhabiting Damaged Land*. Boston: Beacon Press, 1995.

Mollison, Bill. *Introduction to Permaculture*. Tyalgum, Australia: Tagari, 1991, 1995.

Monaghan, Patricia. *Goddesses and Heroines*. St. Paul, Minn.: Llewellyn Publications, 1997.

Moon, Sheila. *Changing Woman and Her Sisters*. San Francisco: Guild for Psychological Studies, 1985.

Moraga, Cherrie, and Gloria Anzaldua. *This Bridge Called My Back: Writings by Radical Women of Color*. Watertown, Mass.: Persephone Press, 1981.

Noble, Vicci. *Motherpeace: A Way to the Goddess Through Myth, Art and Tarot*. San Francisco: Harper & Row, 1983.

Noble, Vicci. *The Motherpeace Tarot Playbook: Astrology and the Motherpeace Cards*. Berkeley, Calif.: Wingbow Press, 1986.

Noble, Vicki. *Down Is Up for Aaron Eagle*. San Francisco: HarperSanFrancisco, 1993.

Ochs, Carol. *Women and Spirituality*. Totowa, N.J.: Rowman & Allanheld, 1983.

Ochshorn, Judith. *The Female Experience and the Nature of the Divine*. Bloomington: University of Indiana Press, 1981.

Oda, Mayumi. *Goddesses*. Volcano, Calif.: Volcano Press, 1988.

Olsen, Carl, ed. *The Book of the Goddess Past and Present*. New York: Crossroad, 1985.

Orenstein, Gloria Feman. *The Reflowering of the Goddess*. Elmsford, N.Y.: Pergamon Press, 1990.

Orlock, Carol. *The Goddess Letters: The Myth of Demeter and Persephone Retold*. New York: St. Martin's Press, 1987.

Outwater, Alice. *Water: A Natural History*. New York: Basic Books, 1996.

Paris, Ginette. *Pagan Meditations: The Worlds of Aphrodite, Hestia, Artemis*. Dallas: Spring Publications, 1986.

Perera, Sylvia. *Descent to the Goddess*. Toronto: Inner City Books, 1981.

Piercy, Marge. *The Moon Is Always Female*. New York: Knopf, 1985.

Plant, Judith. *Healing the Wounds*. Santa Cruz, Calif.: New Society Press, 1989.

Plaskow, Judith. *Standing Again at Sinai: Judaism from a Feminist Perspective*. San Francisco: Harper & Row, 1990.

Plaskow, Judith, and Carol Christ, eds. *Weaving the Visions: New Patterns in Feminist Spirituality*. San Francisco: Harper & Row, 1989.

Postman, Stevee. *The Cosmic Tribe Tarot*. Rochester, Vt.: Destiny Books, 1998.

Potts, Billie. *Witches Heal*. Ann Arbor, Mich.: DuReve, 1988.

Preston, James J., ed. *Mother Worship: Theme and Variations*. Chapel Hill: University of North Carolina Press, 1982.

Quinn, Daniel. *Ishmael*. New York: Bantam, 1992.

Rakusin, Sudie. *Dreams and Shadows: A Journal*. Brooke: Sudie Rakusin Journal, 1984.

Ranck, Shirley A. *Cakes for the Queen of Heaven*. Boston: Unitarian Universalist Association, 1986.

Ray, Paul. *The Integral Culture Survey: A Study of the Emergence of Transformational Values in America* (Research Report). Sausalito, Calif.: Institute of Noetic Sciences, 1996.

Redmond, Layne. *When the Drummers Were Women*. Harmony Books, 1997.

Reed, Ellen Cannon. *The Witches' Quabala: The Goddess and the Tree*. St. Paul, Minn.: Llewellyn Publications, 1986.

Reis, Elizabeth, ed. *Spellbound: Women and Witchcraft in America*. Wilmington, Del.: Scholarly Resources, 1998.*

Rohrlich, Ruby. "State Formation in Sumer and the Subjugation of Women." *Feminist Studies* 6, no. 1 (Spring 1980): 77–102.

Rohrlich, Ruby, and Elaine Hoffman Baruch, eds. *Women in Search of Utopia: Mavericks and Mythmakers*. New York: Schocken Books, 1984.

Rohrlich, Ruby, and June Nash. "Patriarchal Puzzle: State Formation in Mesopotamia and Mesoamerica." *Heresies* 4 (1981), no. 1, Issue 13: 60–63.

Roszak, Theodore, Mary E. Gomes, and Allen D. Kanner, eds. *Ecopsychology: Restoring the Earth, Healing the Mind*. San Francisco: Sierra Club Books, 1995.

Ruether, Rosemary Radford. *Sexism and God-Talk: Toward a Feminist Theology*. Boston: Beacon Press, 1983.

Ruether, Rosemary Radford. *Womanguides: Readings Toward a Feminist Theology*. Boston: Beacon Press, 1985.

Ruether, Rosemary Radford. *Women-Church: Theology and Practice*. San Francisco: Harper & Row, 1986.

Ruether, Rosemary Radford, and Rosemary Skinner Keller, eds. *In Our Own Voices: Four Centuries of American Women's Religious Writing*. New York: HarperCollins, 1995.*

Ryan, M. J., ed. *The Fabric of the Future: Women Visionaries Illuminate the Path to Tomorrow*. Berkeley, Calif.: Conari Press, 1998.*

Sahtouris, Elisabet. *EarthDance: Living Systems in Evolution*. Alameda, Calif.: Metalog, 1996.

Shulman, Alix Kates. *Drinking the Rain: A Memoir*. New York, Farrar, Straus & Giroux, 1995.

Sjoo, Monica, and Barbara Mor. *The Great Cosmic Mother: Rediscovering the Religion of the Earth*. San Francisco: Harper & Row, 1987.

Spretnak, Charlene. *Lost Goddesses of Early Greece: A Collection of Pre-Hellenic Myths*. Boston: Beacon Press, 1981.

Spretnak, Charlene. *States of Grace: The Recovery of Meaning in the Postmodern Age*. San Francisco: HarperSanFrancisco, 1991.

Spretnak, Charlene, ed. *The Politics of Women's Spirituality*. Garden City, N.Y.: Anchor, 1982.

Starhawk. *Dreaming the Dark: Magic, Sex and Politics*. Boston: Beacon Press, 1982.

Starhawk. *Truth or Dare: Encounters with Power, Authority, and Magic*. San Francisco: Harper & Row, 1987.

Stein, Diane. *The Kuan Yin Book of Changes*. St. Paul, Minn.: Llewellyn Publications, 1985.

Stein, Diane. *The Women's Book of Healing*. St. Paul, Minn.: Llewellyn Publications, 1987.

Stein, Diane. *The Women's Spirituality Book*. St. Paul, Minn.: Llewellyn Publications, 1987.

Steinem, Gloria. *Revolution from Within*. Boston: Little, Brown, 1993.

Stewert, R. J. *Earthlight*.

Stone, Merlin. *Ancient Mirrors of Womanhood*. Boston: Beacon Press, 1979.

Stone, Merlin. *Three Thousand Years of Racism: Recurring Patterns in Racism*. New York: New Sibylline Books, 1981.

Streep, Peg. *Sanctuaries of the Goddess: The Sacred Landscapes and Objects*. Boston: Little, Brown, 1994.

Swimme, Brian. *The Universe Is a Green Dragon*. Santa Fe, N.M.: Bear & Co., 1985.

Teish, Luisah. *Jambalaya: The Natural Woman's Book of Personal Charms and Practical Rituals*. San Francisco: Harper & Row, 1985.

Teish, Luisah. *Carnival of the Spirit*. San Francisco: HarperSanFrancisco, 1994.

Teubal, Savina J. *Sarah the Priestess: The First Matriarch of Genesis*. Athens, Ohio: Swallow Press, 1984.

Tucker, Naomi, ed. *Bisexual Politics, Theories, Queries and Visions*. New York: Haworth Press, 1995.*

Valiente, Doreen. *Natural Magic*. Custer, Wash.: Phoenix Press, 1978, 1986.

Valiente, Doreen. *Witchcraft for Tomorrow*. Custer, Wash.: Phoenix Press, 1978, 1987.

Vaughn, Genevieve. *For-Giving: A Feminist Criticism of Exchange*. Austin, Tex.: Plain View Press, 1997.

Volk, Tyler. *Gaia's Body: Toward a Physiology of Earth*. New York: Copernicus, 1998.

Waldherr, Kris. *The Book of Goddesses*. Hillsboro, Oreg.: Beyond Words Publishing, 1995.

Walker, Alice. *The Color Purple*. New York: Harcourt Brace Jovanovich, 1982.

Walker, Alice. *In Search of Our Mothers' Gardens*. New York: Harcourt Brace Jovanovich, 1983.

Walker, Alice. *The Temple of My Familiar*. San Diego: Harcourt Brace Jovanovich, 1989.

Walker, Barbara G. *The Secrets of the Tarot*. San Francisco: Harper & Row, 1983.

Walker, Barbara G. *The Woman's Encyclopedia of Myths and Secrets*. San Francisco: Harper & Row, 1983.

Walker, Barbara G. *The Crone: Woman of Age, Wisdom, and Power*. San Francisco: Harper & Row, 1985.

Walker, Barbara G. *The I Ching of the Goddess*. San Francisco: Harper & Row, 1986.

Walker, Barbara G. *The Skeptical Feminist: Discovering the Virgin, Mother and Crone*. San Francisco: Harper & Row, 1987.

Walker, Barbara G. *The Woman's Dictionary of Myth and Symbol*. San Francisco: Harper & Row, 1988.

Waskow, Arthur. *Seasons of Our Joy: A Celebration of Modern Jewish Renewal*. Toronto: Bantam, 1982.

Weigle, Marta. *Spiders and Spinsters: Women and Mythology*. Albuquerque: University of New Mexico Press, 1982.

Weinstein, Marion. *Positive Magic: Occult Self-Help*. Custer, Wash.: Phoenix Publishing, 1984.

Weinstein, Marion. *Earth Magic: A Dianic Book of Shadows*. Custer, Wash.: Phoenix Publishing, 1986.

Whitmont, Edward C. *Return of the Goddess*. New York: Crossroad Publications, 1982.

Wolkstein, Diane, and Samuel Noah Kramer. *Inanna, Queen of Heaven and Earth: Her Stories and Hymns from Sumer*. New York: Harper & Row, 1983.

Worth, Valerie. *The Crone's Book of Words*. St. Paul, Minn.: Llewellyn Publications, 1986.

Wynne, Patrice. *The Womanspirit Sourcebook*. San Francisco: Harper & Row, 1988.

Zahava, Irene. *Hear the Silence: Stories of Myth, Magic, and Renewal*. Freedom, Calif.: Crossing Press, 1986.

Resources

There are now so many great Pagan organizations, publications, magazines, and Web sites that I can't even think of compiling any sort of representative list. Here are just a few of the groups I either belong to or have worked with, and a few good Web sites to get you started.

Reclaiming
P.O. Box 14404
San Francisco, CA 94114
(The extended network of groups I teach and work with. We publish a quarterly magazine, and our sister communities offer classes and public rituals in many areas.)
Web Page:
www.reclaiming.org/cauldron/
(This Web page links to my personal page, to our Web page for the *Pagan Book of Living and Dying*, and to many others. It includes a calendar of events for all of our extended sister communities, and information about our Witch camps, weeklong intensives offered around the United States, Canada, and Europe.)

Covenant of the Goddess
P.O. Box 1226
Berkeley, CA 94701
(league of covens and individuals across the United States, and a legally recognized church)

Rowan's Web page for the Northern California Local Council of COG is highly recommended as a good overall resource:
www.conjure.com

Covenant of Unitarian Universalist Pagans
P.O. Box 640
Cambridge, MA 02140
(The league of Pagans within the Unitarian Church.)

Serpentine Music
P.O. Box 2564
Sebastopol, CA 95473
phone: 707–823–7425
fax: 707–823–6664
www. serpentinemusic.com/serpentine/

A great source for Pagan music, including Reclaiming's tapes of chants and ritual music.

Mary Ellen Donald
Mary Ellen Books
P.O. Box 7589
San Francisco, CA 94120–7589
phone: 415–826-DRUM

Mary Ellen Donald is my drum teacher. This is the source for her tapes, books, and videos for learning Middle Eastern percussion.

Another great drumming resource is Layne Redmond, who can be reached through her Web site at www.layneredmond.com, where she offers her book, tapes, and videos.

Belili Productions
P.O. Box 410187
San Francisco, CA 94141–0187
www.webcom.com/gimbutas/

The small film/video production company I formed together with Donna Read to produce a documentary on the life of Marija Gimbutas.

Other Recommended Web sites:
www.circleround.com

Our Web site for *Circle Round: Raising Children in Goddess Traditions,* and for continuing information and resources around Pagan parenting.

The Witches' Voice
www.witchvox.com

Up-to-date news about the larger Pagan community, reports on legal battles, networking, and so forth.

Index

Abram, David, 8
Absolutism, 217, 219, 222–23
Acacia, Alan, 97, 129–30
Acrostic eye/vision, 216
Adams, John Quincy, 31
Adams, Samuel, 31
Addictions, 21, 22, 249, 253, 255
Adler, Margot, 5
African slave trade, 31, 249–50
Afro-American religions, 176, 225–26
Afro-American traditions, 108, 176,
    225–26, 242, 247, 249–50, 254
Agape, 49
AIDS, 8, 18, 21, 279
Air, 87–88, 104, 242, 283
Air Meditation exercise, 87–88
Alan, 61–62, 63
Alcohol, 21, 172, 249, 254–55, 275
Alcoholics Anonymous, 21
The All, 50
Allen, Paula Gunn, 232
Allison, 9
Alpha rhythm, 176
Amber, 64–65
American Academy of Religion, 17
American Witchcraft history, 31
Amor, 49
Anchoring energy, 169–70, 277
Anderson, Cora, 16

Anderson, Victor, 16, 26, 136, 172, 241,
    255
Anger, 107, 122
Anger Spell, 143
Angles-Sur-Anglin, 55
Animals, 27–29, 126–27, 161, 165n.5
Anna, 227
Antithetical, 218
Apple, 106
The Apple exercise, 75
Apprentices, 77–79, 188, 189. *See also*
    Covens; Initiations
Aradia, 108
Archer of Love, 48
Arthur, King, 109
Asherah, 108, 282
Ashimah, 108
Aspecting, 273
Aspects of life, 289–93
Astral body, 161, 162, 170
Astral colors, 169
Astral energies, 169
Astral plane, 161
Astral projection, 170, 171
Astral vision, 169, 275
Astrology, 140, 183, 221
Athame, 83, 87, 96, 185, 271, 274
Athame or Sword Meditation exercise,
    88, 242–43

Athena, 271

Aura, 161–62, 163–64

Authority, 61–62, 127–28, 226

Awareness, 43–44, 110–11, 164, 171, 175, 176, 220

Baker, Diane, 267

Banishing, 85–86, 271

Banishing exercise, 85–86

Banishing Pentacle, 76, 185

Barley Mother, 28

Basque gods, 46

Baths (ritual), 86, 190

Bay Area Center for Alternative Education, 63

Beauty, 110

Beltane (May 1), 125

Beltane (May 1) ritual, 204–5, 259

Beshderen, Mevlannen, 272

Beyond God the Father (Daly), 33

Binding a Spell exercise, 141

Binding spells, 141–42, 152–53

Birth stage, 90

Bishop of Ossory, 29

Bishopric of Trier, 31

Black Power Movement, 136

Blessing Over Cakes and Wine, 184

Blue, 45–46

Blue God, 41, 45, 52, 267–68

Book of Blessings (Falk), 282

Book of Shadows, 59, 78–79, 95, 216

Boredom, 176

Brain hemispheres, 43–45, 233. *See also* Left hemisphere; Right hemisphere

Br'er Rabbit, 246

Brigid (Candlemas, February 2), 125

Brigid (Candlemas, February 2) ritual, 202–3, 258, 277

Brigid doll, 9, 277

Brook (man), 247–48

Brook (woman), 72

Brown, Barbara, 45, 167

Brythonic Celts, 91

Budapest, Z., 15

Buddha, 33, 51, 127, 224

Burning Times, 30–31, 35, 60, 83, 129

Business, 290

Cabalists, 46, 83

Caffeine, 275

Campbell, Joseph, 47, 49, 54, 193

Candle Gazing exercise, 76

Candlemas (February 2), 125

Candlemas (February 2) ritual, 202–3

Cantlon, Marie, 17

Castaneda, 42

Casting of a circle, 38, 80–83, 83–84, 97–100, 100–101, 170, 240–41

The Casting of the Circle (Daly), 80–83

Cata Hüyük, 55

Cats, 165n.5

Cauldron Meditation exercise, 93–94

Cauldron of the Goddess, 109–10

Cautions, 176–77, 254

Cautions exercise, 176–77

Celts, 29, 109–10

The Censor, 252

Center of circle, 93–101

Ceremonial Magic school, 87

Ceridwen, 109

Chants, 68–69, 111–18, 129, 160, 182, 241. *See also* Invocations

Character, 138

The Charge of the Goddess (adapted by Starhawk from Valiente), 14, 102–3, 118n.1, 244–45

Charms (herbal), 149–51

The Child (Blue God of love), 52

Children, 10, 11

Chinese Moon Festival parade, 70

Chinese Yin/Yang, 51

Christ, Carol, 5, 17, 33, 264

Christianity, 17, 29–32, 33, 35, 55, 60, 106, 120–21, 133, 222, 260–61. *See also* Western religions

Circle, 239

Circle of community, 25, 261

A Circle for Healing During Struggle (Acacia), 97–98

Circle Round: Raising Children in Goddess Tradition (Starhawk, Hill, and Baker), 267, 272, 273, 277, 279
Circles: casting, 38, 83–84, 240–41; center of, 93–101; formal breaking of, 184; innovations for casting, 97–100; Opening the, 185, 255; protection of energy field of, 100; quartered, 86, 242; stone, 28, 31, 83–84, 232; visions of future lives in the, 227–29
Circle of Self, 225
Circle of the Sun (CD), 273
Circle Visualization, 78
The Circle Visualization Exercise, 94–95
Clinton, Bill, 275
Cogul, 55
College of Mysteries, 59
Colleges of the Druids, 29
Comforter, 124–25
Commoner, Barry, 155
Community, 2, 25, 261. *See also* Pagan communities
Compost coven, 16, 62, 63, 238
Cone of Power, 159, 250–51, 282
The Cone of Power exercise, 159
Confrontation, 173–74
Connection, 155
The Conqueror, 252
Consciousness, 42, 168, 170, 175, 186, 221–22, 233, 280
Consciousness energy, 161–62
Consciousness-raising techniques, 66
Consecrating a Tool exercise, 95–96
Consolet of Hearts, 125
Constructive criticism, 270
Consummation of love, 105–6
Cord, 95
Corn dollies, 55
Courtot, Martha, 216
Covenant of the Goddess, 16–17, 238
Covenant of Unitarian Universalist Pagans, 238
Covens: all-women and all-male, 133n.6; conflicts within, 70, 174, 239; described, 59; of the Faeries, 29;

finding one to join, 65, 66, 239; Guardian confrontation and support of, 173–74; history of, 60; information sources for, 266; initiation into, 38, 38–39, 59–60, 64, 65, 188–92, 255–56, 269, 276; leadership in, 64–65, 240; life span of, 9; male members of, 60, 238; of modern Witchcraft, 35, 60–61, 65–67; structure of, 237–40; taking on new members, 77–79. *See also* Groups
Coyle, T. Thorn, 268
Coyote of Southwest, 246
Craft oral tradition, 39n.1
The Craft. *See* Witchcraft
"Creating Religion: Toward the Future" (*Spiral Dance*), 1
Creation myth, 41–42, 48, 233–35, 267
Creative work, 291
Creativity, 44, 106, 128, 171, 246, 291
Creatrix-Destroyer, 106–7
Criticism, 270
Crone, 53, 104
Croning Ceremony, 282
Crusades, 29
Crystal gazing (scrying), 176, 179–80, 181–82
Cults, 172
Culture: creating life, 215–17; diversity of matrifocal, 219; historical reports of matrifocal, 55; rediscovery of matrifocal, 103
Cup, 89
Cup Meditation exercise, 89
Cushen, Karen Lynd, 113
CUUPs chapters (Unitarian churches), 65, 239
Cycle of life, 51

Daily practice, 270
Daly, Mary, 33, 83
Damping and Projecting Energy exercise, 163–64
Dance, Rose May, 240
Dark and Light Twins, 53

Dark Maiden, 90

Dark Moon Ritual, 195–96

Dark Serpent, 53

David, 9

Death: associated with love, 126; cauldron restoration from, 109–10; as final initiation, 272; followed by rebirth, 124–25; as initiation theme, 188, 189

Death force, 51

Death stage, 90

Deep Self (God Self): described, 45–46, 56, 233; as energy, 162; female and male consciousness in, 169; Goddess speaking to, 107; Star card (Tarot) symbol of, 16

Deep witnessing, 277

Demeter, 271

Denial, 172

Deosil (clockwise) direction, 86

Descent and return myths, 256

Devil, 120–21

Devil's "marks," 30

Devoking, 255

The Diamond exercise, 76

Diana, 108

Diane, 64

Dianic/separatism, 121, 247

Dianic Witchcraft, 13, 35, 50, 121, 247

Dian Y Glas (Blue God), 45, 46

Diary, 78–79. See also Book of Shadows

Diner, Helen, 263

Dionysus, 124

Di Prima, Diane, 216

Dismissal of the Goddess and God, 185, 255

Diversity, 35, 37, 219, 226

Divination, 23, 183–84, 240

Divine Child, 28

Divine Child Sun, 52

Divine Hunter, 125

DNA, 220

Dogs, 165n.5

Donald's Three Rules of Critique, 270

Don Juan, 42–43, 172

Door of Dreams, 175

Door Without a Key, 175

Double ax, 107

The Double Spiral exercise, 107–8

Doumbec, 243

"Dragon" cult, 31

Drawing Down the Moon (Adler), 5

Dreaming the Dark (Starhawk), 18, 231, 232, 239, 250, 263, 269, 280

Dream log, 175

Dreams: explored through scrying, 181–82; objective elements of, 175; Starhawk on own, 16

Dreamworld, 126

Drug experimentation, 46, 47, 174–75, 221, 253, 275–76

Druidic mysteries, 29

Drumming, 243

Dualism, 106, 218, 280

Duncan, Robert, 135

Dying God, 124–25

Earth, 18, 34–35, 89–90, 220, 242, 285

Earth environmental damage, 22

Earth Goddess, 104

Earthing Power, 38, 69

Earth Meditation exercise, 90

The East, 87–88

Eastern meditations, 75

Eastern religions, 32, 36, 48–49, 162, 226, 242; influence of, 221–22, 261; male images of divinity in, 264; rebirth concept of, 51. See also Religions

Ecological balance, 34–35

Ecology, 155, 264–65

Ecstasy, 49–50, 109, 155

Ectoplasm, 161

Ehrenzweig, Anton, 33, 44

El Día de los Muertos (November 2), 10–11, 279

Elegba of the Yoruba, 246

Elemental energy, 161

Elements, 88–90, 242, 283–85

Eleusinian Mysteries, 183

Elfland, 29

Eliade, Mircea, 49

Eliot, T. S., 120

Eloquence charm, 150

Emotion, 139, 250

Enemy spell, 152–53

Energy: anchoring, 169–70, 277; astral, 169; awareness of, 164; of Craft rituals, 66–67; as ecstasy, 155; magically charging object with, 86; molded into form of cone, 159–60, 250–51; projecting, 77; protection through circle, 100; *raith* type of, 59, 78, 161, 170; relaxation to enhance, 72–73; spells and directing, 139–40, 155, 274; spiral flows of, 156; three basic types of, 161–62. *See also* Spells

Engstrom, Donald, 270

Enhancement, 272–73

Environmental damage, 22

Eostar Ritual (Spring Equinox, March 20–23), 203–4, 259, 278

Equinox Invocation of the Male Aspect (Acacia), 129–30

Ereshkigal, Queen of Death, 245

Erhard, Werner, 33, 224

Eros, 49, 124

Esbats, 60, 193

Essentialism, 279–80

Etheric substance, 161

Ethics, 35–36, 265

Eve mythology, 217

Evil spirits, 172–73

Evohe, 129, 134n.17

Exercises: Air Meditation, 87–88; The Apple, 75; *Athame* or Sword Meditation, 88, 242–43; Banishing, 85–86; Binding a Spell, 141; Candle Gazing, 76; Cauldron Meditation, 93–94; Cautions, 176–77; The Circle Visualization Exercise, 94–95; The Cone of Power, 159; Consecrating a Tool, 95–96; Cup Meditation, 89; Damping and Projecting Energy, 163–64; The Diamond, 76; The Double Spiral, 107–8; Earthing Power, 69; Earth Meditation, 90; Fire Meditation, 88; Formal Grounding, 160–61; Full Moon Meditation, 105; Grounding: The Tree of Life, 68; Grounding and Centering, 74; Group Breath, 67–68; Group Salt-Water Purification, 84–85; The Hammer, 77; The Iron Pentagram, 91–92; The Knot, 75; Memory, 180–81; Mirror, Mirror, 76–77; Pendulum Exercise, 162; The Pentacle, 75; Pentacle Meditation-The Five Stages of Life, 90–91; The Pentagram of Pearl, 92–93; Permanent Protective Circle, 100–101; Place of Power, 178; Power Chant, 68–69; Protective Circle, 100; Protective Filter, 142; The Rainbow: Emerging, 178–79; The Rainbow: Trance Induction, 177; Relaxation, 73; Rhythm Play, 44, 266; Ritual Induction, 182–83; The Rock, 77; Salt-Water Purification, 84, 241; Scrying, 179–80; Seeing the Aura, 164; Sensing the Aura: Direct Method, 163; Sensing the Aura: Pendulum Method, 163; Sensing Group Energy, 67; Shadow Play, 44, 266; Simple Visualizations, 74–75; Trance Into a Dream, 181; Transformation Meditation, 93; Wand Meditation, 88–89; Waning Moon Meditation, 105; Water Meditation, 89; Waxing Moon, 104; Womb Chant, 160; Word Association Trance, 71–72

Expanded consciousness, 42, 66, 161–62, 168, 221–22, 280

Eyes symbolism, 107

Faery traditions, 16, 28–29, 31, 35, 45–46, 49, 55, 64, 87–90, 108, 189, 233, 265, 266–67

Fair Folk (Faeries), 28, 29, 31, 35, 45

Falk, Marcia, 282
Fall Equinox, 126
Fall Equinox ritual, 61–63, 208–9
Familiars, 161, 165n.5
Farewell to the Goddess and God, 185
Father God, 33, 34, 122–23, 128, 222, 245, 247
Fathering, 247–48
"Father's Blessing" (*Circle Round*), 273
Feasting, 184, 254–55
Female body, 56, 123, 127
Female energy, 20
Female force, 50–51, 52, 267
Female-male polarization, 3, 267
Female power, 32–33
Feminism, 14, 19, 35, 61, 121, 133, 156, 216, 225, 237, 244, 247. *See also* Women's movement
Feminist covens, 35. *See also* Covens
Feminist religion, 224, 281–82
Feminist spirituality, 17, 50, 217–19, 224–26, 237
Fire, 88, 106–7, 284
Fire Meditation exercise, 88
First Truth of Buddhism, 51
Fool of the Tarot, 246
For Eloquence herbal charm, 150
For Inner Power herbal charm, 150
Formal Grounding exercise, 160–61
For Protection herbal charm, 149
Fortune, Dion, 38, 42, 136, 155
Frazer, Sir James, 53, 54
Freedom: from slavery, 109; as great reward, 11; price of, 42–43, 47
Freud, Sigmund, 33, 175, 221, 224
Full Moon Meditation exercise, 105
Full Moon Ritual, 194–95, 276

Gaelic Celts, 91
Gardening, 8
Gardner, Gerald, 35, 244
Gender power, 20–21. *See also* Men; Women
Genesis, 48
Gimbutas, Marija, 3, 264

God: Blue, 41, 45, 52, 267–68; compared to Goddess, 121–22; described, 245–47; Dying, 124–25; father and, 122, 123–24, 247–48; as Green One, 41, 268; Horned, 46, 52, 64, 120–21, 123, 268; as the Hunter, 26, 28, 52, 120, 125, 226, 249; sacrificing, 53–54; as Self, 122, 126–27; symbols of, 124; women and, 248. *See also* Father God
Goddess: compared to God, 121–22; Craft understanding of, 108–11, 244; enhancement through, 272–73; guises throughout history, 28–29; Hebrew, 225; historical sources on the, 118n.2, 263–64; as Lady of the Mammoths, 27; manifest in nature, 226; as mermaid, 48; political activism and spirituality of, 7–8; reawakening of, 5, 39, 103–4; significance to men, 34, 111, 123–24, 245; symbolism of, 32–34, 103, 105–7; worship of, 55
Goddess Demeter, 271
Goddess figures, 55
The Goddess in the Kingdom of Death (traditional Craft myth), 187–88
Goddess of Night, 214
Goddess religion, 28–29, 55, 220, 221, 224–25, 244, 265
Goddess religion principles, 22
Goddess Self, 221
God Self. *See* Deep Self (God Self)
Goidelic tree alphabet, 91
"Going forth by night," 175
Goldberg, Herb, 34, 120
The Golden Bough (Frazer), 53, 54
Goldenburg, Naomi, 35
Goodall, Jane, 220
Grandmaster, 60
Graves, Robert, 46, 48, 53, 263
"the great conversation," 272
"Great Man" model, 33, 127
Greece, 28, 47–48, 108, 124
Greeley, Andrew, 264

Green One, 41, 268

Grounding: The Tree of Life exercise, 68

Grounding, 69, 74, 156, 165; by familiars, 165n.5; defining, 239; purpose
of, 161; of ritual power, 185

Grounding and Centering exercise, 74

Grounding exercise, 69

Group Breath exercise, 67–68

Group purification, 271

Groups: conflicts within, 70, 174, 239,
253, 270; learning trace state in,
176; renewing energy of, 156; superiority strategy used by, 173; trace
experience of, 181–82. See also
Covens

Group Salt-Water Purification, 84–85

Group trust, 66–67

Growing food, 8

Growth movement, 180

The Guardian, 171, 172, 173–74

Guardian of the Gates, 189

"Guardians of the Watchtowers," 86

Guardian of the Threshold, 188

Guidot, 62

Guilt, 173

Hallie, 158

Halloween (Samhain), 126, 209–12,
214, 256–57, 260, 278–79

The Hammer exercise, 77

Hanged Man, 126

Harding, M. Esther, 43

Harrison, Kat, 272

Harrow, Judy, 272

The Hazards of Being Male (Goldberg),
34

Healing, 21, 51, 137, 140, 141; aspects
of, 291–92; broken heart charm, 149;
using own suggestibility for, 171

Healing Image Spell, 151–52

Heavenly bodies, 286–89

Hebrew Goddess, 225, 282

Hebrews. See Judaism

Herbal charms: listed, 149–51; to
charge, 151

Herbalism, 30, 51

Herbs, 8, 274

Heterosexuality, 20, 235

Hexes, 141–42, 153n.4, 250. See also
Spells

The Hidden Order of Art (Ehrenzweig),
44

High John the Conqueror root, 249–50

High Priest, 21

High Priestess, 21, 253

High Self, 233. See also Deep Self (God
Self)

Hill, Anne, 267

Hinduism, 221–22

History, 26–31, 54–55, 121, 231–32. See
also Burning Times

Hitler, Adolf, 37

Holidays. See Sabbats

Holly's dream, 181–82

Holy Grail, 109

Homosexuality, 20

Honesty, 138

Honeysuckle coven, 62, 63, 65, 238

Honor, 36–37, 110

Honor to the Goddess, Lady of Many
Names to Demeter, The
Immeasurable One, & to the Maiden
(Cushen), 113–14

Horned God, 46, 52, 64, 120–21, 123,
268

Human body, 56, 123

Human potential movements, 223

Human sacrifice, 54, 55, 56

Humor, 47, 175

The Hunter, 26, 28, 52, 120, 125, 226,
249

Hurston, Zora Neale, 249

Hussein, Saddam, 280

Hypnosis, 171, 186

Iamanja, 48

I Ching, 240

Idols, 169–70

Iglehart, Hallie, 250

Illusion, 36, 48

Immanence, 22
Immortality, 110
Inanna, 245
Inclusiveness, 19
Indians. *See* Native American traditions
The Indrinking Spell, 143–44
Infinity sign, 45
Initiations, 38, 59–60, 64, 65, 188–92, 255–56, 269, 276
Initiation stage, 90
Inner Power charm, 150
Innocent VIII, Pope, 29
Inquisition, 29–30
Institute for Culture and Creation Spirituality, 235, 261
Intentions, 251
Interconnection, 22, 155
Intuition, 16, 95, 220–21
Invocations, 25–26, 41–42; A Circle for Healing During Struggle (Acacia), 97–98; endings of, 241; Equinox Invocation of the Male Aspect (Acacia), 129–30; Invocations from the Summer Solstice Ritual (Starhawk), 99–100; Invocation to the Goddess and God (Valerie), 130–31; Invocation to the God of Summer, 130; Invocation to the Ground of Being, 131, 249; power channeled through, 111; Repeating Chants (to the God), 129; Repeating Cycle, 129; Song to Pan (Simos), 131–32; Valerie's Rhyming Invocations to the Four Quarters, 98–99. *See also* Rituals
Invocations from the Summer Solstice Ritual (Starhawk), 99–100
Invocation to the Dewy One, 112
Invocation to the Goddess and God (Valerie), 130–31
Invocation to the Goddess as Mother (Stern), 115–16
Invocation to the God (Goldberg), 119–20
Invocation to the God of Summer, 130

Invocation to the Ground of Being, 131
Invocation to the Queen of Summer, 118
Ireland, 29
The Iron Pentagram exercise, 91–92
Isis, 11

Janicot, 46
Jaynes, Julian, 219
Jean, 46
Jesus, 127, 224
Joan, 46
Joan of Arc ("Maid of Orleans"), 29
Job charm, 150
John the Conqueror, 249–50
Jones, Jim, 128
Jonet, 46
Joy, 109
Juan, Don, 42–43, 172
Judaism, 14, 17, 35, 46, 55, 106, 108, 133, 218, 222, 225; joy/ecstasy of, 109; knowledge exchanged with Craft, 83–84; as positive resource, 282. *See also* Religions
Judeo-Christian heritage: concepts of, 35; dualism of, 106, 218
The Judge, 252
Jung, Carl, 33, 221
Jupiter, 288–89
Justice, 35–36, 292

Kali worship, 222
Karmic bond, 237
Kevyn, 216
Kissing during Spiral Dance, 278
Kitchen magic school, 87
Klein, Melanie, 221
Knives, 87, 242
Knot, 75
The Knot exercise, 75
Knowledge, 92, 220
Kore Chant: Spring and Fall Equinox, 114–15
Kramer, Dominican, 29

Krishna, 127
Kyteler, Alice, 29

Labrys, 107
Lady of the Mammoths, 27
Lady of the Wild Things, 28
La Magdaleine, 55
Land of Eternal Youth, 51
Land of Youth, 109–10, 126
Last Sea for the Dreamland, 126
Laurel, 62, 116–17, 215
Lauren, 244–45
Laussel, 55
Law, 93, 292
Leadership, 21, 61–65, 70, 128, 212,
    224, 226–27, 239–40, 253
Leary, Timothy, 175
Lee, 158
Left hemisphere brain, 43, 44–45, 193,
    233, 266, 273
Lesbians, 133
"Ley" lines, 28, 232
Liberator, 109
Lichtenstein, Marsha, 217, 279
Life (aspects of), 289–93
Life culture, 215–17
Life cycle, 51, 105–6
Life force, 36, 37, 51, 56, 268
Life stages, 90–91
Lilly, John C., 46, 139, 168
Litha (Summer Solstice, June 20–23)
    ritual, 205–7, 259–60, 278
Little People (Stone Age Britain), 35
Logos, 124
Loneliness, 144–45
Lord of the Dance, 125
Lord of the Grain, 28
Lord of Winds, 125
Lords of Mind, 222
Love: as aspect of life, 289–90; associ-
    ated with death, 126; consummation
    stage of, 105–6; God of Witches and,
    123; individualizing force of, 49; as
    law of the Goddess, 109; spells to
    attract, 142

Love charm, 149
Love for life, 36
Love ripening stage, 90
Lovins, Amory, 7
LSD experiences, 46, 175
Lucumi traditions, 31
Lugh, 260
Lughnasad (August 1), 126
Lughnasad (August 1) ritual, 207–8, 260

Mabon (Fall Equinox, September
    20–23) ritual, 208–9, 260
McFarland, Morgan, 133
Macumba traditions, 31
Magic, 37, 42, 47; character required for
    practice of, 138; connection princi-
    ple of, 155; drugs and, 253, 275–76;
    function of, 221; the great conversa-
    tion through, 272; grounding before,
    161; herbs used in, 8; language of,
    137; as part of nature, 159; spell cast-
    ing and, 137–40, 141–42; under-
    standing, 136. See also Spells
Magical diary, 78–79
Magical training, 72
Magical will, 138
Maharaj, 33
Maiden aspect, 104, 108, 125
Male body, 123
Male dominance, 33, 61, 122, 252
Male energy, 20
Male (forces) Principle, 50–51, 52,
    267–68
Male God model, 33, 34
Maleness, 19–20, 50–51, 52, 120, 122,
    122–23, 133, 156, 232, 233–34, 235,
    246, 248. See also Men
Male sorcerers, 39n.1
Malleus Maleficarum, "The Hammer of
    the Witches" (Dramer and
    Sprenger), 26, 29–30
Malta, 55
Manifest deity, 22, 33, 36, 51, 103, 106,
    107, 110, 226, 244
Marcus, Toni, 157

Marian/Miriam/Mariamne/Myrrhine/
    Myrrha/Maria/Marina, 48, 49
Marijuana, 174, 275
Marler, Joan, 264
Marriage, 37
Mars, 288
Marx, Karl, 33
Masculinity: Horned God image of,
    120–21; Western cultural beliefs
    on, 122
The Masks of God (Campbell), 54
The Master of Servants, 252
Material world, 137, 138, 140
Matrifocal civilizations/cultures, 55,
    103, 219, 263–64
May Eve ritual, 47
Maypole winding, 47, 267
Medical establishment, 30–31
Medieval Witchcraft, 120–21
Meditations, 66, 75–76; on aspects of
    Goddess, 104–5; exercises listed,
    87–94, 104–5; names of God used in,
    127; as part of Craft training, 94;
    trance induction through, 175–76
Megalithic era, 83
Mellaart, James, 263
Memory exercise, 180–81
Men: as coven members, 60, 238; essen-
    tialism and, 279–80; impact of
    Eastern religions on, 222; in modern
    Witchcraft, 127–28; polarization of
    women and, 3, 267; significance of
    Goddess to, 34, 111, 123–24, 245;
    significance of God to, 122. See also
    Maleness
Mercury, 287
Mermaid, 48, 121
Metaphors: of magical systems, 221; sci-
    entific, 219–20; of Spiral Dance,
    278; trance perception translated by,
    169; understanding and, 219; of
    Witchcraft, 226; working of magic,
    139, 140
Mettus Curtius, 54
Metzner, Ralph, 265

Mind-altering drugs, 46, 47, 174–75,
    221, 253, 275–76
Minogue, Aine, 273
Miria, 41, 49, 50
Mirror image, 48–49
Mirror, Mirror exercise, 76–77
Misogyny, 30
Mohammed, 224
Money, 290
Money charm, 149
Moon, 26, 27, 58–59, 104–5, 108–9,
    193–96, 256, 274, 286
Moon Goddess, 104
Moon Magic (Fortune), 169
Moonmother (Laurel), 116–17
Moon rituals, 193–96, 256
Morgan, Robin, 124
Moses, 127, 224
Mother, 104
Mother Moth, 87
Mother Winter (Circle Round), 277
Murray, Margaret, 46
Music: invocation set to, 111; of the
    spheres, 49–50
Mysteries, 47, 121, 133, 183, 218
Mystery rituals, 183
Myths: creation, 41–42, 48, 233–35,
    267; of descent and return, 256; Eve,
    217; function of, 20; The Goddess in
    the Kingdom of Death (traditional
    Craft myth), 187–88; Sumerian, 245;
    Wheel of the Year, 52–53, 235–37,
    256–57, 268; of Witchcraft, 46–47

Nada, 16
Nakedness, 71, 109, 272
Names (Goddess or God), 159
National Film Board of Canada, 264
Native American traditions, 225, 245;
    European Pagans joining with, 31;
    Old Religion and, 27
Nature: as daily condition, 9; Goddess
    manifest in, 226; magic as part of, 159;
    respect for, 34–35; strength drawn
    from, 274–75; symbols drawn from, 220

Nazism, 37–38, 265
"Need of anything," 108
Neolithic sites, 55
Neshamah, 46
Neuman, Erich, 263
New Age philosophies, 280–81
The New Diary (Rainer), 79
New Mind, New Body (Brown), 45
New Moon incantation, 58–59
Nicaragua, 18
Night, 214
Nightmare, M. Macha, 268
Nonverbal sharing, 66–67
The North, 89–93
North Star, 89
Nuclear power/weapons, 18
Nudity, 71, 109, 272
"Number One," 54
Nurturing, 123, 248
Nymph, 52–53

Occultism, 37, 46, 139, 161, 162, 165, 168, 170, 171
Old age, 106
Old Gods, 19–20
Old Religion: described, 27; incorporated into Druidic mysteries, 29. *See also* Witchcraft
Olsen, Carl, 232
Olympian Pantheon, 28
Omnipotence, 173, 246
Opening the Circle, 185, 255
Open Universities, 65
Opposites, 125, 218, 233–34
Oracles, 23, 183, 184, 221, 240
The Orderer, 252
The Origin of Consciousness in the Breakdown of the Bicameral Mind (Jaynes), 219
Orishas saints, 31
Ornstein, Robert, 43, 175
Other Side, 161
Other vision, 42
Other way of knowing, 43
Otherworld, 126, 275

Out-of-body, 77
Overworld, 161
Ozone layer, 22

The Pagan Book of Living and Dying (Starhawk, Nightmare, and Reclaiming Collective), 268, 272, 275
Pagan communities: of the Bay Area, 16–17; changes and development of, 17; healing challenges of, 21; neofascist, 37–38, 265; open worship practice by, 10; political activism and, 7–8
Pagan student groups, 65
Paleolithic art, 39n.1
Paleolithic era, 39, 42, 55, 242
Paleolithic shaman's insight, 42
Palmistry, 183–84, 221
Paradox, 48–49
Paranoia, 173, 174
Passivity, 36
Patriarchy, 14, 34, 50, 54, 103, 120, 122, 123–24, 128, 244, 245, 247–48, 260–61
Paul, 62, 78
Peasant revolts, 29
Pelasgians, 48
Pendulum Exercise, 162
Pennsylvania Dutch magic, 153
Pentacle: banishing, 75, 185; engraving, 90; invoking, 75; polarity and, 234
The Pentacle exercise, 75
Pentacle Meditation—The Five Stages of Life exercise, 90–91
The Pentagram of Pearl exercise, 92–93
Permanent Protective Circle exercise, 100–101
Pets, 161, 165n.5
Physical exercise, 78, 240
Picts, 28, 46
Pixies, 28
Place of Power exercise, 178
Plagues, 29
Plaskow, Judith, 5
Play, 47–48

Pleasure, 110, 225
Poemagogic, 33
Poemagogic image, 125
Poetic Colleges of Ireland and Wales, 29
Poetry, 32, 47, 137, 176, 226
Polarity, 3, 20, 48–56, 218, 226, 233–34, 243, 267
Political activism, 7–8, 18–19, 156–58, 217–19, 225
Political rituals, 250
Pornography, 126, 156–58, 224
Power: channeled through invocation, 111; charm for inner, 150; compassion balance to, 110; Cone of, 159, 250–51, 282; coven, 61; grounding of, 156; Horned God model of male, 123; of magic, 136; Pentagram of Pearl, 93; reawakening of female, 32–33; Witchcraft model of male, 128
Power Chant exercise, 68–69
Power-from-within, 61, 142, 245, 269
Power-with, 269
Price of freedom, 42–43, 47
Priest, 21, 54, 55, 121, 184, 227
Priestess, 21, 54, 55, 269; Banishing Pentacle drawn by, 185; blessing over food by, 184; chants by, 111; High, 21; role of High, 253; visualization by, 96
Projection, 77
Projection strategy, 173, 174
Protection (aspects of), 293–3
Protection herbal charm, 149
Protective Circle exercise, 100
Protective Filter exercise, 142
Psychic links, 141–42
Psychic work, 162, 220–21, 293
Psychoanalysis, 45
The Psychology of Consciousness (Ornstein), 43, 175–76
Psychopaths, 56
Psychosis, 47
Purification, 84–85

Quartered circle, 86, 242
Queen of Death, 245

Queen of Elphame (Elfand), 29, 121
Queen of Heaven, 104
Quest, 125
Quietism, 36

"Radical Feminism and Women's Spirituality: Looking Before You Leap" (Lichtenstein), 217
The Rainbow: Emerging exercise, 178–79
The Rainbow: Trance Induction exercise, 177
Rainer, Tristine, 79
Raith, 59, 78, 161, 170. *See also* Energy; Younger Self
Raiths (spirits of four elements), 86
Rape, 37, 224
Raven, Trickster, Creator, 245, 246
Read, Donna, 264
Reagan years, 18
Reality creation, 223–24
Realm of the Ancestors (Marler), 264
Rebirth, 51, 110, 124, 188, 189
Rebirth of the Goddess (Christ), 264
Reclaiming Collective, 5–7, 11, 237, 238, 241, 247, 268, 269, 273, 275, 276
Reclaiming Principles of Unity, 6
Reclaiming Quarterly, 8
Reflection stage, 90
Reincarnation, 110, 124
Relaxation, 72, 78, 175, 176
Relaxation exercise, 73
Religions: Afro-American, 176, 225–26; conflict between science and, 219, 224; feminist, 224, 281–82; future of, 216; Goddess, 28–29, 55, 220, 221, 224–25, 265; trance possession of indigenous, 272–73. *See also* Eastern religions; Judaism; Western religions; Witchcraft
Religious freedom, 10
Repeating Chants (to the God), 129
Repeating Chants (to the Goddess), 111

Repeating Cycle: "Green Bud Leaf," 112
Resilient One, 24
Revelation, 171, 183
Rhythm, 176, 243, 254
Rhythm Play exercise, 44, 266
"Righteousness Syndrome," 218–19
Right hemisphere brain, 43–44, 45, 46, 233, 266, 273
Ring of Sauron (*Lord of the Rings*), 43
Rites of passage for girls, 272
Ritual baths, 86, 190
Ritual Induction exercise, 182–83
Ritual mock death, 55, 268
Rituals: basic structure of, 266; Beltane (May 1), 204–5, 259; Brigid (Candlemas, February 2), 202–3, 258, 277; casting circle to begin, 38, 83–84; Dark Moon Ritual, 195–96; energy of Craft, 66–67; enhancing experience of, 72–77; Eostar Ritual (Spring Equinox, March 20–23), 203–4, 259, 278; essence of Craft, 69–60; evolution of, 4–5, 212n.1, 276–77; Fall Equinox, 61–63; Full Moon, 194–95, 276; initiation, 189–92; Litha (Summer Solstice, June 20–23), 205–7, 259–60, 278; Lughnasad (August 1), 207–8, 260; Mabon (Fall Equinox, September 20–23), 208–9, 260; May Eve, 47; of modern covens, 35; moon, 193–96, 256; Mystery, 183; New Moon, 58–59; playful nature of, 47–48; of the Sabbats, 53; Samhain (Halloween, October 31), 209–12, 260, 278–79; sharing food following, 184, 254–55; Spiral Dance, 5, 27, 258–59, 277–78; "Take Back the Night!" march as, 156–58, 214; true function of, 36; Waxing Moon, 194; Yule (Winter Solstice, December 20–23), 197–202, 256–57, 277. *See also* Invocations
Ritual wine, 271
Robin, 247

The Rock exercise, 77
Rose petals, 276

Sabbats, 29, 53, 60, 125–26, 133, 197–213, 237, 241, 256–57
Sexuality: Goddess religion celebration of, 224–25; of Horned God, 120–21, 123; life force expressed through, 37; women identified with, 30
Sexual preference, 20
Sexual reproduction, 20
Sexual revolution, 224
Shadow fight, 174, 253
Shadow Play exercise, 44, 266
Shadow on the Threshold, 171, 172, 173, 251
Shamanic initiation, 256
Shamanism: ecstasy within, 49; Siberian, 221; spiritual traditions/knowledge of, 232
Shamans, 27; insight of Paleolithic, 42
Sharing, 54
She Who Listens, 46
Siberian shamanism, 221
Sickness defense, 173, 174
The Sidhe, 28
Simos, Bertha, 136
Simos, Mark, 131
Simple Visualizations exercise, 74
Sioux traditions, 42
Skepticism, 139
Slavery: historical trade of African, 31, 249–50; ritual circle freedom from, 109
Slinky toy, 50, 165
Snake, 175
Snyder, Gary, 42
"Solitaries," 38, 66, 233
"So mote it be," 85
Song, 50
Song to Pan (Simos), 131–32
"Song to Pan" (song by Minogue), 273
Sorcerers (male), 39n.1
The South, 88–89
Soviet Union, 280

Spain, 27

Spell for Fallow Periods, 145–46

Spell for Loneliness, 144–45

The Spell of the Sensuous (Abram), 8

Spells: Anger, 143; Binding a Spell exercise, 141; described, 137, 273–74; Healing Image Spell, 151–52; herbal charm, 149–51; hexes, 141–42, 153n.4; The Indrinking Spell, 143–44; metaphors of casting, 139, 140; Protective Filter exercise, 142; Safe Space Spell, 146–47; "so mote it be" ending of, 85; To Bind an Enemy, 152–53; working of, 138–40, 141–42. *See also* Energy; Magic

Spell to be Friends With Your Womb, 148

Spell to Know the Child Within, 147–48

Spiral Dance Ritual, 5, 27, 258–59, 277–78

The Spiral Dance (Starhawk): introduction to tenth anniversary edition of, 13–17; introduction to twentieth anniversary edition of, 1–12; ten years later commentary on, 231–61; twenty years later commentary on, 263–82

Spiral model, 156

Spirit/ether, 285

"Spirit Guide," 46

Sprenger, Dominican, 29

Spring Equinox, 125

Star card (Tarot), 16

Star Goddess, 104, 110

Starhawk, 2, 12, 99–100, 103, 267, 268

Starlight awareness, 220

Starlight vision, 42, 43–44, 56, 66

Star Son, Lord of the Waxing Year, 53

Stealing, 36

Stern, Susan, 115

Stone Age, 103

Stone circles, 28, 31, 83–84, 232

Stonehenge, 220

Stone, Merlin, 263

Subconscious, 45

Suffering, 51, 56, 188

Sumerian Chant, 112

Sumerian myth, 245

Summer-Crowned King, 125

Summerland, 51

Summer Solstice, 53, 125, 277

Summer Solstice ritual, 205–7, 259–60

Sun, 286–87

Sun Child, 125, 249

Sunwise (clockwise), 86

Superiority feelings, 172, 173, 174

Swimme, Brian, 235

Sword, 87, 242

Sword Meditation, 88, 242–43

Symbols: associated with Goddess, 32–34, 103, 105–7; changing response to, 217; drawn from nature, 220; of God, 124; of Goddess as self, 111; of initiation, 188; language of magic through, 137; snake, 175; visualizing, 107

"Take Back the Night!" conference (1978), 156

"Take Back the Night!" ritual march, 156–58, 214

Talamantes, Inez, 268

Tales of Power, 42

Talking Self, 56, 70, 83, 161, 162, 266; described, 45

Tana, 46

Taoism, 221–22

Tarot cards, 16, 23, 183, 221

"That-Which-Cannot-Be-Told," 32. *See also* Witchcraft

That-Which-Is-Brought-Forth, 121

Thealogy, 18, 35, 244. *See also* Goddess religion

"The third eye," 162

To Attract Love herbal charm, 149

To Attract Money herbal charm, 149

To Bind an Enemy spell, 152–53

To Get a Job herbal charm, 150

To Heal a Broken Heart herbal charm, 149

Tolkien, J. R., 43
Tools of Witchcraft, 87, 95, 243, 271
Torture (Burning Times), 30, 121
To Win in Court herbal charm, 150
Trance experiences, 168–72, 174–76, 181–82, 186n.9, 254, 272–73
Trance Into a Dream exercise, 181
Transcendental Meditation, 75
Transcenders, 174
Transformation Meditation exercise, 93
Traveler, 122
Tree alphabet, 91, 243
Tree of Life, 68, 239
Triangles, 107
Trickster, 245, 246
Triple Goddess, 26
Troubadours, 29
Trust, 66–67, 226
Truth, 33, 71, 138, 219, 222–23, 224, 233
Truth or Dare (Starhawk), 18, 231, 239, 247, 249, 250, 251, 260, 263, 269, 272, 280
Twelve Step programs, 21, 22, 253

Ukraine, 27
Unconscious mind, 43, 44, 45, 56, 138, 171. See also Younger Self
Unitarian Churches, 238
Universe: as dance of energy, 167; dynamic nature of, 155; as interplay of moving forces, 42; starlight vision of, 43–44
Ur, Royal Tombs of, 55

Valerie, 62, 63, 130, 238, 253
Valerie's rhyming Invocations to the Four Quarters, 98–99
Valiente, Doreen, 103, 244
Vegetation God, 52
Venice, 15
Venus, 287–88
Vice, 110
Violence, 37, 126, 156, 224, 248
Virgin Mary, 225, 282

Visualization, 66, 72, 73–74, 78, 86, 96, 137, 140, 240
Visualization exercises, 74–77
Voudoun traditions, 31

Wales, 29
Wand, 88
Wand Meditation exercise, 88–89
Waning Moon Meditation exercise, 105
Warrior gods, 28
Wars, 28–29, 34
Water, 48, 89, 242, 284–85
Water Meditation exercise, 89
"Waters of the world," 258
Waxing Moon Meditation exercise, 104
Waxing Moon Ritual, 194
The Well of Remembrance (Metzner), 265
The West, 89
Western culture: focus of the male by, 50; masculinity beliefs of, 122
Western religions: influence of Eastern religions on, 221–22; male images of divinity in, 264; psychology of, 122–23; superiority strategies of, 172; Witchcraft persecution by, 29–32, 60. See also Christianity
Wheel of the Year myth, 52–53, 235–37, 256–57, 268
When God Was a Woman (Stone), 263
The White Goddess (Graves), 53
Wicca, 29
Wiccan Churches, 238
Wiccan Witches, 14
Wicce, 29
Widdershins (counterclockwise) direction, 86–87
Wildness, 248
Will, 138
Williams, William Carlos, 136
Wind Hags coven, 238
Wine, 21, 249, 254–55
Winning (in court) charm, 150
Winter-Born King, 125

Winter Solstice, 125, 126, 197–202, 257–58, 277
Wisdom, 92
"Witch Camps" (Reclaiming), 5
Witchcraft: continuing development of, 217; ecology within, 264–65; empirical nature of, 220; energy of, 49–50; evolution of ritual traditions of, 212n.1; ideals and ethics of, 31, 35–37, 265; knowledge exchange with Judaism, 83–84; media view of, 268–69; men in modern, 60, 127–28; myths and stories of, 46–47; Native American traditions and, 27; persecution of, 23, 29–32, 60; practices of medieval, 120–21; reclamation of, 31–32; as religion, 26–27, 32–38; structural model of, 226–27; tools of, 87, 95, 243, 271; understanding of the Goddess by, 108–11. See also Old Religion
Witches: Book of Shadows kept by, 59, 78–79, 95, 216; commitment and experience levels of, 265–66; cry during Burning Times by, 129; description of modern, 5–7; execution of, 30; familiars of, 165n.5; interest in own history by, 4; persecution against, 23, 29–32, 60; solitary, 38, 66, 233; Wiccan, 14; working of spells by, 138–40, 141–42. See also Covens
Witches' New Year (Halloween), 126, 209–12
Witch Queen (Grandmaster), 60
The Wizard of Oz (film), 70
Woman's Mysteries (Harding), 43
Womanspirit: A Guide to Women's Wisdom (Iglehart), 250
Womanspirit Rising (ed. by Christ and Plaskow), 5, 17
Womb Chant exercise, 160

Women: cultural socialization of, 122; essentialism and, 279–80; honoring, 36–37; impact of Eastern religions on, 222; inviolate bodies of, 56, 123, 127; life cycle of, 105; need for women's spaces by, 218; persecution directed against, 29–32; polarization of men and, 3, 267; reawakening of female power in, 32–33; rites of passage for, 272
Women's movement: Dianic/separatist Witchcraft and, 121, 247, 261; impact of, 19; as mythogenic force, 225; on rise of Goddess religion, 265. See also Feminism
Women's Mysteries, 121, 133, 218
Wonder, 47–48
Word Association Trance exercise, 71–72
Wordplay, 135–36
World Wide Web, 65, 266
Writing, 15–16, 17, 240

Year Child, 256
Yemaya, 48, 108
Yin and Yang, 51
Yoga, 75, 78, 109, 221
Yogis, 162
Yom Kippur, 282
Yoruba-based religion, 272
Younger Self: communication of spells to, 138; creating safe space for, 70; Deep Self connection to, 46; described, 45, 56; dreams and, 175; Goddess speaking to, 107; raith energy of, 78, 162; response to actions and symbols by, 83; terminology of, 266. See also Unconscious mind
Yule (Winter Solstice, December 20–23) ritual, 197–202, 257–58, 277. See also Winter Solstice

Zen meditation, 75